Short Circuiting Policy

Short Circuiting Policy

Interest Groups and the Battle Over Clean Energy and Climate Policy in the American States

LEAH CARDAMORE STOKES

OXFORD
UNIVERSITY PRESS

OXFORD
UNIVERSITY PRESS

Oxford University Press is a department of the University of Oxford. It furthers
the University's objective of excellence in research, scholarship, and education
by publishing worldwide. Oxford is a registered trade mark of Oxford University
Press in the UK and certain other countries.

Published in the United States of America by Oxford University Press
198 Madison Avenue, New York, NY 10016, United States of America.

Library of Congress Cataloging-in-Publication Data
Names: Stokes, Leah Cardamore, author.
Title: Short circuiting policy : interest groups and the battle over clean
energy and climate policy in the American states / Leah Cardamore Stokes.
Description: New York, NY : Oxford University Press, [2020] |
Series: Studies in postwar American political development |
Includes bibliographical references and index.
Identifiers: LCCN 2019047241 (print) | LCCN 2019047242 (ebook) |
ISBN 9780190074265 (paperback) | ISBN 9780190074258 (hardback) |
ISBN 9780190074289 (epub) | ISBN 9780190074296 (OSO)
Subjects: LCSH: Energy policy—United States—States—Case studies. |
Clean energy—Government policy—United States—States—Case studies. |
Climatic changes—Political aspects—United States—States—Case studies. |
Lobbying—United States—States—Case studies. |
Pressure groups—United States—States—Case studies.
Classification: LCC HD9502.U52 S8299 2020 (print) |
LCC HD9502.U52 (ebook) | DDC 333.790973—dc23
LC record available at https://lccn.loc.gov/2019047241
LC ebook record available at https://lccn.loc.gov/2019047242

3 5 7 9 8 6 4 2

Paperback printed by Marquis, Canada
Hardback printed by Bridgeport National Bindery, Inc., United States of America

This book is dedicated to all living beings.
May the fossil fuel era end.

CONTENTS

LIST OF FIGURES

ACKNOWLEDGMENTS

Something is wrong, I know it, if I don't keep my attention on eternity.
May I be the tiniest nail in the house of the universe, tiny but useful.
May I stay forever in the stream. May I look down upon the windflower
and the bull thistle and the coreopsis with the greatest respect.
  —Mary Oliver

This book began as a dissertation at the Massachusetts Institute of Technology (MIT). For a strange and unknowable reason, Larry Susskind, Judy Layzer and JoAnn Carmin saw fit to admit me to a PhD at MIT a decade ago. That decision altered the course of my life, like a river finding a new route. The five years I spent at MIT found me taking courses in planning, political science, public policy, engineering, and science. Traipsing across campus, from department to department, made it possible for me to understand the energy system in a deep way, and through it, grasp the climate crisis. My many mentors at MIT included Larry Susskind, Judy Layzer, Andrea Campbell and Chris Warshaw, who advised my dissertation, as well as Noelle Selin, Jessika Trancik, Henry Lee, Ignacio Perez-Arriaga, Kathy Thelen, Deborah Stone, Danny Hidalgo, Jens Hainmueller, Ken Oye, and Adam Berinsky. It was a moment in time in a very specific place. I will spend the rest of my life deepening the foundation of knowledge I laid while I was there.

Over the seven years it took to write this book, I had an enormous amount of help from research assistants. Jeff Feng was my right hand as I revised, always ready to complete yet another fact check. Rebecca Garverman was instrumental during the field work. Sydney Bartone appeared right when I needed her, helping me push this book over the finish line. Patrick Hunnicutt, Geoff Henderson, Lillian Zhou, Nikayla Jefferson, Sabrina McGraw, Rebecca Sugrue, and Kathryn Buggs all provided invaluable research support.

When I moved to the University of California, Santa Barbara, I gained a deep bench of colleagues on environmental politics: Eric Smith, Hahrie Han, Paasha Mahdavi, Sarah Anderson, Mark Buntaine, Matt Potoski, David Pellow, and Matto Mildenberger all provided inspiration for the work. Several of these colleagues also helped me organize a book workshop on campus, providing valuable feedback. Larry Jacobs, Paul Pierson, Andrea Campbell, and Alex Hertel-Fernandez went out of their way to attend the workshop, giving me sound advice on the project. Others provided valuable feedback on drafts, including: Michael Aklin, Dave Anderson, Parrish Bergquist, Gabe Chan, Colin Cunliff, Ranjit Deshmukh, Chase Foster, Kristin Goss, Jake Grumbach, Richard Hirsh, Jesse Jenkins, Matt Kasper, Robert Keohane, Robert Lifset, Kate Marvel, Alan Nogee, Eric Patashnik, David Pomerantz, Tobias Schmidt, Narayan Subramanian, and David Vogel.

Where would we be without our friends, our companions who walk beside us along the slow road to academic publication? By a strange stroke of fortune, I gained five best friends while writing this book: Hanna Breetz, Laura Chirot, Chad Hazlett, Alex Hertel-Fernandez, and Trish Tan. My time at MIT was full of friendships across campus and Cambridge, including: Isabelle Anguelovski, Kathy Araujo, Parrish Bergquist, Eric Chu, Ross Collins, Ryan Cook, Ellen Czaika, Justin de Benedictis-Kessner, Dan de Kadt, Graham Denyer Willis, Pearl Donohoo, Greg Epstein, Chase Foster, Amanda Giang, Kian Goh, Alicia Harley, Kelly Heber, Devin Helfrich, Claire Houston, Jason Jackson, Chris Jones, Lily Knorr, Vig Krishnamurthy, Christa Lee-Chuvala, Megan Lickley, Krista Loose, Nick Marantz, Claudia Octaviano, Kelly Pasolli, Jackie Piltch, Lily Pollans, Danya Rumore, Rebecca Saari, Nidhi Santen, Todd Schenk, Alexis Schulman, Linda Shi, Chris Smith, Abby Spinak, Kerry Spitzer, Mia White, Tess Wise, Patricio Zambrano-Barragan, and Laurie Zapalac. When I moved to Santa Barbara, I made some new friends, chiefly Kathy Burba, who never failed to ask if I'd finished my book yet (I had not). I also had the great fortune to meet Lacey Baldiviez, Kathryn Barnes, Katie Hershfelt, Megan Mahdavi, Briana McCarthy, Samantha Narang, Ryoko Oono, Tannis Thorlakson, and an entire community at Friday ceramics with the great Bernie Sayers. And to my friends who knew me before this adventure began and saw me through the process: Bernice Chau, Amy Gordon, Sandy Hudson and Danielle Westbrook. Thank you also to Lynn Bratman, Olivia Scobie and Beth Sternlieb for having my back and lighting the way.

At UC Santa Barbara, I found a wonderful home to continue this research. When I first arrived, I had the great fortune of being assigned David Pellow and Eric Smith as mentors. Across the campus, my colleagues have supported my work, including: Sarah Anderson, Bruce Bimber, Kate Bruhn, Mark Buntaine, Ranjit Deshmukh, Paige Digeser, Joan Dudney, Charlie Hale, Hahrie Han,

Robert Heilmeyr, Allison Horst, Scott Jasechko, Kent Jennings, Alison Keleher, Paasha Mahdavi, Matto Mildenberger, Julia Morse, Clayton Nall, Neil Narang, Will Nomikos, Andrew Norris, Debra Perrone, Matt Potoski, Elana Resnick, and Grace Wu. We are building a community on this campus dedicated to solving environmental problems. I hope we succeed in making this world a better place.

Through my work on climate and energy, I've made new friends and colleagues across the country and the world, who have all supported me through this long project: Michaël Aklin, Daniel Aldrich, Steve Ansolabehere, Sarah Anzia, Graeme Auld, Michael Bectel, Thomas Bernauer, Steven Bernstein, Ryan Briggs, David Broockman, Sanya Carley, Steve Cohen, Pat Egan, Nicole Goodman, Kristin Goss, Avi Green, Jessica Green, Matt Grossmann, Jacob Hacker, Jennifer Hadden, Erin Hartman, Mary Heglar, Tanya Heikkila, Richard Hirsh, Matt Hoffmann, Thomas Homer-Dixon, Larry Jacobs, Jesse Jenkins, Josh Kalla, Robert Keohane, David Konisky, Frank Laird, Gabe Lenz, Jonas Meckling, Rob Meyer, Megan Mullin, Jonas Nahm, Julian NoiseCat, Brendan Nyhan, Paul Pierson, David Pomerantz, Barry Rabe, Shira Rascoe, Sarah Reckhow, Molly Roberts, Michael Ross, Costa Samaras, Eric Schickler, Tobias Schmidt, Henrik Selin, Noelle Selin, Theda Skocpol, Narayan Subramanian, Chris Tausanovitch, Dustin Tingley, Sarah Tjossem, Mike Tomz, Johannes Urpelainen, David Victor, David Vogel, Gernot Wagner, Lee Wasserman, Elizabeth Wilson, Abby Wood and Yiqing Xu.

I found the perfect home for this project at Oxford University Press. Dave McBride shepherded the manuscript with skill and was responsive to any question I had. Emily Mackenzie, Richa Jobin and Andrew Pachuta all provided additional support during the book production process. Frank Laird and two anonymous reviewers gave valuable feedback that made the book stronger. Lisa Camner McKay skillfully helped me rewrite parts of the book. Karl Spurzem brought his talents to designing the cover. And Phillip Glass composed the Orphée Suite, which I listened to over 1,000 times while writing this book.

To my family, thank you for your support and encouragement. To my sisters, Elaisha and Jessica for decades of love, laughter and phone calls. And for lending me your cats when I didn't have one of my own. To the cat that eventually came, Delilah, for levity. To my grandparents: thank you for supporting my undergraduate education, for giving me the gears, and for your unwavering love. To my father, for urging me to go to MIT, for always telling me I was smart, and for helping me with math in my teens—turns out it came in handy. To my mother, for many phone calls, for helpful visits when I needed them throughout my education, for editing my resumes and papers for far too long, and for all your encouragement. When I was doing fieldwork for this project, my computer broke, and my mother bought me a new one. I wrote the entire project on that computer over six years. To both of my parents, for everything. And finally, to my husband who has given me love, friendship, and a life of ideas, purpose and joy. We have worked together, side by side, researching environmental problems and solutions for 15 years now. Lucky doesn't begin to describe it.

The usual academic disclaimers apply: I have done my best to root out errors, but I am sure many remain. Alas, I must claim them as mine and mine alone.

Over one hundred policy experts generously shared their experience, ideas and advice with me while I was researching this book. For the sake of anonymity, I will not thank specific people. But I will say that many people gave me hours of their time. I was continuously surprised by the openness policy professionals demonstrated. To everyone I spoke with: thank you. It was inspiring learning from you over the past several years.

Renewable energy advocates have worked tirelessly for decades to try to transform the electricity system into one that meets Edison's vision from over a century ago: an electricity system that does not require us to burn down our homes or poison our neighbors. May this project continue. May the tide begin to turn. And may the fossil fuel era finally end.

Santa Barbara, California

LIST OF ABBREVIATIONS

Organization Names

AECT	Association of Electric Companies of Texas
AEP	American Electric Power
AFP	Americans for Prosperity
ALEC	American Legislative Exchange Council
AriSEIA	Arizona Solar Energy Industries Association
AWEA	American Wind Energy Association
EDF	Environmental Defense Fund
EEI	Edison Electric Institute
ERCOT	Electric Reliability Council of Texas
FPL	Florida Power & Light
GCC	Global Climate Coalition
IEU-Ohio	Industrial Energy Users of Ohio
KCP&L	Kansas City Power & Light
NELA	National Electric Light Association
NRDC	Natural Resources Defense Council
OMA	Ohio Manufacturers' Association
Oxy	Occidental Energy Ventures Corporation
PG&E	Pacific Gas & Electric Company
RUCO	Residential Utility Consumer Office
SEIA	Solar Energy Industries Association
SRP	Salt River Project
TAM	Texas Association of Manufacturers
TASC	The Alliance for Solar Choice
TCCE	Texas Coalition for Competitive Electricity
TEP	Tucson Electric Power

TIEC	Texas Industrial Energy Consumers
TREIA	Texas Renewable Energy Industries Association
TURN	The Utility Reform Network
TUSK	Tell Utilities Solar Won't Be Killed
TXOGA	Texas Oil and Gas Association
TXU	Texas Utilities Energy
UCS	Union of Concerned Scientists

Legislation, Government Entities, and Other

ACA	Affordable Care Act
ACC	Arizona Corporation Commission
ANWR	Arctic National Wildlife Refuge
CBO	Congressional Budget Office
CCS	Carbon capture and sequestration
CES	Clean energy standard
CHP	Combined heat and power
CPUC	California Public Utilities Commission
CREZ	Competitive renewable energy zones
DG	Distributed generation
DOE	Department of Energy
EERS	Energy-efficiency resource standard
EIA	Energy Information Administration
EPA	Environmental Protection Agency
EPS	Environmental portfolio standard
EWGs	Exempt wholesale generators
FERC	Federal Energy Regulatory Commission
FIT	Feed-in tariff
IOU	Investor-owned utility
IRP	Integrated resource plan
ITC	Investment tax credit
KCC	Kansas Corporation Commission
NEM	Net energy metering
NEPA	National Environmental Policy Act
NGO	Nongovernmental organization
NREL	National Renewable Energy Laboratory
PAC	Political action committee
POU	Publicly owned utility
PTC	Production tax credit
PUC	Public utility commission

PUCO	Public Utility Commission of Ohio
PUCT	Public Utility Commission of Texas
PUHCA	Public Utility Holding Company Act
PURPA	Public Utility Regulatory Policies Act
QFs	Qualifying facilities
QSEs	Qualified scheduling entities
R&D	Research and development
RES	Renewable electricity standard
REST	Renewable energy standard and tariff
RPS	Renewable portfolio standard
SEC	Securities and Exchange Commission
TVA	Tennessee Valley Authority
VRPS	Voluntary renewable portfolio standard

1

Introduction

In 1999, an innovative clean energy law passed in an unlikely state, known more for its abundance of fossil fuels than for leading on environmental policy: Texas. The policy was enacted through a large bill that reformed the entire electricity sector. This law, like many others that would follow it, required the state to meet timelines for building clean energy technology. It was good news for climate change, helping the state to reduce the amount of carbon its electricity system emitted. The policy was implemented well and led to rapid increases in clean energy in the state. The year the renewable energy law was passed, the state's electricity system was 88% fossil fuel–dominated—less than 1% came from renewable energy sources. A decade into the policy experiment, Texas got 12% of its electricity from wind energy, having built more wind energy than most countries (Hurlbut 2008).[1] When Texas governor George W. Bush ran for president in 2000, he trumpeted this law as one of his successes, vowing further action on climate at the federal level. Texas was leading the country in wind energy.

With this shift toward clean energy, advocates hoped that the stranglehold fossil fuel companies had over the political system would also begin to erode. Texas and other states across the country have long relied on coal, natural gas, and even oil to power their electricity grids. For a century, the companies using and supplying these energy sources—electric utilities and fossil fuel producers—exerted significant influence over energy policy, blocking progress on energy efficiency and renewables (Hirsh 1999a). Setting ambitious targets for clean energy was a new idea that held the promise of disrupting polluters' political influence. The idea caught on: from the mid-1990s to 2011, most American states passed at least one clean energy law.

Environmental advocates hoped that these laws would result in new interest groups—renewable energy companies and their industry trade groups—that would ally with environmentalists and drive the adoption of more ambitious climate laws. Many predicted a positive spiral upward, with the laws bolstering clean energy advocates, who in turn championed ever more ambitious laws. If

Short Circuiting Policy. Leah Cardamore Stokes, Oxford University Press (2020). © Oxford University Press.
DOI: 10.1093/oso/9780190074265.001.0001

successful, these state laws promised to make the United States a world leader in clean energy and create a pathway to addressing the climate crisis.

Initially, Texas's renewable energy laws developed in the way that advocates had hoped. The state's modest goals were quickly surpassed. Wind energy projects provided jobs and local revenue for school districts in rural, conservative parts of the state. Texas's first clean energy law built a strong coalition of interest group advocates and bipartisan politicians who pushed to expand the policy. In 2005, they won. A more ambitious clean energy target was enacted alongside a large investment in electricity transmission, to build the wires necessary to bring the wind energy to market. Texas would eventually spend $7 billion on transmission—a very large sum in a state known for tight purse strings. Environmental advocates' plan to build political power and clean energy through implementing the initial law seemed to be working.

But the good times didn't last. When the advocates pivoted to promoting solar energy, the fossil fuel industry mobilized to undermine their plans. Very little solar had been built in the Lone Star State. With no policy framework for solar energy, the industry struggled to gain traction. In 2005, a modest solar energy target passed in the same law that invested in wind energy and transmission lines. The advocates were ecstatic at their victory. As it had done for wind, Texas was poised to lead the country in solar energy. But this policy was never implemented. The fossil fuel industry ensured this outcome by increasing the ambiguity in the bill's language. Advocates believed the bill promised a new solar requirement, while opponents argued during implementation that it was a nonbinding plan. In Texas, fossil fuel companies successfully stymied solar energy for another decade.

Hence, the story of Texas's landmark clean energy laws is more complicated than many believe. Some estimate that Texas has the greatest potential for solar in the country (Lopez et al. 2012). Yet by 2018, it had only installed as much solar as Massachusetts—a much smaller and more northern state. By then, California had installed 10 times as much as Texas.[2] Nor did Texas continue to expand its wind energy policy after 2005. Despite its early efforts, Texas has fallen behind on clean energy. In the electric power sector, carbon emissions only declined 5% from 1999 to 2016.[3] In fact, Texas is a below average state in clean energy production. The state is not doing enough to clean up its electricity sector and contribute to solving the climate crisis.

This pattern is not unique to Texas. Progress on clean energy across the United States has been much slower than it needs to be. If we focus only on the current costs of clean energy, we miss a broader pattern. After more than three decades of climate denial, utilities have switched to promoting delay. And this delay matters not just for the climate's stability but also for utilities and other fossil fuel companies' balance sheets. These companies win by stalling—by keeping their coal plants open, or by digging up more fossil fuels. Delaying policy action provides these companies with money.

We can see climate delay across the states. Between 2008 and 2018, natural gas grew by almost 14 percentage points (p.p.)—an annual growth rate of 1.2 points. By contrast, renewables had an annual growth of around half that rate, at 0.74 points annually. They only increased by around 7 p.p. over the same decade. Since 2011, opponents have blocked clean energy laws from being passed in new places, leaving many states without any target. Others have begun to rollback or weaken clean energy policies. When these strategies failed, electric utilities and other polluting companies made the fight bigger, using the public, the parties, and the courts to short-circuit progress on climate policy.

How can we understand this loss of momentum for clean energy laws that were designed to ratchet up in ambition over time? To understand climate policy, we must put politics at the center of our theories (Victor 2011). On the one hand, policies do remake politics, through a pattern political scientists call "policy feedback" (Campbell 2003; Mettler 2005; Pierson 1993; Skocpol 1992). Policies can reshape politics by changing interest groups' and individuals' resources, identities, and preferences. Usually, policy feedback research shows how policies reinforce themselves over time: creating constituencies that drive positive feedback and policy expansion. This pattern is referred to as "path dependence" or "lock-in": once a policy course is set, it is difficult to reverse (Pierson 2000). In the case of clean energy laws, we would have expected this kind of self-reinforcing cycle to lock in the energy transition, with policies growing in ambition over time.

Yet, it's not clear that path dependence holds for many public policies. Instead, we often see policy reversals. As Eric Patashnik and Julian Zelizer put it, "the capacity of public policies to remake politics is contingent, conditional, and contested" (2013, 1072). Why do we see ongoing conflict over policy, even after policies are passed that we expect to generate feedback? I argue that we must place interest groups at the center of our theories of policy change.

While this view is somewhat out of favor today, earlier research in political science argued that interest groups are central to understanding conflict over policy (Dahl 1961; Schattschneider 1960). As E. E. Schattschneider put it, "Pressure politics is a method of short-circuiting the majority" (1942, 189). Most recently, this idea has been articulated by Jacob Hacker and Paul Pierson (2010a), who argue that policy change is a function of "organized combat" between interest groups. The status quo is shaped by the winners of past battles over policy, and for this reason, it favors incumbents (Baumgartner et al. 2009; Moe 2005, 2015). These vested interest groups often seek to prevent or reverse policy change. If we want policy to lock-in, and drive long term change, we have to destroy the political status quo (Patashnik 2008). This is not easy to do.

In this book, I place interest groups at the center of a theory of policy change, examining the conditionality of positive feedback and path dependence. My argument proceeds in several points. First, I show that ambiguity plays a central role in policy change. I call this dynamic the "fog of enactment"—the gap between actors' expectations and the policy's actual outcome. Second, I argue that implementation is a key step in policy feedback. Examining policy changes over long periods, we can see that ambiguity shrinks after implementation. As actors learn, they update their beliefs and come to attack policies they previously ignored or underestimated. Third, I show the mechanisms through which interest groups try to drive policy changes after implementation. Policy changes are contingent on interest groups' knowledge and networks, their direct lobbying of legislators and regulators, and their use of the parties, the public, and the courts.

To understand the limits of policy feedback and path dependence, we must examine cases that a theory of positive feedback fails to predict. To do this, I studied a policy that was enacted across numerous jurisdictions. The policy needed to be one that aimed to create positive, amplifying feedback. I could then look at several cases to see where and why the policy failed to produce lock-in. I chose four cases where clean energy policy has stalled or been reversed: Arizona, Kansas, Ohio, and Texas. These cases of retrenchment represent surprising developments. Clean energy laws are precisely the kind of policies we would expect to lock in over time because they create new industries. This detailed account of the internal statehouse politics shows how interest groups use a variety of mechanisms to change policy, even in cases where we would expect policy feedback to buffer laws from retrenchment.

Policies that involve dramatic redistribution of wealth across society do not lock in without a long fight (Aklin & Urpelainen 2013, 2018; Thelen 2004). Thinking of politics through the lens of organized combat reminds us that policy fights continue and that opponents do not disappear. Policies may prove less path-dependent than our theories would predict, particularly in an age of federated interest groups working across state lines and growing partisan polarization.

Battles over climate policy are fundamentally material: they are about who will get to own the assets of the energy system and the resulting profits. We should not expect the interest groups facing an existential threat from climate policy—fossil fuel companies and electric utilities—to go quietly into the night. For the past century, these companies have maintained vast amounts of carbon-intensive infrastructure and fossil fuel reserves—which they plan to continue to operate and extract, even if their actions erode climate stability. Along with their wealth, they have cultivated significant political power. It will take considerable time and effort for clean energy advocates to contest this power. This book tells the story of the clean energy battles playing out in statehouses across the country and, through it, tells us about our prospects for addressing the climate crisis.

A Theory of Interest Group–Driven Policy Change: The Book's Argument in Brief

In this book I develop a theory that places interest group conflict at the center of policy change. Tracing institutions and actors over time, I argue that organized combat between interest groups is at the heart of American politics (Hacker & Pierson 2010a). In policy battles, interest groups take sides—advocating either for or against policy. Yet advocate and opponent interest groups battle over policy on an uneven terrain. When advocates and opponents fight over proposals, they do not come with the same power. The incumbents—groups that "won" previous battles and gained their preferred policy—usually have greater sway than newcomers. Hence organized combat is often asymmetric: incumbent interest groups retain more power than new entrants. With sufficient relative influence over their adversaries, groups can capture the spoils from policy change. The prize is a change in legislation or regulation in that interest group's preferred direction. These battles continue through later rounds of policy enactment and implementation. Hence, there is an iterative relationship between policy and politics.

Still, new entrants who want to change policy can sometimes succeed in beginning a policy feedback process, despite vested opponents. New policies may be packaged as part of larger reforms, causing interest groups to have divided attention or an inability to block provisions. In addition, policies' potential outcomes are hard to predict, particularly with innovative laws that have not been trialed extensively in other jurisdictions. I argue that interest groups and politicians can struggle to forecast policies' likely consequences because of the fog of enactment. I identify four specific factors that increase this fog: novel policies that have not been implemented widely elsewhere; major reforms that involve complex and detailed rules; policies in technical domains; and policy areas that have overlapping jurisdictions across the state and federal government. These factors all held for early clean energy policies. Shrouded in a thick fog, carbon-intensive actors sometimes failed to invest adequately in policy battles, and reforms passed that later proved costly to their bottom line. Advocates in early-mover states were able to use ambiguity to their advantage before opponents learned and began resisting laws. But with each passing year, this became harder for advocates to pull off.

Opponents do not passively accept policy defeat. With experience, they become wiser to advocates' proposals. Working through interest group networks that cross state lines, opponents can gain new information and update their preferences. Using these networks, opponents can work to ensure that their adversaries' proposals will not be passed or implemented as easily in the future. These cross-state networks are increasingly important to understanding American politics (Hertel-Fernandez 2019; Hopkins 2018). The policy agenda across the country is more unified because interest groups work on the same policies in different states, crossing borders to lobby. Networks play three important roles: they help interest groups learn to anticipate policies' consequences, they help interest groups disseminate effective political strategies, and they facilitate collective action. Overall, networks help interest groups marshal their forces and reduce each individual member's cost in contesting policy. They can also create policy feedback spillovers: when one state acts to pass a law, it can create new interest groups that move into other states to lobby for policy expansion.

These networks of interest groups exist across the political spectrum. Important networks on the right include the American Legislative Exchange Council (ALEC), the State Policy Network (SPN), and Americans for Prosperity (AFP) (Dagan & Teles 2016; Hertel-Fernandez 2014, 2019; Skocpol & Hertel-Fernandez 2016). These groups have helped drive the Republican Party to more extreme policy stances including through the use of model bills, and they are particularly influential with junior legislators who lack capacity (Hertel-Fernandez 2014; Kroeger 2015; Skocpol & Hertel-Fernandez 2016). Overall the left has struggled to challenge the dominance of the right-wing networks in the American states (Hertel-Fernandez 2016, 2019). On energy and environmental policy, these groups have promoted climate denial and worked to undermine clean energy laws.

That said, historically environmental groups have managed to contest these right-wing anti-environment groups. From the mid-1990s onward, the Energy Foundation crafted a cross-state network to drive new clean energy laws. Their efforts found early success in several states, including Texas, California, and Massachusetts. As clean energy companies grew in these places, they crossed over into other jurisdictions to support renewable energy laws elsewhere. In Kansas, a cross-state network of wind advocates defended that state's laws. Similarly, solar companies from California worked to support clean energy laws in Arizona. Policy feedback did not just affect the early-acting states; it spilled over, as advocates took their policies and strategies elsewhere.

However, as opponent fossil fuel corporations and electric utilities realized these laws could add significant costs to their bottom lines and threaten their existing assets, their resistance grew. These interest group opponents undertook major efforts to block, weaken, or rollback climate policies. Opponents worked across state lines though networks, most notably ALEC and AFP, as well as the private electric utility association the Edison Electric Institute (EEI). Through a number of strategies described in detail in this book these right-wing groups put repealing clean energy laws on the agenda in many states. In 2012, the Koch-backed, climate-denying Heartland Institute drafted the "Electricity

Freedom Act" model bill alongside ALEC, and promoted it in legislatures across the country.[4] This bill aimed to repeal clean energy laws. In early 2014, ALEC, working with EEI, began promoting a new model bill on "Updating Net Metering Policies."[5] While advocates attempted to counter these efforts, crossing state lines to defend clean energy laws, they lost many policy battles.

Without opponents' effort, the forces of policy feedback would have succeeded in ratcheting up clean energy laws' ambition. Instead, we have seen many states fail to act and others weaken their laws. These dynamics mirror developments in other policy domains. Across state lines, interest groups have used well-established networks to push conservative healthcare and labor policies (Feigenbaum et al. 2018).

Interest Group Strategies to Drive Policy Change

After implementation of a new policy, interest groups working through networks can push for policy stability, expansion, or retrenchment. By "expansion" and "retrenchment," I mean changes to policy that strengthen or weaken it. To drive policy change, these actors can work either *directly* with politicians and regulators or *indirectly* through the parties, the public, or the courts. When interest groups are empowered with sufficient influence over legislators' or regulators' behavior, they will work directly, leveraging their relationships and using lobbying and campaign contributions to try to shift policy. They may also work directly through the regulatory system, resisting policies' implementation or capturing regulators. In some cases described in this book, fossil fuel companies and electric utility opponents had sufficient influence to work directly with legislators to weaken the policy. In others cases, they worked to capture state regulatory commissions and undermine bureaucratic interpretations of laws.

When opponents seek to reverse policy but lack direct access to legislators and regulators, they can work through three indirect channels: the parties, the public, and the courts. Here, I build on and update Schattschneider's (1960) conception of expanding the scope of conflict to include the parties, the public, and the courts as mechanisms through which organized combat over policy unfolds.

First, the parties are an important route for interest group influence in American politics. As the UCLA School of Political Parties has argued, interest groups are central to party agendas, acting as intense policy demanders (Bawn et al. 2012; Cohen et al. 2009). Building on this work, I argue that interest groups drive partisan polarization in state legislatures and, through it, drive policy change.[6] Asymmetric polarization has emerged as a central trend in American politics (Bonica 2014; Hacker & Pierson 2014; McCarty et al. 2006; Shor 2015). The states are an area of particularly pronounced polarization (Grumbach 2018a; Shor 2015). There is evidence that interest groups have also driven polarization on trade, infrastructure, healthcare, and other policies (Dar & Lee 2014; Hertel-Fernandez 2019; Hertel-Fernandez et al. 2016; McCarty 2007; Nall 2015; Sinclair 2014). In this book, I show that interest groups contribute to polarization by providing resources to politicians and primary candidates who are on the extremes on policy. Even if primary challengers prove unsuccessful or never come, I show that the threat of a primary or loss in campaign funds can drive an incumbent politician to change their position on policy.

The position of the Republican Party on clean energy and climate change is an excellent illustration of how interest groups have driven polarization. Renewable energy is good for economic growth and job creation, two outcomes that Republicans traditionally support. In the 1990s, Republicans actively supported clean energy. However, since 2010, support among Republican politicians has eroded. Fossil fuel companies have threatened to primary or successfully challenged Republican climate champions, shifting incentives within the party. The case of Senator John McCain, who was a climate champion until a serious primary challenge occurred in 2010, shows this dynamic. Similarly, Koch Industries successfully primaried Bob Inglis, a conservative South Carolina Congressman, after he started supporting climate legislation in Congress (Leonard 2019).

While early renewable energy laws had bipartisan support, today Republicans are driving retrenchment efforts. In many Republican-controlled states, opponent interest groups have used contributions and the primary system to convince the Republican Party and specific GOP politicians that opposing climate policies is more important than renewable energy job creation. This is not surprising given that the GOP has maintained fossil fuel corporations as a core part of its base (Karol 2019). By siding with climate deniers, the GOP is on the wrong side of history—ensuring a stable climate is foundational to society.

Second, organized opponents can use public opinion to undermine policy feedback and drive retrenchment. In this book, I emphasize how public opinion is a constructed phenomenon in American politics (Jacobs & Shapiro 2000). Organized interests can mobilize groups strategically and present biased versions of public preferences to legislators. While the public can try to communicate majority preferences, it is far less organized than interest groups (Olson 1965). Instead, the public is often a tool that advocates and opponents use to try to influence decision-makers.

One way that fossil fuel companies and electric utilities have constructed public opinion is by convincing Republicans that the climate crisis is a hoax. These corporations played a key role in spreading climate denial. They funded organizations that denied the scientific consensus on climate change from the

1980s to the present (Anderson et al. 2017; Oreskes & Conway 2010; Supran & Oreskes 2017). The exact language used in denial reports permeated the public discourse, ending up in the media and in presidential speeches (Farrell 2015). The steady drumbeat of this well-funded campaign eroded support for climate policy among Republicans, driving partisan polarization (Dunlap & McCright 2008; Mildenberger 2020).

In 2006, climate change and clean energy were bipartisan. Support for clean energy was extremely high. Yet, as the threat of climate action accelerated in 2007, interest groups ratcheted up their efforts to deny climate science as part of their campaign to block climate policy. Fossil fuel companies brought the public into a debate over climate science, successfully driving polarization. As Matto Mildenberger and Anthony Leiserowitz (2017) show, between 2008 and 2011, belief in climate change among Republicans fell precipitously. While some may believe that the financial crisis played a role in driving polarization, their careful causal identification shows this is not the case. Instead, they find evidence that elite polarization played a role. For example, the GOP presidential primary at that time involved many candidates changing their positions on climate.

Fossil fuel corporations and electric utilities played an important role in driving this elite polarization. Around 2007, ExxonMobil and Koch-affiliated groups began promoting the idea that CO_2 is good, as part of their climate denial efforts (Farrell 2016). Utilities and fossil fuel companies similarly began ramping up their spending on lobbying against climate action (Brulle 2018). The public responded to these campaigns, and support for renewable energy plunged between 2008 and 2013 (Figure 1.1). It is not surprising that public polarization took place at the same time that interest groups had increased their spending on climate denial and anti-renewables campaigns. Fossil fuel companies were not just trying to influence politicians and drive elite polarization—they were also trying to undermine public support for climate action. Among Republicans and Independents, this strategy paid off, with public support falling around 30 points.

In addition to these aggregate, national trends, we can see interest groups using public opinion as a weapon in their fights over state-level clean energy laws. In Kansas and Arizona, clean energy advocates and opponents tried to organize and mobilize the public. The opponents relied heavily on fake grassroots campaigns—sometimes called "astroturfing"—while advocates tried to bolster and communicate genuine support from rural and Republican parts of the state. Interest groups on both sides aimed to expand the scope of conflict. Yet clean energy companies have struggled to be as effective as their opponents. These advocates, who have far fewer resources, have often run less successful public campaigns.

While it is not the primary focus of this book, the courts are a third channel through which interest groups indirectly battle to shift policy. Interest groups

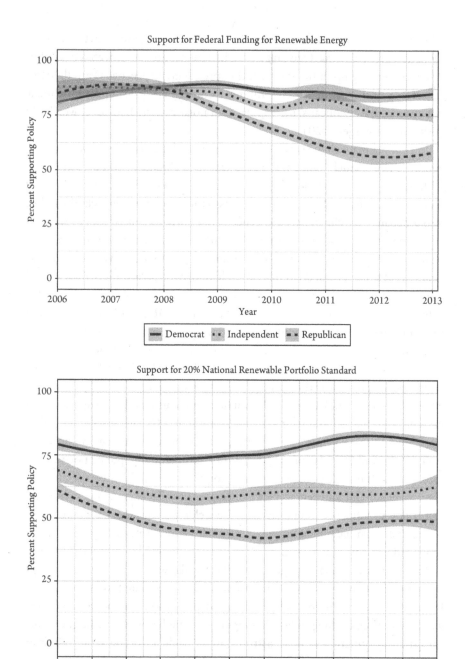

Figure 1.1 Polarization in Support for Renewables in the United States. (Data sources: Pew Research Center for the People and the Press Political Survey, 2008–2012, and Yale Project on Climate Change Communication, 2008–2019 [see Ballew et al. 2019].)

may use this approach as a last resort as it is riskier than working directly with legislators and bureaucrats or indirectly through the parties or the public. As Chapter 3 shows, the Supreme Court's decision to side with the Federal Energy Regulatory Commission (FERC) in important cases in the 1980s was crucial to kickstarting clean energy, helping to scale up the American renewables industry for the first time in California. These legal decisions empowered advocates and placed the United States in the lead globally in clean energy. More recently, opponents' attempts to undermine Colorado's clean energy laws through the courts have proven unsuccessful. Thus, in the case of clean energy retrenchment, the courts have not proven a successful strategy for opponents.

Identifying Interest Group Influence in the American States

Placing interest groups at the center of a theory of policy change in American politics is not without debate (Baumgartner et al. 2009; Baumgartner & Leech 1998; Kingdon 2011; Patashnik 2008). As many have argued, studying interest groups is challenging (Baumgartner & Leech 1998; Hojnacki et al. 2012). When scholars have looked for interest group influence at the federal level—for example, by studying the relationship between groups' campaign contributions and roll call votes—they have often struggled to show an effect (Ansolabehere et al. 2003). Yet, because this approach ignores the content of laws, non-decisions and anticipated reactions, it likely understates influence (Anzia 2018; Crenson 1971; Fairfield 2015; Hacker & Pierson 2010b). By contrast, new research is increasingly showing interest group influence in American politics at various scales and through a variety of mechanisms (Anzia 2011; Gilens & Page 2014; Fouirnaies & Hall 2018; Hertel-Fernandez 2018, 2019; Hertel-Fernandez et al. 2019; Kalla & Broockman 2016). As Sarah Anzia (2018) argues, studying interest group influence at the state level may hold particular promise—for one, it is easier for researchers to gain access to state politicians, their staff, and lobbyists.

In this qualitative study of state energy policy, I find strong evidence for interest group influence. Given the central role energy plays in the economy, incumbent electric utilities and other fossil fuel companies have been granted a privileged position at the policymaking table for over a century. As advocates attempted to push clean energy policy and climate action, these companies dragged legislatures, bureaucracies, the public, the parties, and the courts into a debate over climate science and the need for clean energy. And on balance, it is a debate they have won. Despite more than 40 years of effort from advocates, clean energy laws across the United States have barely shifted the needle. The American electricity system's carbon emissions remain dangerously high.

While the book's arguments are built from cases of energy policy, the theory travels to other policy areas, such as welfare and financial regulation.

For example, while the Dodd-Frank Act had the potential for lock-in through policy feedback (Patashnik & Zelizer 2013), Congress weakened the policy substantially in 2018. Similarly, changes to welfare policy in the mid-1990s did not shore up public support for the program as intended (Soss & Schram 2007). Ultimately, this book aims to build a general theory, describing the conditions and mechanisms through which interest groups are able to short-circuit policy by undermining policy feedback.

The Climate Problem and Clean Energy Solutions

It is hard to overstate the trouble we are in with the climate crisis. At the end of 2018, the main global scientific body on climate change issued a report that implicitly warned we had just 12 years to begin significant transformations to our energy systems. The end goal for many is for society to stop emitting carbon entirely by 2050, and limit warming to 1.5° C (Intergovernmental Panel on Climate Change (IPCC) 2018). Significant changes must happen by 2030 to put us on a path toward this zero carbon society—within this next decade we must aim to cut our emissions in half. Research has shown that building any new fossil fuel infrastructure is incompatible with limiting warming to 1.5° C (Tong et al. 2019). Further delay would mean exacerbating the deadly impacts we are already seeing: heatwaves, wildfires, droughts, extreme precipitation, and coastal flooding.

Economists and climate scientists have struggled to price the cost of climate inaction, but it is on the order of trillions globally (Burke et al. 2018; Ricke et al. 2018). And the costs and consequences will "happen faster than we think" (Xu et al. 2018). Why? First, as emissions accelerate, so too will warming. Second, efforts to clean up air pollution, for example, by closing coal plants, have the perverse impact of reducing the particulate matter in the air, which slows warming by reflecting sunlight back out to space. Third, the planet goes through natural climatic cycles, and there are signs we are entering a warming phase. All of this is on top of the fact that scientific assessments have tended to *underestimate* the pace of climate change (Brysse et al. 2013). This is not a problem for the future. Climate change is happening now, and impacts will only worsen if we continue to delay.

A big part of the changes necessary to address this crisis must come through our energy system (Hoffert et al. 2002; Jamieson 2011). Energy is fundamental to the functioning of modern industrialized societies: it powers our buildings, fuels our transportation system, and drives our industry. Without it, the world as we know it would grind to a halt. Unfortunately the energy source we have used to industrialize—fossil fuels—has a dirty little secret: it is destroying the stable climate that is just as fundamental for society.

Despite the threats climate change poses, we have not lost our appetite for fossil fuels. Hence, global carbon emissions continue to grow. In 2018, emissions both globally and in the United States rose at a faster pace than they had in almost a decade (Jackson et al. 2018; Rhodium Group 2019). Rather than *declining*, US greenhouse gas emissions went up by 3.4%. Even in the American electric power sector, considered the bleeding edge of climate action, emissions rose almost 2%. Why? Electricity demand grew, and even though coal plants retired, natural gas filled the gap more than clean energy. This pattern holds around the world as scientists have summarily captured in the title to one recent paper: "Global Energy Growth Is Outpacing Decarbonization" (Jackson et al. 2018). Removing carbon emissions from societies' energy system is and will remain an extremely difficult undertaking.

Despite calls for a clean energy transition since the 1970s, fossil fuels continue to dominate the world's energy supply. Coal, oil, and natural gas provided 81% of global primary energy production in 2017—a mere 13% decline from 1970—all while total fossil fuel consumption continued to rise.[7] Even in the best of years, dangerous greenhouse gas emissions have flattened globally, not declined.[8] In the United States, 95% of transportation energy and 64% of electricity came from fossil fuels in 2018.[9] There is still a long way to go to remove carbon from the electricity system.

Decarbonizing the electric power sector in the United States is arguably the first linchpin globally to solving the climate crisis. As the largest economy in the world, the technologies America develops will spill over to other markets. There are many clean energy technologies, but renewables—including wind, solar, biomass, and geothermal—are the most popular (Ansolabehere & Konisky 2014). Renewable energy is slowly increasing around the world: excluding hydropower, renewables produced 10.5% of electricity globally in 2018.[10] The US percentage is very close to the global level: excluding hydropower, in 2018 renewables produced around 10% of the electricity supply.[11] Given that these technologies have existed since the 1980s, these numbers are small. Even with hydropower included, renewables only provided 17% of the US electricity mix in 2018.

The pace and scale of cleaning up the electricity system are not secondary issues but the central challenge (Figure 1.2). Given significant delay in acting on the climate crisis, we must make dramatic reductions in the carbon intensity of the electricity system by 2030 to be on track toward zero emissions by 2050. At the same time we must also expand the electricity system dramatically, to "electrify" other sectors—transportation, buildings, and industry. This approach will allow the economy to decarbonize. But it will not be easy. On average, models suggest an increase of 50%–120% in the size of the US electric power sector by 2050 (Iyer et al. 2017; Jenkins et al. 2018; Williams et al. 2014).

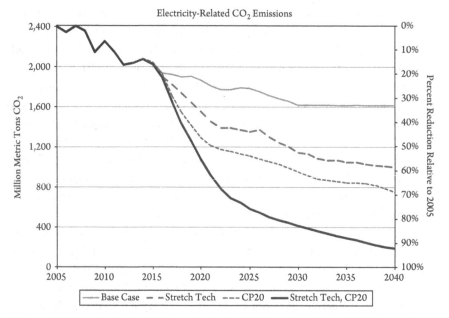

Figure 1.2 Decarbonization Trajectories for the US Electricity Sector, CP20 is a carbon price of $20/tonne (Adapted from: U.S. Department of Energy, "Energy CO2 Emissions Impacts of Clean Energy Technology Innovation and Policy," January 2017).

What would this dramatic change in the US electricity system look like in practical terms? Some estimates suggest that onshore wind energy must increase 10-fold—from around 1,000 projects in 2015 to 10,000 in the coming decades (Davis et al. 2013; Hawken 2017; Pacala 2004). And to move that electricity from where it is generated in the center of the country to where it is needed on the coasts will require a massive transmission network (MacDonald et al. 2016). Building wind energy offshore is another important piece of the puzzle, particularly since this resource is far more reliable. Yet, it too would require exponential growth—in 2019, only one offshore wind project was operating in the United States despite decades of efforts. The point is simple, if very difficult: we need to build an enormous amount of clean energy infrastructure over a very short time period to avert climate disaster.

To drive the clean energy transition, governments have used two policy levers: altering the relative *prices* or *quantities* of clean energy and fossil fuels (Breetz et al. 2018). More recently, these ideas have been combined through proposals like the Waxman-Markey bill or the Green New Deal. Prices can work to drive clean energy in a number of ways. Governments can raise the cost of fossil fuels, for example, through a price on carbon. While efforts at the federal level in the United States have consistently failed, some states have created limited carbon markets (Mildenberger 2020; Rabe 2018; Rabe & Borick 2012). Instead of taxing fossil fuels' for the harms they cause, significant subsidies remain in the

United States and globally (Ross et al. 2017; Victor 2009). If anything, fossil fuel subsidies are forecast to *increase* in the future from $2.2 billion in 2018 to $3.8 billion by 2028.[12] And in addition to direct subsidies, the health and environmental damages from fossil fuels in the United States alone amount to around $650 billion annually.[13] Given the political power of the fossil fuel industry, raising the cost of pollution has proven very challenging (Mildenberger 2020).

Governments can also reduce the cost of clean energy through research and development (R&D) funding, tax incentives and other policies. In the United States, total energy R&D expenditures at the Department of Energy (DOE) peaked in the 1970s at $8 billion annually and declined to around $2 billion by 2000. During the financial crisis, a 1-year spike occurred, where spending topped $13 billion.[14] But overall, the United States has failed to provide stable or adequate funding for energy R&D—particularly for renewables (Anadon et al. 2011). Between 1978 and 2018, renewable energy R&D accounted for 18% of the total spending—over the same time period 24% of R&D was spent on fossil fuel innovation.[15] One promising institution for innovation in clean energy is the Advanced Research Projects Agency-Energy (ARPA-E), created in 2007. The agency initially operated without funding, until it received $400 million in the 2009 stimulus (Bonvillian & van Atta 2011). Unfortunately, this was the high-water mark for ARPA-E funding—on average, the agency has received $250 million in annual funding. Still, in 2019, ARPA-E received over $350 million despite President Trump's calls to eliminate it.[16] Overall, the United States could spend significantly more money on clean energy R&D.

Deployment incentives are also crucial. The federal government's Production Tax Credit (PTC) and Investment Tax Credit (ITC) are both examples of this approach (Bird et al. 2005; Stokes & Breetz 2018). The PTC, enacted in 1992, provides a small tax credit per-unit-of-energy (cents per kilowatt hour) produced from clean energy sources. It has primarily supported wind energy projects. The ITC, enacted in 2005, allows companies to write off some of their tax liability if they invest in renewable energy projects. This policy has primarily benefited solar energy projects.[17] While fossil fuel subsidies are permanent, these renewable energy tax credits expire, leading to constant battles in Congress. At the time of this writing, the PTC was phasing out, and scheduled to expire in 2021 and the ITC was scheduled to begin phasing down on January 1, 2020. While there were efforts in Congress to extend these policies, they did not pass as part of a December 2019 spending bill. In 2019, the Treasury estimated that tax expenditures for renewable energy would decrease from $8.4 billion in 2018 to $3.5 billion by 2028.[18] Without stable policy, renewable energy deployment could slow rather than accelerate (Lewis & Wiser 2007; Stokes 2013).

Alternatively, government climate policy can focus on setting quantities— a minimum requirement for electricity from clean energy sources or a maximum limit on fossil fuels. In practice, governments have pursued clean energy requirements far more than bans on fossil fuels. Renewable portfolio standard (RPS) policies are the primary instrument used to set clean energy requirements in the United States. An RPS sets a requirement for the percentage of the state's electricity to come from renewable energy technologies by a certain date.[19] Efforts in the 1990s and 2000s to pass these policies at the federal level failed, forcing advocates to focus on the states to make progress (Laird & Stefes 2009).

Absent federal action to price carbon pollution or requirements for more renewables, states have proven the most important venues for climate policy in the United States. This book tells a political history of state-led clean energy laws, examining their genesis and how they have changed over time. In some ways, state leadership is not surprising. Since the early twentieth century, states have held primary jurisdiction over electricity markets through public utility commissions (PUCs) (Hirsh 1999a). Early efforts to support renewables in the 1970s and 1980s were small and short-lived. By the mid-1990s, however, a vibrant policy debate was unfolding in states across the country over the best way to spur growth in renewable energy.

An Energy Foundation–funded network of nongovernmental organizations (NGOs) fueled this debate. Beginning in the early 1990s, this foundation cultivated a long-term network of NGOs to shape and spread policy ideas and lobbying strategies across the American states. Within a given state, it relied on a two-pronged insider–outsider funding approach: supporting a technical policy-oriented insider NGO to work on negotiating policy details; and, funding a grassroots outsider NGO focused on public mobilization to get the policy on the agenda and passed. When policymaking windows of opportunity emerged— such as electricity restructuring—this strategy allowed advocates to drive policy change both directly through lobbying and indirectly through the public. Advocates succeeded in advancing two main policies: RPS and net metering.

After several decades of advocacy in statehouses across the country, by 2011 almost 80% of states had passed an RPS policy (Figure 1.3).[20] There were two major waves of RPS adoption: between 1994 and 2002, when they were packaged as part of electricity restructuring laws, and from 2003 onward, after electricity restructuring fell out of favor, when many states enacted stand-alone RPS laws.[21] In addition, from 2005 onward, several states enacted voluntary RPS policies, whose goals were not legally binding. Since Kansas passed its RPS in 2009, only one new state has adopted a mandatory policy—Vermont in 2015. While more than 20 states have expanded their RPS goals and a handful have passed ambitious 100% clean energy targets, a dozen have failed to ever enact a clean energy target, primarily states in the South. In 2018, only 55% of the US electricity supply was covered by an RPS policy (Barbose 2018).

Over the same time period, 44 states passed net metering policies, also called net energy metering (NEM) (see Figure 1.4). These laws set the rules

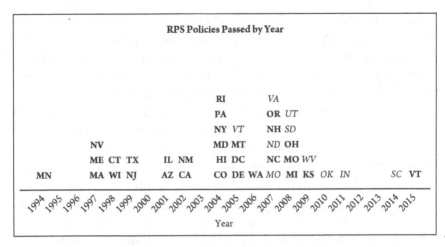

Figure 1.3 State Renewable Portfolio Standard (RPS) Policies, Enacted Post-1990
RPS policies are shown by year; non-binding goals are shown in italic font. MO is listed twice because a ballot initiative overturned a law with non-binding goals passed in 2007. IA is not shown since it passed its law in 1983. MN's first RPS only applied to Xcel Energy, until it was modified in 2008. AZ originally passed an RPS in 1996, along with restructuring; but when this process was frozen, the RPS did not proceed, hence 2001 is given as the date.

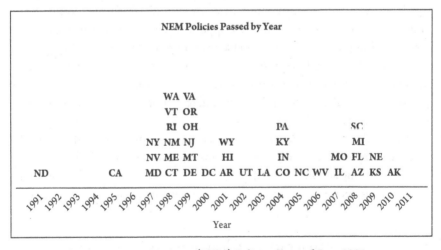

Figure 1.4 State Net Energy Metering (NEM) Policies, Enacted Post-1990
Six states that passed NEM policies before 1991 are not shown: MA and WI (1982), NH and MN (1983), IA (1984), and OK (1988). Although ME had a policy from 1987, it only applied to combined heat and power plants until 1998.

for how to compensate individuals and organizations that supply energy to the grid from small-scale, distributed generation—primarily through solar panels. Typically, net metering policies pay customers the same price that it costs them to purchase electricity. For example, if a citizen decides to put a solar panel on their roof and does not use or store all the electricity they produce, that citizen can provide excess energy to the grid. Full retail-rate NEM pays the customer the same amount for the electricity as the retail purchase price. In other words, the customer is billed the "net" amount of electricity that passed through the meter. Although several states passed NEM policies in the 1980s and early 1990s, California's 1995 law marked the beginning of a wave of modern NEM policy adoption across most states. As with RPS policies, no new NEM policies have passed since 2011. Instead, numerous legislatures have considered retrenching these laws—with many weakening or repealing them altogether. Nearly every state is revising its net metering program in the wake of massive solar growth—in 2018, 47 states plus DC engaged in some policy action around NEM.[22]

In summary, since the 1990s, a majority of US states have adopted RPS and NEM policies. In many cases, these laws created strong policy feedback—states expanded their laws over time as new industries grew and the public participated in the policy. Until the early 2000s legislative and public support was bipartisan. However, over time, electric utilities, fossil fuel corporations, large industrial companies, and other opponents sought to repeal clean energy targets and impose large monthly charges on net metering customers. At the same time that these interest groups lobbied for retrenchment and repeal, public opinion and legislators' positions on clean energy policy became increasingly polarized. Through lobbying politicians and regulators, and driving polarization in the parties, the public, and the courts, these opponents often succeeded in weakening clean energy laws. It is these cases, where policies have slid backward rather than spiraled upward, that this book explores in detail. Combined with the lack of strong action at the federal level, these paltry state efforts have left the US electricity sector behind on addressing the climate crisis.

Challenges to the Clean Energy Transition

Apart from opponents delaying the clean energy transition, there are other challenges to decarbonizing the electricity grid that we would be unwise to ignore. First, renewable energy technologies have some significant downsides. There are ongoing academic debates over exactly how much of the US and the global energy supply renewables can cost-effectively provide (Clack et al. 2017; Heard et al. 2017; Jacobson et al. 2017). Given abundant wind and solar resources, some academics argue that renewables can meet all of the United States and the world's electricity needs by 2050 (Delucchi & Jacobson 2011; Jacobson et al. 2015; Jacobson & Delucchi 2011). By contrast, papers with higher-resolution modeling suggest that renewables can likely supply around 80% of the electricity demand in that same time frame under reasonable cost limits (Clack et al. 2017; Jenkins et al. 2018; MacDonald et al. 2016).

One key challenge for renewable energy is intermittency: the wind does not blow and the sun does not shine all the time. For this reason, wind and solar are often referred to as "variable renewable energy sources." To address this problem, renewables need supportive infrastructure, including storage, transmission lines, and flexibility in both the supply and demand side. First, batteries or other storage technologies could be used to help balance the supply and demand of electricity. For example, a battery can store solar energy collected during the day for use at night. Second, transmission may be particularly important. Connecting geographically dispersed renewables allows for the variations in weather to be smoothed out, creating a more stable supply of electricity. Transmission would also allow high-quality resources in the center of the country to be connected to the coasts. One study shows that if a United States–wide transmission network is built, a combination of natural gas and renewable energy could reduce carbon emissions by up to 80% without increasing the cost of electricity (MacDonald et al. 2016). But new transmission has proven difficult to build because of costs, local resistance and overlapping federal and state jurisdiction (Klass & Wilson, 2012; Vajjhala & Fischbeck, 2007). Third, flexible low-carbon energy sources that can match the variability of wind and solar could be used—including nuclear, hydropower, geothermal, and bioenergy. Natural gas used in combination with renewables could provide backup power—although this approach results in carbon emissions. Fourth, the demand side could be made more flexible by deploying smart meters and appliances that shift their consumption to use more electricity when wind and solar power are abundant and reduce their consumption when the grid does not have adequate supply. Regardless of the solution to intermittency, these infrastructure investments will be very large, particularly given the need to expand the electricity sector to electrify other sectors.

In addition, renewable energy technologies often face problems with local acceptance (Stokes 2013, 2016). To produce the same amount of energy as conventional power plants, wind and solar energy require more land. Consequently, these technologies will need to be built in communities across the country. While solar is broadly popular,[23] both onshore and offshore wind energy often face backlash at the local level—and transmission capacity to support wind energy exacerbates siting challenges. When we consider that a 100% renewable energy system will need to be overbuilt so that it can supply electricity around the clock, every day of the year (Davis et al. 2018; Jenkins et al. 2018), the task and timeline become more daunting. For these reasons, an electricity grid powered exclusively from renewable energy sources likely has significant drawbacks.

What could we rely on if we struggle to deploy enough renewable energy and supportive infrastructure fast enough? There are several other options to reduce carbon in the electricity sector: energy efficiency, nuclear power, hydropower, fossil fuels with carbon sequestration, negative emissions technologies, and natural gas as a theoretically lower-carbon fossil fuel. Like renewables, each of these solutions has significant challenges.

Electricity consumption could be reduced through aggressive energy efficiency and conservation. Efficiency is particularly important in the short term since the electricity system is currently carbon-intensive (Trancik et al. 2014). However, this solution has proven remarkably difficult to unlock at scale, despite decades of optimistic forecasts that claimed untapped potential for profitable efficiency interventions (Charles 2009; Dietz 2010; Jaffe & Stavins 1994; McKinsey & Company 2009). Still, increasing the flexibility of the demand side may prove essential to balancing intermittency issues with high levels of renewable energy penetration (Jenkins et al. 2018).

Nuclear power is a second option. Once operational, nuclear plants do not generate greenhouse gas emissions. However, since it was first introduced in the United States in the 1950s, nuclear power has become expensive and politicized. As Chapter 3 discusses, many nuclear projects had large cost overruns. Since the Three Mile Island nuclear accident, new nuclear power plants have proven difficult to build in the United States. Concerns about environmental harms, including waste, continue to lead majorities of Americans to oppose new nuclear plants in their area (Ansolabehere & Konisky 2009).

That said, there is growing support for existing nuclear among environmental advocates, such as the World Resources Institute and the Union of Concerned Scientists, because it is the largest source of clean energy both in the United States and globally (Clemmer et al. 2018). And in the areas directly surrounding nuclear plants, public support can be higher (Aldrich 2008). In recent years, states have passed clean energy standards (CES), which include nuclear as an eligible technology. For example, Indiana passed a CES in 2011 that allowed 30% of the goal to be met with nuclear or "clean coal." Other states, such as Illinois and New Jersey, passed policies that offer financial incentives for struggling nuclear plants. New York similarly established a zero-emission credit program that stands alongside the RPS. In 2018, California's 100% CES policy theoretically opened the door for new, advanced nuclear reactors—even while the last plant in the state is currently slated for retirement in 2025.[24] Efforts are also underway to build a next generation nuclear plant at Idaho National Laboratory.

Unfortunately for climate mitigation efforts, more nuclear capacity is currently being removed from the US electricity system than added, after 20 years of no growth (Richards & Cole 2017). Shutting existing, safe plants is very problematic for climate mitigation efforts as 55% of clean power came from nuclear in 2018. One-third of the nation's nuclear plants are already closing or at risk of closing.[25] However, if nuclear operating costs remain high and natural gas prices remain low, nuclear could shrink by half by 2030 and drop down to a fifth by 2050.[26] Unless the politics and economics surrounding nuclear energy change dramatically, this technology will continue to struggle—and that is bad news for the climate.

Expanding hydropower would also prove useful for climate mitigation. But in the United States, most large hydro sites were developed by 1980, with little growth since 1995.[27] Even if all the remaining hydropower sources were developed, they would likely only supply an additional 5% of current US electricity consumption.[28] In addition, climate models predict drought for parts of the United States, with potentially negative impacts on hydropower generation (Christensen et al. 2004; Kao et al. 2015). These factors mean hydropower is unlikely to be a large part of the solution.[29]

Another option is to employ carbon capture and sequestration (CCS) technology—wherein carbon from fossil fuel combustion is captured and pumped into underground reservoirs. Scaling up this technology quickly will likely prove challenging—the scale of carbon sequestration necessary if fossil fuels continue to be burned is on the order of existing oil and gas infrastructure (Benson & Orr 2008). This solution has proven difficult to deploy in a cost-competitive way, despite significant government investment in R&D. In 2010, Secretary of Energy Steven Chu committed almost $5 billion for CCS R&D and deployment.[30] Most of the projects that the government supported never became operational.[31] There is now one major plant operating in Texas, Petra Nova, and several other smaller-scale industrial plants (Jenkins 2015). Apart from these sites, most CCS currently involves pumping CO_2 into oil fields to enhance oil recovery—a practice that many criticize as unproductive for climate mitigation. These efforts were further bolstered in 2018, when Congress passed the 45Q program, which provided a tax credit for carbon sequestration and utilization. That said, there is hope that innovation could come through these policies, which would ultimately lead to meaningful carbon reduction.

In addition, negative emissions technologies must play an important role in addressing the climate crisis. Most models that aim to meet a 2° C warming target rely extensively on negative emissions, including bioenergy with carbon capture and storage and direct air capture (Fuss et al. 2014; IPCC 2018; Rockström et al. 2017). Yet, these technologies are not commercially viable. At present, pilot projects do not remove carbon from the atmosphere long term. Still, if innovation enables these technologies to store significant carbon or displace fossil fuels by creating new synthetic fuels—for example by capturing carbon from the air—they would be revolutionary. Similarly, innovating new processes that allow carbon to be captured and stored in cement or other materials would be a huge breakthrough (Davis et al. 2018; Xi et al. 2016).

In addition to these technological approaches to negative emissions, afforestation—adding forests where they do not exist—and increasing carbon storage in soils may also help drive negative emissions (Griscom et al. 2017). The downside with these natural approaches, however, is that they do not permanently remove carbon from the atmosphere since forests can be cut down and soils can be disturbed. Climate change is already making forests even less stable sites for carbon storage (Griscom et al. 2017). And there is already strong competition for land use in other sectors, including for renewables. Some argue that if clean energy can grow fast enough, negative emissions technologies may not be necessary and indeed may be counterproductive (Anderson & Peters 2016). But, given the cases described in this book, that would require a politically unrealistic acceleration of clean energy.

Currently, natural gas is displacing coal in the United States—and, theoretically, this fossil fuel may have lower carbon emissions. It is also cleaner from a conventional air pollution perspective. Given the boom in hydraulic fracturing, the cost of natural gas has declined precipitously in the United States since 2008.[32] Still, there are significant concerns with increasing natural gas in the electricity sector. Leakage, wherein methane escapes into the atmosphere before being combusted, is problematic because methane is an extremely potent greenhouse gas. If natural gas leaks at a rate of 3.2% or higher, scientists estimate that this fuel source is worse than coal from a climate perspective (Alvarez et al. 2012).[33] Accurate leakage rates are very hard to estimate, but it is likely that the official Environmental Protection Agency estimates are too low and that leakage may be around 2.3% (Alvarez et al. 2018). While many see natural gas as a bridge fuel, given high leakage rates, it may prove to be a bridge to nowhere.

It's clear that there are trade-offs and challenges in transitioning our electricity system, whether we rely on renewables or other technologies. If we are serious about solving the climate crisis, we should be aware of these problems. Regardless of the approach taken, the fact is we must increase the rate at which we remove fossil fuel infrastructure from our energy system. This will involve building renewables; accelerating energy efficiency; keeping existing, safe nuclear plants open; maximizing hydropower capacity; investing heavily in R&D for low-carbon technology; deploying negative emissions technologies; protecting land for natural carbon storage; building batteries and transmission; and enacting and sustaining policies that support renewable energy technologies. Solving the climate crisis will require massive government investment and stable public policy. It requires doing everything possible to avert climate disaster. This is not a simple problem.

Case Selection, Methods, and Policy Effectiveness

Since this book aims to use an interest group–centered theory of policy change to understand the limits of path dependence, I examined cases that a theory of positive feedback fails to predict. Here, I study clean energy laws that were retrenched in some way, despite having the potential for lock-in. The empirical chapters construct a political history of clean energy policy across four states where clean energy retrenchment has already occurred: Arizona, Kansas, Ohio, and Texas. Despite the potential these laws had for path dependence, we saw rollbacks and delays. Studying these cases allows us to understand how interest groups engaged in organized combat over policy can undermine policy feedback.

Still, given concerns about selection on the dependent variable, I also include one case where policy feedback theory is predictive—Texas's wind energy laws. In related work published elsewhere, I have studied several states where policy feedback prevailed (Stokes 2015). For example, California has consistently ramped up its renewable energy targets. In that case, advocates worked over many years to build a formidable coalitions of labor, consumer groups and environmentalists. Overtime, opponents had lost significant power and influence in Sacramento. Similarly, in Colorado, despite legal challenges and other attacks on renewable energy laws, advocates were successful at resisting retrenchment. These cases, which are not developed in this book, are examples of when advocates overcame their opponents in organized combat. They are places where the patterns we expect from policy feedback theory do play out. I come back to these more hopeful stories, including other current developments in state clean energy laws, in the conclusion.

The book relies on process tracing to understand the causal relationship between actors and events. Process tracing draws on history, archives, interviews, news articles, and other sources "to see whether the causal process a theory hypothesizes or implies in a case is, in fact, evident in the sequence and values of the intervening variables" (George & Bennett, 2005, 6). To trace policy changes and their causes, I undertook in-depth, longitudinal case studies in the tradition of historical institutionalism. In each case, I examined multiple instances of policy enactment, implementation, and revision. I do not focus on comparing across cases, as other qualitative studies in political science often emphasize (King et al. 1994). Instead, I rely on *within*-case analysis, examining a sequence of events in a given case over time (Fairfield & Charman 2017). This approach is also distinct from policy analysis—it is more concerned with understanding the causes of policy change than with policy effectiveness.

I developed the historical case studies necessary for process tracing through semistructured interviews with political actors, bureaucrats, policy advocates, and policy opponents as well as by analyzing policy documents. Between 2013 and 2019, I conducted 108 interviews with experts on these five cases, as well as individuals involved in US clean energy policy more broadly. Political actors interviewed included state legislators, commissioners, political staff, utility executives and employees, bureaucrats in energy agencies and public utility commissions, interest groups, activists, and citizens. Interviews were largely conducted confidentially, and for this reason, a list of interview subjects is not provided. When specific quotations are given, they are not attributed to an individual or organization but, rather, the broader group that individual represents—such as a utility or a renewable energy advocate at an NGO. Full details on the interviews are given in the Appendix. The analysis also relies on primary and secondary archival documents on the legislative and implementation process. I drew on state legislatures' official records, such as bill versions, bill analyses, and roll-call votes. I also relied heavily on dockets from proceedings at state public utility commissions. During the research process, I gathered and analyzed several clean energy organizations' archives with thousands of pages of documents, including newsletters, emails, memos, and reports.

The goal was to reconstruct historical events, including political actors' behavior that took place publicly and in behind-closed-doors negotiations. In practice, there are serious challenges to studying interest group battles over public policy. It requires understanding interest groups' actions and motives in an environment where secrecy is a central political strategy. Not only is political spending often intentionally obscured, but negotiations inside a legislature are impossible for the public to see directly. Given that most policy negotiations happen in private, constructing accurate political narratives is more often the work of investigative journalists than political scientists or policy scholars. In addition to my interviews, I lean on the excellent work of these journalists throughout this project.

There are times when the evidence I have uncovered for interest group influence is strong. And there are times when the evidence is weaker—when I am less certain about who did what and why. I aim to be transparent about when there is uncertainty over who was in the room or what a given actor's intentions were. Hence, you will find words like "likely" or "may" or "conceivable" in the empirical cases—these are cues to the reader about where I am making informed judgments based on publicly available evidence as well as my confidential interviews. Readers can then judge for themselves whether they find the facts convincing in any given case. My goal is to not overstate the evidence but to provide it transparently alongside its limitations.

Policy Effectiveness and Clean Energy Benchmarks

While this book is focused on building a generalized theory of policy change via organized combat between interest groups, inevitably the reader will wonder, *what about policy effectiveness?* Here, we can think about outputs or outcomes (Fiorino 2011). Outputs concern whether a policy met its targets. However, when organized interests water down a policy's goals during the negotiation process, targets may be weak and ineffective at solving the problem. Thus, we must also consider outcomes: did the policy meaningfully solve the problem? When it comes to addressing the climate crisis, this question should be central to any policy analysis. It is not enough to pass symbolic policies and declare victory. Policies must bring us closer to addressing climate change—whether directly reducing greenhouse gas emissions or indirectly innovating low-carbon technology that can be used around the world. We must have solutions at the scale of the crisis.

States with RPS policies have deployed an order of magnitude more renewables than states without these policies. However, we do not know if this is a causal effect, given significant identification challenges. Some research has raised questions about RPS policies' effectiveness, particularly compared to hypothetical carbon taxes (Greenstone et al. 2019; Upton & Snyder 2017). Yet these research papers have flaws. For one, there are significant challenges with using econometric techniques to estimate policy effects when spillovers occur across jurisdictions. In the case of clean energy laws, as one state acts, it lowers the cost of other states acting. Further, the theoretical stringency and political acceptability of a carbon price are different from what a carbon price would look like in practice. Hence, comparing actual policies that were negotiated under organized combat between interest groups to hypothetical, economy-wide carbon pricing is an apples-to-oranges comparison. In addition, it is clear that there are substantial health benefits from clean energy adoption that these papers underestimate (Dimanchev et al. 2019).

Whether or not RPS policies work to drive new renewable energy adoption depends on how the policies were designed and implemented (Carley et al. 2018; Delmas & Montes-Sancho 2011). Arizona passed many renewable energy laws, beginning in the 1990s, that utilities simply ignored. When these policies are input into econometric models, they are deemed ineffective—when in fact their inability to deliver is a reflection of a broader problem of regulatory capture that a carbon price would also face. Similarly, in Texas, the solar target was written to be toothless. We will see throughout this book that policies are often designed for ineffectiveness because of powerful opponent interest groups.

Here, I take a different approach—thinking about the laws we need, rather than simply evaluating the laws we have. We can begin by setting simple benchmarks for low-carbon electricity, including wind, solar, geothermal, biomass, nuclear, and hydropower (Figure 1.5). If we start in 2000 with 100% dirty electricity and draw a straight line to 2050 when we have 100% clean electricity, we must grow clean energy 2 p.p. every year. With this metric, states should have been producing 36% of their electricity from clean energy sources by 2018.[34] On the surface, we appear to be on track—the United States got just over 36% of its electricity from low-carbon sources in 2018.[35] However, just 17% of the electricity supply came from renewables. Instead, 19% of the electricity system is nuclear energy—a problem given the slate of retirements scheduled and the lack of new plants being built. Renewable energy needs to grow fast enough to beat out retiring nuclear. Unfortunately, so far this isn't happening—natural gas is filling more of the new capacity needs than renewables.[36] Unless this trend reverses, we could see the US electricity system increase in carbon intensity, as has occurred in Germany.[37] In short, we have been living on borrowed time, relying on decades-old nuclear and hydropower plants as we slowly ramp up renewables (Figure 1.6). But we have run out of time to delay any longer.

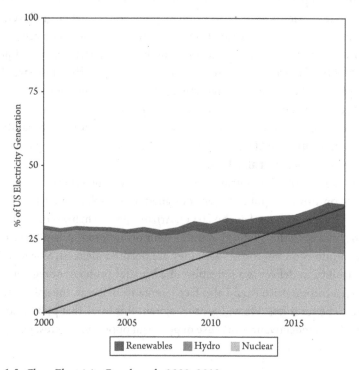

Figure 1.5 Clean Electricity Benchmark, 2000–2018

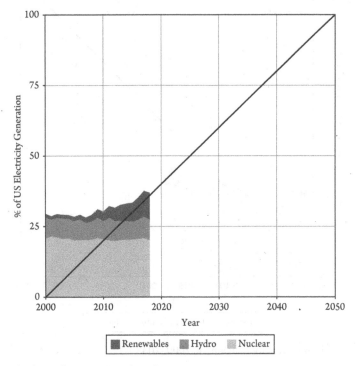

Figure 1.6 Clean Electricity Benchmark, 2000–2050

Even this 2050 benchmark may prove too lax, given the climate impacts we are already experiencing. Instead, we may want to set a goal of having 100% clean electricity by 2035 (Figure 1.7). In that case, if we start in 2000 and draw a straight-line out to 2035, we should already have just over 50% of the electricity supply from clean energy sources. By this benchmark, we are around 15 p.p. behind schedule. If we want to meet this 2035 target, then renewables must grow by more than 4 p.p. annually, to make up for lost time. Given the annual growth rate was just 0.7 p.p. over the past decade, this would represent an almost six-fold increase over historic rates.

Yet even this benchmark underestimates the challenge we face. To cut emissions in half by 2030, in line with what the IPCC has said is necessary to limit warming to 1.5° C (IPCC 2018), we need to make progress on cleaning up two sectors that combined made up 57% of US carbon emissions in 2018: electricity and transportation. In practice, this means making the electricity system about twice as big to electrify cars, trucks and other vehicles. Hence, the 2035 goal is perhaps better understood as a target of 200% clean electricity, compared to the electricity system of 2018. We can draw a straight line out from 2018 to 2035, when the electricity system is twice as large and only comprised of clean

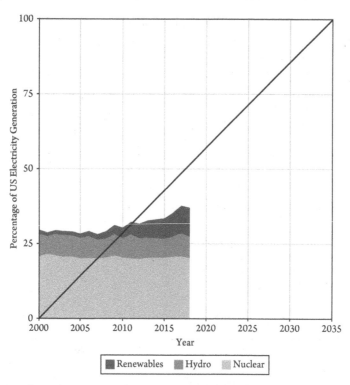

Figure 1.7 Clean Electricity Benchmark, 2000–2035

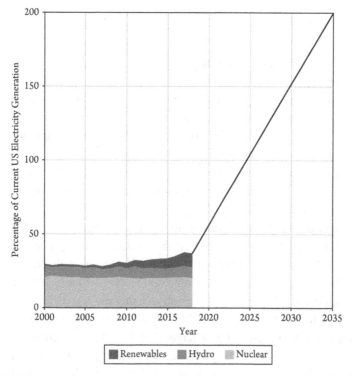

Figure 1.8 Narwhal Curve

electricity. The angle of the "narwhal tusk" in this figure gives a sense of the rate necessary (Figure 1.8). It is, to say the least, daunting. Of course, if we invest heavily in energy efficiency, the tusk will be less steep. And if we keep safe nuclear plants open, it will also be easier to make progress. But regardless the fact is clear: we have procrastinated on cleaning up the electricity system for too long.

How do the states in this book stack up against these benchmarks? By 2018, Texas and Ohio were clearly failing. Despite running ahead on clean energy, Texas was only producing 26% of its electricity from clean sources, putting it 10 and 24 points behind on the 2050 and 2035 benchmarks, respectively.[38] Ohio was doing even worse: at 17%, it was 19 points behind on the easier 2050 benchmark.[39] A quick comparison with California and Iowa shows that these states could have been further along the pathway toward the clean energy future. Respectively, these states had 53% and 43% clean energy by 2018, putting them ahead of their own goals as well as the 2050 benchmark.[40]

On the surface, Arizona appeared to be doing better: it had 39% of its electricity from clean sources in 2018, beating the 2050 goal by 3 points.[41] However, compared to a 2035 goal, the state is more than 10 points behind schedule. Worse, most of Arizona's clean energy came from one nuclear power plant built in 1986, which is slated for retirement beginning in 2045. This creates significant risk, if, for example, the nuclear plant faces problems before then. On renewables, Arizona is consistently behind on its own targets—in 2018, it only produced 5% of its utility-scale electricity supply from renewables.[42] If renewables continue to grow at their best pace in recent years, by 2045 when Arizona's nuclear plant is scheduled to retire, the state will only have around 40% renewable energy sources.[43] Clearly, the state lacks a plan for 100% clean electricity by 2050, particularly given the need to grow the electricity sector to support other parts of the economy decarbonizing.

The Kansas case, however, is much more hopeful. Despite concerted and successful efforts to repeal the state's clean energy law from the Wichita-headquartered Koch Industries and its affiliates, associated groups to repeal the clean energy law, we are still seeing progress in this windy state. By 2018, the state had 37% of its electricity from renewable energy sources alone and an additional 18% from nuclear, putting it a ahead of both the 2050 and 2035 benchmarks and well beyond the state's modest, repealed targets.[44] In Kansas, advocates were smart to sacrifice the RPS policy in exchange for forgoing a new tax on wind energy.

Looking at other states, we see there are many more clean energy laggards— in 2018, 24 states were beating the 2050 benchmark, while 26 were failing. For example, Florida only had 15% clean energy in 2018.[45] Utilities have spent decades beating back efforts to enact an RPS law in that sunny state. West Virginia, which repealed its RPS in 2015, was the second worst state in the country: only 5% of its electricity system was from low-carbon sources.[46] Taken together, these facts suggest that growing and decarbonizing the electricity sector is going to remain very challenging. Hence, the cases in this book are not outliers. More than half of the country is behind on clean energy, even if we count aging nuclear plants and ignore the need to massively expand the electricity system.

We can also see these facts playing out in the financials. New investment in clean energy in the United States peaked in 2011 at $62 billion. For the past half-decade, spending has been flat, hovering around $56 billion annually.[47] Consequently, US states are falling further behind in their efforts to address the climate crisis. Today, China and the European Union have pulled ahead of the United States in wind energy—both regions now have twice as much installed as the United States.[48]

We do not have the necessary laws in place at the state or national level to de-carbonize the US electricity sector. While conflict rages in legislatures and public utility commissions, newspapers run a simple story: wind and solar energy are finally cheap enough. We are on a short path to powering our societies without pollution. States and cities in the United States are policy leaders, solving the climate crisis! It is true that renewables have declined dramatically in price over the past decade. But any student of politics and policy knows that economics are never the entire story. Just because a coal plant is uneconomic does not mean it will close: if utilities have debt and equity in that plant, they will work hard to keep it open.

In the absence of federal action, US states' and cities' actions are not adding up to solving the crisis. What's more, a backlash against clean energy policy is growing across the country, led by interest groups with a vested stake in the fossil fuel status quo. Environmental advocates, including renewable energy companies, have attempted to counteract the backlash; and since the election of Trump in 2016, clean energy advocates have gained some momentum. But we must recognize that almost half the country's electricity system still lacks clean energy targets (Barbose 2018). The transition is not happening fast enough.

Plan of the Book

The following chapters explore organized combat in the American energy system. Chapter 2 provides the book's theory and core argument. I review models of policy change that emerged from debates over social policy in advanced democracies at the national level. Drawing on this research, I define the book's key concepts, including interest groups, policy expansion, and retrenchment. I then develop a new model of policy change focused on the fog of enactment and organized combat, outlining both direct and indirect pathways that advocate and opponent interest groups exploit to influence policy after implementation. Drawing on original survey data from US state legislators and their staff, I provide evidence for my theory, supplementing the historical institutionalist case studies in the rest of the book.

In Chapter 3, I examine the historical roots of the current conflict over the electricity system. Private electric utilities have long held a privileged position in energy policy, controlling state regulatory bodies for most of the twentieth century (Hirsh 1989; Hughes 1983). Early regulatory decisions surrounding electricity ownership and pricing structures paved the way for contemporary conflicts over renewable energy policies. Notably, utilities used their power to shape policy and technology to their advantage in three ways: they resisted innovation, they advocated for rate structures that exacerbated environmental harms, and they denied the climate crisis and other environmental problems. Taking a historical view, we can see that the electricity system developed the way it did—with large, fossil fuel plants and expensive, privately owned, and poorly maintained electric grids—because it served the interests of these powerful private utilities. Thus, like Naomi Oreskes and Erik M. Conway's book *Merchants of Doubt* (2010), this chapter shows how utilities' delay and denial have undermined progress on climate change. It was only with the energy crisis and the rise of the environmental movement in the 1970s that utilities' dominance began to be challenged.

Chapters 4 through 8 present the book's contemporary empirical cases. Across these chapters, I trace iterative cycles of policy enactment, implementation, and revision over several decades. In Chapters 4 and 5, I examine one of the earliest and most prominent renewable energy laws in the United States: Texas's RPS, enacted under then-governor George W. Bush in 1999. Chapter 4 provides the early history of clean energy leadership in Texas, when wind energy grew rapidly. Relying on original archival research and primary interviews with both advocates and opponents, I explain why Texas acted on clean energy before California and other more progressive states. I show how savvy advocates used public opinion to drive policy change during windows of opportunity. More broadly, this case reveals a classic positive feedback dynamic: a growing wind energy sector increased its influence over the legislature and successfully expanded clean energy policy. Here, advocates relied on the fog of enactment to get a clean energy target and an ambitious infrastructure spending bill passed in the legislature. They also worked through the public to convince legislators that clean energy leadership was important for Texans.

In Chapter 5, I conclude the Texas story on a sad note. Over time, fossil fuel companies and industrial energy consumers came to oppose Texas's renewable energy policies. Given their political influence over both politicians and regulators, these opponents were able to block reforms from passing in the legislature or being implemented through regulatory bodies. While a solar energy policy was passed in Texas in 2005, it was never implemented. Clean energy opponents succeeded in blocking the law's implementation because they were influential with the legislature and with regulators. One fossil fuel industry lobbyist reportedly worked from a desk in a key senator's office. In this chapter, we see how opponents can directly undermine policy, even if advocates have previously won policy conflicts and started positive feedback. We also see how opponents can use the fog of enactment strategically to resist policy during implementation.

In Chapter 6, I explore a case of retrenchment by a thousand cuts. Kansas first implemented a clean energy law in 2009, through a political bargain. In exchange for a renewable energy target, Democratic governor Mark Parkinson agreed to approve a coal plant. But the coal plant was never built, and the opposition to the RPS grew. The state seemed poised to withstand retrenchment attacks, due to strong growth in the wind energy industry. However, the opponents—including Koch Industries and their allied AFP—returned year after year and eventually wore down the advocates. Unable to directly overturn the law through the legislature, the opponents worked to weaken support for the policy. They backed politicians in primaries and secured appointments in vacant seats for anti-renewables candidates. They also funded astroturf campaigns. Advocates responded by organizing the public, but they were less politically influential— particularly after the Republican Party made supporting the clean energy rollback a litmus test for party financing. Despite the established wind energy industry backing pro-renewables Republicans in primaries, the fossil fuel opponents were eventually able to retrench the law. This case shows that when policy feedback begins to take hold, it can threaten policy opponents. When these incumbent opponents have sufficient political influence, they can undermine feedback even in cases where feedback has effectively created or supported advocates.

In Chapter 7, I examine a different renewable energy law: net metering. These laws have been crucial across the country for the development of the solar market. They set the rules for how to compensate individuals and organizations supplying energy to the grid. After passing a series of clean energy targets in the 1990s and early 2000s that the state never implemented, Arizona finally began to get serious about renewable energy in 2008, passing a net metering law that year. After this policy, solar energy grew rapidly as companies from earlier acting states crossed into Arizona, in a case of feedback spillovers. However, the state regulator made a series of decisions from 2013 to 2017 that weakened and ultimately retrenched the state's solar policies. Here, regulatory capture was key to electric utilities' success in controlling the policymaking process. One utility, Arizona Public Service, spent at least $55 million across several elections to block clean energy policies and elect anti-solar politicians. This chapter shows how opponent interest groups can directly drive retrenchment through regulatory capture.

In Chapter 8, the final empirical chapter, I examine how networked interest groups can learn about policies in other states and use this information to swiftly drive retrenchment. Ohio was one of the last states to enact a renewable energy target. For this reason, electric utilities understood more quickly that the policy would undermine the financial viability of their existing fossil fuel assets. When states are followers rather than leaders, the fog of enactment is less likely to occur. ALEC, which has electric utility and fossil fuel companies as members, played an important role in Ohio, putting retrenching clean energy "mandates" on the agenda. Opponents worked over several years to freeze the policy, creating an uncertain future for renewable energy companies in the state. They also changed the rules around wind energy siting, locking the entire industry out of the state. At the same time, these utilities pressured their regulators and the legislature to pass subsidies to keep their polluting coal power plants open longer. In 2019, the utilities finally succeeded in repealing the state's efficiency and renewables standards, replacing them with a bailout for coal plants. In this case, we see how policy feedback can fail when opponents networked across the states learn from earlier policies' implementation and weaken the policy before it is able to generate lock-in.

In Chapter 9, the book's conclusion, I chart a path forward, both theoretically and empirically. I show how using a more complex model of policy feedback enables a better understanding of the conditions under which retrenchment is likely. This chapter makes the case that understanding organized combat between policy advocates and opponents is crucial to explaining policy change. I also show how advocates and states can get climate policy back on track, reviewing more hopeful recent developments in state clean energy laws. For too long, a small set of interest groups has captured the regulatory process—the very mechanism that is supposed to serve and protect the public interest. They have used their power to imperil the health and well-being of all people on the planet. To address climate change, policy advocates need to win policy conflicts more often. Clean energy advocates must learn from their opponents' success in retrenching policy.

The final chapter provides lessons from the opponents' playbook over the past 100 years. Until our policies are able to effectively challenge fossil fuel corporations and electric utilities as vested interest groups, the lives of billions of people and even more animals, species, and ecosystems are in grave danger.

Climate change is the largest threat the United States and all societies currently face. We need to radically alter the energy sector's politics if we hope to begin to solve this problem. Advocates cannot just focus on building the future. They must also dismantle the past. To transform our energy system and address the climate crisis head on, we must undermine opponents' political power. The fossil fuel era must end.

When New Policies Fail to Create a New Politics

The plan to reform California's electricity sector began in the mid-1990s and took years. The aim was to move away from the nearly 100-year-old regulated system toward a market-based approach to electricity. Like many major reforms, it was a complicated task. Experts weighed in. Politicians pored over the details in draft bills—and so did interest groups. The private electric utilities the law would transform went to great lengths to influence the process. By the time the Electric Utility Industry Restructuring Act (AB 1890) passed in 1996, it was 67 pages long.

After implementation in 1998, electricity in California was no longer a monopoly business. Companies other than utilities were now allowed to sell electricity. In this way, the law created new interest groups—independent power producers and electricity brokers. This is exactly the kind of transformative reform we would expect to create a positive feedback cycle, locking itself in over time. The law even created an institution—the Independent System Operator—to oversee the new market.

But the history of California's electricity restructuring is not one of path dependence and lock-in. The market was active for less than 3 years. Rolling blackouts and electricity shortages were rampant throughout 2001, leading to a political crisis. By the end of 2003, Governor Gray Davis faced a recall election, which he lost. The policy was rolled back, reverting to nearly the same regulatory structure that monopoly utilities had faced for the past century. Rather than a positive feedback cycle, the law's implementation led to a rapid reversal. This was negative feedback, not path dependence.

Why did the policy fail to lock-in? Reformers could not predict the policy's consequences when they undertook the reform. And no wonder: complex policies enter a world full of uncertainty, with independent decision makers responsible for interpreting and implementing laws, all while interest groups weigh in. Policymakers were working through a thick fog: dealing with a novel

Short Circuiting Policy. Leah Cardamore Stokes, Oxford University Press (2020). © Oxford University Press.
DOI: 10.1093/oso/9780190074265.001.0001

policy, undertaking a major reform, and working in a technical domain. In this and many other cases, policies' consequences are very hard to predict.

This chapter provides the theoretical foundation for the empirical cases that follow. It also contains original empirical evidence from surveys of state legislators and their staff that reinforce the book's theoretical arguments. I argue that novel policies with the potential to create positive feedback are often passed with considerable uncertainty or as part of major reform packages. As a result, opponent interest groups and politicians struggle to predict policies' consequences during the legislative drafting process. I call this dynamic the "fog of enactment." It is only during implementation that policies' consequences become clearer—as resources, incentives, and information change. When policy opponents realize that new policies do not serve their interests or when a shift in political power provides them with an opportunity, they may try to weaken policies.

Understanding whether or not policies will reinforce themselves through path dependence requires centering interest groups. Interest group conflict over policy is not limited to policy enactment—it often intensifies during and after implementation. Even in cases where policy feedback has occurred, interest groups are still engaged in a continual process of organized combat over policy. One group may be weakened from the policies' implementation, but if it still exists, it will fight to shift the law.

To weaken policies during and after implementation, opponents must first gain greater political influence relative to advocates. They can then try to retrench policies through both *direct* and *indirect* pathways. If political opponents are sufficiently empowered relative to advocates, they can work to directly revise a policy by lobbying a legislature. They can also work directly with bureaucrats to shift a policy's interpretation, for example, by capturing the regulator or implementing body.

But this is not the only route forward. If opponents do not have sufficient political influence to weaken policies directly, they can engage in three indirect strategies. First, they can use the party system to drive polarization. Interest groups can support candidates in primary elections to threaten incumbent politicians. This tactic changes who is making the decisions and the incentives for other politicians. Second, opponents can attempt to shape politicians' perceptions of public opinion. This can be done in two ways: via interest groups mobilizing the public, what Ken Kollman (1998) calls "outside lobbying"; or via fake public campaigns, often called "astroturfing" (Walker 2014). Third, opponents can challenge laws and their implementation through the courts.

Throughout this process, interest groups build and maintain networks that allow them to work across state borders. No state is an island: interest groups regularly move across jurisdictions to influence policy elsewhere. If a policy creates new advocates in one place, these advocates can work to drive policy changes in other places. In this way, policy feedback spillovers can occur. Cross-state networks play three important roles: they help interest groups learn to anticipate policies' consequences; they help interest groups disseminate effective political strategies; and they facilitate collective action. Hence, opponents use networks to reduce the fog of enactment and increase their effectiveness in blocking and weakening their targeted policies. Using all these tactics, opponents can cause policy feedback to stall. In these cases, policies can fail to reshape politics over the long term.

Clean energy targets are an ideal policy to study the diverse ways that path dependence can fail. These laws set specific goals, allowing scholars to benchmark progress. In fact, these policies were designed with policy feedback in mind. Their goal was to kick-start new industries, empower advocates, and reduce technology costs over time (Schmidt & Sewerin 2017). Yet many of these policies are failing to create such a virtuous cycle. And worse, they are failing to move the electricity system away from fossil fuels fast enough to avoid climate catastrophe.

Defining Policy Feedback

Policy change can be spurred by external shocks (Baumgartner & Jones 2009; Sabatier 1993). Natural disasters, terrorist attacks, foreign interventions in elections, globalization, innovation in technologies, and economic crises are all examples of exogenous forces that can create opportunities for policy change. But policy change can also come from shifts inside the political system, from interest group behavior and public opinion. Theories of path dependence and policy feedback are concerned with these internal modes of policy change. "Policy feedback" is the idea that public policies can reshape the political landscape, changing both the content of policy and the likelihood of its passage. These studies reverse the traditional arrow in political science, which typically points from politics to policy. Instead, they seek to explain how, according to E. E. Schattschneider, "new policies create a new politics" (1935, 288).

Over the twentieth century, numerous scholars have pointed to the importance of policy feedback in policy change. Theodore Lowi described feedback as how "policies determine politics" (1972, 299). And Hugh Heclo wrote that the "content of a policy can itself be a crucial independent factor in producing effects on the policymaking process. . . . Even the most innovative creations are decisively shaped by the content of previous policy" (1974, 5). Theda Skocpol's *Protecting Soldiers and Mothers* (1992) was a landmark empirical book that fleshed out how feedback unfolded in practice, examining the welfare state's development in the United States. As Skocpol (1992, 58) put it, "policies, once enacted, restructure subsequent political processes."

When Paul Pierson gave his now classic description of policy feedback in 1993, he argued that policy feedback could not be denied when "public policies were not only outputs of but important inputs into the political process, often dramatically re-shaping social, economic, and political conditions" (1993, 595). As he has subsequently pointed out, studying these developments requires a longitudinal approach toward institutions (Pierson 2004). Numerous applied studies of policy feedback followed (Baumgartner & Jones 2002; Campbell 2003; Mettler 2005). Thus, for several decades now, policy feedback theories have offered a valuable contribution to the study of public policy, historical in-stitutionalism, and comparative political economy.[1] The topic has grown to the point where the term yielded almost 17,000 results in an April 2019 search on Google Scholar.

Despite this impressive theoretical flourishing, policy feedback has often proven a confusing concept to define. First, we must understand what the term "feedback" means: it describes a change in a variable, X, that initiates a causal sequence that eventually leads to further change in X. The impor-tant thing to note is that feedback involves causal loops. Feedback comes in two forms. "Positive" feedbacks are amplifying causal chains, where a change in X eventually leads to further change in X in the *same* direction as the ini-tial change. "Negative" feedbacks involve dampening causal chains, where a change in X eventually leads X to change in the *reverse* direction of the initial change. Within political science, other terms are often used to describe these dynamics, such as "self-reinforcing" and "self-undermining" (Jacobs & Weaver 2015; Pierson 1993).

A few practical examples can help explain the difference between posi-tive and negative feedback. Feedback loops are important in climate science. Scientists are concerned about the role of positive feedbacks in amplifying global warming. Increases in temperature can lead to more water vapor in the atmosphere, which further increases global temperatures because water vapor is a greenhouse gas. Similarly, increases in global temperature reduce arctic ice cover, which decreases the reflective capacity of the planet (the albedo), which further increases global temperatures. In both of these examples, warming leads to further warming through a complex causal chain. Hence, these are clear examples of positive feedback. Negative feedbacks are also present in the cli-mate system. For example, some clouds will change as global temperatures rise, allowing them to reflect sunlight back into space. Here, an increase in warming leads to a decrease in warming. Hence, this is an example of negative feedback. Unfortunately, there are more positive than negative feedbacks in the climate system—which is bad news for global warming.

Now that we understand the idea of feedback broadly, we can unpack its meaning when applied to public policy. Importantly, feedback does not unfold in a deterministic way in social systems, as it can in natural systems. In a political setting, actors must interpret policies, and those interpretations vary depending on the actor. In addition, power relationships are involved—some groups have more ability to shape policy change than others. Because opponents and advocates engage in organized combat over the content and implementation of policy, we cannot assume that new policies will necessarily stick. Powerful actors may anticipate the potential for policy feedback and block policy change. Thus, feedback in social systems operates with greater contingency.

As Figure 2.1 shows, existing theory argues that policy feedback can occur either through the mass public or through elites, most notably interest groups. In political science, there are numerous cases of positive feedback in mass politics ranging from welfare reform to the GI Bill to social security to healthcare policy (Campbell 2003, 2012; Mettler 2005; Schneider & Ingram 1993; Soss & Schram 2007). For example, Andrea Campbell (2003) describes how growth in social security led to greater resources for seniors to engage politically. The program also strengthened seniors' public policy preferences and their identity as a collective group. Together these factors amplified seniors' participation in politics, which fueled congressional attention to social security, eventually leading to further growth in social security. She demonstrates that social policies can change political behavior by giving citizens new resources, altering their self-efficacy, and changing their political interests (Campbell 2003). Similarly, as Suzanne Mettler

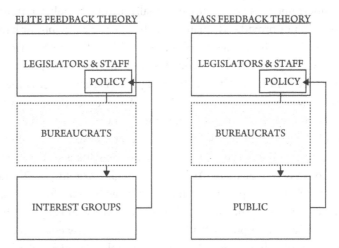

Figure 2.1 Policy Feedback: Existing Theories
This figure shows the actors involved in existing policy feedback theories. Most research examines either elite feedbacks or mass feedbacks independently. The implementation phase where bureaucrats play a role may or may not be emphasized.

and Joe Soss write, policies can shape mass politics by "defining membership; forging political cohesion and group divisions; building or undermining civic capacities; framing policy agendas, problems, and evaluations; and structuring, stimulating, and stalling political participation" (2004, 55). Overall, a large part of the political science literature on feedback examines the public.

There is also significant research showing the way that policy can reshape interest groups and elites (Anzia & Moe 2016; Goss 2010; Hacker 2002; Hertel-Fernandez 2019; Skocpol 1992). In her classic book, Theda Skocpol (1992) shows that women's groups engaged with early government policies were able to successfully propel larger social reforms over time. More recently, Sarah Anzia and Terry Moe (2016) have demonstrated how public-sector collective bargaining laws fueled growth in public-sector unions. Overall, work on elite feedbacks shows that policies can expand existing groups, create entirely new interest groups, modify group identities, and reshape groups' preferences (Campbell 2003, 2012; Hacker 2002; Mettler 2002; Patashnik 2003, 2008; Pierson 1993; Skocpol 1992).

In this project, I build on research at both the elite and mass levels, proposing a meso-level approach that integrates both of these processes and looks at positive and negative feedback simultaneously. There are strands of this approach in the literature. For example, Kristin Goss (2010) builds a multilevel model of policy feedback where organized civil society structures individuals' actions. Both elite and mass politics are involved in her feedback theory. Other scholars have also treated mass and elite effects simultaneously, including examining retrenchment. For example, Kent Weaver (2010) shows that pension system design can undermine these programs, eventually leading to policy retrenchment. If programs do not provide adequate benefits, operate equitably, or have an acceptable correlation between contributions and benefits, both mass and elite support for these programs may drop. This loss in program support can eventually drive decision makers to cut the program (Fernández & Jaime-Castillo 2013). In this way, a policy can undermine itself over time. These approaches are quite similar to my own. Thus, while my model is new, it builds on earlier work.

Much of the policy feedback literature also emphasizes how policy design can affect politics. The distribution of costs and benefits is usually highlighted as an important design element. As both R. Douglas Arnold (1992) and James Q. Wilson (1980) argue, policies with concentrated benefits for interest groups are more likely to arise and survive than policies with diffuse benefits for the public. Similarly, as Campbell (2012) shows in her review essay on mass feedback, a number of policy design elements matter: the size of a policy's benefits; its visibility, traceability, and duration; the way beneficiaries are distributed geographically; and a policy's mode of administration. Although enactment and policy design were the focus in early policy feedback research, more recent work emphasizes implementation (Moynihan & Soss 2014). Implementation is a crucial step between enactment and later policy changes for two reasons: first, it is during the implementation process that resources are redistributed among various political actors; second, implementation provides another opportunity to change policies through interpretation. Similarly to this more recent work, I emphasize implementation as a crucial step in feedback. After laws are implemented, actors obtain new information about the policy's effects and may come to support or oppose the policy in the future.[2]

Retrenchment and the Limits of Positive Feedback

Early work on policy feedback assumed that path dependence in policy was likely to occur. As Pierson put it, "self-reinforcing [positive feedback] processes make reversals very difficult" (2004, 10). And to date, research has largely supported this view, with numerous studies showing how policies lock in through path dependence. Scholars have identified successful policy feedback leading to path dependence in social security (Campbell 2003), the GI Bill (Mettler 2005), and the Head Start program (Bruch et al. 2010). Most of the policy feedback literature emphasizes positive feedback and lock-in.

However, sustained positive feedback may not be as common as the literature suggests. As Andrea Campbell (2012) has pointed out, research in this area has tended to select on the dependent variable for cases where feedback worked. As social scientists, we can be prone to studying successful cases of policy change. There is much less work on the conditions under which feedback can fail (Patashnik & Zelizer 2013; Pierson 2006; Weaver 2010).

Some scholars have begun to push back against a deterministic of path dependence (Béland 2010; Pierson 2004; Thelen 1999). In their working paper on the limits of policy feedback, Eric Patashnik and Julian Zelizer (2009) identify three causes that commonly undermine feedback: weak policy design, inadequate or conflicting institutional supports, and poor timing. As they put it, "policies sometimes fail to remake politics." This work builds on Eric Patashnik's earlier research on what happens after large policy reforms (2003, 2008). Overall, he does not find that path dependence or positive policy feedback is the norm. As he concludes, "The long-term durability of general-interest reforms simply cannot be taken for granted. . . . Sustaining broad-based reforms against the threats of corruption and reversal may be, if anything, an even more politically challenging task than winning the passage of those measures in the first place" (Patashnik, 2003, 226).

Other scholars have uncovered additional factors that limit feedback. In her review article on policy feedback, Andrea Campbell argues that new policy may not always create powerful advocates. As she puts it, "The constituency that emerges may be too weak to take on entrenched business interests or other clienteles" (Campbell, 2012, 346).[3] Alan Jacobs and Kent Weaver similarly argue that policy feedback can be undermined when powerful incumbents realize that the costs of the new policy are greater than they anticipated: "Public policies will sometimes work out badly for actors with substantial political resources, and thus a capacity to apply effective pressure for policy change" (2015, 446). Other studies have applied these ideas to specific empirical cases, finding negative feedback in practice (Lockwood 2013). Across the board, these theoretical and empirical research projects have shown that feedback is a contingent and contested process.

The consequence of negative feedback is retrenchment. What do I mean by "retrenchment"? Building on Paul Pierson's (1994) definition, retrenchment is policy change that: 1) repeals or weakens policy targets or funding; 2) restructures policies in a way that reduces their efficacy at addressing the problem; or 3) alters the policy's context in a way that increases the potential for retrenchment. Retrenchment and other forms of policy revision are quite common. For the first 10 years of a federal policy, a program has around a 5% chance of being modified or repealed each year—meaning that about 40% of the time federal policies change in their first decade (Berry et al. 2010). Hence, retrenchment is common, and it does not just occur when laws are repealed outright.

As Kathleen Thelen, James Mahoney, and Jacob Hacker argue, policies can be modified in complex and subtle ways, through displacement, layering, drift, and conversion (Hacker 2004, 2005; Mahoney & Thelen 2009; Thelen 2004). "Displacement" involves laws or regulations being rewritten directly. Legislation can also be subject to "layering," when new rules are added onto an existing policy regime, in some cases undermining the policy. This can also involve building parallel institutions that serve competing interests (Schickler 2001). Policies can suffer from "drift": if the policy regime stays stable while the world outside changes, the policy is unlikely to be able to address growing or new problems (Hacker 2005). In this case, if a modest goal is surpassed but a problem continues to grow, then policy drift occurs. Finally, "conversion" is the use of old rules for new ends through reinterpretation, for example, by actors exploiting ambiguities.

In this book, I build on this research, arguing that organized interest groups engaged in conflict over policy are a particularly important pathway for retrenchment. In four of the five cases in this book, retrenchment has occurred. In the case of Texas's solar law, the retrenchment came during implementation, when the law was never put into practice. In fact, this is an example of conversion: the words on paper stayed the same, but the way actors interpreted them changed.

In the cases of Kansas, Arizona, and Ohio, retrenchment involved repealing or weakening the policy directly, through displacement, as well as layering on new rules that made it harder to build clean energy. In many other states, drift has occurred: clean energy targets have been passed, but the state has failed to raise the target after it was met. Hence, across the board, we are seeing retrenchment in clean energy in the American states.

An Integrated Approach to Studying Policy Feedback

While significant research has examined successful policy feedback at either the elite or mass level independently, less work has tried to understand both simultaneously. In this project, I look at interest groups, the public, and the interactions between the two, proposing a more complex, meso-level theory of policy feedback (Figures 2.2 and 2.3). The goal is to identify generalizable conditions under which we might expect policy feedback to fail. In psychology, there is a long tradition of studying disease to understand how a healthy process works. I adopt that approach here: if we learn from the cases where policy feedback fails, we can use this knowledge to understand the conditions that are necessary for it to succeed. In this way, although I emphasize cases where we do not see successful policy feedback, I am still contributing to building a theory of policy feedback more broadly.

My theory of policy feedback emphasizes two key elements. First, I argue that policy changes are often adopted under a fog of enactment (Figure 2.2). This fog is thicker for novel policies, major reforms, in technical policy areas, and in cases where policies cross jurisdictional boundaries. Second, I show that implementation is a key stage in determining the success or failure of policy feedback—it is then that resources, incentives, and information are redistributed. After implementation, both interest groups and the public respond, helping to shape further policy changes and leading to policy expansion or retrenchment.

The feedback cycle initiates when legislators, working with their staff, write a bill. The bill-writing process is inherently complex, with significant ambiguity and uncertainty. There is a fog surrounding enactment, with politicians, interest groups, and the public struggling to predict proposals' likely consequences. The fog of enactment is particularly notable under a number of conditions. First, in early-acting states that pioneer policies, the uncertainty surrounding a bill's consequences is large. This is because interest groups have not yet experienced the policy first-hand and passed that information through their networks to states that act later. Networks allow information to be pulled in from elsewhere,

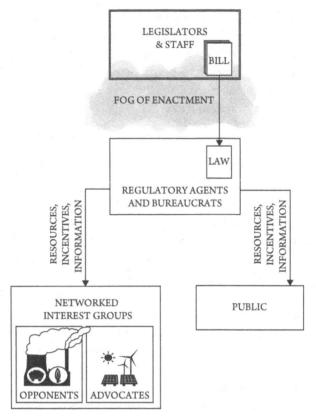

Figure 2.2 Enactment and Implementation After Policy Change
Bills can often be difficult to understand because of the fog of enactment. After
implementation, these laws can begin the feedback cycle by redistributing resources,
shifting incentives, and providing new information.

reducing ambiguity in states that enact policies later. Second, uncertainty is
greater for major reforms that involve long and complex language, which is difficult for all actors to process. Such reforms may also involve trade-offs, forcing
groups to compromise. Given the ambiguity in the policy's likely consequences,
with hindsight these compromises may not prove to be the right decision for
some groups. Third, technical policy areas are particularly prone to uncertainty,
in part because of innovation. Fourth, uncertainty is pronounced in policy
domains that interact across jurisdictions, with federal, state, and local rules
being overlaid on one another. When these factors are present, a given policy's
effects can be highly ambiguous.

After a bill becomes a law, bureaucrats and regulators take over as the primary decision makers. This is a crucial stage for feedback. During implementation, laws are interpreted and rules and regulations are issued. Depending on the

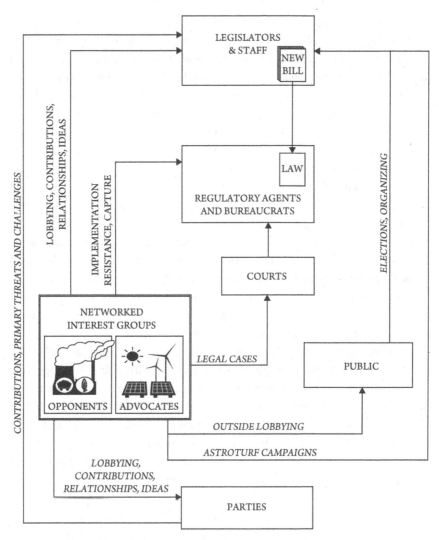

Figure 2.3 Organized Combat Post-Implementation: Retrenchment Pathways
After implementation, networked interest groups can try to undermine policies that have
a potential for feedback. Direct pathways of interest group influence are shown in normal
font; indirect pathways of interest group influence are shown in italic font.

specific policy, interest groups or the public may be affected as laws change resources, incentives, and information. Laws can provide new resources to specific
groups or incentives for individuals to invest in a technology. Through implementation, they can provide new information, for example, on how the policy
will affect outcomes.

After these changes in resources, incentives, and information, political actors react (Figure 2.3). Interest groups and the public may update their beliefs,

preferences, and even group identities after implementation, in a kind of political learning process. With this new information, actors decide whether to advocate for a policy's expansion, stability, or repeal. Feedback is thus contingent on interest groups' strategic reactions to policy (Patashnik & Zelizer 2013).

After implementation, interest group advocates may have grown in political power relative to opponents because of the resources the policy provided them. But incumbent opponents may still remain more influential in absolute terms. If after implementation opponents have updated their beliefs and preferences and are now against a policy, they will seek to undermine it. Opponents may be particularly successful at driving retrenchment if a change in government has opened up a policy window that increases their access to legislators and regulators. This is a form of exogenous policy change. But policy feedback theories remind us to also look for endogenous changes. Under existing feedback theory, opponents drive policy changes directly through lobbying, contributions, relationships, and ideas. Opponents are able to undercut policy feedback when they are relatively empowered compared to advocates, with sufficient influence with legislators. Opponents can also directly challenge policies by capturing the regulatory system or engaging in what I call "implementation resistance."

I demonstrate that when opponents are less powerful, they can still try to weaken policy *indirectly*—using parties, the courts, and the public. By supporting primary challengers against incumbent politicians who are not on their side, opponents may try to shift the politics and cut off feedback (Bawn et al. 2012). Over time, this can drive partisan polarization in a policy domain and make path dependence less likely. Opponents can also use the public to try to shift policy. They can construct public opinion both by working with the public and by creating fake public campaigns through astroturfing. Interest groups can also use the courts to challenge and undermine policy.

In this model, organized opponents who operate through networks are more likely to drive retrenchment than the public. Compared to the public, interest groups have greater resources and information and suffer less from a collective action problem (Olson 1965). That said, if policies primarily shift resources for the masses and the public successfully organizes, it can also respond to policy change. In these cases, the public may demand the government keep or shift a policy. If politicians are convinced public concern is large enough to warrant a risk for re-election, they may respond. We see this, for example, when carbon taxes are rolled back after raising energy prices.

Overall, if opponent interest groups are successful at gaining influence compared to policy advocates, policy feedback can fail, resulting in retrenchment or policy drift. The rest of this chapter unpacks each of these stages in greater detail, fleshing out this meso-level theory. In particular, the feedback process is contingent on whether: 1) interest groups are successful at driving partisan polarization through primary challengers winning campaigns or scaring incumbents into falling in line; 2) interest groups are able to organize the public such that it now appears to politicians that the public has shifted toward opposition; and 3) judges rule in favor of the opponent interest group. Advocates and opponents engage in organized combat in each of these areas, trying to move politicians, regulators, parties, the public, and the courts in the process. Hence, this book emphasizes power and resources, rather than framing, to understand when policy changes are likely to occur.

Starting the Feedback Cycle: A Theory of the Fog of Enactment

In 2010, when the Affordable Care Act (ACA) was wending its way through Congress, Nancy Pelosi infamously said, "We have to pass the bill, so that you can find out what's in it, away from the fog of the controversy." Republicans used this quote, out of context, to pillory Pelosi for years. But she was speaking to a deeper truth in American politics: there is ambiguity surrounding policy enactment. I call this dynamic the "fog of enactment." In this section, I examine when and why it occurs. Ambiguity is a fundamental part of policymaking for at least three reasons: the negotiation process, the intentional use of ambiguity by some actors, and the future's fundamental unknowability. I also identify four specific factors that enhance the fog of enactment: policies that have not been implemented widely elsewhere, major reforms that involve complex rules, technical policy domains, and policy areas that have overlapping jurisdictions.

In policy domains with strong incumbent opponents, enactment represents a puzzle for theories of path dependence. How do policies that might engender positive feedback become law in the first place if powerful opponents are present to block the proposal? We know that interest group policy monopolies exist in many domains and that they resist changes that do not benefit their interests (Baumgartner & Jones 2009). As a result, policy tends toward stasis rather than change. Why would these dominant interest groups, which maintain a monopoly over policymaking, allow a policy to pass that could spur feedback and undermine their position?

The reason is the fog of enactment: interest groups and politicians do not always understand a policy's likely consequences, creating a gap between actors' expectations and the policy's actual outcome after implementation. Ambiguity, uncertainty, and unintended consequences all play a role in policymaking (Bergquist 2018). Ambiguity occurs when rules are left open to multiple interpretations. This creates space for cooperation and compromise, facilitating negotiation during enactment (Arnold 1992). As Deborah Stone argues, ambiguity is often intentional. It allows individuals to project different visions onto the same policy, making a policy "two things at once" (Stone 2002, 161). As she put it, "A type of policy analysis that does not make room for the centrality of ambiguity in politics can be of little use" (Stone 2002, 157). Similarly, John Kingdon's work on the policy process placed ambiguity at the center, particularly with respect to coalition-building (Kingdon 2011; Zahariadis 2007).

Uncertainty also plays a role. In policymaking, there is always unknown or imperfect information. In this way, the fog of enactment is similar to "bounded rationality"—the idea that decisions do not unfold with perfect information (Cohen et al. 1972; March & Olsen 1976; March & Simon 1993). The idea is also related to unintended consequences—outcomes that are not foreseen or intended when an actor takes a purposive action (Merton 1936). As Lindblom (1959) put it, "A wise policy-maker consequently expects that his policies will achieve only part of what he hopes and at the same time will produce unanticipated consequences he would have preferred to avoid." These are commonly seen in environmental problems—indeed, climate change is an unintended consequence of fossil fuel combustion. All of these factors—ambiguity, uncertainty, and unintended consequences—play a role in the fog of enactment.

My argument here thus centers interpretation—a factor that was highlighted in early research on policy feedback: "The process through which individuals choose a course of action does not involve a simple calculation of easily discernible costs and benefits" (Pierson, 1993, 611). However, this argument was not central to later research on feedback. In this project, I flesh out this interpretivist view in greater detail. It is not just material effects that can affect actors' preferences—their *beliefs* about future material effects are crucial.

How do ambiguity, uncertainty, and unintended consequences lead to a fog during enactment? First, the negotiation process within legislatures plays a key role. As Alan Jacobs and Kent Weaver put it, "Policy choice [in democracies] is typically a collective activity. . . . Policymaking procedures thus frequently contain substantial complexity and incoherence rather than a single policy logic" (Jacobs & Weaver 2015, 445). As bills are negotiated, they move from chamber to chamber, bouncing back and forth, and a variety of actors weigh in. The bargaining environment is not clear because advocates and opponents do not always sit down at the same table together (Susskind & Cruikshank 1987). When a given interest group negotiates over specific provisions, it may not know what it is trading off against, making the counterfactual condition unclear. Different groups also have varying ability to access the negotiating table. While public committee hearings are open to everyone, backroom negotiations where politicians act as brokers are very common—and not everyone is invited to this table.

Second, interest groups can strategically use the fog of enactment to gain an advantage. As Douglas Arnold (1992) argues, some politicians will leave bills ambiguous to provide themselves cover. Power asymmetries are important here. Not all political actors have the same resources to reduce ambiguity and uncertainty or anticipate consequences (Curry 2015). We can think of actors' ability to understand the potential consequences of laws as akin to Philip Tetlock's (2005) distinction between foxes and hedgehogs. Some political actors bring considerable expertise that allows them to forecast the future like a fox. As Lee Drutman (2015) shows, corporate lobbyists act like foxes, holding more information than legislative staffers or public interest groups. Other political actors are hedgehogs—stuck within a given paradigm that does not allow them to evaluate potential outcomes well.

Still, the fog of enactment is most surprising for politicians, their staff, and highly professionalized interest groups operating in a specific policy area. These actors pay the most attention to policy in the United States. For some interest groups, such as regulated electric utilities, understanding government policy is at the core of their business. Yet, even these actors can fail to anticipate policy outcomes. Dominant interest groups may become staid institutions, fixed in their ways and unable to nimbly forecast the future. As the next chapter will show, electric utilities are one example of a hedgehog-like interest group. But we can think of other examples, like banks. Before deregulation, many other industries that maintained monopolies, from telecommunications to airlines, would have also fit this description (Patashnik 2008).

Hence, the fog of enactment can be asymmetric—certain actors can predict policy implementation and feedback better than others. The challenge of understanding legislation is not equally distributed. Politically influential parties can see more of the negotiating landscape because they have closer ties to politicians and are therefore better placed to extract information. This is similar to James Curry's (2015) argument that party leaders in Congress have more knowledge than rank-and-file members. Indeed, leadership may deliberately leave members in the dark to ensure that they support bills. If knowledge is power, some actors may choose to keep information to themselves. A better-informed party can use the fog of enactment as a weapon against its opponents.

These factors are only exacerbated for the public, which almost always acts like a hedgehog. People hear about policies filtered through politicians, interest groups, and the media. Understanding bills typically requires legal training, making it difficult for the public to directly participate in policy debates. This also makes it easy for interest groups to manipulate public perceptions of legislation to their advantage. Hence Pelosi's point—the public can be left in the dark during bill negotiations, presented with ideological or interest-based representations more than facts. In the case of the ACA, that included arguments that the bill would create "death panels" that would adjudicate healthcare decisions. When it comes to policy, the public is usually wandering blind, led by interest groups with a stake in the outcome.

Third, the fog of enactment is a result of the future's fundamental unknowability. When policies are passed, politicians and interest groups make guesses about the future. They do not know what will happen. We know that individuals can suffer from myopia, assuming the future will be like the present (Levitt 1960; Quoidbach et al. 2013). When politicians think about the future, they are more likely to focus on short-term rather than longer-term consequences (Jacobs & Weaver 2015). Similarly, the Congressional Budget Office forecast the effects of legislation assuming no future policy change; given potential interactions between policies, this is likely a poor—if necessary—assumption. For some policy areas the future may turn out to be quite different from forecasts, particularly when uncertainty is high. According to Pierson (1993), we should expect forecasting to be a function of policy complexity. New industries that are rapidly expanding are particularly hard to predict. Overall, uncertainty is high when policies are enacted, leading to unintended consequences.

There are thus good theoretical reasons to assume that a fog of enactment looms over policymaking. But is this true in practice? Survey data can speak directly to this question. In 2017, I fielded a survey of politicians and their staffers in state legislatures across the country. Overall, the resulting sample was fairly representative, and around 400 respondents answered each question. I asked politicians and staffers to identify two policy domains from a list: the one they knew the *most* about and the one they knew the *least* about. The list included, healthcare, education, environmental, energy, criminal justice, immigration, and economic policy. After selecting two policy areas, state politicians and staff were asked a series of questions to test whether there is evidence for the fog of enactment.

Politicians and their staff were asked to recall specific bills that passed their chamber in the two policy areas they chose. Did the policies do what the respondent expected them to do when they were passed? For those areas state politicians and staffers said they knew the *most* about, more than half of respondents said the policies did not do what they expected, or only partially did what they expected (Figure 2.4). These results suggest that even for the laws that policymakers and their staff pay the most attention to, there is still considerable ambiguity and uncertainty. The results are even more dramatic for policy domains that politicians and staff are less familiar with: about 90% were at least partially surprised by policies' impacts in areas they knew the least about.

State politicians and their staff were also asked how well they believed they were able to predict policy impacts. Did they believe they could see the future during policymaking? Here again, politicians and their staff displayed

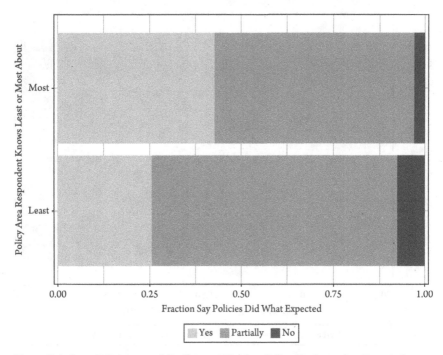

Figure 2.4 State Politicians and Staffers on Whether Policy Performed as Expected

considerable uncertainty. As Figure 2.5 shows, only 20% of respondents believed they could be very certain of a bill's impacts in the policy domain they knew the most about. This fell to only 3% for the policy domain respondents said they knew the least about. Clearly, there is a lot of ambiguity and uncertainty in policymaking. The fog of enactment is common.

The Fog Thickens: Novel Policies, Major Reforms, Technical Domains, and Multiple Jurisdictions

While it is arguable that all policies experience some amount of fog during enactment, certain factors make the fog particularly thick—increasing political actors' difficulty in anticipating a policy's consequences. I identify four factors that amplify the fog of enactment: when policies are novel, during major reforms, in technical policy domains, and when policies interact across scales of government.

First, when a policy is novel, there is greater uncertainty about its likely effect post-implementation (Volden et al. 2008). When policies are enacted, there are many unknowns: the nature of the problem, whether the solution will fix the problem, how the solution will interact with other policies, whether forecasts are correct, and so on. These unknowns decline over time as more jurisdictions

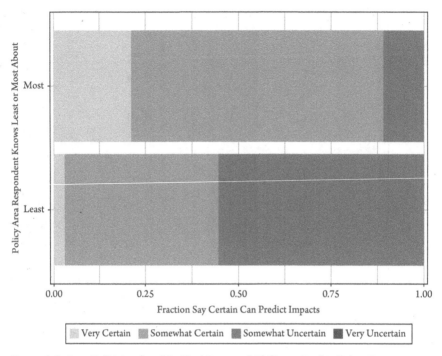

Figure 2.5 State Politicians' and Staffers' Reported Ability to Predict Policy Impacts

implement a given policy (Pawson et al. 2011). For example, in the case of clean energy, before any state had adopted and implemented a renewable portfolio standard (RPS), it was very difficult to predict how the policy would impact revenue streams for both clean energy and fossil fuel sources. Once 12 states had passed an RPS law, there was a considerable wealth of precedent available. This type of learning can happen between the states, from the federal level, and even across national borders. As a result, the fog of enactment decreases as laggard states follow leaders. Who is doing the learning? Unlike previous accounts (Volden et al. 2008), I view cross-state networks of interest groups as key to this process. Both advocates and opponents learn about the policy from early-acting jurisdictions. In states that have never acted to pass the policy, opponents who have learned from elsewhere may block the policy from ever passing. In this way, learning spills across state lines, as interest groups gather new information and share it through their networks.

Second, major reforms increase uncertainty and ambiguity. When bills are long and complex, it is more likely that legislators, their staff, the public, and even expert interest groups will struggle to understand all the provisions and their interactions. Yet bills in Congress are getting longer. According to data from the *Federal Register* compiled by the Brookings Institution, bills are now an average of around 20 pages.[4] This is a 10-fold increase since the late 1950s. Important and technical bills stretch into the hundreds of pages—the Energy Policy Acts of 1992 and 2005 were 357 and 551 pages, respectively. In 2009, Representative John Conyers commented, "What good is reading the bill if it's 1000 pages and you don't have two days and two lawyers to find out what if means after you read the bill?" Like Pelosi, he too was pilloried for this statement. But it was honest. With 97,000 pages published in the *Federal Register* in 2016, it is fantasy to believe that all members and senators are reading everything they vote on. Although compiled data are not available at the state level, similar trends in bill length are likely occurring there, at least in professionalized legislatures.

At both the federal and state levels, complex bills may be rushed because some interest groups have a strategic interest in maintaining ambiguity. For example, President George W. Bush's final prescription drug plan was over 1,000 pages long. Legislators were given less than 24 hours to review the bill before voting on it.[5] Pharmaceutical manufacturers likely believed that pushing the plan through quickly would benefit their bottom line (Oliver et al. 2004).

Major reforms also divide actors' attention. With a complex bill, politicians, interest groups, and the public are unlikely to have time to digest, anticipate, and lobby on all the different parts of the legislation. Political actors must prioritize issues, particularly with limited negotiating capital (Binder & Lee 2015; Jones & Baumgartner 2005). If actors are rational, they should pay attention to the issues that they believe matter the most to their interests. It may simply turn out that they are wrong about which provisions will prove the most important. To add to the complexity, each chamber's bill can have different clauses. At any given time, it is unclear what the final rules will be, meaning that actors do not necessarily know which provisions to focus on. When the bill is reconciled, its exact meaning may be unclear because of interactions between different parts of the law from the different chambers or because of last-minute additions.

Third, technical policy areas may be particularly susceptible to the fog of enactment because of uncertainty and unintended consequences. As Jennifer Pahlka, the founder of Code for America, put it, "All technical decisions are unintended."[6] This is because technology changes quickly, making it difficult for politicians or interest groups to forecast. In a brilliant illustration of this dynamic, Hanna Breetz (2013) shows how congressional targets for biofuels were wildly optimistic with hindsight. Clearly, the lawmakers failed to understand how their plans on paper would run into technological limits. This is a common issue in technical policy areas, where innovation is occurring—or failing to occur—alongside policy changes.

Fourth, and finally, policies' impacts can be difficult to predict because of how institutional changes interact across levels of government. Typically, scholarship focuses on one level of government, whether federal, state, or local. This is

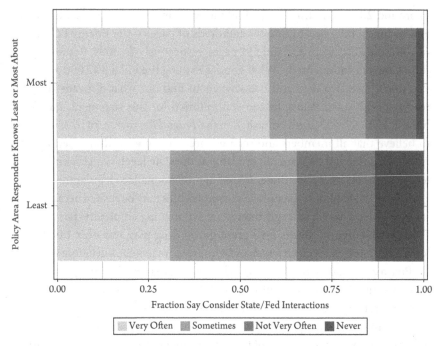

Figure 2.6 State Politicians and Staffers on Whether They Consider Potential State–
Federal Interactions During Policymaking

understandable given the challenge of understanding policy in any given jurisdiction. However, many policies interact across jurisdictions. Uncertainty can arise during enactment because of how a new law will relate to existing institutions and policies, particularly at other levels of government. When actors agree to a policy in a given jurisdiction, they do not know what other governments are going to do or even how previous policies elsewhere could interact with this new policy. This phenomenon is particularly salient in federalist systems where different levels of government share authority over a policy domain.

For example, changes to economic policy at the state level, such as altering taxes or the minimum wage, can shift wage markets and politics across state borders. Healthcare similarly has strong federal–state policy interactions. If the federal government changes payments to insurers, it dramatically alters the viability of states' health exchanges. In this case, the federal government has devolved implementation to the states, further increasing uncertainty (Jacobs & Callaghan 2013; Jacobs & Skocpol 2015). In practice, politicians and their staff report paying considerable attention to state and federal policy interactions. As Figures 2.6 and 2.7 show, this holds across policy domains they know the most and the least about. It is particularly pronounced for energy and healthcare policy—areas where there is considerable overlap in jurisdiction.

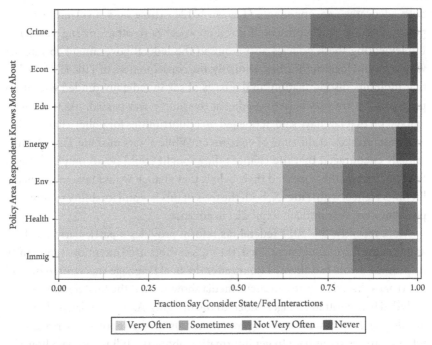

Figure 2.7 State Politicians and Staffers on Whether They Consider State–Federal Interactions in Policymaking: Most Knowledgeable Policy Domain

Applying the fog of enactment to the cases in this book can help illuminate its usefulness. As the next chapter will show, utility companies were ill equipped to understand how transformative renewable energy technologies could be to the electricity regulatory consensus. In the early days of RPS and net energy metering (NEM) policies, some opponents—including many incumbent utilities—did not understand renewable energy policies' potential effects. These were novel laws, in a technical area, with overlapping state and federal jurisdiction. Initially they were also put in major reforms to the electricity system. If utilities could have forecast the future accurately, they would never have agreed to RPS or NEM policies in the first place. However, utilities, like many actors, are poor at predicting policy impacts. As one advocate put it, "The utilities were victims of their own beliefs. They thought that renewables were some tiny market that would never grow."[7] This inability to see past enactment into implementation, or to forecast technology change, meant that utilities often agreed to more ambitious policies than they would have with hindsight.

This dynamic is not limited to the policies I studied at the state level. At the federal level, advocates are often caught in a similar fog, with prominent examples including the Clean Air Act and the Clean Water Act. When these policies were passed in the 1960 and 1970s, their long-term consequences were obscure to both advocates and opponents (Layzer 2012). These laws involved technical policy domains and represented novel approaches to attacking big problems. Implementing these policies also required the federal government to interact with state and local authorities. Similarly, the consequences of Title IX—the law that prohibits discrimination on the basis of sex in federally funded education programs—were very hard to predict at the time it was passed.[8] As those who worked on that law have said, it opened up opportunities for policy changes that were not foreseen at the time of enactment. While actors pushing Title IX were initially encouraged that the changes they sought could be accomplished in a few short years, they updated their beliefs that change would take more than a lifetime. Hence, with Title IX, both the uses of this law and its ability to solve the problem were very difficult to predict in advance.

More recently, the 2017 federal tax reform provides a particularly vivid example of the fog of enactment. First, the bill's authors used intentional ambiguity by pushing a vote less than 24 hours after the final language was written down.[9] Politicians shared pictures on social media showing that the final Senate version included handwritten changes added to the margins. As a result, lawmakers had no idea what they were agreeing to. Numerous media reports described how interest groups scrambled to get information about the bill to evaluate how the proposed changes might affect them. The negotiations—happening across both chambers and with the executive branch—were extremely complex. The pace of the voting and the bill's length—more than 1000 pages—meant no one inside or outside of Congress knew exactly what was going on. For example, the bill was written in such a way that it failed to clearly establish the lowest corporate tax bracket, forcing politicians to return to their chambers to pass another version of the bill.

Once implementation of the tax reform began, it became clear that the law's consequences were more ambiguous than politicians on the Hill had assumed. State and local governments began to allow citizens to pay their tax bills earlier and to creatively get around the changes in deductions. And media reported on a billion-and-a-half-dollar provision that had gone mostly unnoticed during enactment—economic opportunity recovery zones. One advocate involved with that provision stated, "if it's successful, we'll look back 10 years from now and say this was one of the most important parts of the tax bill, and one we didn't talk nearly enough about."[10] The ramifications of the tax bill are only beginning to become clear. According to the 2019 Institute on Taxation and Economic Policy's *Corporate Tax Report*, 60 of the biggest Fortune 500 companies avoided all federal income taxes in 2018.[11] Electric utilities, such as American Electric Power, benefited enormously from the tax bill, receiving a $32 million federal tax rebate.[12] Overall, because tax loopholes remained in place yet the statutory rate decreased, corporate tax revenues fell by 31%.[13]

Of course, policymaking is not always caught in a thick fog. In some cases, opponent interest groups may not like all the provisions in the law and understand that the reform will prove problematic to them in the future. Yet, they do not have enough influence with decision makers to block the policy. During implementation, they may seek to resist provisions they were unable to block during enactment. It is to this issue we now turn.

Implementation and Political Learning: Restructuring Politics Through Changing Resources, Incentives, and Information

If enactment creates the seed for changes in politics, then implementation is where this seed may germinate. The critical word here is "may." Simply because a law is passed does not mean it will be implemented in line with actors' expectations during enactment. Implementation's importance for policy change can be seen in cases where the rules are never enforced, and therefore the politics do not shift. Governments routinely violate their own laws, miss their own targets, or fail to implement provisions. Rules can be structured during enactment so that they are easier to break. If laws are never implemented, this directly undermines any potential feedback, making them easier to retrench. It also provides justification for retrenchment: opponents can argue that the rules were never implemented *because* they were untenable.

Implementation is a stage where the executive branch has considerable discretion and can block feedback. We see this dynamic unfolding clearly at the federal level under the Trump administration, which is not enforcing numerous regulations, most prominently those at the Environmental Protection Agency (EPA). Similarly, the mercury rule under the Clean Air Act was not implemented for several decades. When environmental rules are not implemented, industry's behavior and the politics of the issue remain the same as before enactment.[14] Focusing on implementation reminds us to think about the difference between the rules on paper and the rules in use.

If government policy is poorly implemented—whether intentionally or unintentionally—then feedback is less likely to take hold. The case of how the nonprofit Code for America improved food stamps' usage in California illustrates this fact well. This nonprofit works to improve government implementation and aimed to make food stamps easier to access. Like other states, it is very difficult for individuals to apply to receive food stamps in California. After Code for America rewrote the application, it helped reach more than 140,000 people in 2017 and 200,000 in 2018.[15] Improving a program's implementation helps to make policy stickier—these people are a potential constituency who can be organized and mobilized by interest groups if the policy is attacked.

In cases where laws are put into practice, implementation still does not automatically create policy feedback. Rather, it causes new resources, incentives, and information to be distributed to interest groups and the public. Through implementation, specific decisions are made that affect the scale of resources given to or taken away from different groups or individuals. Implementation can create entirely new interest groups. It can also reshape identities. For example, Suzanne Mettler (2005) illustrates how implementing government policy—in her case the GI Bill—can shift politics. As she puts it, "Program implementation conveyed to [veterans] powerful messages not only about the value of one particular program but also, more broadly, about government's responsiveness to people like them. . . . This suggests that the way in which government implements social programs can have a direct effect on the kind of citizens it produces" (Mettler 2005, 59). She documents how citizens receive messages during implementation that reshape their identities, beliefs, policy preferences, and ultimately political behavior.

Information also shifts during implementation allowing political actors to learn. The term "learning" is often associated with bureaucrats eager to improve laws (Heclo 1974). But it is not just neutral learning about policy effectiveness that is occuring. Implementation is also the site of political learning (May 1992; Sabatier 1988; Soss 1999). What these interest groups learn is not neutral information about how the policy could be improved. Instead, they learn about how the policy affects their interests, and they update their preferences accordingly. Implementation is when the ambiguities in laws and interest groups' positions are resolved.

Is there evidence that implementation is an important stage for learning? Looking back at the survey data can help to illuminate this question. When state politicians and their staff were asked to recall specific bills in the policy domains they knew the most about, *not a single respondent* said that she or he did not pay attention to what happened to policy during implementation (Figure 2.8). Instead, 60% said that they were fully aware of what happened to a law after implementation. Even for policy domains that politicians and their staff knew the least about, 100% of the survey respondents said they were at least partially aware of what happened to the laws during implementation. Clearly, implementation is an important stage that politicians, staffers, and interest groups pay attention to. It is a key stage when interests and preferences change as more information is revealed.

Learning also occurs more quickly in jurisdictions that follow policy leaders. Interest groups are not isolated within a single jurisdiction; rather, they interact across state borders. Networked and federated interest groups are increasingly

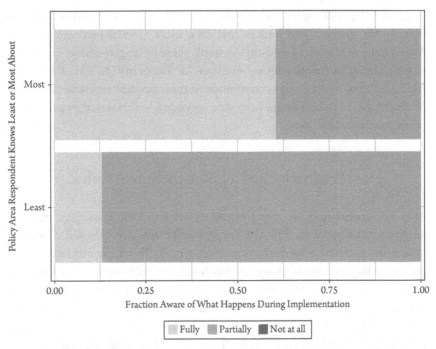

Figure 2.8 State Politicians and Staffers on Whether They Pay Attention to Policies During Implementation

important to state politics, in part because these groups are organized at the level that matters to influence politics (Skocpol et al. 2000). Prominent networks that try to influence legislators by providing an ideological view on laws and their effects include right-wing groups like the American Legislative Exchange Council (ALEC) and the State Policy Network, and left-wing groups like the State Innovation Exchange and the State Priorities Partnership. The nonpartisan National Conference of State Legislatures (NCSL) also tries to disseminate information about the effects of legislation that is relevant across the ideological spectrum. As actors in one state learn about the policy through implementation, they communicate with others. In this way, the fog of enactment can diminish in jurisdictions that are slower to enact policies, leading to policy changes being blocked during enactment, resisted during implementation, or outright retrenched. Later versions of the same policy passed in a different jurisdiction can face faster retrenchment.

Opponents are particularly effective when they deploy their attacks through networked, federated interest groups that cross state lines. Working through networks, interest groups can change politicians' incentives. In the case of renewable energy laws, cross-state interest groups pressured GOP legislators, putting RPS and NEM repeal on the agenda in many states. ALEC is particularly successful at providing legislators with an agenda that is certified as business-friendly for conservative leaders that lack ideas (Hertel-Fernandez 2014). Across most of the cases I study in this book, there are fingerprints of cross-state actors pushing for repeal, such as Americans for Prosperity (AFP) in Kansas and ALEC in Ohio. These groups communicated that opposing renewables was part of what it meant to be a Republican state legislator. In this way, they polarized a previously bipartisan issue.

How Feedback Can Fail: Retrenchment Pathways

After implementation, we might expect policies to lock in, as they create or reinforce constituencies. When a law has politically strengthened advocates, opponents will have a harder time undermining it. This is the central lesson of policy feedback research. However, this is not the only potential outcome. As Kathy Thelen puts it, "Institutions do not just generate positive feedback, they also 'generate grievance'" (2004, 295). The United States may have institutions that are particularly supportive of political losers' repeated efforts to dismantle policies. In Daniel Carpenter's (2010) words, "institutional strangulation" can occur as laws are slowly chipped away at. Or, as William Riker argues, losers continue to search for opportunities to change the status quo (see Shepsle 2003). Merely establishing a law in the United States does not guarantee its longevity (Berry et al. 2010).

Once opponents realize a policy undermines their interests, they may attack it. As Figure 2.3 shows, there are both direct and indirect pathways to drive policy change post-implementation. If opponents want to undermine existing legislation, they must first gain influence with decision makers. This power is relative: opponents can either undermine policy advocates' influence or increase their own. In this way, my framework builds on earlier research about the balance of power across different interest groups (Dahl 1961; Gaventa 1980). Interest groups compete in political combat to try to change policy in their desired direction. When they are empowered, opponents will work directly with legislators and regulators to rollback policy. When they do not have sufficient power, opponents can work indirectly through the political parties, the public, or the courts to try to short circuit policy. Through either direct or indirect means, interest group opponents may ultimately undermine policy, even after feedback has taken hold. Still, contestation is a hopeful sign. It means there are advocates available to defend the policy. The alternative is quiet politics or non-decision-making—which both point to the dominance of opponents (Crenson 1971; Culpepper 2010; Fairfield 2015; Gaventa 1980). Policy conflict means that the balance of power is shifting. In the rest of this section, I unpack both the retrenchment pathways in greater detail. Examining when policy feedback fails helps us to understand both American politics broadly and inaction on climate change specifically.

Retrenchment via Direct Means

Opponents are often incumbents who are well established prior to a new policy's enactment. In these cases, direct policy retrenchment may be easier because advocates remain insufficiently empowered. This can happen when a policy is poorly implemented and, as a result, advocates do not notably increase in numbers or resources. Under these conditions, opponents retain sufficient dominance in the legislative and regulatory process to push retrenchment. Thus, even if a policy has increased advocates' absolute levels of power or influence, these gains may be paltry compared to incumbent opponents' power. Who has the edge in organized combat is not just a function of the last marginal redistribution of resources, incentives, or information, but also the historical distribution of power.

We typically think of interest groups influencing legislators and regulators directly, through lobbying, relationships, contributions, and ideas. Lobbying has grown dramatically in the United States over the past several decades—in terms of both the number of corporate lobbyists and the amount of money they spend (Drutman 2015). Over time, lobbyists build strong relationships with legislators and their staff, providing them with information (Hansen 1991). As Lee Drutman (2015) shows, lobbyists sometimes become de facto additional staff members for legislators. Given that organized interest groups' agendas are distinct from the public interest, lobbying may undermine democratic representation (Baumgartner et al. 2009). To increase their political influence, opponents can strengthen their relationships with legislators, leaving them well positioned if and when an opportunity for policy retrenchment arises.

If opponent interest groups cannot convince legislators to directly undermine policies, they may instead lobby for other policies that undermine a law's efficacy. For example, in Vesla Weaver's (2007) work on resistance to civil rights legislation, she describes how opponents can change their tactics after they lose in enactment. Unable to defeat civil rights legislation from passing in the first place, opponents created a powerful countermovement that reinforced racial discrimination in the penal system. After civil rights activists ushered in reforms, opponents worked to undermine these gains by passing discriminatory laws, including mandatory minimum sentencing. Hence, policies can be undermined when opponents successfully lobby for parallel institutions.

Campaign contributions can also help interest groups influence politicians and their staff. As Lynda Powell (2012) shows, there is a relationship between state legislators' receipt of contributions and specific bills and votes. Campaign contributions' effects increase when there are no term limits and when issues have lower salience with the public. As she puts it, "the influence of contributions is in the details of legislation. Even a few words in a bill may be of great importance to a donor" (Powell 2012, 202). This is what Jeffrey Lax and Justin Phillips (2012) have called the "democratic deficit" in the states. After the *Citizens United v. Federal Election Campaign* decision that political spending is a form of protected speech that corporations have a right to use, state-level campaign contributions increased. As Douglas Spencer and Abby Wood (2014) have shown, this increased funding has been funneled through organizations and political committees that allow for greater anonymity. These dynamics are explored in this book in the Arizona case. But more generally there is significant evidence that campaign contributions are changing public policy in the states.

With a longer-term strategy, opponents can also use the power of ideas to create the conditions for retrenchment (Layzer 2012). Ideas may come in the form of a compelling report that resonates with a politician's ideology. Opponents may also target the public with narratives that challenge a policy's legitimacy. This dynamic is at play in the case of gun control policy, where gun rights advocates used ideas to change the interpretation of the Second Amendment over several decades (Goss 2008). Ideas need not only be constructive. Interest groups may also aim to discredit advocates' ideas, for example, by critiquing their reports. We see this clearly in the case of climate denial.

Interest groups do not just target politicians for direct policy revision, however. They also target the bureaucracy. Policy opponents have a variety of tools they can use in the regulatory process to engage in what I call "implementation resistance." Actors can try to have laws reinterpreted for new ends, by working to influence regulators and agencies. As Lowi (1979) argued, interest groups are more likely to dominate in regulatory bodies because these venues are less visible to the public. Terry Moe (1989) has similarly shown that interest groups try to structure bureaucracy to meet their goals. As Jacob Hacker (2004) argues, existing public policies can be reinterpreted in a process he calls "conversion." As he points out, "In general, the conversion of a policy should be easier when it delegates administration or lacks clear overarching rules or aims" (Hacker 2004, 247). One way actors can do this is by moving a policy from the legislature to an executive agency (Baumgartner & Jones 2009). Actors can also try to shift the venue to the courts to seek a reinterpretation of existing rules. The US federalist system supports this search for new venues to oppose policy, through its shared governance across levels of government. This can change the interpretation of existing policy and alter actors participating in the process or their relative influence, particularly if policy opponents have managed to capture a regulator (Stigler 1971). Given that interest groups are more organized than the public, particularly for low-salience issues, regulatory capture is often possible (Kalt & Zupan 1984). Regulatory capture can unfold in a variety of ways, including through bribes, rent-seeking, threats of legal challenge, social capture, and a revolving door between the regulated and the regulator (Carpenter & Moss 2014). Overall, interest groups wield significant influence during implementation (Yackee & Yackee 2006).

Retrenchment via Indirect Means

When opponents are not sufficiently empowered over advocates to directly retrench policy, they may instead try indirect strategies. Retrenchment can occur even after policy feedback has increased advocates' influence or the public's support for the policy. Indirect tactics involve targeting the parties, the public, and the courts to undermine policy. Some approaches are lower-profile (Hacker 2004; Layzer 2012). Others are about expanding the scope of conflict, to make the fight bigger and more visible (Schattschneider 1960).

The first indirect strategy opponent interest groups use is working through political parties. As the UCLA School of Political Parties argues, interest groups are intense policy demanders, central to crafting party agendas (Bawn et al. 2012; Cohen et al. 2009). In the empirical chapters, I show how interest groups can try to influence party agendas through elections, lobbying, contributions, relationships, and ideas. Interest groups can make certain policies litmus tests for partisans. If they are successful, politicians will fear retribution from activists, party elites, and primary voters if they stray from a particular position. They can also try to influence party platforms through constructing and disseminating ideas. The result is increasing partisan polarization, as the parties move further apart on issues. When policies are already in place that they oppose, opponents' goal in intervening in the electoral process is to elect sympathetic politicians, open to retrenching policy. Given current law, interest groups can participate in elections with considerable anonymity. They can even encourage their employees to support their preferred candidate (Hertel-Fernandez 2018). When interest groups succeed in changing which party is elected to state legislatures or governorships, the effect on policy liberalism is large—and even larger than it was in the past (Caughey et al. 2017).

We can see how interest groups use the parties to shape policy through primaries—a place where elections, lobbying, contributions, relationships, and ideas all come together. When they hold sway over a policy domain in a party, opponents can threaten incumbents who are off side. Threats can be the loss of interest group funding or party funding, or support for primary challengers. The potential for a strong primary challenger from their own party can create incentives for incumbents to fall in line. There is evidence that even the threat of a primary alters congressional representatives' behavior (Kamarck & Wallner 2018). When primary challenges are successful, they result in incumbents losing their seats, shifting *which* politicians are making policy decisions (Hacker & Pierson 2006). In this way, interest groups can use the party structure to change who is in office into someone who shares their policy positions (Bawn et al. 2012). Partisan swings in who governs can be particularly important for undermining policy because it gives different interest groups access to decision makers (Berry et al. 2010).

Does this happen regularly? There is evidence that interest groups are now vetting candidates for primary challenges to an even greater extent than parties do (Rauch & La Raja 2017). And interest groups are investing in primaries with larger and larger contributions. In 2016, outside groups contributed $38 million to competitive primaries, compared to $5 million in 2008 (Rauch & La Raja 2017). These donors are on the extremes in their positions—and individuals associated with interest groups are particularly influential in primary nominations (Grumbach 2018b).

Interest groups' ability to shape the parties through primaries is pronounced at the subnational level. Nominations and general elections in the states are low-information. As a result, the public has trouble following the intricacies of policy debates, making it a particularly favorable terrain for interest group influence. At the state level, interest groups face less competition to propose or vet primary candidates. We can see this clearly in Arizona, where one utility was able to capture its regulators by playing a dominant role in primaries and general elections. Similarly, in Kansas, only a few actors—the Chamber of Commerce and Koch Industries—were investing in primary challengers. Hence, there was little competition from other groups to influence the process. Interest groups' role in shaping nominations in higher-profile, more information-rich nominations, such as the presidency, is likely lower (McCarty & Schickler 2018). Overall, given extreme polarization driven in part by a dense interest group environment and skyrocketing spending in primaries, policy feedback is unlikely to be as strong a force today in state politics.

Interest groups also use the public in their battles over policy. In the US, as in other democratic systems, the public exerts an important influence over politicians and their staff. The public is crucial to how politicians think about policy decisions (Fenno 1978; Hertel-Fernandez et al. 2019). Through elections, public opinion polls, contact with elected officials' offices, and other means, legislators become aware of the public's preferences. These preferences matter for politicians' re-election prospects, and consequently, politicians and their staff pay significant attention to the public (Fenno 1978; Hertel-Fernandez et al. 2019). The public can directly support policy change through elections. Yet, as Gabriel Lenz (2012) argues, the public struggles to understand policy independently from elites. Hence, groups are key brokers for the public. Interest groups explain policy to the public and construct versions of public opinion for politicians. If regulators are elected, interest group construction of the public extends to agencies.

There is evidence that interest groups are driving a wedge between public opinion and politicians' perceptions of public preferences (Broockman & Skovron 2018; Hertel-Fernandez et al. 2019). In research with Alexander Hertel-Fernandez and Matto Mildenberger (2019), I show that senior congressional political staffers systematically mis-estimate public opinion. This gap between what the public wants and what staffers and legislators think the public wants is partially explained by interest group contact and contributions. David Broockman and Christopher Skovron (2018) similarly show that in statehouses politicians often misperceive their citizens' policy views. Their paper demonstrates a "conservative bias"—politicians believe their constituents are *more* conservative than they are. They argue that this is because Republican citizens are far more likely to contact state politicians. Although they do not explicitly point to interest groups organizing right-wing citizens to contact politicians, their argument is consistent with this hypothesis. It is quite likely that interest groups are mobilizing certain citizens whose views are more extreme than those of the median voter. In the age of big data and the Internet, public communication with politicians is rarely spontaneous. Interest groups are getting better at targeting citizens to contact their representatives.

Interest groups are not trying to objectively measure and communicate public preferences—they aim to construct a particular view in line with their interests (Jacobs & Shapiro 2000). Outside lobbying, wherein interest groups mobilize citizens to contact or pressure decision makers, is one important strategy that interest groups use to construct versions of the public (Kollman 1998). But, in contrast to Ken Kollman's argument, I conceive of public opinion as less of a *constraint* on interest group influence and more as a *tool* interest groups use to influence legislators. Interest groups selectively mobilize specific groups in policy campaigns and elections and even ask leading questions on surveys (so-called push polls). They can construct opinion so that it appears that the public does not support the status quo policy. This can involve raising the policy's salience with the public—for example, by highlighting costs—to increase the likelihood of retrenchment.

In even more extreme cases, interest groups can go around the public but still shape legislators' and their staffs' perceptions. As Edward Walker (2014) shows, public affairs professionals organize participation in contemporary American politics. In its most nefarious form, interest groups circumvent the public entirely, creating fake campaigns—called "astroturfing." In these campaigns, interest groups suggest there is grassroots mobilization supporting or opposing a policy proposal. In truth, the public is not rising up—vested interests are just lying. In these cases, it's up to journalists to investigate and tell the truth about these campaigns' origins. Otherwise, interest groups' fake public campaigns may prove effective with politicians. In addition to astroturfing, interest groups may run false political ads (Walker 2014). Fossil fuel companies regularly rely on this technique. Apart from the cases described in this book, coal companies in West Virginia have developed front groups that purport to represent the public but are actually run by the industry (Bell & York 2010). In one extreme case, a utility in New Orleans—Entergy—hired actors to attend a public hearing, pretending they were concerned citizens. These actors were told to speak out against clean energy and in favor of a natural gas plant.[16]

This is not to say that the public can never independently exert influence over policy. In some cases, the public has an effect on policy change or stability, particularly when policies have created mass feedback effects through new resources. Hahrie Han (2014) demonstrates throughout her research that the public's voice can be heard through organizing and activism. Still, in contemporary American policymaking, interest groups' voices are usually much louder than the public's. Increasingly, the public is used as a tool by interest groups in their battles over policy.

The third indirect way that interest groups try to shift policy is through the legal system. Opponents can use the courts to contest policy they were not able to block during enactment or weaken during implementation. Steven Teles (2012) shows that conservatives have attempted to undermine liberal dominance in the courts. The result is that the same polarization trend that is affecting legislatures is also shaping the judicial branch (Binder 2008). This matters because judges have significant discretion over policy interpretation. As Judy Layzer (2012) shows, conservatives have used the judicial branch to make low-profile changes to policy, driving retrenchment over time.

Opponent interest groups can simultaneously deploy all of these direct and indirect strategies. When better-resourced opponents continually attack a policy, policy retrenchment can occur by a thousand cuts. After sustained attacks over many years, advocates may change their preferences and become willing to lose a policy because the alternative is an ongoing expansion of conflict. This is shown clearly in the case of Kansas's renewable energy laws. As resources are cut off from advocates, advocates' coalitions fracture. With scarcity, coalitions can break apart as advocates fight for their narrow survival, rather than allying for the broader common cause.

Conclusion: Examining Feedback Failures to Understand Politics

This chapter has argued that policy feedback often begins from a place of considerable ambiguity and uncertainty—from a fog of enactment. This dynamic lessens over time, with each round of policy revision, as the relationship between the words on paper and their implementation in practice becomes clearer. Hence early-acting states, complex reforms, technical policy domains, and cases with overlapping jurisdiction all involve greater ambiguity and uncertainty than late-acting states, simple reforms, nontechnical domains, and issues without federal interactions.

Implementation represents a key moment when political actors can learn. After implementation, policy changes how resources, incentives, and information are distributed across interest groups and the public. In response, these actors may change their beliefs, preferences, and even identities. Consequently, when policies are revised or retrenched, there is more information available about a given policy's consequences in the relevant jurisdiction or from similar policies passed in other jurisdictions. In some cases, opponents may seek to retrench policy. To do so, they can use both direct and indirect channels to gain political influence over advocates. Overall, policy feedback is less common in today's era of growing partisan polarization. Federated and networked interest groups play a particularly important role in spreading policy agendas from state to state, fueling retrenchment (Hertel-Fernandez 2019).

While this theory focuses on cases where path dependence fails, it does not just teach us about politics when feedback is disrupted. More generally, it provides a deeper understanding of how policymaking and implementation operate. Using detailed, longitudinal histories, we can unpack interest groups' relationship to policy over time (Pierson 2004). These histories need to describe what happened to get a policy on the agenda, passed by the legislature, implemented, and either expanded or retrenched. These cases also need to cover significant time in order to show how the political dynamics evolved. The same approach can be used to understand organized combat between interest groups and policy feedback in other policy domains, such as social policy, tax policy, or healthcare policy. In the rest of this book, I present detailed cases of interest group battles over clean energy policy. To enable the reader to follow these stories of organized combat over climate policy, we must begin with the longer history of electricity politics and climate inaction. It is to this issue we now turn.

3

An Institutional History of Electricity Politics and Climate Inaction

*Why, we have just begun to commence to get ready to find out about elec-
tricity. This scheme of combustion to get power makes me sick to think of—
it is so wasteful. . . .*

*You see, we should utilize natural forces and thus get all of our power.
Sunshine is a form of energy, and the winds and the tides are manifestations
of energy. Do we use them? Oh no! We burn up wood and coal, as renters
burn up the front fence for fuel. We live like squatters, not as if we owned
the property.*

—Thomas Edison, 1910[1]

All political institutions are resistant to change. But the regulations governing
electricity are particularly sticky. In part, this is because of the nature of the technology. Unlike other goods, electricity supply and demand must match in real
time, moment by moment—otherwise, the grid will grind to a halt. But technology is not the whole story. Politics have also made electricity institutions
stable. As this chapter will argue, electric utilities have ossified institutions,
shaping the regulatory structure to their benefit. To understand why utilities
were able to undo policy feedback, we need to examine their privileged position
in policymaking (Lindblom 1977).

In a pattern common to other policy areas, from healthcare to welfare to economic policy, a grand bargain was struck between the regulator and the regulated
(Hacker & Pierson 2002; Hertel-Fernandez 2019; Jacobs & King 2016). In the
early twentieth century, state governments gave private electric utilities monopoly status. In return, these companies would take advantage of economies of
scale to provide cheap and reliable energy. This decision locked in an incumbent
that relies on outdated technology, leading to significant delays in addressing
climate change. As a result, the status quo system increasingly operates at cross
purposes with the demands of transitioning the grid toward low-carbon sources.
In the electricity sector, as in many others, we see asymmetric organized combat

Short Circuiting Policy. Leah Cardamore Stokes, Oxford University Press (2020). © Oxford University Press.
DOI: 10.1093/oso/9780190074265.001.0001

with opponents to renewable energy technologies—fossil fuel companies and electric utilities—holding a privileged position. To unpack this dynamic, we need a political history of electricity policy in the United States, from its inception to the present, to provide context for contemporary conflicts over the electricity system. Here, I introduce the political actors who will appear repeatedly in the empirical chapters that follow.

Throughout the twentieth century, governments have structured electricity regulation to meet various public policy goals: price reduction in the early twentieth century, capacity expansion mid-century, conservation and supply diversity in the 1970s, price reduction in the 1980s and 1990s, and environmental goals most recently. These goals roughly correspond to the five historical periods covered in each section of this chapter (Figure 3.1). Drawing on primary and secondary sources, as well as energy historians' research, I explain how key decisions on technology, pricing, and regulation remain important today. I demonstrate that the organized conflict between interest groups over clean energy policies traces its roots to the earliest decisions on electricity pricing and regulation. The last section—climate change and the rise of renewable energy—presents a national overview of the politics unfolding in the empirical cases in the rest of the book.

Despite this rich institutional history, contemporary debates over renewable energy policy tend to be ahistorical. Advocates and opponents advance arguments about the relative merits of policy instruments, the validity of rate structures, and the right way to pay for distributed generation's grid costs without reference to the basis for the status quo regulatory system. Yet, to evaluate these arguments, we need to understand how path dependence led to contemporary

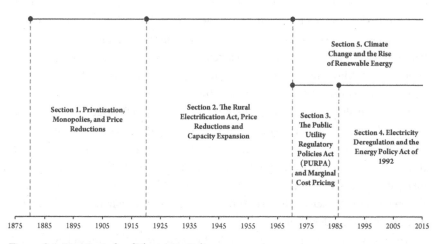

Figure 3.1 Five Periods of Electricity Policy

electricity regulation. This requires understanding the electricity system's institutional history.

History shows us that electricity is priced through political negotiations between utilities and their regulators, with occasional influence from other actors including academics, environmentalists, independent power producers, and citizens. In the United States, the level of government responsible for managing the electricity system has shifted over time. Municipalities were largely responsible in the late nineteenth century, with state governments gaining control from 1907 onward, and the federal government becoming increasingly interventionist beginning in the 1970s.

While utilities have at various times pushed for and resisted these jurisdictional changes, they have most consistently favored state-level regulation. Why? In the early twentieth century, electric utilities managed to secure a regulatory bargain at the state level that allowed them to maintain a monopoly over the power system and a privileged position in policymaking. Utilities used their power to shape policy and technology to their advantage in three problematic ways: they resisted innovation that would disrupt their business model, they shaped the rate structure in ways that exacerbated environmental harms, and they ignored or actively disputed the growing climate crisis and other environmental impacts from the energy system.

First, utilities resisted innovation (Hughes 2004). Once monopoly rights were granted, innovation in electricity technologies slowed. Instead, utilities focused on increasing profits rather than adopting new technologies (Hirsh 1999a). The radical inventiveness that characterized early electricity companies declined as corporate managers took over and focused on existing technologies, building ever larger coal plants. Utilities also used their market power, as the exclusive provider, to price electricity in a way that drove decentralized technology and industrial cogeneration out of business. This had the effect of increasing overall energy consumption and the environmental consequences of the electricity system. Private utilities were extremely effective during much of the mid-century at driving out competition, blocking industrial electricity production, and thereby securing their monopoly status.

Second, utilities, along with their regulators, shaped prices in a way that increased environmental harms. As Karl Polanyi (1944) convincingly argued, markets are fundamentally constructed with and by governments. Thus, electricity pricing is a function of both government policy and interest group privilege; it is not a simple function of economics. Understanding contemporary debates over electricity rate structures requires an understanding of historical electricity pricing decisions.

The rate structure was built alongside the centralized plant model in the mid-twentieth century when fuels were cheap. Until the late 1970s, electricity bills whose marginal costs *declined* with additional consumption had the effect of increasing the energy system's negative environmental and health impacts (Hirsh 1999a). In other words, the more electricity you bought, the cheaper it got. The government supported this structure because it was focused on building new capacity, particularly in rural areas (Spinak 2013). Utilities supported this pricing structure because it allowed them to expand their capital investments and electricity sales, thereby increasing their profits. Cost-based regulation made this the clearest pathway to increased profits for monopoly utilities. With greater sales, they could build new plants and apply for rate recovery. This kind of regulation creates an incentive to overinvest in capital to increase profits—a dynamic referred to as "gold-plating" or the "Averch-Johnson effect" (Averch & Johnson 2017). As a result, utilities maximized capital costs rather than focusing on efficiency (Boyes 1976). Consequently, private utilities did not prioritize energy conservation and efficiency before governments required it after the 1970s oil crises. And even then, they resisted.

This history shows us that while private utilities sometimes claim otherwise, economically rational electricity pricing has never occurred. It simply does not exist. Despite current reliance on economic arguments to justify their hostility to clean energy policies, utilities themselves have often resisted changes that would bring electricity policy in line with economic principles. Instead of favoring economic principles, like all businesses, utilities favor their bottom line: profit.

Third, for decades utilities have promoted climate denial and cast doubt on the science behind other environmental problems including acid rain and mercury pollution. Throughout the twentieth century, private electric utilities waged an organized denial campaign to discredit environmental science and delay state and federal action. These efforts succeeded in postponing environmental policy that would have mitigated the energy industry's harms.

From the 1980s onward, private utilities—organized through their industry association, the Edison Electric Institute (EEI)—actively spread climate denial. For example, in 1991 EEI and several utilities worked on a public campaign to " 'reposition global warming as theory' and not fact."[2] This denial of climate science continued for three decades. As recently as 2017, Thomas Fanning, the chief executive officer (CEO) of Southern Company, a private utility based in Georgia, claimed that climate change had been happening for millennia and that human emissions were "not the issue."[3] When he made those statements, he was chair of the EEI. And climate change is not the only environmental problem that utilities denied. In the 1980s, utilities claimed acid rain was not real (Oreskes & Conway 2010). Throughout the 1990s, they cast doubt on the science of mercury—a highly toxic element, extremely harmful to human health (Harley 2011). For all three issues, the science was clear during this time period. Denial of scientific facts for the sake of profit continues to permeate electric utilities at the highest ranks.[4] Like other fossil fuel companies, utilities also allied with and funded conservative think tanks to promote climate denial (Jacques et al. 2008; Layzer 2012).

But it is not just a matter of denying science. Private utilities also waged a campaign to delay environmental policy. Electric utilities successfully blocked the mercury rule, passed under a Republican president, for two decades. And climate policy is perhaps the issue they fought the hardest. Electric utilities engaged intensively in the 2000s to block federal emissions trading, a policy which would begin to address the climate crisis (Mildenberger 2020). As sociologist Robert Brulle (2018) estimates, utilities spent $554 million lobbying on climate policy at the federal level between 2000 and 2016. More recently, electric utilities have turned their attention to resisting state clean energy laws—the focus of this book.

When efforts were made to pass a federal clean energy standard (CES) through Congress in the 1990s and early 2000s, utilities successfully resisted.[5] Targets ranged from 4% to 10% renewables by 2010, with proposals from Representatives Ed Markey and Dan Schaefer as well as Senators Jim Jeffords and Dale Bumpers.[6] The failed Waxman-Markey bill from 2009 contained a renewable electricity standard that would have required 20% renewables for each state by 2020, with efficiency able to meet 8% of the target. While this 12% target was seen as relatively weak, it would have made a difference: in 2018, only 9.7% of the US electricity supply came from renewables, and 34 states fell below the target they would have been required to meet 2 years later.[7]

Interestingly, while the largest coal companies uniformly opposed Waxman-Markey, several electric utilities provisionally supported it, in a compromise to forestall a worse outcome—what we call "strategic accommodation" (Downie 2017; Grumbach 2015; Hacker & Pierson 2002; Kim et al. 2015). Other, coal-dominated utilities, particularly in the Midwest and South, lobbied legislators to weaken the renewable electricity standard.[8] Ultimately, the Waxman-Markey bill failed in the Senate, and no clean energy target has ever passed federally despite decades of effort from advocates. Periodically, politicians in Congress try again to pass a clean energy target—the latest iteration being Senator Udall's Renewable Electricity Standard Act of 2019, which would require utilities to generate 50% of their electricity from renewable sources by 2035. But carbon-intensive utilities have managed to keep this policy from passing at the federal level.

As Amory Lovins (1976) argued in the 1970s, there was a road not taken for American electricity policy. It is not difficult to imagine an alternative history where innovation was privileged over profits, energy conservation was incented, and clean energy was promoted. Such a system would have been much more favorable to renewable energy technologies today. Taking a historical view, we can see that the electricity system developed the way it did—with large and polluting fossil fuel plants and expensive, privately owned, and poorly maintained electric grids—because it served the interests of private electric utilities and other fossil fuel interests.

While the historical details in this chapter are specific to electricity, the arguments are generalizable to other policy domains. Healthcare is another highly technical area, driven by regulation. In that case, providers and insurers play the dominant role in shaping policy (Jacobs & Callaghan 2013; Olson 2010). Like electric utilities, they have high upfront capital costs and long investment horizons. Given the technical and esoteric nature of health regulation, the consequences of policy changes can similarly be hard to predict in advance. And the public rarely pays attention. These are both examples of what Pepper Culpepper (2010) calls "quiet politics"—low-salience and high-complexity policy domains that leave significant room for business influence because the public and the media are not paying much attention. As he argues, interest groups are able to control policy in these kinds of domains because legislators defer to interest groups, believing they hold greater expertise. We see the same pattern of quiet politics with electric utilities for much of the twentieth century.

My goal with this chapter is to take a historical institutionalist approach and bring energy and environmental policy onto an equal footing with other policy domains studied in political science and related fields. While understanding electricity policy can be technical, the same can be said for other policy areas. Understanding the eligibility requirements for Medicare and Medicaid, state-by-state rules on firearms and immigration, and financial reform is challenging. Yet, political science and public policy research are able to grapple with these issues. Given the climate crisis and other environmental problems, we urgently need to understand the political dimensions of our energy system. I hope this chapter will serve as a primer for those interested in gaining literacy on this most pressing challenge.

Of course, the topics covered here do not address all aspects of energy or environmental policy; but the goal is to provide a basis for understanding the case studies in the following chapters. And for those already familiar with electricity policy, this chapter will provide a political lens to understanding how our electricity system has evolved over the past century.

Privatization, Monopolies, and Price Reductions (1880–1920)

To understand electric utilities' privileged position and their durable influence on energy institutions and policy, we must begin in the late 1800s, when electricity was a new and expensive commodity. In 1879, electricity was first used for city lighting in place of natural gas lamps (Bradley 1996; Hughes 1983). Edison himself only formally patented his electric light bulb technology in 1882 (Hargadon & Douglas 2001). During the 1880s, very few homes or businesses had access to electricity because it was very expensive. At the time, private utilities, operating in small urban areas, were attempting to commercialize new technology. Electric utilities were competing against each other and against the established gas light business. It was a crowded marketplace for a new service to become profitable.

Initially, there was no policy framework for managing this new technology. Municipalities debated three different regulatory options. Option one would allow private companies to operate as exclusive monopoly franchises within the city. Private electric utilities largely favored this model. They argued this structure could reduce costs, given electricity's large upfront fixed investments. But it could also lead to anticompetitive behavior from private corporations, which could potentially increase costs. Although it was not recognized at the time, this monopoly-centralized plant model would favor revenue growth over resource efficiency (Yakubovich et al. 2005), exacerbating environmental problems.

Option two was allowing multiple private companies to compete against each other in a given city. This would allow competition to theoretically drive down prices and would likely create more on-site generation rather than grid expansion. Equipment manufacturers like General Electric tacitly favored this option as it would allow them to sell more equipment (Yakubovich et al. 2005). On-site generation would also prove more resource-efficient as both the electricity and the steam from combustion could be used, for heating and lighting, respectively. By contrast, electricity generation led to wasted energy because the steam could not be used for other purposes.

Option three was municipal ownership through publicly owned utilities. Many argued at the time that municipalities could own the system's assets, provide service at a lower price, and generate municipal revenues. In places where municipal utilities were established, they were initially able to provide electricity for lower costs than private utilities (Rudolph & Ridley 1986). Many municipal governments favored this third, public power option. But electric utilities did not want municipal ownership and preferred to operate as private monopolies. They lobbied city councils across the United States for private and exclusive franchise rights, in some cases resorting to outright bribery to block municipalization (Hughes 1983).

At that time, Samuel Insull, a businessman, was the most prominent leader in the electricity industry. He opposed municipal ownership and decentralized systems, favoring vertically integrated utility monopolies. Insull worked for Thomas Edison, helping to found Edison General Electric. In 1892 he became president of Chicago Edison. Examining Insull's political influence can help us understand the roots of utilities' ability to influence energy policy today. According to one historian, "Insull was for about thirty-five years the most powerful political operator on the American business scene" (Hughes 1983, 205; McDonald 1962). Drawing on his expansive network and by lobbying regulators, Insull created significant innovations in the way electricity was sold and regulated in the United States. Insull shaped electricity in three ways that remain influential today: the technology, the economics, and the policy framework.

Although he is best known as a businessman, Insull made important contributions to technological change. At the time, electricity was generated in the building or through small stations for localized consumption (Hughes 1983). He did not embrace this version of the electricity system, where industry co-generated electricity and steam near where they were consumed through distributed generation. Instead, Insull admired large hydroelectric dams with significant transmission capacity and believed that economies of scale would achieve greater efficiency and profits. Along with other utility leaders, he pushed for an electricity system organized around centralized plants and electric grids. In Chicago, he built his company through ever larger coal plants.[9] He either did not realize the energy efficiency losses and environmental harms he was creating in the process or did not care.

While he shaped electricity technology, he also worked to change its economics through influencing the way electricity was priced. One significant challenge with electricity is that demand can swing over the course of days and weeks: from low and relatively stable demand to high and variable peaks. When demand is low, electricity infrastructure sits idle. This was particularly the case in the early days of electricity in the mid-1890s when it was mostly used at night for lighting. Large idle times without revenue to cover debt created high fixed costs, high prices, and, subsequently, little demand for an expensive commodity.

The first key innovation in electricity pricing was the move away from flat charges per lightbulb toward volumetric charges as measured through a meter. One story claims that Insull visited Brighton in the United Kingdom in 1894 and met a manager of a small municipal station who had begun to charge customers for their actual consumption and their potential peak consumption (McDonald 1962). Using meters, electricity was sold in Brighton on a volumetric basis rather than as a flat charge. When Insull returned to the United States, he began to use meters to sell electricity by volume, calculating consumption in kilowatt hours (kWh), rather than charging by the lightbulb.[10] In the mid-1890s, he also pioneered long-term, low-priced contracts with large customers to grow the customer base and consumption (McDonald 1962). Consequently, demand was smoothed, the company's load factor grew, and electricity costs dropped. With lower rates, more customers would buy electricity, continuing the positive spiral (Hughes 1983; Yergin 2011).

Through the industry associations he dominated, Insull pressured other utilities across the country to price electricity in the same way. At the time, there were significant debates among utility executives about the best way to price electricity. Two main options were discussed: efficiency-oriented versus growth-oriented pricing (Yakubovich et al. 2005). The efficiency system aimed to make maximum use of existing infrastructure by charging customers not only for the amount they consumed but also for the time of day they used it. Since electricity assets were sitting idle outside of evening hours when demand for lighting was highest, this system would more efficiently use existing assets to gain new customers. Although this was not considered at the time, from an environmental perspective, this approach would have also resulted in greater resource efficiency. Insull, however, was a proponent of the growth-oriented pricing structure, wherein customers were charged the same rates regardless of when they used electricity. This pricing system would push the electricity system toward centralization, vertical integration, and private utility monopolies because it would require greater upfront fixed costs (Yakubovich et al. 2005). Insull preferred increased revenue and growth over efficiency and he worked to convince his peers that this was the correct path forward.

Having convinced the industry, he launched a campaign to convince the regulators. Allied with other utilities, Insull aimed to secure regulatory decisions that would favor private monopolies running large centralized plants. Through the National Electric Light Association (NELA)—the first utility association and the precursor to the EEI—Insull and other utility managers met to discuss pricing, technology, and public policy.[11] In places where municipalities had chosen option two—creating significant competition between different utilities—Insull developed a frame that would come to define regulation. He argued that electricity was a natural monopoly because of its large fixed costs and networked nature. Hence, franchise rights should be limited to a small number of companies in each service area. He viewed replicated infrastructure as unnecessarily costly, contributing to high electricity rates.

The association also aimed to stem the tide of municipal public power, ensuring that private utilities would reign. Of course, many municipalities wanted to own the power system's assets. Consequently, the private utility association began a campaign to move electricity regulation from municipalities' jurisdiction to the states, in a classic example of venue shopping. This move had three goals: first, to facilitate private utility expansion; second, to reduce the number of municipal utilities; and third, to circumvent municipal corruption

(Hughes, 1983, 207). The association aimed to secure monopoly status through state governance.

However, by the early 1900s, monopolies were seen as dangerous economic entities that used their market power to charge high and unfair prices. To gain the monopoly status at the state level, then, NELA and Insull had to concede to greater government oversight. As historian Richard F. Hirsh argues, a "utility consensus" was forged in the early twentieth century between private electric utilities and the states. In return for the right to operate as a monopoly, private utilities would be required to have state oversight to ensure reliable and cheap power. A limited number of companies would have the right to sell electricity, with state regulators overseeing rates (Hirsh 1999a). In this framework, regulation was supposed to guard against monopoly power (Stigler & Friedland 1962). This change also limited growth in public, municipal utilities.

These ideas formed the basis for the public utility commission (PUC), the main regulatory institution for electricity still used today. Beginning in New York, Georgia, and Wisconsin in 1907, PUCs rapidly spread to two-thirds of all states by 1913 and three-quarters by 1922. Commissions became the institutional venue for ensuring that utilities were able to recoup their costs without abusing their monopoly power (Anderson 1981; Stigler & Friedland 1962; Troesken 2006). This was achieved through the PUC overseeing utility costs and allowing utilities to charge "cost-of-service" rates with regulated profits. Rather than municipal governance, PUCs became the primary governing body regulating electric utilities.

Using propaganda tactics from World War I, utilities sold their business model to the people, dramatically increasing acceptance of private ownership and eroding the push for public power (Hughes, 1983, 208). Consequently, municipalities lost significant control over power regulation. In places where public, municipal utilities already existed, they were left outside the PUC process. This decision to allow municipal utilities to operate independently continues to have significant consequences today. Just over 100 years later, municipal utilities see themselves as sovereign self-regulators, exempt from the latest regulatory fashion at the PUC: whether that be deregulation in the 1990s or renewable energy requirements in the 2000s.

Public Utility Commissions remain quasi-judicial, quasi-legislative regulatory institutions led by a group of commissioners. The commissioners are usually appointed by the governor, as is the case in Texas, Ohio, and Kansas; but in a few states, including Arizona, commissioners are elected. The PUC is the implementing agency for electricity legislation. As such, it sets rules and prices, conducts ratemaking proceedings, and oversees contracts. PUCs have long been tasked with overseeing electricity rates and deciding whether utility costs and investments were reasonable. The fact that utilities would operate as monopolies made consumer protection electricity regulation's central goal during its first 50 years. Meeting this goal came to be defined as efficiency, economy, and reliability. Other goals, such as equity and environmental protection, were largely left off the agenda.

This regulatory bargain between private utilities and state PUCs led to incredible reductions in the price of electricity over time. Although contemporary electricity debates focus on rising prices—particularly with reference to renewables—the larger secular trend over the past century is falling prices. As Vaclav Smil (2003) demonstrates, electricity prices declined 98% over the twentieth century. In 1902, when the first electricity pricing data are available, the national average price was 16 ¢/kWh, equivalent to $2.50/kWh in 1990 dollars (Smil 2003). In 2017 the average price for residential electricity in the United States was a mere 8 ¢/kWh in 1990 dollars.[12] The most dramatic price declines happened between 1900 and 1920, precisely when PUCs and monopolistic regulation were unfolding across the United States. But price declines continued through the 1960s due to technological and managerial innovation, giving governments little reason to re-examine the regulatory consensus (Joskow & Schmalensee 1983).

Through this consensus, the state delegated a critical, societal function to private companies. Although the PUC is theoretically independent, in practice, this bargain empowered utilities to capture the regulatory process as the main and most influential stakeholder (Hirsh 1999a). As long as electricity prices remained low, utilities were welcome to continue to act as monopolies, expanding capacity and increasing their profits.

In the early twentieth century, utilities became a particular manifestation of Charles Lindblom's privileged position of business (Lindblom 1977). Energy was and remains the backbone of American prosperity. This can be seen easily in the correlation between gross domestic product (GDP) and energy consumption.[13] While this tight relationship is weakening over time, energy has and continues to play a foundational role in all societies.[14] This was even more true historically. By the 1920s, electricity production was the biggest industry in the US economy (Carley 2009). Here we see the state delegating a key economic input—electricity—to private corporations rather than requiring public ownership. With this deference, Lindblom tells us, also comes significant power. And so utilities have had a privileged seat at the table in negotiations over energy policy from the 1920s to the present. It was only with the stock market collapse in 1929 and the subsequent depression that we saw the first challenges to private utilities' privileged position.

The Rural Electrification Act, Price Reductions, and Capacity Expansion (1920–1970)

Initially, innovation was at the core of the utility industry's business model. But by the early 1920s, the sector had abandoned its roots in radical invention (Hughes 2012). As Hirsh (1999, 52) puts it, "For the next fifty years [from 1920 to 1970], managers and their allies in manufacturing firms sought to stifle radical inventions that could upset the central station paradigm and threaten established financial interests." Private utilities had turned away from innovation, focusing instead on scaling up through technology and profits. While new technology was largely discouraged, innovative financing models and corporate structures flourished. Insull, in particular, became famous for buying up electric utilities across the country and constructing complex holding companies (Spinak 2014). But he was not alone. At the time, banks were loaning large sums to utilities. Utilities used this money to buy up competitors (McDonald 1962). It was a time of significant consolidation in the sector as corporations attempted to create economies of scale.

With the stock market collapse in 1929 and the resulting economic insecurity in the early 1930s, utility companies' stock eroded (Figure 3.2). Here, New York bankers played a key role. In their attempts to take over the Insull Group's assets, they aimed to devalue its holding companies (McDonald 1962). Under this predatory action, the Insull empire eventually collapsed. However, the bankers largely escaped blame. Instead, the private utilities were seen as highly culpable, due to the complex legal and financial arrangements they had used to drive consolidation in the 1920s. These developments began to upset the regulatory consensus. Utilities were seen as less trustworthy, and their privileged status began to erode. As part of New Deal–era reforms, the federal government stepped in to place significant restrictions on utilities (Hirsh 1999a). Two major changes were made: first, politicians returned to advocating more vocally for publicly owned power; second, the government increased limits on what private utilities could do.

In the 1930s, the federal government began supporting public power through the New Deal. Congress passed the Tennessee Valley Authority (TVA) Act in 1933, establishing the large public utility. The TVA sold power at very low prices across seven southeastern states, aiming to raise citizens' standard of living. It was a social project, steeped in progressive ideals, and directly counter to the notion that private utilities should profit from electricity as a public good (McCraw 1971; Tobey 1996). An executive order by President Franklin D. Roosevelt followed in 1935, creating the Rural Electrification Administration. The aim was

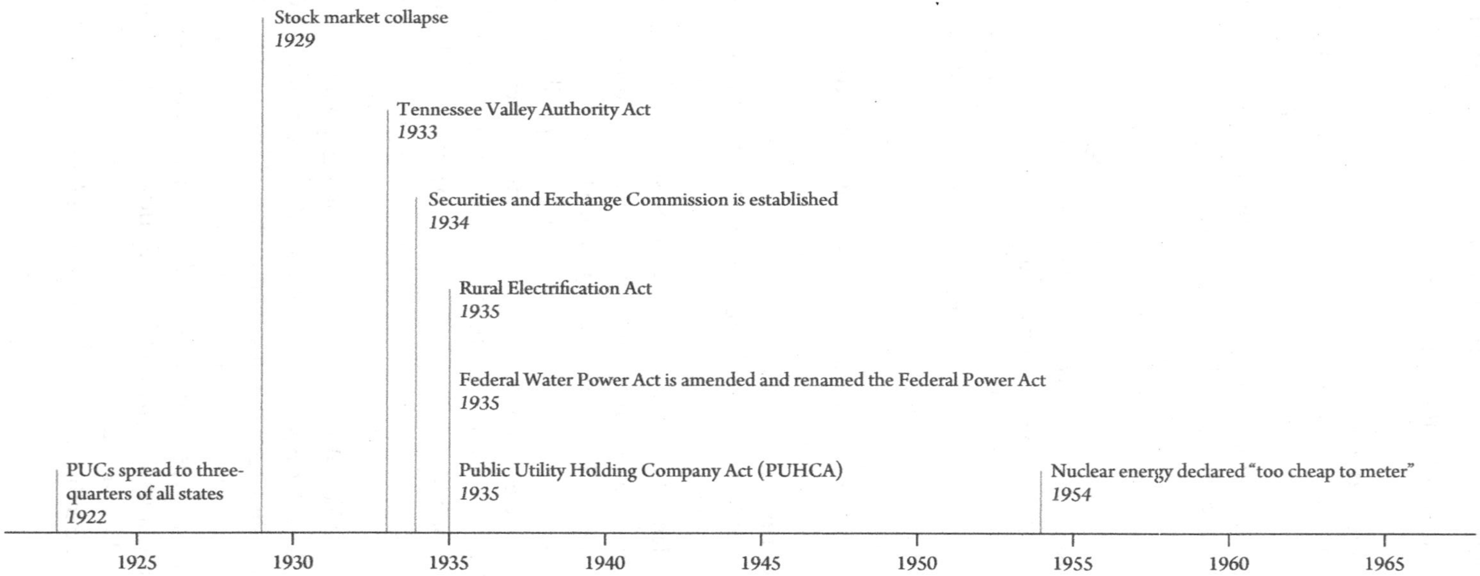

Figure 3.2 Major Events in Electricity Policy, 1920–1970

Stock market collapse
1929

Tennessee Valley Authority Act
1933

Securities and Exchange Commission is established
1934

Rural Electrification Act
1935

Federal Water Power Act is amended and renamed the Federal Power Act
1935

Public Utility Holding Company Act (PUHCA)
1935

Nuclear energy declared "too cheap to meter"
1954

PUCs spread to three-quarters of all states
1922

1925 1930 1935 1940 1945 1950 1955 1960 1965

to provide electricity to parts of the country that private utilities had long neglected, using cooperatives rather than public or private utilities. It is important to note that this was not a new phenomenon—during the 1920s utility managers worked with land grant universities to expand electricity to rural areas (Hirsh 2018). That said, Roosevelt's policy dramatically accelerated rural electrification. It also helped address inequalities in electricity access that cut across both class and racial lines (Harrison 2013, 2016). Congress supported this policy in 1936, passing the Rural Electrification Act. Through these two policies, rural cooperatives—the third main type of utility still operating today—proliferated across the country (Spinak 2014).

The federal government made several other changes to utility regulation and operations during this era that increased federal oversight. In 1934, Congress established the Securities and Exchange Commission (SEC). The SEC included provisions to inspect utilities' financial arrangements. This was followed the next year by the federal Public Utility Holding Company Act (PUHCA), designed to limit the kinds of corporate structures available to utilities (Hirsh 1999a). The PUHCA also limited private utilities' geographic scale in an attempt to increase PUC oversight. These two laws reduced utilities' ability to take large financial risks and to engage in complex financial arrangements. Third, the Federal Water Power Act was amended and renamed the Federal Power Act in 1935, giving the Federal Power Commission—now the Federal Energy Regulatory Commission (FERC)—the authority to regulate all interstate electricity sales and transmission. This law aimed to ensure just and reasonable power prices in the states (Wolak 2003). Together, these laws began the slow march toward federal oversight of PUCs and electric utilities.

But these regulatory modifications were insufficient to disrupt the utility consensus (Hirsh 1999a). State PUCs remained the central governing body. And private electric utilities continued their growth, outpacing public utilities and cooperatives to retain their dominant position. In the post–World War II era, private utilities across the country focused on capacity expansion. Given cost-of-service regulation, the primary way utilities could make a profit was through owning the system's assets and applying for rate recovery through PUC proceedings. As monopolies, utilities were outwardly hostile to independent power producers. Allowing other groups to participate in electricity production would reduce utilities' profits.

Thus, utilities used their monopoly power to drive out competition. For example, they aimed to shrink co-generation, a technology often used at industrial facilities to generate both heat and electricity simultaneously. This technology is more efficient and therefore has a lower environmental footprint. In the mid-twentieth century, utilities offered industrial users low rates to disincentivize them from making their own efficient electricity through co-generation. These efforts worked, driving a centralized, utility-dominated electricity system. In 1902, 60% of the electricity system's capacity was non-utility assets; but, by the late 1970s, this number had fallen to just 3% (Hirsh 1999a, 82). As they focused on their own profits, private utilities proved ineffective at pursuing economic or environmental goals. In an effort to sell more electricity, a declining block rate structure was used during this period: as customers purchased more electricity, their marginal price would fall.[15] This pricing paradigm incented greater consumption and thereby increased utilities' profits. Utilities favored this structure despite the fact that it poorly aligned with economic principles (Anderson 1981, 66–68) and worked against conservation. Taken together with their drive to eliminate co-generation, private utilities dramatically increased the energy requirements for the US economy during this period—leading to significant waste. But in the postwar period, policymakers believed there were abundant energy resources, and they placed little focus on negative environmental repercussions.

Private utilities' strategy proved successful at meeting one regulatory goal, however: cost reduction. With their monopoly status secured, the utilities invested in economies of scale, and the price of electricity dropped. Between 1952 and 1968, energy prices fell in real terms (Laird 2001). Further cost declines were predicted with the rise of nuclear plants. As the chair of the Atomic Energy Commission famously said in 1954, nuclear energy would be "too cheap to meter" (Bodansky 2008).[16] Nuclear plants were proposed in large numbers across the states, with exponential growth in permits between 1965 and 1975. This was an age of technological optimism—economies of scale would bring low-cost, abundant energy sources. Endless energy would lead to global progress and peace.

However, the age of energy optimism would prove short-lived. Nuclear energy's costs grew alongside opposition to the technology and safety and security requirements at plants. Projects were taking longer and longer to build, with protests and new safety standards. Over time, large cost overruns would be incorporated into rates, increasing electricity prices (Joskow 2006). Additionally, nuclear waste rose in prominence as a thorny political issue (Aldrich 2008; Slovic et al. 1991). Environmental concerns about the entire energy system started to mount as the antinuclear environmental movement grew. At the same time, oil shortages drove up prices. Politicians and regulators no longer saw abundant and cheap energy. With mounting costs, the utility consensus began to erode.

The Public Utility Regulatory Policies Act and Marginal Cost Pricing (1970s)

After more than 50 years of regulatory stability, utilities' interests in increasing profits and society's interests in maintaining low and stable energy prices came into conflict. Utilities, profiting off of electricity expansion, had no incentive to reduce consumption. With cost-of-service regulation, utilities can grow their rate base by building more plants, then sell more electricity, and thereby increase their profits. With these incentives, utilities expanded capacity and encouraged citizens to buy new appliances to increase demand (Spinak 2014; Tobey 1996). And they eschewed more efficient technologies, like district heating and industrial co-generation.

Overall, the industry stopped investing in improving technologies. Instead, utilities entered a period that historian Richard Hirsh (1989) has called "technological stasis." Electricity prices started rising. Previously, technological improvements had mitigated the effects of inflation (Hirsh 1989). However, the industry's movement away from innovation magnified inflation's effects. With the energy crisis, rising fuel costs exacerbated this problem (Lifset 2014). Electric utilities were no longer supplying cheap power—they were failing to hold up their end of the regulatory bargain (Hirsh 2013).

With private utilities struggling to provide low-cost power, jurisdiction over electricity regulation once again moved up to a higher level of government. After the 1973 Arab oil embargo, the federal government began to question whether all this wasted energy and excess consumption was problematic (Figure 3.3). The Ford administration proposed creating a new agency that would spur alternatives to imported oil, for example, by developing synthetic fuel technologies (Breetz 2013). But Congress rejected this proposal. When the Carter administration took office, the federal government began to actively encourage energy conservation, efficiency, and changes to electricity regulation.[17]

Drawing on economic ideas, most notably from Alfred Kahn, the Carter administration sought rate reform at the federal level. The government wanted to require marginal cost pricing, to align consumer signals with conservation goals—an idea that Kahn promoted. By this time, marginal cost pricing for electricity was already being used in Europe (Chick 2007). And although it was far from the norm in the United States, in the early 1970s, several state PUCs held hearings on the topic, including New York and California (Joskow 1976; Mitchell et al. 1980). Kahn himself served as the chair of New York's PUC when it transitioned to marginal cost pricing. This idea, along with other strategies to drive energy conservation, was advanced through Carter's proposed National Energy Plan (Hirsh 1999a).

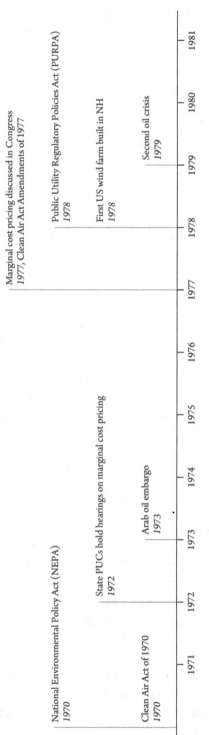

Figure 3.3 Major Events in Electricity Policy, 1970–1980

When President Carter sent the plan to Congress in 1977, however, it proved controversial, with broad opposition from many interest groups (Breetz 2013). Although parts of Carter's blueprint passed the House, the Senate broke up the energy reform into several bills, arguing that the diversity of topics covered was too large for one package. Some of these disaggregated bills aimed to reform the electricity rate structure, while others would impose new taxes on fuel-intensive vehicles. The utilities were largely focused on a debate over whether coal would be converted to oil and natural gas, as well as limiting the electricity rate reform's scope and extent (Breetz 2013). They paid little attention to other bills in the legislative package (Hirsh 1999a, 1999b). Utilities' lack of ability to forecast and their divided attention were key factors in allowing significant reforms to pass. In a pattern we will see repeated in the chapters that follow, the fog of enactment was operating. As with many reforms that have the potential to reshape policy through feedback, these laws' consequences were difficult for incumbent opponents to predict in advance. Further, with a large and complex reform, the utilities could not focus on all the bills' provisions simultaneously.

A largely overlooked bill was included in the reform package—the Public Utility Regulatory Policies Act (PURPA). President Carter's plan aimed to revive on-site production through co-generation plants. The goal was to increase energy efficiency while also expanding supply diversity. PURPA included Section 210, which would allow more small-scale power production. As historian Richard Hirsh lays out in exceptional detail, Republican Senator Charles Percy of Illinois and Democratic Senator John A. Durkin of New Hampshire both played key roles in drafting this section of the bill. Their motivations were diverse. Senator Percy was eager to avoid another oil crisis and viewed renewables as the energy sources of the future (Hirsh 1999a). As a result, the bill was drafted to require 75% of eligible independent power producers' energy to come from biomass, waste, solar, wind, or geothermal (Devine et al. 1987).[18] In the 1970s, renewable energy was still a bipartisan issue.

Senator Durkin's goals were less idealistic. Wheelabrator-Frye Corporation, a company based in his home state, operated a waste-to-energy plant. The company approached him with an interest in selling electricity from co-generation and potentially moving into biomass-based electricity production. Working with lobbyists for this firm, Senator Durkin secured several changes to PURPA's sections 201 and 210 that would aid the company: increasing the maximum project size from 30 to 80 megawatts; ensuring that the federal government would set the rules around pricing, rather than the states; and ensuring that these federal rates included both capital and variable costs. These changes were agreed to largely because utilities perceived this section as unimportant compared to other energy bills' provisions. Senator Durkin's proposals were viewed as constituent-oriented and focused on a niche industry, rather than systemic to the electricity

sector as a whole (Hirsh 1999a). Enacting these federal energy bills took another year. But the House eventually agreed to a resolution that would bind
all five bills together to ensure that the entire package passed. President Carter
signed the bills in November 1978, noting that the law would ideally kick-start
innovation in solar energy in the United States. Here we see our first example of
how policy feedback can be started during a time of significant legislative uncertainty and ambiguity, through a fog of enactment. This one small company
kicked off a much larger positive feedback cycle—one that was not predicted in
advance. Once implemented, this law would come to undermine utilities' monopoly status.

Still, the enacted legislation did not guarantee a new group of independent
energy producers that would rival the utilities' monopoly over the electricity
supply and their regulators. As I argue, feedback does not take hold until laws
are effectively implemented and resources, identities, and preferences are re-
cast. The federal energy regulator, FERC, had to first interpret the law before its
transformative effects could be felt.[19] One key issue was how to treat this new
class of independent power producers, called qualifying facilities (QFs) under
PURPA. After significant deliberation, FERC decided on generous terms. It also
removed the requirement for QFs to go through the same bureaucratic approvals
as utilities. Given their much smaller size, this lower regulatory burden would
prove important for reducing transaction costs. It would also ensure that QFs
avoided direct conflict with utilities through PUC proceedings.

The commission made other implementation decisions that bolstered new
projects' economic viability. They defined avoided costs to mean the cost of the
utility's own power production. This interpretation meant that payments to QFs
would not be based on the new plant's costs but on the costs utilities would theoretically avoid spending. This decision held the potential to provide independent
producers significant profits. It also enabled a diverse range of technologies to be
developed. From FERC's perspective, more generous payments were justified
because QFs were taking on significant risk. This stood in marked contrast to the
monopoly utilities—they had little to no risk, since the PUC process guaranteed
profit margins above their costs. Finally, FERC allowed QFs to buy electricity at
the standard consumer rate while selling it at the higher, avoided cost rate. This
arrangement was codified over the opposition of utilities, which would have preferred a net metering approach, wherein the power purchased is valued at the
same price as the power sold. But FERC argued that QFs should pay the same
electricity prices as any other consumer (Hirsh 1999a).[20] FERC's interpretation
of PURPA paved the way for significant policy feedback through the creation of
a new group of electricity companies that could challenge utilities' policy monopoly. It also acted as the first, proto-feed-in tariff policy.

Once FERC issued these rules, the law faced resistance from opponent utilities. During implementation, the utilities had updated their expectations about the policy's likely effects. They now perceived significant threats to their business from FERC's expansive interpretation. Opponents legally challenged the implementation decisions through two cases, which both went to the Supreme Court. Here we see an example of an opponent interest group trying to stop policy feedback before it takes hold by working indirectly to resist policy through the courts. The first case against FERC came in 1982 in *Federal Energy Regulatory Commission v. Mississippi*. It was brought by the state and its PUC. Mississippi challenged the constitutionality of PURPA Section 210, arguing that Congress did not have jurisdiction to interfere with state PUCs setting rates because of the Tenth Amendment and the Commerce Clause. The Supreme Court ruled with FERC, arguing that utilities were a form of interstate commerce (Martin 1983). The second case, *American Electric Power Service Corporation v. Federal Energy Regulatory Commission*, occurred in 1983. The Ohio-based utility American Electric Power (AEP) argued that FERC's interpretation of the law went too far (Martin 1983). It claimed that QFs should have to go through PUC hearings before interconnecting with a utility and that avoided costs should not have been interpreted as the utility's marginal costs. Drawing on the House–Senate conference report, the Supreme Court again sided with FERC, stating that the law's intent was not to keep prices low but to diversify fuel supply as a long-term safeguard against scarce fossil fuels (Hirsh 1999b). Further, it argued that interconnection approval requirements would paralyze QFs' ability to operate, undermining the law's intention. Through these two Supreme Court decisions, PURPA's strong implementation was secured.

After these cases concluded, state PUCs began to set PURPA rates. FERC had left the specific avoided cost calculations to the states. In practice, a wide variety of methodologies were used. Differences in marginal electricity costs across states also led to significant variation in rates (Loiter & Norberg-Bohm 1999). States like California and New York set high avoided cost rates since their incumbent utilities also had high costs. For example, California's PURPA rate was 3 ¢/kWh (Devine et al. 1987).[21] States with significant hydropower resources, like Washington and Oregon, had much lower rates, between 1 and 2 ¢/kWh (Righter 1996a). This variation in rates, alongside other differences in states' implementation of PURPA and their adoption of complementary policies, would dramatically affect independent energy producers' ability to finance projects in different states. These factors would lead to significant variation in the type and scale of renewable energy projects that were developed across states (Loiter & Norberg-Bohm 1999).

Once states' rates were finalized, hundreds of stalled energy projects started moving. Within a few short years, PURPA was used to develop renewable energy projects. The first wind farm in the United States was built in New Hampshire in 1978 when U.S. Windpower (later called Kenetech) erected 20 windmills (Righter 1996a). Shortly thereafter, California began the largest investment in wind energy in the world up to that time.

PURPA represents a classic case of positive feedback. The law undermined utilities' monopoly status by creating a new set of actors with divergent interests. Utilities tried to stir controversy over these new independent power producers, asserting unwarranted costs and capacity (Lesser & Su 2008). But they were largely unsuccessful. Through this law, utilties had lost "much of the power they once held in the utility system" (Hirsh 1989, 100). These independent energy companies began to cultivate influence with politicians, and they held different goals for energy policy from the utilities. While electricity policy would continue to be dominated by interest group preferences, there was no longer *one* interest group at the PUC. As the next two sections will show, these independent power producers would prove critical in the coming decades, both to debates over deregulation and to the rise of renewable energy.

Electricity Deregulation and the Energy Policy Act of 1992 (Late 1980s–2005)

While earlier challenges to the regulatory consensus focused on *increasing* utility regulation, by the 1980s the aim had reversed. Now politicians wanted to *reduce* regulation. Alfred Kahn was key to getting deregulation on the agenda when he published an influential, two-volume book, *The Economics of Regulation*, in the early 1970s (Kahn 1971). The work advanced a theory that government regulation should prioritize economic efficiency and that institutional arrangements should be crafted to best meet this goal. In addition, Kahn re-examined the case for monopolies. He argued that in many instances utilities provide a mix of goods: some parts of utility's products were true monopolies, while others could be sold through competitive markets. He targeted numerous monopoly industries, from telecommunications to natural gas transmission to air transportation. Kahn would go on to become the chair of the Civil Aeronautics Board, which was in charge of deregulating the airline industry—a deregulation that both Republicans and Democrats lauded as wildly successful (Stelzer 1982). The Carter administration drew on Kahn's work to push marginal cost pricing for electricity in its late-1970s energy reforms. His ideas proved extremely influential—not just at the federal level but also with state legislatures and PUCs.

In the electricity sector, these ideas helped put deregulation on the agenda.[22] Public Utility Commissions typically oversee a wide variety of utilities, including telecommunications and natural gas. After these industries underwent successful deregulation, electricity appeared to be a natural next step for state regulatory reform. Key justifications for monopolies in the electricity sector included economies of scale, difficulties of obtaining capital, and market efficiency. However, all of these principles were challenged once PURPA was implemented in the early 1980s. Independent power producers had clearly demonstrated that they could provide power cheaply, for as little as a few cents per kilowatt hour. The burden of proof now fell to utilities to justify their monopoly status. Through policy feedback, PURPA's successful implementation had reshaped the political landscape, changing the balance of power across interest groups.

By the early 1980s, a handful of economists were applying Kahn's work to the electricity system. Using engineering-economic models developed in the 1970s at the Massachusetts Institute of Technology and the University of Texas at Austin, academics started to examine what restructuring would look like in practice (Baughman et al. 1979). Paul Joskow and Richard Schmalensee, in particular, began questioning whether electricity required monopolies. They did so first in a report to the DOE in 1982, and later in their 1983 academic book, *Markets for Power* (Joskow & Schmalensee 1983). Electric utilities had secured their vertically integrated monopoly status by arguing that their good was a natural monopoly that only required one set of wires to be transmitted to market. Like Kahn, Joskow and Schmalensee instead argued that this monopolistic structure made utilities' electricity expensive and that a market would bring efficiency through competition. They believed that while some parts of the electricity sector might be monopolistic in nature—namely, distribution and transmission systems—generation could theoretically be run through a competitive market. Separating out these functions and creating competitive markets was seen as one solution that would enable restructuring.

Joskow and Schmalensee wrote their book on the heels of a decade of financial woes in the electric industry. By the late 1960s, electricity price declines and coal power plant efficiency had both stagnated (Smil 2003). Utilities were no longer lowering their costs. Given that cost-of-service regulations guaranteed cost recovery plus profit, electricity prices stopped declining. Instead, prices began to rise as utilities invested in excess capacity and nuclear plants with cost overruns (Devine et al. 1987). With nuclear power, it was no longer clear that increasing the plant's scale would decrease the average costs (Grübler 2010; Trancik & Cross-Call 2013). Further, the costs of utilities' existing coal investments rose as new environmental regulations were implemented in the 1970s. Although there were technological innovations in natural gas combined-cycle turbines, utilities were not building these plants. Without increasing demand, they had little incentive to develop new infrastructure, even if it would lower operating costs or make plants less polluting. Notably, these dynamics are still at play today: throughout the South, uneconomic coal plants continue to operate despite the availability of cheaper and cleaner alternatives. Since utilities have sunk debt and equity into these plants, they want to keep them open.

Given that utilities had stopped innovating or reducing costs, economists argued that their monopoly status was outdated and inefficient. They believed that introducing competition would help fix some of these problems. If independent power companies built the latest technologies, they could offer lower electricity prices (Hirsh 1999a). Moreover, the latest natural gas technologies no longer showed economies of scale, further undermining the argument that monopolies were necessary in this sector. Together, these facts eroded the case for monopoly electric utilities. Private utilities were increasingly viewed as stagnant, uneconomic, and harmful to human health and the environment.

While the idea gained traction and the Reagan administration became a strong advocate for deregulation across the economy, little progress was made on electricity restructuring in the 1980s. Instead, a number of states began implementing centralized government planning through integrated resource plans (IRPs) in late 1980s (Duane 2002). This approach put an emphasis on both supply- and demand-side concerns. As social and environmental costs figured more prominently in IRPs, both regulators and environmentalists grew in power, and the utility consensus further eroded.

It was only during President George H. W. Bush's administration that electricity deregulation reached the federal policy agenda (Figure 3.4). In part, the decision to proceed with restructuring in England and Wales in 1990 influenced US policy (Joskow 2003). But more directly, yet another oil crisis—triggered by the 1990 Gulf War—opened a policy window (Hirsh 1999a). In response, President Bush announced a national energy strategy in 1990 and again in 1991, focusing significant congressional attention on energy policy.

These ideas were taken up in Congress in 1992 through the proposed Energy Policy Act (Stokes & Breetz 2018). This complex bill had a large number of provisions on electricity deregulation. It proposed competition in power generation at the wholesale level. It also allowed states to choose whether they would implement retail competition—enabling customers to choose their electricity supplier. The bill also proposed modifications to PUHCA, to allow utilities to operate in larger geographic areas. It would also modify PURPA, extending the exemptions QFs were receiving to other independent power producers and creating a new class of actors, exempt wholesale generators. With these changes, independent power producers would be able to operate more broadly, even outside of PURPA's purview (Hirsh 1999a). The bill also proposed changes to electricity transmission rules. To enable generators to get their power to market,

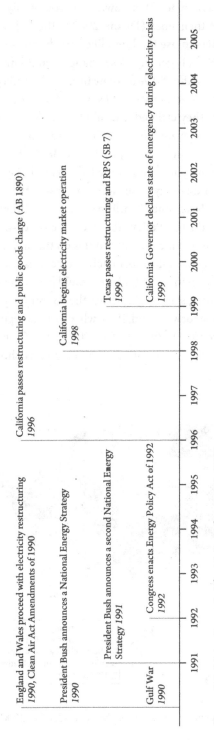

Figure 3.4 Major Events in Electricity Policy, 1990–2002

transmission would need to be open-access. Up until this point, utilities owned and operated transmission for their own use, voluntarily "wheeling" other utilities' power across their lines (Duane 2002). The bill would change that, allowing other providers to use the lines, like cars driving on a public highway (Watkiss & Smith 1993). Together, these changes would dramatically restructure the electricity sector after 80 years of institutional stability.

Utilities opposed the electricity reforms in the bill under the banner of reliability (Hirsh 1999a). They claimed it would be difficult to supply power consistently under this deregulated system. The private utility association, EEI, particularly opposed the transmission provisions. But by this time, utilities had lost considerable influence, including at the federal level. Electricity prices were no longer declining. And energy crises were increasing the attention Congress and presidents paid to these issues (Carlisle et al. 2016). Eventually, and despite utility opposition, the Energy Policy Act of 1992 passed—albeit with slightly more generous terms for the incumbent utilities on transmission rights.[23]

Still, the federal law did not immediately create a cascade of deregulation across states' electricity sectors. First, FERC would have to interpret and implement the law; and second, state PUCs across the country would have to decide whether or not to move forward and, if so, what form deregulation would take in their state (Joskow 1997). By October 2000, 90% of the states had begun restructuring their electricity sector to some extent, as shown in Figure 3.5 (Hirsh 2013).

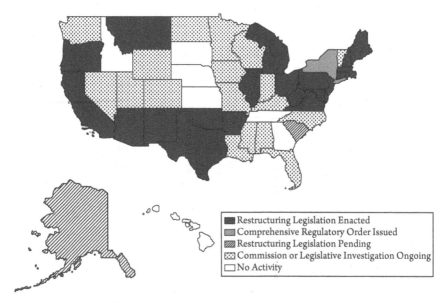

Figure 3.5 Status of Electricity Restructuring by State, October 2000.
(Source: Hirsh 2013.)

Ultimately, both California and Texas are well known for adopting restructuring policies in the late 1990s—policies that had nearly opposite results. California, ever a front runner in electricity policy, acted first by passing AB 1890 in 1996. Its market began operating in 1998. However, in California deregulation ended in disaster, with high electricity prices, rolling blackouts, a utility declaring bankruptcy, and the governor declaring a state of emergency. The crisis had many causes: low rainfall, high natural gas prices, and Enron engaging in price fixing (Hirsh 2013). It ultimately cost around $40 billion, with the California government stuck holding costly long-term contracts for electricity (Borenstein 2002; Joskow 2001). It also cost Governor Gray his position in a 2003 recall election. After this highly publicized failure, six other states suspended their restructuring programs, including neighboring Arizona.

Texas, by contrast, had already moved forward with restructuring in 1999. Its system is often seen as a success, particularly for retail competition (Joskow 2006). The Northeast, parts of the Midwest, and Oregon all restructured their electricity systems to various extents from the late 1990s onward (Figure 3.6). Across the country, deregulation proved a mixed success, with retail participation rates—the share of people signing up to change their electricity provider—hovering around 5% for most states by 2009 (Hirsh 2013). With these results, deregulation stopped being the central policy issue at PUCs by around 2005. Instead, renewable energy and climate change took center stage in state electricity policy, becoming the largest challenge to utilities' dominance over electricity policy.

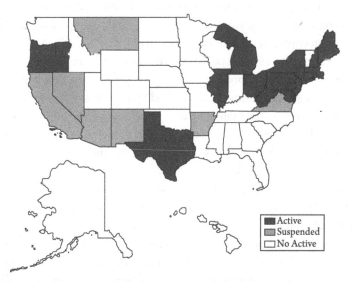

Figure 3.6 Status of Electricity Restructuring by State, September 2010. (Source: Energy Information Administration, 2010.)

Climate Change and the Rise of Renewable Energy (1970s–2015)

To understand how debates over renewable energy came to eclipse deregulation as the main issue on states' electricity policy agendas, we need to look back further in time. Utilities' decisions during the mid-twentieth century exacerbated the energy system's environmental harms. Initially, state regulators did little to address this growing problem. By the 1960s, extreme smog events were killing hundreds of citizens at a time, particularly in New York City, Pennsylvania, and Los Angeles (Greenburg et al. 1967; Jones 1975). Some states responded to these crises by passing clean air laws, including California (1947) and Texas (1965). But it was only with federal action that significant progress on air quality was made.

The 1970s were a watershed period for federal environmental laws. The decade began with a massive demonstration of 20 million Americans for the first Earth Day. This large scale social mobilization resulted in landmark environmental legislation being passed at the federal level. Given that the energy system contributes heavily to environmental problems, many of these landmark environmental policies applied to electricity (Laird 2001). In 1970, President Nixon signed the National Environmental Policy Act, requiring environmental assessments before construction of new power plants (Johnstone 2011). Later that year, the federal government created the Environmental Protection Agency (EPA) and Congress passed the Clean Air Act. This law, which remains crucial today, was aimed squarely at the power sector. It required new power plants to start dealing with the negative harms they caused, through installing best available pollution control technology (Layzer 2012).

In the wake of the 1973 oil crisis, one environmental activist, Amory Lovins, seized upon the moment, promoting a singular vision for a new energy system (Lovins 1976). As Lovins saw it, the United States was at a fork in the road—it could either take the "hard energy path," prioritizing environmentally harmful technologies including fossil fuels and nuclear, or it could take the "soft energy path," turning toward renewables and energy efficiency. It was unclear which path the United States would take.

During the 1970s, the federal government began supporting renewable energy technologies through tax credits. In 1973, a small, $300,000 program kicked off federal investments into wind energy (Galbraith & Price 2013). Under President Carter's administration, renewable energy's importance expanded. Funding for wind energy grew from 1977 onward, peaking at around $160 million annually in 1983. However, this did not represent a wholesale adoption of new technologies. Federal funding for renewables paled in comparison to nuclear energy investments, which peaked in the early 1980s at $3.5 billion annually (Nemet & Kammen 2007).[24] The so-called energy transition from utility-supported technologies with polluting side effects—oil, coal, natural gas, and, to some advocates, nuclear and even hydropower—toward renewables and energy efficiency had hardly begun by the end of the 1980s. Despite two decades of advocacy, the utilities with their polluting technologies maintained political dominance (Hirsh 1999a).

Still, the 1970s and early 1980s was a period of important experimentation for renewables and energy efficiency, particularly in California. When Governor Jerry Brown was first in office, the state focused significant effort on energy efficiency (Charles 2009). In 1982, California introduced "decoupling," wherein the relationship between utilities' profits and their sales volume was broken. This allowed utilities to promote efficiency without eroding their revenues. The policy proved wildly successful, allowing California to grow its economy dramatically but keep electricity consumption flat. While decoupling has been on the agenda in other states for decades, the movement largely did not see progress until the 2000s.[25] As of March 2019, 24 states have undertaken rate reforms that decouple utility revenues from sales.[26]

California was also an important early leader in renewables. In 1978, Governor Brown supported a bill to create state renewable energy income tax credits (Righter 1996b). California's incentives, combined with the federal tax credits, allowed for a potential 50% tax write-off. And that was in addition to PURPA payments. Given these favorable terms, by the mid-1980s, California had developed the largest amount of wind energy, geothermal, and biomass technologies anywhere in the world (Morris 2000; Righter 1996a; Sawyer 1985). These technologies were new and expensive. But they represented the biggest attempt yet to move away from the polluting, centralized plants the electric utilities had promoted for the past century. Had we watched these developments in the late 1970s equipped with policy feedback theory, we would have predicted stable or growing government support for this budding industry.

However, by 1986 both state and federal policies supporting renewables were retrenched. Even though these policies had enabled the United States to become *the world leader* in renewable energy technologies, there was no path dependence. Instead, the policies that kept these businesses alive collapsed. Under the Reagan administration, renewables were not promoted. While solar and geothermal technologies had some minor tax credits extended, these expired in 1988. After the oil crisis ended, Congress paid less attention to the energy problem and even less federal funding flowed toward renewable energy research and development (Carlisle et al. 2016). The lack of policy stability had catastrophic effects on the nascent renewable energy industry and its ability to innovate and bring down technology costs. As a result, little non-incremental innovation occurred in wind energy technologies (Nemet 2009). Similarly, the solar hot water boom, fueled by tax incentives, left little innovation behind. Instead, there were a number of bankrupt companies and many poor-quality, leaking systems (Nemet 2012). During this period, the United States lost much of its human capital and technological advantage in renewables. The lucky companies were sold for 10 cents on the dollar, and Europe rapidly pulled ahead in renewables technology (McDowall et al. 2013). In the 1980s, the United States ultimately failed to drive renewables adoption, innovation, or cost reductions.[27]

But despite the policy rollback—and the loss of technology and human resources—renewable energy technologies remained important because they solved a number of challenges the electricity sector was increasingly facing: high costs and environmental problems. In terms of costs, conventional technologies presented growing challenges. Nuclear was declining in popularity among both the public and regulators, particularly after the Three Mile Island accident in 1979. And by the late 1980s, it was clear that nuclear energy was no longer showing declining costs as the technology increased in scale. Instead, constructing new nuclear plants was become more expensive (Grübler 2010; Lovering et al. 2016). Many nuclear projects ran years over schedule and billions over budget.

Supply diversity and fuel costs were growing concerns in the energy sector. Given repeated energy crises, there was widespread concern over "peak oil" and secular declines in other fossil fuels. Although it would eventually become clear that a stable climate was the true limit on fossil fuels, not resource availability (Rogner 1997), this was not clear to many political actors in the 1980s.[28] Instead, there were concerns that fossil fuel's costs would grow in the future. Throughout the mid-twentieth century, coal plants' capital costs declined through experience, as predicted by the learning-by-doing hypothesis (Arrow 1962). This helped bring down electricity prices. However, coal *fuel* costs showed a flat trend. This meant that the price of coal created a floor on coal-fired plants' costs (McNerney et al. 2011). This trend extended to other fuels, whose prices had remained largely flat or even increased over time in real terms (Smil 2003). Since all fossil fuel–based electricity sources by definition require fuel, this trend suggested that further cost reductions in fossil fuel sources were unlikely.[29] When fuel costs spiked, so too would the price of power.

Environmentalists also understood that the electricity system posed significant threats for climate stability and human health. By the late 1980s, climate change had emerged as an important environmental problem. Dr. James Hansen testified in front of the Senate Energy and Natural Resources Committee in 1988, explaining that fossil fuel combustion was leading to global warming (Layzer 2011). Concerns about conventional air pollution were also heightened. In response, in 1990 the Clean Air Act Amendments passed, requiring tighter controls for nitrogen oxide, sulfur dioxide, and mercury.

Advocates framed renewable energy technologies as solutions to climate change, air quality, and a lack of supply diversity. Renewable energy technologies typically do not emit carbon and other kinds air pollution. And, unlike conventional fossil fuel technologies, they do not require fuel as an input.[30] Advocates were particularly interested in getting the government to support new and more expensive technologies that had lower environmental impacts: wind, solar (photovoltaic, thermal, and concentrated solar power), geothermal, and biomass. Since these technologies were young, innovation in manufacturing and installation could theoretically still bring large cost reductions.

Initially, electric utilities, like other fossil fuel companies, understood and accepted the science of climate change. Like the fossil fuel industry, the electric utility industry undertook research on the greenhouse effect and consistently found that the earth was warming (Anderson et al. 2017). In 1977, the Electric Power Research Institute (EPRI) testified in front of Congress that if climate change "turns out to be of major concern, then fossil fuel combustion will be essentially unacceptable, an important justification for expanding the nuclear and solar energy options."[31] Throughout the 1970s and 1980s, many articles ran in the utility industry's trade magazines that confirmed the scientific consensus of climate change (Anderson et al. 2017).

But by 1989 the private utilities were actively promoting climate denial. As climate policy began to gain traction on the national agenda, electric utilities understood that they could stand to lose a lot of money. Dealing with the environmental harms from coal and natural gas plants was inconvenient. Hence, utilities waged a war on environmental science, casting doubt on climate change, acid rain, and mercury pollution (Anderson et al. 2017; Oreskes & Conway 2010). Particularly active utilities in climate denial included Southern Company, AEP and Duke Energy, as well as the association of private utilities, the EEI.

Beginning in the mid-1970s, AEP ran advertisements in *The New York Times* and *The Washington Post* arguing that coal use should be expanded. In 1991, EEI alongside the utility Southern Company started a public campaign to "'reposition global warming as theory' and not fact."[32] They designed ads that said climate change was like Chicken Little—claiming there is "no hard evidence it is occurring."[33] From 1989 and throughout the 1990s, electric utilities—alongside EEI, EPRI, and the National Rural Electric Cooperative Association—were part of the Global Climate Coalition (GCC), a prominent climate denial organization. Participating utilities included AEP, Ameren, Consumers Power Company, Duke Energy, PG&E, and Southern Company. Southern Company played a particularly active role, for example, hosting meetings for the GCC in 1996. Southern Company, Duke Energy, FirstEnergy (then Ohio Edison, later Energy Harbor) and EEI were all on the board of the GCC in the 1990s, along with the National Rural Electric Cooperative Association.[34] These utilities also attended workshops, developed climate denial policy memos, and helped disseminate misinformation, particularly in the mid to late 1990s.

Even after the GCC disbanded in 2002, utilities continued to deny climate science. For example, the Intermountain Rural Electric Association circulated a memo in 2006 challenging "the legitimacy of the 'alarmist' science about climate change." The memo specifically mentioned that Koch Industries, AEP and Southern Company were working together on producing climate denial content.[35] Until 2015, Southern Company funded a prominent climate denier, and in 2017 their CEO publicly disputed climate science on television (Anderson et al. 2017). Recent utility efforts to delay climate action have been organized through the Utility Air Regulatory Group (UARG), the American Legislative Exchange Council (ALEC), and other groups. Through their denial campaign, electric utilities successfully managed to delay policy enactment for decades. This history is all the more problematic given that monopoly utilities funded their denial campaigns using guaranteed profits from captured customers who could not choose to buy their power from other, more ethical companies.

Still, in the late 1980s there was reason to hope for action on climate change. Under President George H. W. Bush, energy prices began rising once again, focusing federal attention on the issue. In 1991, a large omnibus bill, the Energy Policy Act, began wending its way through Congress, passing in 1992 (Stokes & Breetz 2018). Controversial provisions in the bill—on nuclear energy regulation, oil development of the Arctic National Wildlife Refuge (ANWR), and emissions standards for cars—captured lawmakers' attention. By contrast, a small provision on renewables received little notice. Through a production tax credit (PTC), the bill proposed to create a 1.5 ¢/kWh tax credit for 10 years for eligible renewable energy projects, most notably wind.[36] This would turn out to be one of the most important parts of the complex law, though opponents missed its far-reaching consequences during the negotiations. In other words, the fog of enactment was operating.

Unlike fossil fuel subsidies, this meager funding for renewables was not permanent—it would need to be renewed regularly by Congress. The federal PTC would lapse and be extended many times over the coming decades. Combined with state policies, it would prove critical to financing renewable energy projects (Bird et al. 2005). But that fact was difficult to foresee in 1992. More than a decade had already been spent trying to kick-start renewables with very little success. Constantly shifting policy incentives at both the federal and state levels undermined progress. Outside of California, few renewable energy projects had even been piloted. Hence, advocates and analysts began to call for policy stability as one crucial ingredient in any renewable energy revolution (Rader et al. 1989; Rader & Hempling 2001; Wiser & Pickle 1997).

At the state level, there were few renewable energy projects in the pipeline by the early 1990s. Instead, advocates focused their attention on blocking coal plants. Before deregulation, many states had transitioned to IRP processes. In theory, this planning approach was supposed to bring public benefits like environmental harms into utilities' proposals. It largely worked: advocates advancing energy efficiency and renewables in IRPs were often winning. But with deregulation, the IRP process would disappear from many states (Duane 2002; Wiser et al. 2000). Thus, advocates had to change tactics and find new policy ideas that could be tacked onto the agenda of the day: electricity restructuring.

Advocates working through a cross-state network saw restructuring as a policy opportunity. The Energy Foundation—a foundation started in 1991 that provides grants to clean energy advocates—funded this advocacy network.[37] The group met regularly to discuss policy ideas and political strategies. To build capacity offline, the foundation set up a list-serve where members could share and debate. Key groups in this network in the mid-1990s included the American Wind Energy Association (AWEA), the Environmental Defense Fund (EDF), the Natural Resources Defense Council (NRDC), Public Citizen, the Sierra Club, the Union of Concerned Scientists (UCS), and the Utility Reform Network (TURN).

In specific states, the foundation would strategically fund groups when policy opportunities arose. This funding strategy involved a blend of insider groups, who could sit at the table and negotiate policy; and outsider groups, who could build grassroots campaigns to pressure the negotiations externally. Over time, this strategy evolved, and eventually the Energy Foundation saw itself as funding three kinds of groups: pillars, specialists, and local groups.[38] Pillars led regional efforts across the country, providing professional staff and technical expertise—these groups included UCS, the Renewable Northwest Project and the Conservation Law Foundation. Specialist groups had a narrow focus, only working on one topic such as energy efficiency. Local groups had relationships and credibility in a given state and the ability to drive grassroots mobilization. In practice, this funding model sometimes failed to incorporate local groups into national campaigns or would result in national groups parachuting into local debates last minute. That said, even those groups that did not receive foundation funding, such as state Public Interest Research Groups and Environment America, built relationships with the network and provided critical grassroots support. Many of the EF-funded groups also worked together to try to get a federal clean energy target on the agenda during the 1990s, although that effort ultimately failed.

The advocates struggled in the early days of this foundation network to agree on which policy to advance (Wiser et al. 1998). There were three main options: voluntary green power purchasing, a systems benefits charge, and the renewable portfolio standard (RPS). Voluntary green power purchasing would allow consumers to choose to buy clean energy, by paying more on their electricity bills. This view fit the ideals of the day, pushing the system toward "markets, not mandates." Today, these ideas are echoed in companies that sell power with higher renewable energy content, as well as current movements in California to create community choice programs.

A second group of advocates favored a system benefits charge.[39] This policy involves collecting small, volumetric charges from customers and creating a fund for renewables. The approach catalyzed energy efficiency in the late 1980s and early 1990s through programs that included customer loans and incentives. Some advocates wanted to expand this policy for renewables, and they succeeded in many states. By 2013, 16 states had public benefits funds, with most created during the 1990s when this network of advocates was active (Hirsh 2013; Wiser et al. 2000).

A third group wanted to create a new policy, called a Renewable Portfolio Standard or RPS—a term coined in the early 1990s by a California advocate, Nancy Rader (Lauber 2004; Rader & Norgaard 1996). This policy would require the state to meet targets for the amount of renewables built by a certain date. Whereas UCS supported the policy from the start, other groups such as EDF and NRDC, were initially opposed to advocating for RPS policies. Eventually, this policy would prove the most successful of the three ideas. According to one foundation employee, "RPS was our go to policy because it solved problems. It broke down the resistance to buying higher priced power sources in the utility procurement process."[40] Ultimately, the foundation coordinated the effort to push for state RPS policies and supportive federal policy throughout the 1990s.[41]

But it was not clear at the time that the RPS would prevail. It both fit and clashed with the dominant policy agenda of the day: restructuring the electricity system. On the one hand, an RPS was a "mandate." It did not trust a market to fix the problem of a dirty energy system. Hence, it fit more squarely within a centralized IRP process than a market-based system.[42] On the other hand, the RPS could facilitate greater competition since it would require new technologies that incumbent utilities were less familiar with and largely uninterested in developing. Since renewable energy technologies are usually smaller in scale, independent power producers could build them more easily. Ideally, investment would also bring their costs down over time. But the most important factor for RPS policies' success was its simplicity. It was easy for politicians to understand and simple to sell to the public. The RPS also didn't highlight costs—as a systems benefits charge would, through a new line item on customers' bills. As one advocate put it, "it's easier to build a campaign around an environmental goal [than a new electricity bill cost]."[43]

Ultimately, many renewable energy advocates were able to use restructuring as a policy window to push clean energy policies, with the RPS proving the most successful. When the California PUC endorsed an RPS in the mid-1990s as part of its deregulation plan, this increased renewable energy advocates' interest. It was now seen as a politically viable policy to include in restructuring laws. Eleven states would pass RPS policies between 1994 and 2002, mostly in electricity restructuring laws, with Massachusetts enacting the first modern RPS and a system benefits charge in 1997 (Hogan 2008). As the next chapter will explore, in 1999 Texas passed its RPS policy as part of its deregulation bill. Similarly, Ohio passed its RPS policy in a revision to its restructuring law in 2008. Through this issue linkage, deregulation came to benefit renewable energy (Kim et al. 2014). Once electricity restructuring fell out of favor, many states enacted stand-alone RPS policies.

In the 1990s, advocates also began to push legislatures to enact another policy that would prove crucial for solar energy: net metering. Net energy metering (NEM) allows individuals to connect small systems to the grid and get compensated for the power they provide. The rate they are paid to sell electricity is the same as the rate they paid to buy it—hence, it is a "net" accounting system. When these policies were enacted, it was unclear how important they would be for solar's development across the United States. Since there were very few small-scale solar projects and even fewer that were grid-connected, it was difficult to anticipate how many people would choose to have utilities buy the power they produced. The utilities at this point subscribed to a paradigm that renewables would struggle to develop, so they were not very threatened by NEM laws. As one advocate put it, "[Net metering] it's so simple, it's elegant and fair. The utilities were victims of their own beliefs. They thought that renewables were some tiny markets that would never grow. And they passed many of those net metering laws with limits to ensure they wouldn't be too big anyway."[44]

Before 1995, only a handful of states had NEM policies on the books (Stoutenborough & Beverlin 2008). By the late 1990s, net metering grew rapidly, with 16 states adopting laws between 1997 and 1999 (Carley 2011). Grassroots, state, and national renewable energy advocates fueled their growth, with help from EPA regional offices (Faden 2000; Stoutenborough & Beverlin 2008). Again, the Energy Foundation funded one particularly important advocate based in California, Tom Starrs.[45] He was effective, going state by state to promote and pass net metering laws in numerous legislatures in the 1990s. After this initial wave of adoption, many other states copied the idea. And when the federal government required states to consider the policy, even more acted. By 2011, 43 states had net metering policies. Most of these policies were passed without significant opposition from utilities. It was clear that utilities did not believe net metering would be a consequential policy. And for two decades, it wasn't.

But federal policy changes in 2005 revealed net metering's hidden potential. The Energy Policy Act of 2005 raised the existing 10% tax credit to a 30% investment tax credit (ITC) for commercial and residential solar (Stokes & Breetz 2018).[46] Tax credits for residential projects were capped at $2,000. While the ITC was only authorized for 2 years, the financial crisis created a policy window, enabling an 8-year policy expansion as well as the removal of the residential cap. The policy would have expired again at the end of 2016—but by then it had created new actors: solar leasing companies. In the late 2000s, solar leasing companies began cropping up, particularly in California. As the Arizona case explores in detail, these companies combined the federal ITC policy with state net metering policies to finance residential solar projects. When customers enter a solar lease or power purchase agreement with these companies, in effect they "rent" a solar panel and agree to pay a fixed monthly amount rather than paying the upfront costs of installation. This business model made it much easier for many homeowners to adopt solar. With these policies and this financing model, the solar industry grew dramatically. Here we see how federal and state laws can interact in ways that are hard to predict in advance. When the federal policy was set to expire in 2015, the now much larger solar industry successfully lobbied for a long-term extension of the ITC through 2021. In other words, these laws kicked off policy feedback.

The financial crisis also opened a policy window for wind energy developers. While the federal tax credits were useful, they required projects to pay the full costs of the project upfront and to find tax liabilities. By contrast, a government grant would provide developers with easier to access capital. The American Recovery and Reinvestment Act of 2009 created a new policy: the 1603 grant, which lasted until 2012 (Aldy et al. 2018). If developers chose the 1603 grant option in lieu of the ITC, they received a cash payment of 30% of their investment costs. The program helped to propel 100,000 projects, of which 98% were solar projects. Still, given wind energy's higher capital costs, half of the program's expenditures were spent on wind projects. The total government investment through this program was $26 billion. Given California's aggressive focus on clean energy during this period, it benefited the most from these grants.[47]

Once these state and federal incentives were in place, solar and wind projects expanded significantly. By 2007, there was a new solar installation every hour.[48] State RPS policies combined with federal incentives spurred large growth in wind projects. Consequently, the price for both solar and wind came down throughout the 2000s as a result of innovation and learning (Arrow 1962; Fri 2003; Nemet 2009). This innovation occurred not just because of US deployment but also because of significant investments made around the world, especially in Germany, Spain, Italy, and China (Candelise et al. 2010; Nemet 2006; Reichelstein & Yorston 2013). By 2014, investments in other countries had brought down costs for solar and wind projects in US states, making some projects competitive with fossil fuels (International Renewable Energy Agency 2015). Finally, clean energy could start to compete financially.

But just as the economics began to make sense, opposition against renewable energy policy mounted. Utilities and other fossil fuel companies began attacking RPS policies, believing these laws would limit their ability to make profits off of their existing assets. In 2012, ALEC and the Heartland Institute drafted the "Electricity Freedom Act" model bill, and promoted it in legislatures across the country.[49] Koch Industries likely played a role in this model legislation, as many of the organizations participating in this effort had ties to Koch (Leonard 2019). This model bill was introduced in many states, including Ohio. Utilities in that state simultaneously attacked RPS targets and requested subsidies to keep their coal and nuclear plants open. They claimed that renewables were too expensive. In fact, research has shown that inexpensive natural gas is more important to making utilities' other assets unprofitable, for example, driving nuclear offline (Jenkins 2017). But utilities were happy to scapegoat renewables and their government "mandates."

Over time, utilities' opposition to net metering also grew. As consumers began to use state and federal incentives in greater numbers to deploy small-scale solar, pressure began to mount on the electricity rate structure. As a result, distributed solar started to pose a threat to utilities' conventional assets. Customers opting out of receiving electricity from the grid most of the time reduced their payments to the utilities. Utilities went to their regulator to argue that the grid's fixed costs would have to be recuperated from a smaller number of customers. As these remaining customers' rates increased, utilities became fearful that more customers would opt out as well, choosing to produce their own energy and further exacerbating their ability to recuperate their fixed costs. By 2011, this dynamic—termed "the death spiral"—became a major issue at utility conferences (Blackburn et al. 2014; Kassakian & Schmalensee 2011). Utilities increasingly saw net metering as a Trojan horse that would fundamentally challenge the utility model. If individuals and independent power producers owned the electricity system's assets, utilities would lose their monopoly in generation— and the regulated profits that came from it. Compounding these problems, utilities also faced flat or declining sales and aging infrastructure that needed investment.[50]

As a result of these factors, many utilities became hostile toward NEM policies and distributed generation customers. In January 2013, the EEI published a prominent report called *Disruptive Challenges* (Kind 2013). The report noted the rapid decline in the cost of solar photovoltaics—falling 77% in

4 years.[51] Combined with increased utility rates in some parts of the country, by 2013 solar was competitive in around 16% of the US retail electricity market, where prices were 15 ¢/kWh or greater. Of course, the report neglected to note that this rise in utility prices was, largely, utilities' own making. And while tax incentives had been available to corporations for decades, the fact that they were now available for citizens through solar leasing companies threatened utilities. Given these cost declines and the increase in ratepayers' ability to access solar, the report painted a dire picture for monopoly utilities. It was an alarm bell— utilities realized they needed to mount a challenge to renewable energy laws. In late 2013, EEI began working with ALEC to draft a model bill on net metering repeal, innocuously called "Updating Net Metering Policies."[52]

In the interest of their profits, utilities have come to argue that NEM policies are inequitable, leading to cross-subsidization between solar and non-solar customers. Of course, this narrative neglects the fact that the electricity system has long set rates with cross-subsidization in mind, albeit across income groups through "rate tiers" and across sectors through "customer classes" (i.e., residential, commercial, industrial). Nevertheless, utilities commissioned studies that used economic models to demonstrate that solar customers imposed large costs on their neighbors. In response, solar companies—particularly California-based solar leasing companies—argued that they provided valuable services, such as emissions reductions, that were not adequately priced in these studies. They wrote rival reports whose economic models demonstrate that solar photovoltaic's benefits exceed the retail rate. Depending on the politics of the state and the political makeup of the PUC, the utilities' or the solar companies' narratives prevailed. Given these rival reports, in 2016 Congress asked the Department of Energy to review recent studies on net metering. The resulting 2018 report by the ICF found that of the 15 studies conducted since 2014, only three factors were consistently included—avoided energy generation, avoided generation capacity, and avoided transmission capacity.[53] Few studies included environmental benefits from solar, such as the benefit of avoiding carbon pollution.

Over time, attacks on net metering laws have grown considerably. Utilities have asked PUCs for large fixed charges on customers' monthly bills related to net metering: in 2015, there were 61 requests for bill increases, and by 2018 the number rose to 77.[54] Since 2014, around 125 utilities in 34 states have requested fixed charge increases.[55] Overall, a majority of utilities have succeeded in getting at least some of the charges they requested. For example, of the requests PUCs received from investor-owned utilities (IOUs) in 2018, PUCs granted increases about two-thirds of the time.[56]

The dynamic whereby utilities have attempted to place large, monthly charges on NEM customers will be explored further in the Arizona case. But the key point here is that arguments over who should pay for using the grid must be rooted in a historical understanding of the electricity system. One could argue that utilities received adequate payments to build the grid while the utility consensus dominated regulation. Such an argument could be grounds for making the grid a public asset, an idea that was seriously considered in the wake of the California electricity crisis (Duane 2002). Had such a policy been implemented, a very different political dynamic for distributed generation would likely have emerged across the United States.[57] Similarly, governments could invest in the grid and require that all generators—commercial and retail alike—have access to it. In some ways, Texas undertook just such an investment in transmission starting in 2005. This alternative pathway for the electricity system could ameliorate significant conflict between private utilities and renewable energy, particularly for small-scale distributed generation.

Conclusion

Who sets the rules for our energy system and, through them, the harms our energy system imposes on people and the planet? Throughout most of the twentieth century, it was private, profit-motivated electric utilities and their largely captured regulators. Operating as economic monopolies and providing a fundamental input for the US economy, utilities and other fossil fuel interest groups held a privileged position. They maintained a near monopoly over the policy agenda across the states. Richard Hirsh (1999a) has called this stable regulatory structure the "utility consensus."

But by the 1980s, this consensus began to erode. Economists first critiqued monopoly utilities for failing to provide low prices. Environmentalists added that they were failing to innovate, exacerbating environmental harms, and resisting new regulations. While these attacks have made a dent in private utilities' power, they still exert considerable control over policy. Utilities remain the dominant interest group in electricity policy debates. The rest of this book will show how utilities, across various states, have used their power to rollback clean energy laws and prevent their expansion.

With this history in hand, it should not be surprising that utilities have often won policy battles. Renewable energy advocates are small, fledgling actors compared to these large private utilities receiving guaranteed profits from the state. In 2017, the private utilities' association, EEI, had operating revenues totaling $364 million. That was 17 times and 50 times higher than the wind and solar energy associations' revenue, respectively.[58] In policy feedback, the deck is not evenly stacked for new advocates compared to incumbent opponents. Or as historian Thomas Hughes (1969) put it, once an existing technological system has momentum, it becomes more difficult to change.

Although this analysis places significant blame on utilities for resisting clean energy policies and technologies, regulators also hold responsibility for their failure to address climate change. Public Utility Commissions, like the utilities themselves, resisted changing their operations—whether to accommodate renewables or increase competition. Thus, it is not economics alone that has driven decisions in this sector but also politics. As Paul Sabin, an energy historian put it,

> The supply and demand of energy—the price of energy—has a deeply political history. . . . The rhetoric of price shares the common assumption that cost is a meaningful independent variable, which we can calculate easily and compare. In this capitalist ideal, a free market determines prices, except when government intervenes through regulation or subsidies. But . . . the free market, supposedly independent of government interference, is a mythical concept that we should have discarded long ago. (Sabin, 2005, xiv–xv)

The government has worked with utilities to get us into this mess—where we now have very little time to address the climate crisis. Regulators have advanced narrow goals, including capacity expansion and economic growth, at the expense of innovation, public health, and climate stability. They have a responsibility to change that, and start valuing climate stability and air quality more highly.

Still, whatever little progress we have seen so far in clean energy is a credit to advocates and the government, not electric utilities. Mandating that private utilities generate a portion of the supply from renewables has proven critical to our meager action on climate to date. Yet it is not just private utilities that are a problem. In one-third of states with binding RPS laws, public utilities and cooperative utilities have avoided having to comply, in part because they are not subject to PUC oversight. In two-thirds of states with net metering laws, these same utilities are not required to participate.[59] Overall, private, public and cooperative utilities and made little progress. History shows us that utilities simply would not have switched to renewables on their own. Instead of acting on climate change, private and, to a lesser extent, public utilities, have promoted climate denial and delay from the 1980s onward (Anderson et al. 2017).

With this background on the US electricity system's history and institutions, it is now possible to examine how policy feedback has failed in the electricity sector, looking at specific cases. As was the case with PURPA and federal renewable energy tax incentives, in each state the politics of enacting a clean energy law have differed from the politics of implementation. While advocates have managed to enact modest clean energy laws in many states, these laws have not fundamentally restructured utilities and other fossil fuel companies' power. Instead, these organizations have used their privileged position to rollback clean energy laws, delaying progress on addressing the climate crisis.

Policy Feedback Takes Hold

Networked Advocates Use the Public to Drive Clean Energy Leadership in Texas

To understand how advocates can win political battles against opponents, it is useful to first examine a case where policy feedback created path dependence. Texas was an unexpected early leader in clean energy, acting even before California. Renewable energy advocates from Texas—working with a network across the country—developed the idea of a renewable energy target.[1] When they had the opportunity to get this idea onto the policy agenda in the mid-1990s, when the state was restructuring its grid, the advocates were ready with their proposal. As a result, in 1999, Texas passed an ambitious set of environmental policies as part of its electricity restructuring law.

After the policy was implemented, the Texan wind industry grew. Allied with NGO advocates, this burgeoning clean energy industry lobbied for policy expansion. They were successful: in 2005, the Texas legislature expanded the renewable energy target. Per the predictions of policy feedback theory, a Republican legislator whose rural district had experienced economic benefits from wind energy sponsored the bill. In a rare move in Texas, the legislature also invested $7 billion into an infrastructure program to support clean energy. Policy feedback was working—the law was expanding, enabling a shift away from fossil fuels in the electricity sector.

This chapter describes the first decade of clean energy policy in Texas, when wind grew rapidly. Here, we can see the fog of enactment operating clearly, enabling advocates to gain a foothold. Given that Texas was an early actor, uncertainty was particularly pronounced. Although fossil fuel companies and electric utilities believed there would be costs from renewable energy laws, in 1999 these costs were not yet clear. It was hard to predict how technologies would mature or how policies would interact across jurisdictions. Yet, environmental NGOs and other renewable energy advocates could see the future more clearly than their

Short Circuiting Policy. Leah Cardamore Stokes, Oxford University Press (2020). © Oxford University Press.
DOI: 10.1093/oso/9780190074265.001.0001

opponents in 1999. As a result of foundation funding, they had strong networks that helped them understand the potential these laws held. Since the opponents had not yet mobilized against renewables, the issue was not yet polarized—both Democrats and Republicans supported the policy in its early years. The advocates also used the public as a tool to get clean energy laws on the agenda and passed. These factors allowed for an initial decade of successful policy enactment, implementation, and expansion. Eventually, opponents would learn through implementation. In the second decade, they worked to undermine clean energy policy and drive polarization. In the next chapter, I show how opponents blocked progress on solar energy. But this first decade, covered in this chapter, was a hopeful time in Texas, particularly for wind energy.

Networked Advocates Use the Public to Enact a Renewable Portfolio Standard During Electricity Restructuring

Given fossil fuels' centrality to the Texan economy, oil and gas companies have held significant power in the Longhorn State for over a century. Texas is extremely energy-rich. Since oil was discovered at Spindletop in 1901, fossil fuels have consistently made up a large portion of the Texan economy (Hinton & Olien 2002). Oil and gas extraction contributed over 10% to Texas's gross domestic product in 1963—almost as much as the entire manufacturing sector.[2] Today, the stretch of land from Houston to Galveston Bay has the highest density of petroleum refineries, petrochemical companies, and other oil and gas infrastructure in the world (Weisman 2008).

Texas's economy was built on this backbone of cheap and plentiful energy. Heavy industry consumes large amounts of fossil fuels and electricity. With abundant energy supplies, the state has done little to invest in conservation: it is well known as one of the worst states for energy efficiency.[3] Why save energy when there is so much of it and it's so cheap? Not surprisingly, the companies that own and operate all this energy infrastructure are also large and politically influential. Their aim is to maintain the status quo—irrespective of the energy system's environmental harms. In Texas, fossil fuel companies and electric utilities, with strong ties to politicians and regulators, are well placed to win in organized combat over any given policy.

Given this political and economic arrangement, electricity regulation came to Texas 50 years later than other states. Texas has long maintained its own, sovereign grid—one that does not cross state boundaries—in part to avoid federal regulation. At the state level, the electricity system was largely unregulated and without a public utility commission (PUC) for most of the twentieth century (Anderson 1981). However, in 1967, utilities began to increase their rates. These growing costs caused lawmakers to continuously raise the idea of establishing a regulator until 1975 when a law established the Public Utility Commission of Texas (PUCT) (Hopper 1976). But this arrangement did not last long.

By the mid-1990s, the rising pressure across the United States to increase competition in the electricity sector reached Texas. When Governor George W. Bush took office in 1995, he appointed Pat Wood III as chair of the PUCT. During his time, Wood worked with the legislature to signal to incumbent, monopoly electric utilities that deregulation was imminent.[4] The legislature took the first steps, passing a small-scale law that paved the way for deregulation in 1995.[5] Given that the Texas legislature only meets every other year, the PUCT had to wait another year for legislative direction.

This delay would prove fortuitous for clean energy advocates. It enabled a public opinion exercise to unfold that they would successfully use in their campaign for a clean energy law. While the commission waited for the legislature to go back into session, it resumed its de facto Integrated Resource Planning (IRP) process in 1995.[6] The plan called for a public engagement component. Around that time, one of the commissioners saw a television program with political scientist James Fishkin discussing his deliberative opinion polling method (Rabe 2004). Inspired by this idea, in 1996, the commission ran a series of deliberative polling exercises within each utility's territory, in partnership with the private utilities.[7] These events featured presentations from various interest groups, including environmental NGOs.

The results were promising for advocates seeking to push a renewable energy law in Texas. Although the expectation was that low costs would prove the most important variable for citizens' attitudes on electricity, in practice reliability and price stability came out as more important (Rabe 2004). Further, citizens overwhelmingly endorsed renewables—even if they cost more money. We might hypothesize that public opinion drove the subsequent adoption of Texas's first clean energy law (Ansolabehere & Konisky 2014). In practice, though, the story is more complicated. In the mid-1990s, advocates used public opinion as a tool in their battle to pass clean energy laws.[8] They shaped and communicated public preferences to push renewable energy onto the agenda during the deregulation debate.

Meanwhile, the utilities were being squeezed. In 1996, the commissioners put the electric utilities through a very difficult rate case, with Chairman Wood leading the process.[9] This was a negotiation tactic: the PUCT was signaling that remaining with the status quo regulatory structure would prove unfavorable for the private utilities—it would be better if they cooperated with the legislature's restructuring plans. As one person put it, "it was clear that the utilities had some exposure under the Pat Wood regime."[10] The utilities had built new infrastructure, and the PUCT indicated that it might not qualify as useful and, therefore, would not be included in rate recovery calculations. When utilities invest in infrastructure but cannot make adequate returns through the regulatory process, they hold "stranded costs."[11] This created a bind for the utilities: whether or not they went along with deregulation, there would be downsides. Thus, the executive branch was working with the legislature to push the utilities toward cooperating.

When the legislature went back in session in 1997, several restructuring bills were introduced, most prominently the Texas Consumer Power Act (SB 684). Given the scale of the proposed changes, both advocates and opponents showed up for the fight. Key advocates for restructuring included Enron and the Texas Coalition for Competitive Electricity (TCCE).[12] A now defunct group formed in 1997, the TCCE members included large fossil fuel companies like Oxy, Altura Energy, and the Texas Oil and Gas Association. The status quo regulatory system created significant uncertainty for these companies because electricity was a large input cost for their operations. They believed a restructured system would bring lower and more stable prices.[13] At the time, newer and cheaper electricity technologies—including co-generation and combined cycle gas turbines—were becoming available. The TCCE believed that deregulation would bring these options to Texas. Given the fossil fuel industry's long-standing influence in the Lone Star State, it held significant sway in the legislature, helping to put deregulation onto the agenda and shaping its design. The TCCE eventually morphed into the Texas Association of Manufacturers (TAM) in 2005—an important group that led the attack on clean energy policy in the second half of our Texas story.

Unsurprisingly, in 1997, the main opponents of electricity restructuring were private utilities, networked through the Association of Electric Companies of Texas (AECT). Competition posed an existential threat for incumbent monopoly electric utilities.[14] They preferred to remain with the status quo regulatory system, despite the recent, difficult rate case. Unexpectedly, the Texan rural electric cooperatives also opposed the plan. They likely believed restructuring was risky even if a competitive electricity system might not directly affect them.[15] Given that these rural co-ops operated in conservative districts, they acted as veto players for many members of the state legislature. Working together, these utilities were able to block the bill,[16] and electricity deregulation failed in 1997.

Despite this failure, negotiations over deregulation continued, with participation from a wider range of interest groups. When the legislature was not in session in 1998, several legislators investigated the issue through a lieutenant governor-appointed Senate interim committee. Republican senator David Sibley from Waco was the chair. The group was very active, even visiting California and the United Kingdom to understand their restructured systems.[17] By the end of 1998, Senator Sibley and Democratic representative Steven Wolens pulled together a group to negotiate a draft bill for the next session. Since the Democrats controlled the House and the Republicans controlled the Senate and the executive branch, a bipartisan effort was necessary. The failed deregulation bill in 1997 also demonstrated that success would require a broad group of stakeholders to agree to a bill's basic provisions. Thus, a broad negotiating table was opened.

At the next legislative session in 1999, strong opponents to the deregulation agenda remained. The private utilities, allied through their trade association, still opposed the plan. If it proceeded, however, their primary focus was on securing provisions to cover their existing investments—their "stranded costs."[18] Deregulation advocates, meanwhile, continued working through their network—the TCCE—believing restructuring would lead to lower electricity rates.

A strange assortment of other interest groups joined forces to support deregulation. In a kind of Baptist–bootlegger coalition, environmental advocates and clean energy companies joined with the fossil fuel industry to support restructuring (Vogel 1995, 2018). By the mid-1990s, there was a small clean energy industry in Texas. After Zond—one of the largest wind companies in the United States—went bankrupt, Enron bought it in 1997.[19] Hence, Enron was interested in policy that would support renewables. That company was also interested in creating a energy market the they could trade in—as it would later do in California, with disastrous consequences. Environmental groups had more complicated motives for joining the effort.[20] Although consumer advocates and environmental organizations were skeptical that deregulation would benefit their cause, some groups, particularly the Environmental Defense Fund (EDF), saw the policy fight as an opportunity to push for environmental protections.

Given the broad interest groups and issues involved, the resulting bill was quite complex. As introduced, the Texas Electric Restructuring Act of 1999 (SB 7) addressed many disparate issues. Initially, the bill did not contain environmental provisions. But as it made its way through the legislature, it broadened, becoming a "Christmas tree"—a bill that every interest group could hang its ornament upon.[21] At the end of the negotiations, three significant environmental provisions were included in the final law: a requirement for old coal plants exempt from the 1971 Texas Clean Air Act to cut air pollution emissions,[22] broad energy efficiency goals, and a renewable portfolio standard (RPS). Where did these environmental provisions come from? They came from interest group advocates. Environmental NGOs and consumer groups used deregulation as an opportunity to push environmental policies through the legislature. In particular, two environmental NGOs—EDF and Public Citizen—played a key role in getting the policy on the agenda and passed.

As is the case with many other complex bills in technical areas, the fog of enactment was operating when advocates negotiated for environmental provisions in Texas's electricity restructuring bill. There were several reasons why uncertainty and ambiguity surrounded the bill: the RPS and efficiency provisions were novel policies, it was a major reform, it was a technical area, and multiple jurisdictions would eventually influence the law's effects. At the time, a clean energy target was a new idea that had rarely been implemented—and certainly not in a market as large as Texas. The bill was also long and complex. Large bills consume interest groups' time and resources. This dynamic gives less influential interest groups an opportunity to push their own smaller reforms, while their opponents are distracted. Fossil fuel companies were focused on the bigger prize of passing a deregulation bill. And the private electric utilities that would prove important opponents to clean energy targets in many other states were distracted by stranded costs and market rules. Their limited bandwidth provided environmental and renewable energy advocates an opportunity. As one industry representative put it, "I think we would have fought harder [against the RPS] but there were other issues that distracted us at the time."[23] The policy's eventual consequences were also difficult to foresee because they would be a function of policy at multiple levels of government: from local siting decisions to federal tax incentives.

Despite this thick fog, some groups had a clearer sense of the future. Clean energy advocates, working through a network that crossed state lines, were able to see through the fog surrounding the proposal. Since the early 1990s, the Energy Foundation had been steadily supporting a group of clean energy advocates across the states.[24] This network provided advocates more information and resources.[25] Over time, the group had developed policy ideas and political strategies to get clean energy laws passed. They were focused on tacking clean energy policies onto deregulation bills. Prior to 2000, all but one state-level RPS policy was enacted as part of an electricity restructuring reform bill (Hogan 2008). In Texas, the foundation supported two key groups: EDF and Public Citizen.[26] Seizing on deregulation as a policy window, these two environmental groups worked to get renewable energy onto the agenda.

It was a fortuitous time for environmental advocates to push their ideas. Unusually in the decades since, environmental groups held influence in the Texas legislature in 1999. With the Democrats in control of the House, the Republicans controlling the Senate and executive branch realized they would need a broader coalition to overcome utilities' lobbying against electricity restructuring.[27] Given their level of influence, clean energy advocates worked both directly and indirectly to get a renewable energy target on the agenda and enacted.

One advocate worked on the inside of the negotiations, directly influencing the legislation. EDF, a pro-market environmental organization, was granted a seat at the table because of its long history in the state and its strong relationship with legislators. It advocated for an RPS as well as tougher air pollution standards for existing coal plants. Given that the Democrats controlled the House, the clean energy target was included in Representative Wolens's bill, introduced in early 1999 (HB 349). This proposal set a starting point for the negotiations: a target of 3% of the electricity system from clean energy sources by 2005, developed in consultation with EDF.[28] On the Senate side, Sibley's initial bill (SB 7) contained no RPS provision.

As the House and Senate worked to reach an agreement on electricity restructuring, a larger negotiating table was established with various interest groups. The fossil fuel companies and industrial energy consumers, working in a network through their lobby association, the TCCE, were well represented. This group was willing to support a target of 1,000 MW around 1.5% of the total electricity system, provided the timeline was stretched out to 2009.[29] EDF's proposal in the House bill would have amounted to about three times as much clean energy in half that time. The conflict over how to set a baseline also caused the negotiations to shift from a percentage target to a capacity target, showing the opponents' influence.[30] Even in these early days, industrial electricity consumers—which include oil and gas companies—were the most important opponents to renewable energy policy. Fossil fuel companies aimed to water down the clean energy policy's ambition.

Eventually, Senator Cain offered an amendment to the Senate bill on March 17, with the same 3% target as Wolens's proposal, albeit with the TCCE's preferred later deadline of 2009.[31] The final bill had a capacity target of 2,000 MW by 2009, amounting to a modest 3% of the electricity system. EDF played a significant role, helping craft the language for the RPS provisions in the final version.[32] To appeal to the Republicans' pro-market sensibilities, a renewable energy credit trading mechanism was also included that would theoretically lower costs. Indeed, some attribute the requirement for a market mechanism in the RPS to Governor Bush himself.[33]

After the negotiations concluded, the bill still had to be passed, signed, and implemented with the clean energy target intact. To ensure that this happened, another interest group advocate, Public Citizen, worked indirectly to influence legislators outside the negotiations. They used the public as a tool in their campaign to support clean energy policy. They strategically targeted specific legislators, using the media and public outreach to push for stronger renewable energy goals and environmental and consumer protections as part of the deregulation package. The advocates knew that the public would be a valuable ally in their efforts to pass environmental provisions in the electricity restructuring bill. So they brought the public into their campaigns.

Public Citizen is an advocacy group focused on grassroots mobilization. In the mid-1990s, it began a public campaign for an RPS, intensifying its outreach as the legislature moved toward restructuring in 1998. Like EDF, Public Citizen had been working with other interest groups across state lines in the Energy Foundation network.[34] In the lead-up to SB 7, Public Citizen targeted two politicians they considered to be crucial to getting the environmental provisions enacted: Representative Wolens, the House leader on restructuring, and Democratic senator David Cain from eastern Dallas, vice chair of the Special Committee on Electric Utility Restructuring in the 1999 session. These politicians were chosen because of the committees they sat on and because Public Citizen thought they might be sympathetic to environmental concerns.[35] To influence these legislators, Public Citizen tabled at state fairs and knocked on doors to try to mobilize individuals to send letters and call these politicians' offices. They also worked to get members of the public into the hearing room. During one hearing, a young advocate with asthma gave emotional testimony on what pollution reductions would mean for him, holding up several inhalers and calling for solutions.[36] Seemingly affected by this personal narrative, Wolens voiced his desire to reduce pollution. Public Citizen also helped form the Wind Coalition, which drew together businesses and wind advocates. This group pooled resources to create job analyses and engage rural areas in their outside lobbying efforts.[37]

Throughout this period, advocates were very focused on how the public could be used to pass new clean energy laws. For example, the Texas Renewable Energy Industries Association (TREIA) described a variety of tactics to build public support for renewables in its summer 1997 newsletter, including a clean energy lobbying campaign aimed at Austin's public utility. But as a trade association, the organization was poorly designed for outside lobbying. TREIA had grown to 70 members by 1999 and included large organizations such as Enron Wind, Vestas, and BP Solar. Utilities were also members, including Texas Utilities Energy, Central and South West Corporation, and Lower Colorado River Authority.[38] Despite its growing membership, it was a niche lobbying organization compared to the fossil fuel corporations allied through the TCCE. Further, having utilities among its membership limited TREIA's ability to influence the restructuring debate, given that these monopolies were opposed to the policy altogether. Even on clean energy policy the association's membership was split on the best path forward.[39] Together, these factors limited TREIA's political influence in the restructuring debate.

Eventually, the bill passed both the House and the Senate by voice votes, with all three environmental provisions intact. The bill made its way to the Governor's desk where it was signed in June 1999. Deregulation provided an opportunity for advocates to enact a landmark clean energy law in Texas. These interest group advocates advanced an insider–outsider lobbying strategy. Given that they had some influence with legislators—particularly Democrats who controlled the House—advocates used direct lobbying strategies to get their ideas on the agenda. Other groups supported these efforts from the outside, using indirect strategies including outside lobbying to construct a vision of Texans allied in support of clean energy.

Alternative Explanations: Executive Leadership, Public Pressure, and Bureaucrats

I have argued that interest group advocates were the driver of Texas's first clean energy law. But this is not the only perspective. As an important early clean energy law, Texas's initial RPS has been well studied. There are three other competing causal narratives in existing research about why the RPS was included in Texas's deregulation bill: leadership from Governor Bush and the executive branch (Galbraith & Price 2013), broad public support for renewables (Ansolabehere & Konisky 2009), and champions in the bureaucracy (Rabe 2004). In this section, I review each of these hypotheses and the available evidence for each claim. Overall, I find stronger evidence that interest groups were the critical factor in getting a clean energy target and other environmental policies enacted in Texas.

The first causal narrative identifies executive branch leadership as key. Governor Bush reportedly said to PUCT chair Pat Wood in 1996, "we like wind. . . . Go get smart on wind" (Galbraith & Price, 2013, 121). It is possible that Sam Wyly, a major donor with close ties to Bush, had influenced the governor. Wyly had become interested in improving air quality through renewables and may have suggested to Bush that wind was a good idea.[40] Years later, when Bush ran for president in 2000, wind energy was included in the Republican Party platform. On the campaign trail, Bush would claim credit for Texas's success in leading the nation on clean energy.

However, the story that Bush championed renewables seems implausible for several reasons. In 1997, Governor Bush and commissioners Pat Wood and Judy Walsh proposed a model restructuring bill, with eight key principles. Renewable energy was not mentioned. As the TREIA newsletter evaluating the governor's plan at that time put it, "virtually nothing that would encourage, much less require, the development of renewable energy generated electricity was in the bill."[41] This was not because an RPS was inconceivable then—TREIA included the idea in its March 21, 1997, policy statement in the midst of the deregulation debate. Rather, renewables were not a priority for Governor Bush in 1997, a year after his remark to Wood. There is no evidence to suggest he changed his opinion in the intervening 2 years. Ultimately, the renewable energy provision would first appear in the Democratic House bill, not in any proposal from the governor.

A second story points to a central role for public opinion. Often, public opinion is viewed as a key variable driving policy change, particularly at the state level (Erikson et al. 1993; Lax & Phillips 2012; Stimson et al. 1995). In the Texas case, some have argued that public support pushed politicians to enact the RPS policy, particularly given the deliberative polling process, which favored renewables (Ansolabehere & Konisky 2014). But even there, interest groups' role in constructing public opinion is understated.

Evidence suggests that environmental groups were actively shaping public support for clean energy in the deliberative polling exercise and later in the negotiations over restructuring. Both EDF and Public Citizen were on the advisory committee that organized the deliberative public opinion exercise (Fishkin 2011). Once these polls were completed, they constructed a simple and clear narrative that strategically highlighted and downplayed results in ways that served their interests. For example, when these groups talked about the outcome of the exercise, they highlighted that most citizens were willing to pay more for renewable energy. This was one result. But the process also had results that ran counter to advocates' interests. For example, after deliberation, more citizens ranked renewable energy *lower* on their priority list. As Luskin et al. (1999, 8) wrote on the results of the process,

> There was some decrease in support for using more renewable re-sources, despite their potential for safeguarding environmental quality. The reason seems to have been increased realism. Before deliberation, many participants had pie-in-the-sky notions of what renewable energy could presently do, and at what cost. During the deliberations, they learned that the large scale use of renewable energy would presently be very costly and might entail some reliability problems.

These complex results were left out of advocates' stories. Instead, they emphasized the "clear" outcome that Texans wanted more clean energy.[42] Years after the deliberative polling exercises concluded, clean energy advocates linked these results to the restructuring debate, ensuring that it remained at the top of legislators' minds.

In truth, the technical nature of the restructuring debate left little room for spontaneous public engagement in the legislative process. Most citizens did not know enough about electricity to construct and voice an opinion. As such, civil society groups needed to make legislators *believe* that the public thought energy and environmental issues were salient and high priorities. For example, in February 1997 an EDF employee said at a briefing at the capitol for legislators, "Recent polls have clearly indicated that Texans want clean renewable energy resources."[43] In another case, Public Citizen targeted two important legislators from Dallas, highlighting the urgent air quality problems in their district and impressing upon them that the public cared about this problem. As one person involved in the campaign at the time said, "So we just flooded their offices with letters and calls from citizens. We set up tables at the natural food stores in Dallas. We went to street fairs and worked their neighborhoods and got thousands of letters into those two representatives."[44] Thus, the evidence suggests it was not public support on its own that got renewable energy onto the agenda. Rather, advocates used the public as a tool, actively shaping and communicating the public's preferences and strategically targeting specific legislators.

A third proposed causal mechanism points to bureaucrats championing renewables. In this story, policy change occurs through learning, with technical bureaucrats watching via bureaucratic networks what policy choices nearby states make and these policies' ramifications. Modern policy problems are complex. Thus, bureaucrats are increasingly specialized and potentially able to dominate the policy agenda (Heclo 1978). In theory, bureaucrats are able to use ambiguities in laws, combined with their autonomy and discretion, to develop rules and institutions in line with their interests. Given the technical nature of electricity policy, we might expect that bureaucrats have political legitimacy and autonomy in this policy domain.

Examining US state energy policy, Barry Rabe (2004) argues that bureaucrats helped diffuse key environmental policies, including RPS policies, across states. As Rabe writes specifically on the Texas case, there was a state agency official "who is widely credited as having been a pivotal policy entrepreneur behind the RPS initiative" (Rabe, 2004, 56). It may be the case that bureaucrats have been important policy incubators, particularly in the early days of renewable energy. However, despite significant effort,[45] I did not uncover this key bureaucratic champion or other evidence for bureaucrats' central role in renewable policy at that time in Texas. As we will see in the next chapter, bureaucrats' influence have only diminished over time, as the issue has become more threatening to incumbent opponents.

Overall, I argue that organized combat between interest groups best explains this case. It is notable that environmental groups and consumer advocates did not just get a renewable energy policy in 1999. The bill also included significant air quality and energy efficiency provisions. These parts of the bill show the clear marks of a network of advocates, working across the states and funded by a savvy foundation to advance exactly these policy goals. Their success suggests that environmental groups were effective lobbyists at that time—working both directly to lobby for specific bill provisions and indirectly through outside lobbying. In the first round of combat in Texas, the advocates prevailed over their opponents.

Advocates Win This Round: Successful Implementation and Policy Feedback in Texas's RPS policies

The spoils from victory in organized combat go to the party whose laws are implemented—not just passed. Conflict between advocates and opponents continues during implementation. In the case of Texas, the renewable energy laws enacted in 1999 faced little resistance during implementation. Potential renewable energy opponents continued to be preoccupied with implementing the larger and more complex deregulation policy. Texas's RPS law was also simple and straightforward in its design (Langniss & Wiser 2005). Both the RPS and the air quality provisions were market-based, making them resonant with the dominant views on regulation. For example, the renewable energy policy was structured with a performance incentive. Because the statutory target was given in capacity (megawatts), implementing the law required it to be translated into an energy value (megawatt hours). If renewables performed well and created more energy (megawatt hours), they would generate more renewable energy credits. There were also automatic compliance penalties established by the PUCT. After a successful implementation, the renewable energy credit market began functioning well.

The wind energy industry took off. Texas's excellent resources were located in sparsely populated areas with little local resistance, allowing wind projects to be built quickly and yield high profits. To give a sense of the scale, almost 1,000 MW, or roughly 750 wind turbines at that time, were installed in the first year alone.[46] By the end of 2001, Texas was ahead of schedule, with wind power going in faster than the targets required (Langniss & Wiser 2003). In part, this speedy growth occurred because the RPS policy was large—projects were able to benefit from economies of scale, leading to low costs of under 3 ¢/kWh on average (Langniss & Wiser 2003). In addition, projects were able to take advantage of the federal production tax credit, which guaranteed 1.5 ¢/kWh in 1990 dollars adjusted for inflation (Stokes & Breetz 2018). This policy reduced the implementation costs for Texas, since the federal government subsidized the state's early action on wind (Moeller 2004). By the middle of the first decade of the 2000s, the RPS was seen as a made-in-Texas success story, propelling the state ahead of California to its current position as the largest wind energy producer in the country. Wind projects brought economic development to rural, Republican districts. Even Republican governor Rick Perry endorsed the technology, creating the Texas Energy Planning Council in 2004 to promote renewables. All indicators pointed to growing political support for clean energy.

The proverbial wind was in the sails of the advocates. After the initial targets were surpassed years ahead of schedule, they began organizing to expand the RPS and pass other complimentary policies to support clean energy growth. Troy Fraser, a prominent Republican state senator, championed the issue in 2005. Senator Fraser's interest in working on wind energy came from seeing the positive results of the first law in his backyard. Geographically, part of his district was in West Texas, an economically depressed area that includes the Panhandle and parts of Hill Country. After the first law, many large wind farms had been built there, and property values had risen. Fraser's hometown of Abilene, in Taylor County, began calling itself the "wind energy capital of the world," with some of the largest wind farms in the country. Parts of Fraser's district left behind their history of being poor cattle towns as wind spurred rural economic development. Politicians whose districts had benefited from the RPS policy had an interest in creating further development opportunities for new wind farms. Here we see clear policy feedback—politicians, like Senator Fraser, were seeing benefits from the policy in their district and therefore sought to expand the policy.[47]

In 2005, Senator Fraser introduced a bill (SB 533) that would expand the RPS policy and invest government funds in transmission infrastructure to support clean energy. Since the RPS target was quickly being exceeded, a new goal was necessary to continue to spur growth in wind. The bill proposed to increase the RPS target substantially, to 5,880 MW by 2015—around 5% of the grid. It also included a longer-term goal of 10,000 MW by 2025. These were solid, but not overly ambitious targets, suggesting that opponents were able to water down the bill to some extent, as they had done with the first target. And they were nowhere near what was necessary to address the growing climate crisis.

More significantly, the bill proposed government spending to build new transmission infrastructure in Texas. This investment would address the growing transmission constraints on the system from new wind capacity. When wind farms are built far away from cities—where the electricity is consumed—power lines are necessary to bring that energy to market. At the time, Texas's electricity market regulator, ERCOT, had a multiyear transmission planning process.[48] Wind developers complained that this long planning process was mismatched with the shorter timelines necessary to finance and build wind projects.[49] They advocates called this the "chicken-or-egg problem": without the transmission capacity, wind projects would not be able to sell their electricity for reasonable rates and without new wind projects, there was no demand for transmission capacity. Thus, to spur more growth in wind energy in Texas, both new targets and an investment in infrastructure were necessary.

Like other technical reforms, this bill granted discretion to bureaucrats to implement the policy. Expanding an electricity grid requires significant modeling, planning, and cost estimation. This was not within politicians' expertise. Hence, the legislators punted the specifics to the PUCT. Still, the lawmakers set ground rules for the plan. The bill stipulated that new transmission would be built through competitive renewable energy zones (CREZ). The PUCT would be given the authority to create these zones based on areas with significant existing, planned, or potential wind energy resources. Next, it would develop a transmission plan that would allow for the power resources in these zones to be brought to market (Zarnikau 2011). As the bill's author, Senator Fraser, wrote to the PUCT, the goal was to expand transmission capacity in a cost-effective manner. The zones would be based on actual or planned projects "to protect ratepayers from having to pay for the construction of transmission in the face of renewable generators that fail to appear."[50] From his perspective, this approach would minimize costs by deferring to the regulator to implement a comprehensive transmission planning process. In practice, deferring to the regulator also shielded the legislature from criticism. The bill left the issue of how much money would be spent on transmission to the PUCT, providing the penny-pinching Texas politicians cover. It also punted conflict to the implementation phase, since the legislators did not have to argue over which districts would benefit from the investment.

This large and complex bill set the stage for another battle between advocate and opponent interest groups. But this time, the first law had left an important legacy: it had built a stronger coalition of advocates. Renewable energy advocates, including TREIA, had long envisioned transmission capacity investments to bring the distant wind resources to the cities. But their policy ideas were not viable without a larger industry with greater political influence in the capitol. After the first clean energy targets were implemented, installed wind energy in Texas grew 10-fold in a few short years, from 184 MW in 1999 to 1,992 MW in 2005.[51] With larger economic interests at the table, enacting the advocates' vision became possible. For example, Florida Power & Light (FPL)—one of the then largest renewable energy developers in the country—lobbied heavily for the infrastructure investment. They were interested in expanding transmission to fix a bottleneck in West Texas that affected one of their wind farms.[52] This large project of over 400 turbines was partly located in Senator Fraser's district.[53] Thus, we see an elite-level feedback: the initial RPS policy's successful implementation brought new interest groups into the legislative process. Using their ties to legislators, advocates pushed for policy expansion.

Once again, the fog of enactment worked in the advocates' favor. In this case, uncertainty about who the policy would benefit enabled electric utilities to support—rather than oppose—the bill. Generators such as Luminant and Reliant and more broadly the AECT became a key constituency supporting the transmission investment. Although these new lines would help wind developers, the argument was made that a transmission investment was technology-neutral: any kind of electricity development could make use of the grid. Since the transmission lines were then mere words on paper, various actors could project into the future, imagining the benefits to their companies from their idealized version of the infrastructure expansion. In practice, most of these future projections would never come to pass. But the key thing is that actors *believed* they would. Thus, uncertainty during enactment caused utilities—previously renewable energy opponents—to support the proposal.

This time, the clean energy target did not need to hide as a provision deep within a large and complex bill. There was enough support from advocates with influence at the Capitol that renewables were the focus. With both the increased RPS goal and the CREZ transmission plan, the proposal gained broad support. Many renewable energy advocates—including FPL, the Wind Coalition, EDF, and Public Citizen—testified in support. The clean energy industry had grown and now had greater influence in the legislature. Notably, TREIA testified in a neutral manner, despite the extremely far-reaching implications of the bill for the renewables industry, suggesting a poorly organized lobbying effort on their part. Even the utilities and their association, AECT, were in favor of the bill.

Still, the bill faced resistance from the politically influential large industrial energy consumers, which testified through the TCCE since the TAM did not yet exist. However, at that time, opposition from the fossil fuel industry was insufficient to derail the bill. Senator Fraser likely believed that economic development from wind energy would prove too valuable for his district to pass up. And although these groups were able to successfully delay the bill from passing in the regular session, it eventually passed in a special session.[54] After policy feedback, the advocates had won: Texas's renewable energy goal grew.

But the opponents did not hang up their hats and go home after losing at the legislature. Instead, they began to actively resist the law's implementation. Unlike the first clean energy target, there was greater controversy in implementing the second law. When the law went to the PUCT for rulemaking in early 2006, conflict increased over planning the transmission expansion. Many state legislators wrote to the commission with their views on how the zones should be identified, particularly if there was potential for their districts to benefit from renewable energy development.[55] There were large economic stakes for many districts depending on the specific transmission plan the PUCT adopted. Thus, both the advocates and opponents enlisted legislators to help make their case to the regulator. Despite the political implications of such a large infrastructure investment, the PUCT was able to manage the process effectively, prioritizing places where wind development was likely.

Further underscoring the fog of enactment, the total cost for the transmission expansion ended up being much higher than politicians, regulators, and interest groups expected. While the legislature and the PUCT's initial cost estimates for the transmission expansion fell between $1 billion and $5 billion, the final costs totaled $7 billion (Fischlein et al. 2013).[56] Giving discretion to the bureaucracy to implement the law left significant uncertainty around spending. As one opponent representing the oil and gas industry put it, "Had consumer groups understood how big that [transmission spending] was ultimately going to be, they wouldn't have agreed to it. The truth is at the time we thought it was not going to be as big of an expansion as it ended up being."[57] These opponents had tried to put a cost limitation in the statute; but they were not successful in convincing the legislators it was necessary, and the provision was not included in the bill. As a result, the PUCT was able to spend significantly more resources on transmission than anticipated. This investment will continue to fuel Texas's growth in wind for the foreseeable future. By contrast, the new renewable energy targets once again proved modest. The state met its new goal 7 years early, in 2008 rather than 2015. Thus, while policy feedback occurred, opponents' efforts to water down the law were clear. As the next chapter shows in detail, fossil fuel corporations and other heavy industries would not tolerate a truly ambitious clean energy law in Texas that would effectively decarbonize the system on the timeline necessary for climate stability.

Conclusion

Why was Texas an unexpected early leader in renewable energy policy? A group of advocates, working in a network with other interest groups across state lines, was able to push two major clean energy laws onto the agenda and ensure that they passed. Their efforts were buoyed by the fog of enactment—a large and complex bill was winding its way through the legislature, and opponents' attention was divided. It was also unclear to potential opponents just how big clean energy could get in Texas—and how fast. In contrast, because the advocates had been working on these policy ideas and political strategies through a foundation-funded network for several years, they were better poised to see through the fog. These environmental NGOs used both direct and indirect strategies to ensure that the law was passed with a number of important environmental provisions intact, including the clean energy target. Working directly with legislators, one group pushed the negotiations from the inside. A second group focused on using public opinion and mobilization to targeted specific legislators, pushing the policy indirectly. These tactics worked, and the electricity restructuring law passed with an important clean energy goal. After enactment, implementation went smoothly in Texas, with initial policy goals met years ahead of schedule.

After the first bill passed, it was easier for the advocates to pass the second law. Policy feedback had kicked in: there were new interest groups ready to make the case to legislators. In their own backyards, politicians had seen the benefits of this new technology for their districts. It brought economic investment, jobs and tax revenue to rural, conservative districts. As a result, Republicans championed the policy's expansion. In line with policy feedback theory, advocates bolstered by the first law gained resources and political influence. They used their growing power to sway politicians to expand the law. Consequently, and despite opposition from fossil fuel companies and industrial energy consumers, in 2005 Texas raised its clean energy goals. It also committed billions for supportive infrastructure, leaving the exact implementation details up to the regulator. Despite delegating responsibility to interpret the law, providing a second opportunity for opponents to undermine the policy, advocates were able to ensure its successful implementation. In part, they worked to mobilize legislators to contact the regulator and explain the legislative intent, undermining opponents' implementation resistance efforts. Overall, in the first decade, advocates prevailed in the battle over Texas's clean energy laws. Policy feedback and lock-in were starting to unfold in the Lone Star State. Given feedback theory, we might expect this upward policy trajectory to continue.

But as the next chapter will show, 2005 was the high-water mark for renewable energy policy in Texas. Since this time, Texas's policy feedback has faltered. When the first two laws were passed, there was considerable uncertainty on the part of clean energy opponents. It was not clear how these new technologies would interact with a deregulated market, federal laws, or technological innovation. Once the large costs to their bottom lines became clearer, opponents mounted a considerable resistance. And they were far more successful in blocking clean energy progress in Texas in the next decade.

A Direct Line to Legislators
and Regulators

Fossil Fuel Corporations Undermine Texas's Solar Energy Law

In 2005, Texas seemed poised to lead the nation in clean energy. As the last chapter showed, the state passed one reform after another, sinking billions of public funds into the effort. The first law spurred economic investment in renewable energy. Once the Texan renewable energy industry grew, it helped lobby for the second law—one that raised the renewable energy target and invested in supportive infrastructure. Politicians whose districts benefited from the first policy sponsored and supported the second bill. Thus, at first glance policy enactment and implementation changed the political landscape, bolstering advocates and enabling policy expansion. However, when the advocates tried to accomplish for solar energy what they had achieved for wind, opponents mounted a much larger resistance. As a result, the state only produced a quarter of its electricity from clean sources in 2018.

This chapter shows how short-lived and narrow policy feedback can be when opponents with political influence wield their power. By 2006, progress on renewable energy policy stalled in Texas. After the first clean energy target was implemented, networked, opponent interest groups gained more information about its likely effects. Opponents were likely concerned about a broad-scale movement away from fossil fuels. These commodities had formed the basis of their corporations' prosperity for decades. Utilities, fossil fuel companies and heavy industry had also learned from places with larger amounts of solar energy that this technology would not serve their interests—solar could decrease their profits from supplying electricity to the grid during shortage hours. Consequently, they doubled down on their resistance to renewable energy policies in Texas.

Short Circuiting Policy. Leah Cardamore Stokes, Oxford University Press (2020). © Oxford University Press.
DOI: 10.1093/oso/9780190074265.001.0001

Although Texas's second clean energy law (SB 20)—discussed in the previous chapter—contained a specific target for solar energy, it was never implemented. After enactment, the Texas Industrial Energy Consumers (TIEC), an alliance of fossil fuel corporations and other industrial companies that rely on cheap energy, intervened aggressively to block this policy at the Public Utility Commission of Texas (PUCT). These opponents argued that a binding legal provision for solar was not the legislators' intent when passing the law. Working through established interest group networks, the opponents easily defeated progress. Eventually, these opponents would weaken Texas' policies, allowing industrial corporations to opt out of paying for renewable energy policies altogether.

As we saw in Chapter 3, fossil fuel companies often maintain a privileged position in policymaking. This is certainly the case in Texas. When clean energy opponents wanted to resist the latest policies in Texas, they did not need to use indirect tools, like the parties, the public, or the courts. With sufficient influence at the Capitol, with the governor, and with regulators, they could work directly and win. Using lobbying, contributions, relationships, and ideas, fossil fuel corporations and other industrial companies reversed the state's course on clean energy. The scale of opponents' power can easily be seen in the case of the fossil fuel industry lobbyist who frequently worked from a desk in a senator's office on Capitol Hill.[1] Which senator? The one leading the energy file, naturally. When this lobbyist wanted to oppose renewable energy policies, he need not travel far. With tight relationships across the branches of government, these opponents had the ear of the key politicians and bureaucrats. They could keep the scope of conflict small and still win.

This chapter shows that advocates can win rounds of political conflict but still fail to convert their victories into longer-term gains through policy feedback. After a mere 6 years, the clean energy industry in Texas was simply not large or established enough to rival the 100-year-old fossil fuel lobby. It had established fewer relationships with politicians and had less political influence. Advocates' ability to rely on a strong network of other interest groups was also much weaker. They had not invested sufficient time or resources into coordinating their policy efforts. When scarcity hit the industry, the coalition fragmented. Thus, it is not just a matter of the advocates winning a policy battle at some point in time. Advocates need to lock in gains to establish greater political influence than opponents. Only then will they be able to protect laws under attack by incumbent industries. In Texas, the advocates had only gained a toehold.

Feedback Begins to Falter: Ambiguity and Implementation Resistance in Texas

In the early 2000s, renewable energy technologies were still new. It was difficult to forecast their costs or clean energy laws' likely consequences. In Texas's newly liberalized electricity market, one unforeseen effect began to develop as wind projects grew in number. Beginning in 2006, negative market prices sometimes occurred in regions with large amounts of wind energy (Zarnikau 2011). This dynamic developed because of interactions between state and federal policies—a common cause of poor policy forecasting.

The federal government's production tax credit (PTC) paid wind projects a small fee for every unit of electricity they produced. Normally, renewable energy projects bid zero into electricity markets, because without fuel costs, their marginal costs are zero. But with the federal PTC, wind developers could bid into the electricity market *below* zero and still make a profit (Zarnikau 2011). For example, if a wind generator bid −1 cent per kilowatt hour (c/kWh), it would still receive 1.5 c/kWh from the federal government, providing a net total of 0.5 c/kWh. Why would wind generators submit a negative bid? It would increase the likelihood that their energy would make it to market, being dispatched in the system the next day. Thus, it made strategic sense for wind generators to bid small negative prices. However, in some limited cases, this strategy led an entire zone of the market to have negative prices (Woo et al. 2011). The dynamic was further exacerbated by limited transmission capacity. When wind produced a surplus of energy in a given region, this oversupply fueled low or negative prices in that area (Zarnikau 2011).

Advocates and opponents competed with one another to frame this problem (Raymond 2016). Opponents focused their narrative on economic costs, while advocates focused on the benefits from job creation and economic development. Even though these occurrences were limited, opponent interest groups successfully used negative prices to advance a narrative that wind energy was costly. They worked directly with legislators and regulators to spread this idea. This view took hold as the PUCT implemented the transmission policy. Using these facts, opponents were ultimately able to change the pro-renewable narrative in Texas. Consequently, by the latter half of the decade, the idea that the government should not be "subsidizing" technologies and "picking winners" became oft-repeated phrases within the Republican Party.[2] Eventually, these ideas would hinder renewable energy policy in Texas.

Despite growing opposition, advocates continued to try to win policy conflicts and expand clean energy in the state. By the early 2000s, advocates set their sights on solar energy. After implementation, it became clear that Texas's first renewable portfolio standard (RPS) was a de facto wind energy goal. Since the policy was based on a trading mechanism, only the lowest-cost technologies were developed. Solar was shut out from growth under Texas's first clean energy law.[3] When advocates were working to expand the policy in 2005, they were rightly concerned that the proposed policy would not benefit any technology other than wind.[4] In fact, Texas was overall a fairly hostile state for solar energy. It did not have—and still does not have—a net metering policy. Consequently, very little solar energy had been developed in the Lone Star State.

Advocates saw the 2005 bill as an opportunity to remedy this problem. As the bill wound its way through the legislature, the renewable energy industry and environmental NGOs worked to advocate for a solar energy policy. They wanted a specific goal for solar—a policy often called "a carve-out." To advance this idea, they used the same strategy they had used with the 1999 bill—working from inside the negotiations and creating pressure from the outside. As one NGO advocate involved with the campaign for the solar target put it, "Basically it was the same formula as 1999. It was grassroots work aimed at the specific committee members. It was jobs analyses. It was working the rural parts of the state that would benefit from solar."[5] The advocates' tactics worked. After several near misses, the final bill included a specific, 500 megawatt (MW) target for non-wind energy by 2015. Renewable energy advocates thought that this clause created a *subset* of the overall binding RPS goal, which the bill would increase.[6] They believed that the bill's passage would finally kick-start the solar industry in Texas.

However, advocates had less influence with legislators than their opponents. While they were involved in earlier negotiations over the bill, environmental and renewable energy groups were not invited to the table when the *final* provisions for the bill were negotiated.[7] Opponents, by contrast, *were* at the table.[8] Specifically, a lobbyist who represented both the Texas Association of Manufacturers (TAM) and the TIEC was present. He gave a strong voice to industrial and fossil fuel companies' interests.

At this point, it is worth pausing our narrative to explain these crucial opponents—the TAM and TIEC—in detail. These groups were and remain highly influential in Texan energy policy. On paper, one of these groups lobbied at the legislature (TAM), while the other lobbied at the PUCT (TIEC). But in practice it is difficult to tell these groups apart. The groups relied on the same lobbyist. The groups also held largely harmonious lobbying views, supporting deregulation and opposing renewable energy and other "costly" environmental policies. And while there is no public membership list for either group, the lists that do exist in regulatory filings contain significant overlap. To understand why the TAM and the TIEC opposed solar energy specifically, we need to examine their membership in detail.

The TAM is the successor network to the Texas Coalition for Competitive Electricity (TCCE). That corporate group—described in the previous chapter—lobbied for deregulation in the electricity sector during the late 1990s. In reviving this association, the group aimed to bring "heavy industry groups under one umbrella" according to an individual working with the network.[9] Formed in 2006, with over 450 companies, it is a much larger association than the TIEC. Given Texas's industrial makeup, the TAM membership is slanted toward oil and gas as well as chemical companies. Large corporate members include ExxonMobil, Occidental (Oxy), Temple-Inland, Huntsman Corporation, Georgia Pacific, ConocoPhillips, Dow Chemicals, Chevron Phillips, Bayer, Marathon Petroleum, Texas Instruments, Hewlett Packard, and Valero. The fossil fuel companies likely play a dominant role in setting the network's agenda, particularly on energy policy. For example, TAM's chair in 2012 was Bill Oswald, the government and regulatory affairs director at Koch Industries, a major petrochemical company.[10]

The TIEC is a similar, albeit smaller, business association formed in 1976, just after Texas established its PUC.[11] It is a lobbying association that grew up symbiotically with its state regulator. The group includes large energy consumers, particularly oil and gas, chemicals, and steel companies. Although they do not make their member list public and do not have a website, TIEC's known participants include a who's who of fossil fuel and chemical corporations: ExxonMobil Power and Gas Services, Chevron Phillips Chemical Company, Shell Oil Products, Huntsman Corporation, Valero Energy Corporation, Oxy, Air Liquide America, and Air Products and Chemicals Inc.[12] Today, the TIEC continues to intervene at PUC hearings. Its goal is to represent the interests of large, industrial energy consumers, which primarily entails trying to keep industrial electricity rates as low as possible. Similarly to the TAM, within the TIEC there is reason to believe that the fossil fuel industry takes precedent in setting the agenda on energy policy.[13] As one person working in the energy industry stated in an interview, "I believe that fundamentally the oil and gas industry, those are the companies that drive policies within the TIEC."[14]

These opponents were powerful, with a direct line to politicians. When the 2005 clean energy bill was being negotiated, both the TIEC and the TAM were influential with the legislative and executive branches. There was a particularly tight link between the Senate energy policy leader, the governor's office, and these fossil fuel and industrial opponents. As several people noted in interviews, the lobbyist for the TIEC and the TAM maintained an extremely close relationship with Fraser's office. One person argued he worked out of the office on occasion: "He sits in Senator Fraser's office. There's an empty desk that he uses. [The lobbyist and the legislator's staffer] are extremely close."[15] Or as another person who used to be a Republican staffer put it, the lobbyist "basically just lives in

[Fraser's] office."[16] Another person characterized his influence this way: "And this goes right to the issue of [the lobbyist for the TIEC and the TAM] and the amount of power he has over the PUC but also Fraser's office but also in the governor's office."[17] Further, one of the lobbyists for TAM was married to a staff person in Fraser's office—a scheduler, who ultimately became Fraser's chief of staff.[18] There were extremely close ties between the Republican lead on energy policy in the Senate and lobbyists for the fossil fuel industries.

These business associations provide a clear example of Charles Lindblom's (1977) privileged position of business—and, more specific to my work, the privileged position of utilities and fossil fuel companies. It is privileged, indeed, for a lobbyist to maintain an informal desk in the Capitol building. Given this lobbyist's close relationship with both legislators and regulators, numerous interview subjects argued that he was responsible for both the bill's language and its interpretation during implementation.[19]

Using the fog of enactment strategically, these opponents concealed what they were doing. The specific language for the solar energy requirement was as follows: "Of the renewable energy technology generating capacity installed to meet the goal of this subsection after September 1, 2005, the commission shall establish a target of having at least 500 megawatts of capacity from a renewable energy technology other than a source using wind energy." This carve-out provision referred to an earlier clause in the bill that would create the *binding* RPS goal. In addition, the bill included language that set a larger, *non-binding* stretch goal for more renewable energy: "the commission shall establish a target of 10,000 megawatts of installed renewable capacity by January 1, 2025." According to those privy to the negotiations, the word "target" was used deliberately in the solar energy requirement to make it different from the binding RPS "goal" of 5,880 MW and the same as the broader non-binding 10,000 MW "target." In short, the opponents wrote the bill so that both the non-binding target and the carve-out relied on the same legal term. This was a calculated tactic to water down the solar policy during implementation.[20] Opponents hoped this would provide them with ammunition during implementation to kill the solar requirement. The advocates did not understand the bill's likely consequences if it was passed as written. Without sufficient power to gain a seat at the negotiating table, advocates did not know that this was their opponents' plan—and neither did many legislators. The opponents managed to shroud the bill in a significant fog.

During implementation, the question of legislative intent became central. When the law reached the PUCT, its interpretation was contested. Was the legislature attempting to create a binding non-wind target of 500 MW in order to increase solar in the state? Or was the legislature simply signaling that non-wind resources would be a nice voluntary objective, like the broader 10,000 MW stretch target? At the PUCT, opponents argued that the solar carve-out—like the long-term goal—was voluntary. That interpretation would make the new policy meaningless, driving no new growth in solar. Those involved in final negotiations over the bill—including the lobbyist for the TAM and the TIEC,[21] a few Republican legislators, and their political staff—argued that the legislative intent was a non-binding target. As the TIEC asserted in its brief to the PUCT, goals were mandates, while targets were voluntary. Similarly, utilities such as Xcel Energy argued for a "soft target" approach, even while acknowledging that the PUCT had the legislative mandate to pursue a "hard target" with mandatory compliance. Other utilities, including American Electric Power (AEP) and Reliant, wrote to critique the need for additional resources from solar energy given its cost. They too promoted the idea that the solar target was voluntary. The utilities and fossil fuel companies were allied in their opposition to solar energy.

The advocates, by contrast, were unaware that this language would prove so consequential. Otherwise, they would have worked harder during the legislative session to clarify it.[22] Had they realized, they might have been able to sway some politicians to pressure the lead senator to change the bill language. Given the benefits renewables had brought to many districts, these groups held some influence at the Capitol—even among Republicans. At the very least, it would have been an openly discussed issue in committees and on the floor, prior to the final vote.

When the bill went to the PUC for implementation, the advocates believed it would be binding. TREIA, BP Solar, and Vote Solar focused their regulatory comments on how to implement the mandatory target they believed the legislation clearly required. They discussed practical questions, such as how to divide up the target between utility and distributed generation projects. When opponents put the issue of legislative intent on the agenda, the advocates were surprised—and they tried to fight back. They argued that the legislative intent could be seen in different parts of the law from where the opponents were fixated. For example, they pointed out that the bill used the term "shall" and argued that "target" is a clear synonym for "goal." They also pointed out that the non-wind carve-out referred to the part of the bill that was binding (the 5,880 MW goal) rather than voluntary (the 10,000 MW goal).

Given earlier growth in the clean energy industry through policy feedback, these advocates had some influence, and were able to expand the scope of conflict at the commission. Republican senator Todd Staples and Republican representative Roy Blake, Jr.—who had both voted for the bill—shared the advocates' view that the law intended to create a *mandatory* solar target. They wrote to the PUCT in late 2006 arguing that the non-wind target should be implemented.[23]

But the advocates were not well organized in their response. In contrast to the opponent interest groups, which worked together in an extremely dense network, the advocates had a loose coalition. For example, the Wind Coalition—a technology-specific association—did not speak up for the solar industry, making no comment on the carve-out. While the first clean energy law had bolstered wind energy politically, it did not enable a broad coalition for clean energy or for lowering the state's carbon emissions more generally. Here we see how policy feedback can be quite narrow and particularistic.

During implementation, the executive branch gains greater political importance, with significant power to arbitrate ongoing conflict between advocates and opponents over policy. Like regulatory bodies in other policy domains, the governor is responsible for appointing commissioners to the PUCT. These commissioners were charged with resolving the ambiguity in the latest clean energy law.[24] The PUCT initially proposed draft rules that would drive some limited, new solar.[24] Advocates supported this proposal while the industrial opponents dissented. Once again, the opponents had greater influence over the regulator than the advocates. The opponents—specifically, the large industrial companies working through the TIEC—likely lobbied the governor to pressure the PUC to interpret the rule in their favor.[25] These group maintained very close ties with the governor.[26] Between 2003 and 2007, Governor Perry received more campaign contributions from energy companies *than any other state politician in the country*—almost $500,000.[27]

Likely with pressure from the governor, the PUCT changed its final ruling, siding with the opponents against even a modest pro-solar policy. The regulator did not mandate a non-compliance penalty, which would have increased solar under the RPS. As the commission stated in its July 2007 order, "The commission believes there is significant uncertainty about its authority to establish a separate RPS for non-wind renewable resources, but this rule should provide incentives for the development of non-wind renewable resources. If this expectation is not realized, the commission has the latitude to review the rule and amend it in the future." It was clear even then that the incentives the commission was referring to would prove completely ineffective. No solar would be built as a result of this weak policy. It was not even worthy of the paper it was written on. The opponents had succeeding in killing Texas's solar revolution before it even started.[28]

Ultimately, the advocates lacked sufficient influence to gain a seat at a crucial negotiating table. Shut out from the discussions, these groups succumbed to the fog of enactment. Opponent interest groups, by contrast, had very strong influence with legislators and regulators. These groups intentionally created ambiguity in the law during enactment. They then worked during implementation to interpret that ambiguity in their favor. And this was not the end of the conflict over clean energy in Texas.

Opponents Continue to Retrench Clean Energy
Policy in Texas

While on paper Texas expanded its successful renewable energy policies in 2005 to include solar energy, in practice the clean energy laws faced significant implementation resistance. Consequently, the feedback dynamic was interrupted, making further policy expansion unlikely. Advocates would make several more attempts to kick-start new solar energy policy—in a state with the largest solar resources in the country but almost no solar projects. But they would never find success. Rather, in a sign of growing resistance from politically influential opponents, the legislature began rolling back Texas's renewable energy laws.

The first policy retrenchment came in 2007 when Republican representative David Swinford's bill (HB 1090) passed the legislature. This law gave large energy consumers—those connected to the transmission system—the ability to opt-out of the RPS requirement via written notice to the PUCT. Despite the change primarily benefiting large companies, including members of the TAM and the TIEC, their lobbyist did not push for the opt-out. Instead, Representative Swinford thought he could use an opt-out to appease these corporations, to get them to stop fighting the broader renewable energy goals. As one person involved with the negotiations put it, "He wanted to . . . neutralize [the large customers] so that [they] couldn't really complain about that issue anymore."[29] The bill pitted Swinford against Fraser, who did not want it to pass because he wanted the participation of large companies to make sure the clean energy laws didn't get "out of hand."

It proved a poor political strategy. The opt-out allowed the industrials to avoid paying for the clean energy transition—but it did not succeed in neutralizing them politically. The bill passed and was successfully implemented by the PUCT, weakening the state's renewable energy laws. Many members of the TIEC, the TAM and the closely affiliated Texas Chemical Council chose to regularly opt-out, including Occidental Energy Ventures, Valero, Shell Oil Company, Chevron Phillips Chemical Company, Temple-Inland, ExxonMobil Power and Gas Service, and Gerdau Ameristeel.[30] This meant that the public would have to bear more of the costs of transitioning the electricity system, while large fossil fuel corporations were free-riders.

Meanwhile, advocates' repeated attempts to establish policies to support solar failed. In the following legislative session, advocates tried to pass a new bill that would clarify the language in the 2005 law, but this effort failed. Two years later, in 2009, legislators and renewable energy advocates tried again to pass a solar carve-out under the RPS. The activity was significant enough that Senator Fraser deemed 2009 "the solar session"—a phrase trumpeted by many media articles. While there were a wide number of bills proposed in 2009, only two made significant progress.

Once again Senator Fraser took the lead on a clean energy bill (SB 545). His plan included a goal of 3,000 MW of solar by 2020, of which 1,000 MW would be distributed generation.[31] But unlike the previous attempts to craft a solar-specific requirement, Fraser's bill would fund solar projects through utility-based rebate programs. Since funds were collected from ratepayers, the policy would not impact the state budget. This time, the legislature went to great lengths to specify implementation details. In the bill's final version, a volumetric charge was proposed for residential and commercial customers, while industrial consumers would pay a small flat charge of $40 a month. This structure meant that small customers rather than industrial customers would bear the brunt of the program's costs. Fearing a prolonged fight with these opponents, Fraser's office proposed these low costs to the industrials' lobbyist.[32] The legislation also outlined cost caps for the rebates, ranging from $2.40/W for small-scale projects to $1/W for large-scale, wholesale, or industrial generation. Unlike the earlier transmission investment, this bill capped the total amount of money that could be spent on the policy. Still, there was some discretion given to the implementing agency. The bill gave the PUCT the option to extend the program if significant solar manufacturing materialized in Texas. Despite clear limits on industrial customers' costs, the TAM, the Texas Chemical Council, and the Texas Oil and Gas Association still opposed the bill. But support was also broad, from renewable energy companies like Meridian Solar to environmental groups and even one utility, Reliant. The chemical company Dow even broke with its industrial confederates to support the bill.

However, the advocates did not present a united front during this legislative session. One major advocacy group, the Solar Alliance, chose to back a secondary bill (SB 541), which Democratic senator Kirk Watson from Austin had sponsored. When he was the mayor of Austin, Watson had worked on the solar issue with its municipal utility, Austin Energy. His bill more closely resembled a traditional RPS, with a goal of 1,500 MW of additional, non-wind resources by 2020—only half the target in Fraser's bill. There were also incentives for made-in-Texas equipment and new requirements for municipal utilities to increase their renewables. Despite being in the minority party, Senator Watson— a persistent and capable politician—managed to get his bill on the calendar in both the Senate and House. Like Fraser's bill, Watson's had many supporters, primarily environmental and renewable energy advocates. But unlike Fraser's bill, utilities, like Reliant, did not support it. And like Fraser's bill, the TAM registered opposition.

Both bills made progress in both chambers. But neither passed because an unrelated voter ID controversy hung the end of the legislative session, killing

all the bills that remained that year. The outcome left significant bad blood between the bill sponsors and the solar advocates. Overall, the solar community
was poorly organized. Solar industry associations' member companies had few
operations in Texas and few prior relationships with legislators, resulting in poor
lobbying. Unlike the wind industry, there had been no policy feedback from the
RPS to spur the solar industry's political influence.

After this flurry of legislative activity on solar, Governor Perry gave a keynote address at a TREIA event in November 2009. He endorsed renewables
broadly, while at the same time arguing against mandates and "picking winners
and losers." Shortly thereafter, the PUCT once again took up the issue of non-
wind renewables, issuing a strawman proposal in December 2009. The proposal would require that 500 MW of power come from non-wind renewables,
with only 50 MW of solar power by 2014. Advocates, including TREIA and
SunPower, worked with the commission; but the process dragged on for over a
year while the fossil fuel lobby continued to oppose solar-specific requirements.
Unable to come to a decision, the PUCT once again deferred to the legislature
for direction.[33] But when the solar issue was taken up again in the 2011 session, it no longer had traction. By this time, polarization on clean energy had
grown at both the state and federal levels (see Figure 1.1), leaving renewables
associated with the Democrats. Republicans increasingly argued against renewable energy "mandates." This dynamic only intensified with the bankruptcy of
Solyndra in August 2011. With this growing partisan divide, again no solar bill
passed in 2013.[34]

Explaining Opposition to Solar Energy in Texas

Why did these industrial and fossil fuel corporations oppose policy that
would spur solar energy? This question is more difficult to answer than it first
appears. First, the solar carve-out in the 2005 bill was small—500 MW is less
than 1% of Texas's electricity system. It would not dramatically raise electricity
prices. Second, industrial consumers connected to the transmission system had
already secured the right to opt out of the RPS requirements in 2007. These
provisions gave them a clear avenue to avoid cost increases under the Watson
bill, and in the case of Fraser's bill, their monthly charge for solar would only
be $40. Surely, this small monthly expense did not justify the much higher
lobbying expenses. These corporations would not face substantial costs under
a solar-specific policy. In the words of a former Republican staffer "[industrial
companies that are members of the TIEC and the TAM] care partly about electricity prices rising. And that's part of the answer. But, as renewables mature and
become price competitive, that's less and less of the answer."[35]

Instead, large industrials' interests are more clearly understood by paying attention to their energy assets. While all of these companies are large energy consumers, it is easily observed that many are also energy *producers*. Many members of the TIEC and the TAM maintain their own natural gas generation infrastructure. As one Republican political staffer described industrial companies' opposition to renewables, "There's no question—they have interests in the energy sector. More recently they have become their own qualified scheduling entities, QSEs, out of ERCOT [the Electric Reliability Council of Texas]." For example, as of December 2017, Shell Energy had eight QSE-registered plants, ConocoPhillips had four, Oxy had two, and Gerdau Ameristeel had one. More broadly, in 2017 several members of TIEC and TAM were on the list of the 100 largest electricity producers in the United States, including ExxonMobil, Oxy, and Dow Chemicals.[36]

In deregulated electricity markets, generators compete directly with one another. Given how Texas's electricity system operates, generators make larger profits when there is supply scarcity that leads to high prices for "peaker plants"—facilities that operate in peak hours and can cycle up and down quickly. These kind of plants are typically natural gas generators (Dinca et al. 2007). Generators' profits further increase when natural gas prices are low but electricity market prices are high, as has happened since the shale gas boom.

The conflict between natural gas and solar generators arises because solar technologies shave the number of peak hours in a year. This competition is seen clearly in market-based electricity systems with high solar penetration (Hirth 2016). Similarly, the federal PTC allows wind energy to bid negative prices, which suppresses the market price. Consequently, natural gas generators in deregulated markets lose revenues when solar or wind generation increases, putting their interests directly at odds with increased renewable energy. Or, in the words of another advocate who struggled to understand the lengths that opponents had gone to block renewables,

> These companies [that were members of the TIEC and the TAM] saw this as a substantial cost that they did not wish to bear. . . . And the realization I think finally began to dawn on the natural gas guys that wind was starting to cut into their profits and solar was certainly going to cut into their profits. Because under a deregulated electricity system, the most valuable hours are peak. They began to think to themselves: 'We make almost all our money, in a deregulated market, on the 200 hours when it's hotter than hell. And if solar gets deployed successfully, that's when it's going to make the most energy and it's going to take our profits away.'"[37]

In other words, these industrial corporations with generating assets had learned from earlier laws implemented elsewhere that renewable energy was not in their interest. It's not surprising that opponents would not have known about this earlier. Renewable energy technologies were very new when Texas adopted its RPS law in 1999. And the relationship between renewable energy technologies, deregulated electricity markets, and federal subsides was unclear.

Even today, this dynamic in market-based electricity systems is generally underappreciated. Take, for instance, how natural gas is often viewed as the complement to renewable energy technologies because it can theoretically adapt flexibly to intermittent sources. While this may be true from a technical perspective, it is not the case politically or economically. As one former Republican staffer put it, "There's always been talk about how natural gas and renewables are friends . . . but natural gas wants to run everything: vehicles and electricity and manufacturing and everything."[38] More broadly, fossil fuel companies no doubt fear a societal movement away from dependence on their product (Leonard 2019). They do not want to support a clean energy transition that could render their business model worthless.

Texas's Failure to Enact a Net Metering Laws and Ongoing Fragmentation Among Advocates

This pattern of failed policy expansion is not limited to Texas's clean energy goals. The state has also failed to expand rooftop solar—so-called distributed generation—through an effective net metering policy.[39] Texas was one of the first states to act on net metering, passing a rule through the PUCT in 1985 (Stoutenborough & Beverlin 2008). However, implementation proved problematic. The PUCT failed to enforce the law requiring generation to be bought at the retail price. As a result, utilities exhibited anticompetitive behavior and actively resisted solar net metering customers. For example, they did not allow small-scale generators to connect to their grid on the grounds that the systems were not properly insured. In 2007, a bill was passed (HB 3693) that made the net energy metering (NEM) situation worse by using language that stipulated that utilities *may* purchase electricity from customers rather than *shall*. More recently, the state has failed to update its net metering policy and provide a clear framework for distributed generation solar.[40] As a result, the state is widely seen as being without a binding net metering policy.

In Texas, politicians often assume that the market will provide an option for customers who want to install solar if it makes sense economically. However, much like the chicken-or-egg problem with transmission capacity, in practice, the system is caught in an unfortunate equilibrium. Customers will not install solar if they cannot be assured that they will be compensated fairly; and therefore, few customers exist to incentivize companies to offer attractive net metering plans. This dynamic may be overcome in the future if electricity retailers see value in locking in customers through longer-term contracts. But it could be overcome more quickly if the PUCT set a clear framework for net metering and the solar carve-out.

Instead, on solar, Texas is free-riding off the efforts of other states. Once solar technologies are cheap enough, large-scale merchant plants will be built and will bid into the competitive electricity market. This dynamic began to unfold in 2014 when a large First Solar plant was announced. However, it is unlikely that significant numbers of these plants will be built in the near future since this first plant used panels that cannot be warrantied and, therefore, have lower values. While a market-based approach is consistent with the political rhetoric in Texas, it remains flawed. If *all* of the US states acted like Texas, there would be little renewable energy built, little innovation through learning and even less action on climate change.

In the case of Texas, policy retrenchment and implementation resistance have created problems for renewable energy advocates, leading to fragmentation and conflict in their political coalition. In 2015, TREIA changed its name from "Association" to "Alliance," signaling lowered resources. Similarly, a new solar association was established in mid-2014, the Texas Solar Power Association, in essence competing with the Solar Alliance and TREIA. Advocates' inability to work together does not bode well for their ability to change laws in the future.

Conclusion

Many believe that Texas is a clean energy leader, given its early success in wind energy. But a closer look at the facts suggests a much more complicated story. Fossil fuel corporations and other heavy industries have spent the past decade blocking progress in the Lone Star State. Working through a dense network, and with extremely strong ties with the key legislator on the energy file, these opponents learned from earlier policies' implementation and successfully blocked the RPS from including a new technology. Consequently, in Texas, we see an initial period of policy expansion, followed by a period of implementation resistance and later of policy retrenchment.

This case also demonstrates how the fog of enactment can be used intentionally as a weapon against groups with less information. On the solar energy provisions, opponents kept their resistance hidden during enactment, creating ambiguity in the draft bill. Consequently, the advocates left that legislative session believing the language had one meaning; the opponents left with a prefabricated argument that it held another. Opponent interest groups wanted advocates to believe they had made progress while they intended to resist the law during implementation.

Texas's opponents are not unique in using this strategy. In Nevada, solar advocates worked to protect net metering after a 2016 court ruling threatened the policy. Advocates felt they had notched a win with a compromise agreement that net metering customers would receive 95% of the retail rate for exported solar energy. The compromise also firmed up rate design rules to ensure that these customers would not be treated as a separate class. But that didn't stop opponents from trying to create ambiguity in the legislation's provisions. Rather than respecting the 95% retail rate provision through monthly calculations, opponents argued that this system should be applied on a unit-by-unit basis. This threatened to decrease returns for net metering customers. After protests and a public campaign challenging the decision, Nevada governor Brian Sandoval signed a bill in 2017 that reinstated net metering at near full retail rates.[41]

In Texas, the change in the interpretation of the bill during implementation had both climate and technological impacts. Texas's renewable energy laws helped spur existing inexpensive technologies—wind energy—but did nothing to incent solar as a newer, more costly technology. In this way, this case also shows that policy feedback can be narrow. We might expect a renewable energy law to broadly catalyze new industries. But, in practice, it only catalyzed the least expensive technology. Unlike the fossil fuel industry, clean energy advocates failed to work across technological boundaries and build a broader coalition with greater power and influence. Consequently, Texas has not capitalized on its significant solar resources nor contributed to innovation in solar photovoltaic technology. In part, this has occurred because, without a stable NEM policy, solar companies are largely absent from the state. Without these players, there are few actors to advocate.

Texas continues to lag behind in solar. Despite having the largest resources, it was only ranked sixth in the nation overall for solar installations in 2018.[42] Municipal utilities, like Austin Energy, and local electric co-ops, which operate outside the deregulated system and do not have RPS requirements, have driven much of the recent growth in solar.[43] They have taken advantage of lower-cost solar and have supported customer adoption of distributed generation in some cases.[44] With hindsight, Texas could have easily met the 2005 goal that was never implemented. It also could have easily surpassed Fraser's failed 2009 bill, which aimed to have 3,000 MW of solar by 2020—in 2019, this target was met. Opponents resisted even these unambitious policies. Had these laws been passed or implemented, Texas would be further along in solar energy today.

Solar has come to Texas late—only after other states, like California, have paid for the costs of innovating the technology.

It is also notable that while Texas's government has supported clean energy, the state's policy ambition has consistently been weak. Advocates pushed for higher targets but lost out to opponents in negotiations. Thus, policy goals were met years ahead of schedule. As a result, the feedback dynamic was weaker than we might expect with a more ambitious policy. This case can help us understand policy feedback when incumbents are politically powerful. Laws may empower new interest groups, but not enough to rival opponents. Under these conditions, opponents may continue to hold greater influence over politicians. As a result, they are more likely to win organized combat by deploying direct tactics like lobbying, contributions, relationships, and ideas. If opponents successfully resist laws during implementation, they can disrupt policy feedback, causing advocates to lose resources. As their coalitions fragments, this can kick off a downward spiral for both advocates and policy.

Retrenchment by a Thousand Cuts

Koch Industries and Allies Drive Polarization on Clean Energy in Kansas

In 2009, Kansas passed its first clean energy law. As a much later actor, the fog of enactment was less central to driving this policy. By this point, the likely consequences of passing a renewable portfolio standard (RPS) policy were clear. Instead, the RPS was enacted at the urging of the wind industry in exchange for a coal plant permit. These wind energy companies existed because of policy feedback in other states. Hence, advocates enabled by policies passed in other states spilled into Kansas to lobby for the law. The policy was well implemented and faced little resistance. The wind energy industry in Kansas grew rapidly.

But uncertainty still played an important role—albeit not for the clean energy policy. Instead, it was the coal plant that unexpectedly faced implementation resistance. Environmental advocates used the courts as an indirect strategy to block the plant's permit. There were also delays from regulators, and in the interim federal policy changed, undermining the coal plant's viability. Here we see how interactions between policies across scales can fuel uncertainty. The way a policy was negotiated can also affect how feedback unfolds. If the policy was traded in a quid pro quo negotiation, it may have had more opposition than was clear at the time of enactment. If parts of the negotiated deal are never implemented, this failure to follow through may engender significant resentment and opposition.

By 2011, a movement to repeal renewable energy laws was underway across the country, led by groups with ties to fossil fuel companies—most prominently the American Legislative Exchange Council (ALEC). This campaign targeted Kansas as a strategic opportunity. If they could flip the policy there, the opponents reasoned, it might create a cascade across the country. Perhaps other states would follow in weakening their laws—or at least fail to increase their

Short Circuiting Policy. Leah Cardamore Stokes, Oxford University Press (2020). © Oxford University Press.
DOI: 10.1093/oso/9780190074265.001.0001

clean energy targets after they were surpassed. If this campaign was successful, it could slow down society's move away from fossil fuels.

In Kansas, networked opponents worked directly to undermine the clean energy law, lobbying politicians in the legislature and executive branch. Although a number of groups participated in targeting politicians, they all had links to one company: Koch Industries. This company is headquartered in Wichita and is extremely influential in the state and across the country. The company and its two executives at the time—Charles G. Koch and David H. Koch—had been active in funding climate denial for more than two decades.[1] In Kansas, Koch Industries used a variety of other groups to mask its lobbying against clean energy, including its affiliated network, Americans for Prosperity (AFP). Through ALEC, AFP and other groups, Koch worked to get anti-clean energy bills onto the legislative agenda in Kansas.

It is also likely that Koch Industries played a role in convincing the governor to appoint a climate-denying, ALEC-affiliated fossil fuel consultant—Representative Dennis Hedke—to a vacant seat in the House.[2] This appointee quickly became well positioned in the legislature as the head of the relevant energy committee. Opponents must have had the ear of important politicians and party members to secure this central position for an ally.[3] The assignment gave Koch Industries a direct line into policymaking. Why might they have had such influence to appoint an ally to the chamber and, later, a key committee? Koch Industries was a major funder of Republicans in Kansas. It channeled its contributions both directly and indirectly, through the Republican Party and the Chamber of Commerce. At the time, Koch was likely *the most critical* source of campaign funding in governor and statehouse races. As research has shown, interest groups often focus their campaign spending on influencing committee assignments, since well placed allies can facilitate policymaking (Fouirnaies & Hall 2018).

Still, clean energy advocates mounted a significant defense. By 2012, wind companies had grown through policy feedback—both inside and outside the state. Working through their own network, the Wind Coalition, advocates succeeded in holding off retrenchment for several years. Both sides expanded the scope of conflict, bringing the public into the debate. Working in coordination with grassroots NGOs, the wind energy's industry association launched a broad campaign to defend Kansas's policy. This effort included public mobilization, public opinion, and research. Opponents launched a countercampaign, creating fake grassroots ads and reports that estimated higher policy costs. Both sides used ideas—highlighting costs and benefits, respectively—to try to persuade politicians to support their view. Initially, the advocates had the upper hand. Over the first 3 years, the advocates were able to maintain bipartisan support for Kansas's clean energy law.

But the opponents did not stop trying to drive polarization. They leaned on Republican legislators and the governor. They returned annually with new strategies to expand the scope of conflict and weaken the policy. Through their networks, they made the issue a high priority for campaign funding. Koch threatened to withdraw campaign contributions and fielded well-resourced primary opponents against Republicans who resisted their agenda. In the 2014 elections, these threats came to fruition, with many renewable energy supporters facing tough races. While the advocates supported some Republicans through a wind energy political action committee (PAC), their funds could not compete with lost money from the party. By the end of 2014, the opponents had made inroads with the governor, who appointed a vocal anti-renewables legislator with ties to Koch Industries to the state public utility commission (PUC). Eventually, the opponents' efforts succeeded and polarization grew. Fewer and fewer Republicans were voting to keep the clean energy law intact. The advocates were losing a war whose fronts were expanding every year.

By 2015, the opponents had managed to get *taxing* renewable energy on the agenda. This forced advocates into the unexpected position of shifting their strategy from pushing for policy *expansion* to managing a policy *repeal*. They now judged that the RPS policy was more of a liability than an asset. The wind industry surrendered, negotiating a bargain in 2015 that avoided new taxes on wind but also repealed the RPS law and eliminated favorable tax exemptions. The clean energy industry had grown to the point that it had enough political influence to get a seat at the table—but not enough influence to set the terms for the discussion. Thus, while policy feedback was happening, it was still nascent. The advocates eventually lost the war against a much more established opponent.

Policy Feedback Spillovers Enable Kansan Clean Energy Policy

Dorothy immortalized Kansas's windiness. Given the state's abundant resources, it was an early leader in wind technology, if not clean energy policy. Beginning in 2001, large-scale modern wind farms were completed in the state, before Kansas had any comprehensive clean energy policy.[4] Slowly, the industry began to develop, and new advocates emerged. Despite the growing wind industry, there was a general sense that Kansas would not pass a clean energy goal, given the state's conservative bent.

Still, the state government started to focus more on this budding industry. In 2005, Democratic governor Kathleen Sebelius directed the state PUC—the

Kansas Corporation Commission (KCC)—to look at the "full range" of renewable energy's benefits and consider additional investments in this area. She envisioned a voluntary challenge of 1,000 MW of wind by 2015. Given that the KCC has three governor-appointed commissioners, it listened to the governor's direction. The KCC began working on a report on the benefits and costs of wind in Kansas.

While waiting for the final report from the regulator, Governor Sebelius continued to push for a voluntary clean energy goal. She found some support for her policy idea in an unlikely place—some electric utilities were open to increasing renewable energy in the state.[5] By this point, wind energy had started to become competitive in Kansas, given the high quality resources that existed. As long as the utilities were able to build new infrastructure and receive rate increases to cover their costs through the PUC, wind energy would make sense for their bottom line. Given the governor's support for renewables, utilities believed the regulator would approve rate increases resulting from new projects.

In 2007, the governor negotiated a voluntary utility target of 10% renewable energy by 2010 and 20% by 2020. Given the structure of the electricity sector in Kansas, she only had to negotiate with two major private utilities: Westar Energy, which supplies almost 50% of the state's power, and Kansas City Power & Light (KCP&L), which supplies nearly the other half. In response to this policy direction, Westar built three large wind farms.[6] The legislature attempted to follow the governor's lead. That same year there were bills to create a legal RPS policy in Kansas; but these bills died in committee.[7] Overall, while the wind industry was gaining momentum, the state struggled to create policies that would support it.

Surprisingly, early opposition to wind energy in Kansas came from within the environmental community.[8] In 2007, a bill was proposed (HB 2492) that would halt some wind developments. Two conservation groups, the Kansas Audubon Society and the Nature Conservancy, opposed a wind project called Smoky Hills in central Kansas. These groups were concerned about development in areas where the greater prairie chicken, a vulnerable species, is found. Governor Sebelius had opposed wind farm development there, calling for a voluntary ban on a large part of the relevant area in 2004.[9] But this bill would change the process surrounding wind farm siting altogether. It would allow for greater public hearings and create a new petition mechanism that could stall developments. In short, it would likely enable local "not in my backyard" (NIMBY) resistance to wind energy. The Kansas Sierra Club chapter, the Kansas Farm Bureau, and several county rancher associations opposed these measures. With the environmental groups divided and the wind industry opposed, the bill ultimately died in committee.

In early 2008, Governor Sebelius became more ambitious, calling on the legislature to pass a binding RPS policy. It was a fortuitous time for the state to ramp up its policy. The KCC's report had finally come out, and it concluded that Kansas was an excellent place for wind development.[10] At the time, Siemens—a large industrial company with significant wind energy business—was considering creating a major manufacturing center for wind turbines in Hutchison, Kansas. The governor was aware of this and likely thought that creating policy certainty through a mandatory clean energy goal would improve the state's chances of receiving the jobs and investment.[11]

When framing the RPS policy for the legislature, Governor Sebelius specified the same targets as the voluntary agreement she had already negotiated with the utilities: 10% by 2010, 20% by 2020. Even though this first target was only 2 years away, the state had made enough progress that 10% was reachable. But the utilities saw a large difference between a voluntary agreement and a mandatory policy. They resisted codifying the idea in law. KCP&L stated that a mandatory target was unnecessary. Westar was comparably less opposed, given that it had acted early to start building wind energy, but it still resisted.[12] With the utilities in opposition, no RPS bill passed in the 2008 session.

Instead, progress on clean energy policy came from an unlikely place: a utility reliant on coal power. At the time Sunflower Electric Power—the third largest utility in the state, serving around one-tenth of Kansas's electricity—was working to move a bill through the legislature to expand its Holcomb coal plant. This rural electric cooperative had been trying to expand its coal power capacity since 2001, proposing first a new plant and later an expansion at its existing plant. In 2007, the utility had attempted to get an air quality permit from the Kansas Department of Health and Environment but was denied. Consequently, new legislation was necessary to move the project forward. Overall, there was broad support for the coal plant among legislators. In 2008, three versions of a bill that would grant Holcomb the necessary permits passed the legislature, some with "green" add-ons like tree planting.[13] However, the governor vetoed all three bills. And there were not enough votes in the legislature to override her veto. In April 2009, Governor Sebelius left to become the US Secretary of Health and Human Services, leaving no resolution to the Holcomb permit or her plan for a mandatory clean energy target.

When Democratic governor Mark Parkinson took office on April 28, 2009, he made passing an RPS policy a first priority. He knew that Siemens was still interested in locating wind energy manufacturing in the state. To seal the deal, he had to show the company that the state was serious about supporting renewables. According to one interview subject privy to the negotiations, "it would have been next to impossible [for Siemens] to locate in a state without an RPS because so much of their business was predicated on selling wind turbines to states trying to fulfill their RPS. [Siemens was] having extensive conversations with both governors [Sebelius and Parkinson]."[14]

Governor Parkinson decided to use Sunflower's interest in expanding the Holcomb coal plant as leverage, negotiating a package with its chief executive officer and president, Earl Watkins.[15] The two parties came to a settlement agreement in the first week of his governorship, on May 4, 2009. In exchange for the governor not vetoing the air quality permit, the utility would have to enact a mandatory RPS and a net metering policy.[16] The proposed RPS had the same targets as Governor Sebelius's voluntary agreement, albeit with a new interim target of 15% by 2016. Behind the scenes, the governor was also meeting with Siemens. This became clear when, the day after the binding RPS agreement with Sunflower was announced, Siemens announced its intention to build a wind turbine manufacturing plant in Kansas.[17] Since the governor was negotiating with all the parties simultaneously, these announcements were clearly linked. Here we see how policy feedback can spillover, across borders. Advocates enabled through policies in other states had worked to expand a policy in a later acting state.

Once this deal was negotiated with Sunflower, the governor's office reached out to the other utilities to see if they would also agree to a binding RPS. With one utility on board, it would be more "fair" if all the utilities had the same requirements.[18] To persuade the two major private utilities to sign on, his plan included a very low-cost cap of 1%. The governor's office likely had a specific interpretation of what that provision would look like: if a utility could demonstrate its rates increased by more than 1% as a result of the clean energy requirements, it would be exempt from complying further. The first target would also be easy—by 2009 the utilities were already on track to reach the first 10% target in 2010.[19] Given their significant progress on wind energy, the utilities agreed to the package and continued to provide input during the bill drafting.

The idea quickly moved from a deal with the governor's office to a bill (HB 2369). The legislature was keen to finally approve the coal plant and advanced the bill briskly. The bill also established net metering up to 1% of utilities' peak demand. That said, when the deal was translated into legislation, some changes were made that weakened its stringency. Compared to an executive branch negotiation, the legislative process is more visible and includes more parties. In this case, a broader set of opponents was now participating in conflict over the proposal. In the legislature, the utilities likely pushed to make the definition of what counted as "renewable" more generous. The Senate committee broadened the renewables definition to include existing hydropower, new small-scale hydropower, landfill gas, and crop residue biomass. This would increase utilities' ease in meeting the goals. This bill also included an "in-state sweetener"[20]— every 1 MW installed in Kansas would count for 1.1 MW in compliance with the policy. Along with the cost cap, these provisions weakened the policy's potential impact. But it also got the utilities to sign on the dotted line. And the in-state requirements might grow the local advocates necessary to ensure that the policy could be expanded in the future.

Despite the fact that the proposed legislation weakened the Governor's plan, many advocates supported the bill. As a result of earlier policies in other states, as well as the state's excellent in-state resources, a wind energy lobby already existed in Kansas. Earlier RPS policies in states like Texas had grown the wind industry in the United States, allowing policy feedback to spillover to other states. These interest groups had organized in a network, called the Wind Coalition, which represented wind companies across seven southern and Midwest states. Given their experience with existing clean energy targets, these networked interest groups knew that an RPS in Kansas would greatly benefit wind. The Kansas Rural Center also gave its support, understanding the economic benefits for rural areas. However, environmental groups, including the Sierra Club, did not support the deal—they vehemently opposed the coal plant expansion. And the Citizens' Utility Ratepayer Board—the public ratepayer advocate—opposed the policy, arguing it could increase ratepayer costs.

On May 22, 2009, with broad support from the utilities and the wind energy industry, the clean energy policy passed the Senate 37–2 and the House 103–18. In fact, more Republicans than Democrats supported the bill: in the House, 99% of the Republicans voted in favor compared to only 64% of Democrats. Implementing the law at the KCC was simple and straightforward. Unlike other states' RPS policies, many of the details the opponents wanted were worked out in advance in the legislature. The policy seemed poised for success. In 2011, a bill made one small change to the policy (SB 224), but it only strengthened the law by requiring utilities to report progress toward meeting the targets more regularly. Overall, the utilities were on board with wind energy and were ahead of their targets, having installed almost 3,000 MW in the state by 2012.

Advocates Use the Courts, Regulators, and Federal Policy to Delay the Coal Plant's Implementation

The RPS policy was implemented well, with little resistance from opponents. But, the same could not be said for the coal plant expansion. The necessary state-level permit was not issued for more than 18 months, in part because one bureaucrat who personally opposed the projet decided to delay issuing it. Once the developer had the permit in hand, advocates attacked the policy using the courts. In December 2010, the Sierra Club and Earthjustice mounted a legal challenge against the coal plant expansion. They argued that the Clean Air Act required the state government to consider greenhouse gas emissions in the permitting process. Furthermore, they suggested that Kansas had rushed permitting, without considering other air pollutants like mercury and particulate matter.[21] Since the federal rules had not been in place when the coal plant was negotiated a year and a half earlier, it is understandable that the Kansan statehouse didn't anticipate the problem. This is a more subtle version of the fog of enactment: overlapping jurisdictions can change rules over time, which can impede implementation. In this case, both the utilities and politicians had a poor understanding of the broader economic and environmental context for coal power.

The Holcomb project remained tied up in a legal battle that would make its way to the Kansas Supreme Court. Although the court eventually ruled in favor of the coal plant's expansion, by 2017 the project was doomed. The economics of renewables had improved to such an extent that the investment no longer seemed viable. In hindsight, this outcome does not seem surprising. Since 2008, new coal plants have almost never been permitted due to stricter federal air quality regulations, public protests, and lawsuits from environmental groups.[22] But in 2009, the utility and many Kansas politicians thought coal still had a long future ahead. They believed that the project would eventually be built. Holcomb's failure during implementation angered some politicians. They now believed they had made an unfair agreement: trading the RPS and a net metering policy for a coal plant expansion that failed to materialize.[23] This resentment would prove important when opponents began to attack Kansas's clean energy laws.

Meanwhile, after Governor Parkinson's term expired in January 2011, Republican governor-elect Sam Brownback assumed office. Despite this partisan shift in the executive branch, there was reason to believe that Kansas would continue to support clean energy. As a senator in Congress, Brownback had backed renewables: supporting a 10% national RPS policy in 2005 and even co-sponsoring a 25% by 2025 renewable energy goal in 2007.[24] In his first State of the State address, he enthusiastically supported renewables:

> We will expand and start new wind energy projects in the state. If we do this right, we will see the development of a renewable energy corridor between Wichita and Salina that will provide jobs for rural Kansas and clean energy for the world. I want Kansas to be known not only as the Wheat state—but as the Renewable State.[25]

Later in 2011 Governor Brownback wrote a letter to Congress, along with 22 other governors, calling for an extension to the federal production tax credit (PTC)—a letter that, for example, Ohio governor John Kasich did not sign.[26] Brownback's support continued until at least 2013, when he had his own Jimmy Carter moment, installing solar panels on his Topeka home. With this strong record, there was reason to believe that he would continue to support renewable energy in Kansas, leading to further policy expansion.

But Governor Brownback also made other decisions that put renewable energy development at risk. In his first year in office, he more than doubled the area in the Flint Hills protected from wind farm development, raising it to almost 11,000 square miles. That said, Brownback was not driving this policy but merely formalizing a voluntary agreement between the wind industry and local landowners. In fact, Brownback stated when the plan was finalized that he did not wish to convey any negativity toward wind developments. The area already included two wind farms, which could continue being built and operated but could not expand.[27] Thus, it was far from a radical departure from the status quo.

Clean energy opponents, however, were not pleased with the status quo. They began to resist the Kansas RPS policy, using rising electricity rates to advance a narrative that clean energy was costly. The state's electricity rates had increased from the mid-2000s onward. Between 2005 and 2015, the commercial price jumped from 5.95 cents per kilowatt hour (¢/kWh) to 9.67 ¢/kWh, an increase of 60%.[28] Opponents used this upward trajectory in electricity prices to their advantage. In 2012, two conservative think tanks—the Kansas Policy Institute and the Beacon Hill Institute—jointly released a report on the RPS's economic impacts.[29] Among other claims, they argued that electricity rates would rise 45% by 2020 as a result of the RPS law. They concluded by calling for its repeal. The arguments in these reports found a receptive audience with conservative politicians in the state.

It did not matter that renewables were playing little role in electricity rates' rise. In truth, price increases occurred more quickly in Kansas than other places because the state used very little natural gas. Consequently, they did not benefit as much as other states where newly abundant shale gas resources reduced electricity's cost.[30] Nor was it acknowledged that there was already a stringent cost cap in place for the clean energy law, limiting its ability to increase electricity prices. Opponent interest groups constructed a version of the facts, irrespective of whether their argument was based in reality. After these reports, the legislature passed a bill in 2012 (HB 2526), requiring the KCC to issue reports on the RPS policy's rate impacts. Renewable energy opponents likely thought this law would reveal how costly the clean energy target was, eroding politicians' support and fueling retrenchment. They were trying to undermine the policy, to roll it back.

Opponents and Advocates Use Direct Strategies, Working With Legislators on Clean Energy Policy

By 2013, opponents began trying to retrench Kansas's clean energy laws. The first bills were introduced in parallel to the House and the Senate (HB 2241 and SB 82). In February, the chair of the House Standing Committee on Energy and Environment, Republican representative Dennis Hedke, began leading one repeal bill. Representative Hedke was a geoscientist, running an oil and gas consulting company, and a climate change denier.[31] He had published a book in 2011, *The Audacity of Freedom*, which directly criticized Kansas's RPS policy, drawing on Heritage Foundation studies to make his claims (Hedke, 2011, 81).[32] He was not elected to office, but appointed. Just after his book came out, the governor appointed him to an open seat for the district just east of Wichita, where Koch Industries is headquartered. Hedke was also a member of the ALEC. Although we cannot be certain, it would be reasonable to assume that the Kochs played a role in this appointment. Underscoring their close relationship, Koch Industries met with Hedke about the bill behind closed doors.[33]

Two years after taking his seat, before ever facing the public in an election, Hedke became chair of the energy committee—an excellent placement if fossil fuel companies hoped to influence energy policy. In this role, he introduced the bill which would weaken the RPS by pushing the 15% target further out in time and dropping the final 20% goal altogether. This was an interest group-driven attempt to directly retrench the law. Opponents now had a politician who would push their agenda on the inside.

Unsurprisingly, committee hearings on Hedke's bill centered on climate change. By this time, fossil fuel companies had been lobbying and running public campaigns to deny the climate science for many decades (Oreskes & Conway 2010). These denial campaigns were successful at changing both elites' and the public's perceptions. By 2010, public opinion on climate change had become polarized along partisan lines across the country (Mildenberger & Leiserowitz 2017). The same thing was happening at the elite level, with fewer right-wing politicians supporting climate action. Fossil fuel companies, in concert with conservative activists, had succeeded in driving a wedge between the Republican Party and facts by attacking climate science (Brulle 2018; Farrell 2015; Layzer 2012; Oreskes & Conway 2010).

In a pattern we will see again in Ohio (Chapter 8), many important opponents working to undermine Kansas's clean energy laws came from outside the state, brought into the conflict through right-wing interest group networks. Key opponents included the Kansas Policy Institute, the Beacon Hill Institute, AFP, the Heartland Institute, ALEC, and Americans for Tax Reform. These conservative interest groups maintained strong ties with Republicans politicians in Kansas. For example, the Speaker of the Kansas House, Ray Merrick, and the president of the Kansas Senate, Susan Wagle, served on ALEC's board at the time. Grover Norquist, president of Americans for Tax Reform and a prominent conservative, lobbied the Kansas legislature to weaken the clean energy target. Many of these groups were allied with Koch Industries and other fossil fuel companies. Behind the scenes, a Koch Industries–affiliated lobbyist met with Representative Hedke. With a fossil fuel champion on the inside, Koch Industries did not need to publicly testify on the bill. They could keep quiet and still be heard loud and clear by the legislators who mattered.[34]

But by 2013, there were also many clean energy advocates who wanted to keep the RPS policy in place. Through policy feedback, the clean energy industry had grown in Kansas, and it now planned to defend the policy that created the foundation for its own growth. Like their opponents, some of these advocates were networked across state lines, for example through the Wind Coalition. This group gave testimony against Hedke's bill. In addition, several wind energy companies—Vestas, BP Wind Energy, Iberdrola, and NextEra—all gave oral or written testimony opposing the bill. The presence of these large wind companies was a direct result of RPS policies in Kansas and other states, which had spurred dramatic growth in the industry. And their views carried weight in the Capitol: the job creation from wind energy in rural, conservative districts in Kansas could not be discounted.[35]

The clean energy industry was not the only group of advocates ready to defend the existing law. A broader grassroots coalition emerged called Kansans for Clean Energy. This campaign linked several organizations including the Climate + Energy Project, the Kansas Farmers Union, the Kansas Rural Center, the Kansas Sierra Club, and Kansas Interfaith Power & Light. Like the renewable energy companies, these groups attended committee hearings and gave testimony in support of the RPS policy.

Notably, the Kansas utilities did not support a repeal, having already met the standards ahead of schedule. Instead, they stayed neutral and did not give testimony.[36] The fact that Kansan utilities saw an ability to profit off of building new wind capacity greatly reduced the opponents' rhetorical points. Even some of the typically conservative local chambers supported the RPS policy, such as the Hays Area Chamber of Commerce in western Kansas. Together, the Kansas-based industry and grassroots organizations formed a formidable coalition against repealing the RPS policy. Policy feedback was starting to take hold.

Advocates also began using campaign contributions as a tool to increase their influence. The RPS policy had enabled the wind industry to grow to the extent that they could now afford to financially back politicians who shared their views. The case of Republican representative Russ Jennings shows this fact clearly. Jennings was from Lakin in western Kansas and was a member of the Energy and Environment Committee. He was newly elected in 2013, having served in various government roles over the previous few decades. He emerged as the greatest Republican champion in the House working against the RPS repeal. Unlike some of his colleagues, he did not receive money from the Koch-linked Kansas Chamber of Commerce, which strongly supported the rollback. Instead, a wind company—NextEra—was Jennings's largest donor. The Wind Coalition's PAC, the Kansas New Energy Economy, and the American Wind Energy Association likewise contributed to his campaign.[37] He also received smaller donations from two utilities: Sunflower and Westar. Through policy feedback, the growing clean energy industry was able to support politicians, allowing them to challenge their fossil fuel opponents who had long spent significant amounts on politics.

Using campaign contributions to increase their influence with specific politicians helped the advocates in the battle over the bill.[38] In 2013, Representative Jennings worked alongside his colleagues from western Kansas to communicate the benefits of wind energy for their local communities. Like Hedke, Jennings sat on the relevant House committee. He used this position to help delay and undermine the bill. After the bill made its way to the floor, it was referred back to committee, where he was able to leverage his influence to kill it. The second time the bill was to be voted out of the committee, another Republican, Representative Scott Schwab, switched his vote. Consequently, HB 2241 died in committee in 2013.[39]

Although the repeal attempt in the House failed, the advocates were not yet home free. That same year, the Senate Standing Committee on Utilities sponsored another bill that aimed to repeal the clean energy target (SB 82). The chair and vice chair of this committee were Republican senators Pat Apple and Forrest Knox, respectively. Senator Apple, who began serving in 2005, was from a district south of Kansas City, near the KCP&L Lacygne coal plant. Over the years, Senator Apple received significant campaign donations from utilities and fossil fuel companies, including KCP&L, Sunflower, Koch Industries, and ExxonMobil, as well as from the Kansas Chamber of Commerce.[40] Senator Forrest Knox was from the same area as Dennis Hedke, east of Wichita, near Koch Industries' headquarters. He was a newly elected senator in 2013, having served in the Kansas House of Representatives from 2005 to 2012. Similarly, his top sector for campaign contributions was energy, with donors including Koch Industries, Westar, Sunflower, and KCP&L, as well as the Kansas Chamber of Commerce. Both politicians had spoken out against renewable energy "mandates."[41]

Like the failed House bill, the Senate proposal sought to undermine the policy feedback the clean energy law was creating. It aimed to delay progress: the 15% target would be pushed back from 2016 to 2018, and the 20% target would shift from 2020 to 2024. Their aim was to slow down growth in clean energy companies and thereby undermine the advocates. Cutting off resources to the advocates would make it easier for the opponents to further retrench the law in the future. The bill also aimed to enable implementation resistance, with a provision that allowed the PUC to waive compliance if the utility showed "good cause ... [which] includes, but is not limited to, availability of firm transmission service or excessive costs to retail electric customers."[42] This kind of vague language would provide significant latitude to weaken the policy during implementation.

The bill had the same supporters and opponents as the House bill, and it was voted out of committee. But it failed to pass the Senate floor, with a vote of 17 to 23 at the end of February 2013. Interestingly, while all 17 of the bill's supporters were Republicans, nearly as many Republicans—15—opposed the bill. This suggested that policy feedback was working. Republican districts were seeing the benefits of wind energy for economic development. By 2014, one advocate, Kansans for Wind Energy, estimated that the industry had invested $8 billion in capital and generated 13,000 jobs in the state.[43] The advocates had succeeded in fending off the attacks.

Advocates and Opponents Bring the Parties and the Public Into the Conflict

After the repeal bills both failed in 2013, advocates and opponents remained in a standoff. In the lead-up to the next Kansas legislative session, the interest groups changed some of their tactics. Both sides decided to expand the scope of conflict, drawing the parties and the public into the debate.[44] The opponents started by working through the parties. They aimed to polarize the issue by defining the existing policy as against Republican principles and by threatening to pull support from politicians who were off side. Meanwhile, the advocates brought in the public, through a grassroots campaign.

First the opponents tried to influence Governor Brownback's thinking on the issue. There is evidence they were successful—anti-renewable energy statements began to crop up in the governor's speeches. In early 2014, at an informal press conference, Governor Brownback said he supported phasing out the RPS over 4 years, a stark change from his earlier comments. But that evening, his office claimed this was an error. They argued that the governor meant to say he favored phasing out the *federal* PTC, a policy he had championed just 3 years earlier and when he was a member of Congress. It did not make sense for the governor to change his position—this policy gave the Kansas economy significant federal tax credits. Even the Kansas Chamber of Commerce was surprised at the governor's remarks on the PTC.[45]

If we take the governor's initial statement on the RPS at face value, we could note that this shift in position brought him in line with Koch Industries and the Kansas Chamber of Commerce, which were gearing up to aggressively challenge the RPS. Notably, the governor would later appoint Pat Apple to the state's PUC—an RPS opponent who had received significant backing from the Chamber of Commerce and Koch Industries. Taken together, these facts suggest a web of important relationships between the governor, the Koch brothers, and the Kansas Chamber of Commerce. Still, by 2014, Governor Brownback had received *more* money from wind company NextEra than from the chamber, likely accounting for his quick about-face on the RPS. He was being cross-pressured on this issue.

Opponents also used ideas in their campaign to try to drive polarization on clean energy, framing renewable energy "mandates" as overly costly. In 2014, the state PUC issued a report—required by the 2012 law—that estimated that the cost of utilities complying with the RPS was less than 2.2% of electricity rates.[46] By this time, renewables accounted for 15% of the supply, and utilities were actually beating their required RPS targets. With these facts it was difficult for the opponents to frame the policy as costly—but they nevertheless continued to try.

An out-of-state group, networked with opponents in Kansas, intervened in the debate over the likely cost of the state's clean energy law. The Heartland Institute—a major national player in climate denial, funded by fossil fuel companies—produced its own cost estimates in an article from climate skeptic James M. Taylor. This article attributed the larger rise in Kansas's electricity prices since 2009, compared to the national trend, to the state's RPS, stating: "The rise in the state's electricity prices closely tracks and is directly attributable to the increasing generation of costly renewable power."[47] Here, we see opponents using ideas to try to drive polarization—no matter that they had to deny facts along the way. Even the utilities knew this fossil fuel–funded report was poorly done. As one utility executive put it, "The RPS rate impact has been minimal. The KCC cost estimates are within the range that we think they are. There have been other reports that have made bolder claims as far as how costly it is. I don't see that they're really valid."[48] The point was not truth: opponents were just interested in making Republicans believe that renewable energy was expensive and that PUC's cost estimates could not be trusted.

It is unclear why the Heartland Institute, an out-of-state group, decided to intervene in the Kansas case. Notably, the organization had strong ties to the Koch brothers. Around that time, Charles Koch had begun funding Heartland again after a hiatus, and the organization started working on climate disinformation campaigns targeted at the K–12 level.[49] The Heritage Foundation has also received millions of dollars from the Koch-affiliated Claude R. Lambe Charitable Foundation.[50]

Just as the opponents were mobilizing ahead of the 2014 session, advocates also used the legislative break to develop new strategies to counter the effort to rollback the clean energy law. Both public mobilization and public opinion were key tools advocates drew on to resist retrenchment. Two organizations co-led the campaign: the Climate + Energy Project (an NGO) and the Wind Coalition (an industry association). As we saw in the first Texas case, these organizations divided responsibilities. The NGO took the lead on organizing the public through a grassroots campaign, while the association led on fundraising, lobbying, public opinion polls, and testimony.[51]

The Climate + Energy Project aimed to mobilize the public through a "Wind Works for Kansas" campaign launched at the state fair in September 2013. It created a postcard petition and collected over 2,000 pieces of mail to deliver to statehouse representatives. Through its campaign website, citizens could also record personalized voicemails for their legislators. Overall, nearly 1,000 voice messages were sent to legislators in support of the RPS policy, in addition to 1,200 emails.[52] Given Kansas is a small state with only a semi-professionalized legislature, this represented a significant public response. The campaign also actively recruited people to write letters to the editor supporting the RPS policy. Through these strategies, the Climate + Energy Project built an effective grassroots campaign, similar to the Public Citizen campaigns described in chapter 4.

Getting the public involved in Kansan policymaking was a challenging undertaking for the advocates. The Kansas legislature is notorious for its secrecy and lack of public involvement in the legislative process. For example, in 2017, committees introduced 94% of the bills that passed, leaving policies without identifiable sponsors.[53] This made it difficult to target specific legislators with public campaigns. Kansas is also one of the few states that allow "gut and go" legislating, whereby a bill passed in one chamber can be replaced with something completely unrelated.[54] These institutional rules make it harder for the public to organize against controversial bills. Hence, the fact that the clean energy advocates were organizing rural Republicans to contact their legislators represented an important grassroots mobilization.

While the NGO took the lead on increasing public participation, the Wind Coalition funded a public opinion poll.[55] The January 2014 poll found that 75% of Kansans supported the RPS policy and only 16% opposed it.[56] Support was very high among Republicans, at 73%.[57] In sharp contrast with opponents' repeal agenda, majorities of the public also supported *increasing* the RPS. Almost 40% of respondents indicated they would be *more* likely to vote for a politician who supported a new clean energy goal.[58] In news reports, the independent firm that conducted the poll was usually cited, rather than the poll's funder, the Wind Coalition. This lent the poll an air of objectivity. Of course, the advocates were not the only group savvy enough to try to shape and strategically communicate public opinion. Around the same time, the Kansas Chamber of Commerce conducted its own poll, finding rising energy costs were a significant concern for Kansan business owners. In this way, both advocates and opponents were attempting to construct public opinion to shape politicians' views ahead of another conflict in the legislature.

When the 2014 legislative session began, the opponents worked through the parties and their interest group networks to drive polarization and ensure that they had the votes for repeal. Unlike earlier retrenchment efforts, which would only delay the policy, the most prominent bill that year proposed repealing the RPS policy outright (HB 2014).[59] Three closely linked organizations—ALEC, the Kansas Chamber of Commerce, and Koch Industries—applied pressure to move this bill. That year the Republican leadership in both the Senate and House was affiliated with ALEC, as we will see was also the case in Ohio when they moved to repeal their RPS.[60] These majority party leaders made retrenching the clean energy law a priority. They pressured members to support the bill, threatening to withdraw campaign support via the Kansas Republican Party if politicians dissented. This was no small threat—the party was many politicians' largest source of funds. The chamber, another big source of campaign funding, similarly threatened members. As one Republican politician stated,

> The leadership was leaning on people. But it wasn't just the leadership in the chambers. The outside influence was the Kansas Chamber of Commerce. They were very engaged and made it very clear that this was an important issue for them. And that more than anything began to move some votes.[61]

This was a big threat. Republicans who bucked the party line would likely lose their three largest sources of campaign funding. They might even find themselves with well-funded primary challengers from the right. Since 2014 was an election year, many members were worried.

Likely, Koch Industries was the underlying driver of this effort to repeal the clean energy law.[62] The key groups pushing the idea all had links to the Koch empire. The Koch brothers were early funders of ALEC, which awarded them the Adam Smith Free Enterprise Award in 1994. Between 1999 and 2014, Koch Industries gave more to the Kansas Republican Party than any other party committee in the country.[63] Koch Industries was also a platinum member of the chamber at the time. Thus, Koch Industries gave campaign funding both directly to candidates and funneled it through the Republican Party and the chamber. Together, these groups represented the main sources of campaign funding for right-wing Kansan politicians. In the 2012 election, the chamber was the second largest contributor, and Koch Industries was the fourth largest.[64] Here we see a clear example of how interest groups can use campaign contributions to drive polarization and affect policy. Funding can be used to pressure legislators to vote in a certain way for fear of retribution through lost funding or well-financed primary challengers.

As the legislative session continued, both sides redoubled their efforts to use the public as a weapon in their combat over the future of Kansan policy. Opponents focused their efforts on building an astroturf campaign. It is likely that the Kansas Chamber of Commerce, AFP, and Koch Industries funded the Kansas Senior Consumer Alliance, a shell organization that aimed to look like it was grassroots. Although this group purported to represent the views and interests of fixed-income seniors, it was not a spontaneous public movement—it never even had a website or a list of members. The group was able to raise money and send out mailers in one week, making it highly unlikely the effort was truly a public outcry.[65] Instead, the group's founder was a family member of the Kansas Chamber of Commerce's chair. The group's lobbyist had previously worked as AFP's state director and as a lobbyist for Koch Industries. When asked, the lawyer who registered the group told a reporter from the *Topeka Capital-Journal* he worked for AFP, not for a senior's group.[66] When these facts came to light, Representative Don Hineman (R) stated, "That's just further evidence of the kind of dark money campaigning that goes on in Kansas politics these days. Well-funded special interest groups try to hide behind sham organizations in order to try to influence the electorate."[67] Without journalists working to uncover these facts, the campaign might have passed for a true grassroots effort rather than an astroturf shell organization.

This AFP- and chamber-linked group worked to lobby and mobilize the public. They ran numerous television and radio ads and sent targeted postcards to elderly people telling them their electricity bills would rise as a result of the clean energy policy. Records suggest that AFP and other opponents spent at least $445,000 on the effort—around seven times as much as advocates spent.[68] Through mailers and other ads, they were trying to sway parts of the public by constructing an inaccurate view of the policy and its consequences. From the opponents' view, this was an indirect strategy to influence legislators and other politicians, aiding their efforts to repeal the law.

But the advocates were also aware that the public could be a valuable ally. They staged a large "Wind Works for Kansas" day in February 2014, bringing almost 200 people to the Capitol. These in-person participants brought along a giant sign filled with messages collected over the past 6 months showing support for wind energy from across the state.[69] Unsurprisingly, this was not just a grassroots uprising—members from the industry also attended the event.[70] Like the opponents, these advocates were trying to shape the public to influence legislators. They also wielded ideas about the policy's likely effects.[71] For example, the Wind Coalition lobbyist focused her messaging on jobs, highlighting that wind energy had created 13,000 jobs in the state.

As these public campaigns continued, the legislature moved the repeal bill forward. The bill passed the Senate 25 to 15. While all the supporters were

Republicans, seven Republican senators still opposed the bill. When the bill made it to the House, however, it proved much more difficult to pass, failing by a vote of 44 to 77. In one of the final floor votes, as many Republicans supported the bill as opposed it: 44 to 44. Feedback was working: there were simply too many Republicans from the western part of the state where wind energy had benefited rural areas. Using public pressure, political contributions, and ideas, advocates once again kept the clean energy policy stable.

Undeterred, the Republican leadership tried again in May to pass a new RPS repeal bill. This attempt also failed to pass the House. But it raised concerns for the wind industry. The margin was narrower: 60 voted to repeal the RPS and only 63 voted to keep it. An election was imminent in the fall for every member of the House. Behind the scenes, the chamber and Koch Industries were likely warning Republicans that supporting the RPS would cost them campaign funds. They might even find themselves with a primary challenger. The chamber had a history of supporting challengers to Republican House members who did not vote for their repeal efforts.[72] Indeed, Representative Scott Schwab argued that he lost the chamber's endorsement in his 2014 election because he questioned Koch Industries' involvement in the renewables fight, detailing confrontations with their lobbyist.[73] While they left the 2014 session with a legislative win, the advocates were losing ground against a full-scale assault from Koch-backed organizations. The wind was no longer in the advocates' sails.

The Thousandth Cut: Opponents' Efforts to Drive Polarization Pay Off and Kansas's Clean Energy Law Is Repealed

After both the House and Senate repeal bills failed in 2014, there were consequences for some of the politicians who voted against these proposals. Opponents used the primary system to try to drive polarization on the issue. During the fall 2014 state election, the Kansas Chamber of Commerce's PAC targeted several Republican members. This included prominent wind energy champions: Representatives Russ Jennings, Kent Thompson, and Tom Sloan. These legislators had spoken in favor of RPS and voted against the repeal bills. They found themselves with chamber-backed primary opponents. The chamber also pulled funds from other politicians running for re-election.

It became clear that Koch Industries was central to this effort when one Republican representative, Scott Schwab, sent a campaign email that was leaked to the press. Schwab had switched his vote the year prior, preventing an anti-RPS bill from leaving a committee. In 2014, he asserted in an email that the Kansas

Chamber of Commerce did not support him in his race because Koch Industries wanted the RPS repealed, and he had stood in the way. Specifically, he wrote,

> After the meeting [in 2013 on HB 2241], Jonathan Small [a lobbyist af-filiated with Koch Industries] asked if I was supportive of the [RPS re-peal] bill. I responded by asking who was pushing it, and he admitted it was Koch Industries. I told him if he wanted me to vote for the bill, then we needed some Kansas businesses to advocate it because right now it looked as an anti-business vote. He told me at the time only Koch wanted the measure. I recommended that Koch testify then. Jon said if they did that, people would not like them. My response was that people don't like them anyway, so just be honest.[74]

But the opponents were not the only interest group using the party system to try to sway policy in their preferred direction. The advocates were trying to re-sist polarization on clean energy. The Wind Coalition helped some threatened Republicans win re-election, including Jennings, Thompson, and Sloan, fielding their New Energy Economy PAC.[75] With this new support—and despite the loss in campaign funding Koch-linked groups—these Republican incumbents were able to defeat their primary challengers and win re-election. However, many Democrats did poorly in the 2014 election, in a statewide shift that was unrelated to this specific policy fight. These election results would alter the polit-ical terrain, making it harder for the clean energy interest groups. The advocates were now fighting an uphill battle. After the 2014 election, it did not seem likely that they would retain enough political influence over the legislature to with-stand another retrenchment attempt.

The opponents' repeated attempts to influence the executive branch were also starting to bear fruit. The 2014 election was a tough one for the governor. He faced a primary challenger and ran in a tight general election race against a Democratic candidate, winning by less than 4%. Some Republicans had even defected, endorsing the Democrat. Clearly, Brownback needed whatever support he could muster. Losing funds from Koch Industries—a longtime supporter—because of his support for renewable energy would not be ideal. Dependent on this funding, the governor began to grow increasingly hostile toward renewable energy in the lead-up to the election.

Koch Industries' growing influence over the executive branch can be seen in the decisions made in 2014 at the state utility regulator. In March 2014, the governor appointed Republican state Senator Pat Apple to the KCC. When he was a senator, Pat Apple's top donors included Koch Industries. In addition, he received significant funding from the Kansas Chamber of Commerce and the Kansas Republican Senatorial Committee—entities that Koch Industries was also a top donor to. Hence, both directly and indirectly, Koch Industries supported Senator Apple.[76] Given that Senator Apple had sponsored the RPS repeal legislation in his role as chair of his Senate committee for the past 2 years, the choice signaled that the governor was updating his stance on clean energy policy. Advocates were losing influence with the executive branch and, through it, the regulator. They could expect greater challenges to clean energy laws during implementation.

In 2015, the opponents tried once again to repeal Kansas's clean energy target through a new bill (HB 2373). This was the fourth consecutive year the issue was on the legislative agenda. By this time, the fossil fuel industry had managed to polarize the issue and influence both chambers' leadership and the governor. They had helped put anti-renewables champions in all the key positions. In 2015, the climate denier Representative Hedke once again led the effort to repeal Kansas's renewable energy policy in his capacity as chair of the House Energy and Environment Committee. In the other chamber, Senator Robert Olson, chair of the Senate Utilities Committee, led another repeal bill (SB 91). When the energy committees in both chambers took this up as a high-priority issue, advocates knew it would be extremely difficult to keep it off the agenda.

By this point, the comparatively less influential advocates were worn down. Even after the last binding clean energy target was met ahead of schedule in 2015, opponents continued to attack the policy. Why would opponents attack a law that no longer had teeth? First, opponents saw a strategic opportunity in Kansas. If they could repeal the policy there, it might start a chain reaction, encouraging other states to act. It could also change the advocates' behavior. Previously, these groups might have tried to *increase* the RPS policy after an initial target was met. But with the law repealed, it would be even harder to expand.

In 2015, another bill proposed to create a 4.33% excise tax on the sale of renewable energy (HB 2401). At the time, the state was facing a severe budget shortfall due to large income tax cuts Brownback had implemented for the wealthy in mid-2012. Many ideas were being debated to increase government revenue, and opponents were more than happy to put renewable energy taxes on the agenda. The proposed tax would represent a significant burden for renewable energy projects. The Wind Coalition estimated it would cost a medium-sized wind project $5.2 million annually.[77] Putting a tax on renewable energy sales would also be a dramatic departure from the status quo. At the time, renewable energy developments benefited from a permanent property tax *exemption* for the operating life of the project.[78] It is likely Koch Industries did not like that renewable energy projects had longer tax exemptions than fossil fuel projects.[79]

The Wind Coalition began to worry that the RPS was more of a liability than an asset for the industry. As a lightning rod for opponents' attacks, it created uncertainty rather than stability. Even more extreme tactics to stop wind energy were now being trialed in other states, like Ohio, with devastating impacts for the industry. As that case shows (Chapter 8), in 2014, Ohio buried a setback rule in a budget bill, bringing their wind industry to a complete standstill. Likely these networked advocates working across state lines understood what was at stake. If the fight continued, it would undermine the entire industry.

As a result, the interest group advocates decided to sit down with their opponents to negotiate a deal to quell the attacks. In a closed-door meeting in early 2015, the Wind Coalition met with an AFP representative and the president of the Kansas Chamber of Commerce, along with Representative Hedke. The fact that the wind industry was able to craft a negotiation table was a testament to the sector's maturity as a result of policy feedback. Their professional lobbyist had cultivated sufficient political influence to be able to set some of the terms. Notably, other groups without these relationships—such as the solar industry and environmentalists—were not included in the talks.[80] These groups had not benefited as much from existing clean energy policy. Consequently they did not have the same level of influence.

At this meeting, the Wind Coalition's goal was to eliminate the RPS as a contentious issue and focus on creating stability for the industry, particularly on taxes. They agreed to eliminate the RPS law and to phase out property tax exemptions for wind energy projects after 10 years. The latter was a major concession—at the time wind projects had permanent tax exemptions for the project's operating life. But the change put wind and fossil fuels on equal ground where taxes were concerned. The wind industry's lobbyist was also able to secure a compromise date of December 31, 2016, for the phase-out of the tax exemptions. This would protect seven wind energy projects already under development. Although the terms would all be losses for the industry, the lobbyist no doubt viewed this as an attempt to stem the bleeding. According to Jeff Clark, executive director of the Wind Coalition, "This isn't bad. This is long-term tax certainty for us. . . . [Though] it's a step back from what we have now."[81] It was an effort to secure policy stability and avoid an even worse outcome.

In 2015, the governor unveiled this compromise bill, which was tabled in the House and passed the chamber 107–11. Many of the former RPS advocates now found themselves in the odd position of supporting the law's repeal. The opponents had managed to expand the scope of conflict and secure influence throughout the government. When this bill was signed, the lobbyist from the Wind Coalition, alongside a lobbyist who had represented both Koch Industries and AFP, and the president of the Kansas Chamber of Commerce were all at the governor's press conference.[82] It was quite a picture, and it was the end of the road for the clean energy law in Kansas.

Conclusion

In another telling of this story, Kansas is not a failure. The state exceeded its clean energy target ahead of schedule. The wind industry grew dramatically, and so did its political influence. Advocates were able to field a PAC, hold back polarization, and withstand policy retrenchment for many years. They successfully expanded the scope of conflict, investing in public opinion polls that showed support for renewables was high in Kansas, communicating these results to legislators and through the media. The NGOs were also well organized, running public campaigns that mobilized the public against anti-renewables legislation. These organizations received part of their funding from the renewables industry. Thus, we see the clear marks of policy feedback.

But such a telling of this story would neglect the ending. The advocates ultimately lost to their opponents. Koch Industries led an effort to polarize clean energy in Kansas. They used ideas, crafting a narrative that renewables were expensive and that "mandates" were bad policy. They ran a fake public campaign. They also threatened, removed funding from, and primaried politicians who opposed their efforts. They made supporting the RPS policy's repeal a litmus test for Republicans, successfully driving polarization on the issue. Using these tactics year after year, the opponents made progress with the Republican leadership in both chambers and the governor, convincing them that supporting renewable energy was bad policy.

Over time, the opponents managed to shift the agenda from weakening the policy to repealing it and putting a tax on renewable energy. In 2015, the advocates were forced to admit defeat and sit down to work out a compromise. While they framed it as a win for the wind industry, it was actually the avoidance of a worse outcome. As Boog Highberger, a Democratic representative in the state house, described it, the deal was similar to the one made when being robbed at gunpoint: "You get your life, and they get your money. . . . It's kind of a compromise, I guess."[83] The opponents had managed to shift the terms of the negotiation to the extent that policy retrenchment seemed to be in the best interests of the clean energy industry.

The consequences of these tax changes and the policy's repeal have been significant. From 2013 to 2015, the wind energy industry grew 17%; from 2015 to 2016 it grew 28%. But after these policy changes were implemented, the industry's growth rate fell precipitously to 2% from 2017 to 2018. At the Siemens factory that opened as a result of the original RPS policy, more than half of the workers had been laid off as of 2017.[84]

As hard as the repeal has proven for the wind industry, it will likely be even harder on less mature technologies, like solar. Despite having high solar potential,

Kansas underperforms—it is near the bottom in the nation in solar generation.[85] In 2014, net metering also came under attack in Kansas from ALEC. A compromise was reached where customers would be credited on a monthly basis rather than a yearly basis. In the 2018 session, bills to restore net metering to its 2009 origins were quickly defeated in committee. With the KCC approving Westar Energy's demand charge at the end of 2018, solar customers in the biggest utility in the state are now receiving less compensation for their energy. The future of solar energy in Kansas does not look bright.

And repealing the state's clean energy law was not just bad for Kansas. When repeal efforts succeed in some states, it can send a message to other states. Ultimately, Kansas was the second to last state to pass its first RPS bill and one of the first to repeal it. Thus, this story also shows the collapse of a policy idea under the weight of concerted, cross-state opposition from incumbent opponents. Clean energy laws are increasingly falling victim to fossil fuel corporations' attacks.

It is true that in 2018 Kansas had the third highest renewable energy penetration in the country. But given the wind resources available in Kansas, we should expect even more development than has occurred. For example, by the end of 2016 Iowa had more than 1.5 times as much installed wind than Kansas, despite Kansas's larger wind resources.[86] The state, like Texas, consistently surpassed its RPS targets, suggesting weak policy ambition from the start. And despite a strong wind industry, Kansas never increased its RPS target, as we would expect from policy feedback. Instead, the opponents were able to retrench the policy after wearing down the advocates over many years.

Ultimately, policy feedback is not a magic bullet. Ensuring policy lock-in requires sufficient time to shift power toward advocates and away from opponents. When policy feedback begins to take hold, it can threaten incumbents. Once threatened, these opponents can work to undermine feedback if they retain greater power and political influence than advocates. While advocates may effectively thwart retrenchment for a time, they can be worn down when opponents have greater resources to invest in driving polarization and attacking the policy over many years.

Regulatory Capture
Thwarts Feedback

Utilities Undermine Arizona's Net Metering Policy and Clean Energy Targets

Opponents that want to undermine policy may try to capture regulators to increase their political influence. Regulatory capture can allow opponents to undermine policies, even after strong policy feedback. In Arizona, we see an example of this in the symbiotic relationship between a private utility, Arizona Public Service (APS) and its elected regulator, the Arizona Corporation Commission (ACC). Over several years, this utility managed to retrench clean energy policy in Arizona using indirect strategies. APS drove partisan polarization and brought the public into the debate through outside spending in their regulator's elections. Out of state clean energy advocates, spurred by feedback elsewhere, tried to resist. Yet they were outspent six to one. In part, utilities had more resources to invest in these policy fights because they are a monopoly with guaranteed profits. This raises a major democratic concern with the institutional structure for Arizona's electricity policy. If a regulator is elected and regulated entities can make campaign contributions in those races—whether directly or indirectly—regulatory capture is likely.

Regulatory capture can also be seen in Arizona's long history of enacting ambitious renewable energy policies but not implementing or expanding them. Beginning in the 1980s, the commission passed five successive clean energy policies. In this period, there was little polarization on renewables and many Republicans championed these policies. However, most of these policies were never implemented. Consequently, solar was slow to develop in Arizona.

Why didn't the regulator implement the state's clean energy laws? Utilities resisted rules that would require them to change their behavior and cut into their profits. Even when the targets were binding, utilities behaved as if they were not.

Short Circuiting Policy. Leah Cardamore Stokes, Oxford University Press (2020). © Oxford University Press.
DOI: 10.1093/oso/9780190074265.001.0001

They knew they had a direct line to the regulator and could resist policy implementation and face little consequences. We can understand this implementation gap as stemming from opponents' long-standing ability to capture their regulator.

When a net metering policy was finally passed in 2008, clean energy began to grow in Arizona. This new law allowed citizens and companies to build solar energy and be paid a decent rate for excess energy that they produced. During the middle of the first decade of the 2000s, Arizona had the largest distributed generation requirements in the country—a boon for solar companies and the public. Initially, the utilities supported this policy. They did not yet see that their customers had pent-up demand to install solar, that solar costs would dramatically decline, or that companies would combine federal and state policy to create a profitable business model. In short, they were caught in the fog of enactment.

It was only when other states saw dramatic growth in solar projects, after solar leasing companies developed, that utilities began to resist net metering. Policies in states like California spurred these companies. Through policy feedback spillovers, solar companies found their way into the Arizona market. In response, the main private utility, APS, began to perceive a bigger threat from the net metering policy. And they were not alone. By 2011, utilities across the country began to perceive that net metering ran contrary to their interest in owning and profiting from the electricity system's assets. In short order, APS and other utilities began attacking Arizona's clean energy laws.

Without changing its official company policy, APS started intervening in elections for its regulator. Across several elections, the utility would spend at least $55 million. Working through primaries, the opponents were able to select politicians who were the most likely to be lenient regulators. This strategy drove polarization in clean energy policy along partisan lines. In 2012, APS successfully worked to unseat two commissioners and increase its influence. Soon thereafter, the utility gained exceptional, and possibly illegal, access to the chair of the commission. While solar energy advocates mounted a resistance, they had far fewer resources likely spending about half as much as the utility over the same time period.[1]

With its influence secured, APS requested large monthly charges on solar energy users in early 2013.[2] If approved, these charges would have wiped out the industry overnight. Solar companies resisted and were somewhat successful in this first battle. Both sides expanded the scope of conflict, waging public relations campaigns with ads and protests. APS, in particular, poured millions of dollars into campaigns that aimed to link solar to Obama and Solyndra. The advocates responded with their own public campaigns. Given the heightened public's awareness, the commission only approved modest charges for net metering customers. Hence, the opponents got some—but not all—of what they wanted. The advocates had held back full retrenchment.

But the opponents did not just target monthly charges—they also successfully cut incentives for solar. After this policy change, many companies no longer had a viable business model. In response, the advocates fractured into numerous associations rather than unifying. Here we can see policy feedback begin to unravel. As opponents successfully rollback laws, revenue losses can shrink advocates. This scarcity can fragment the industry as those left standing fight among themselves for what little resources are left.

In Arizona, some of the advocates drew on their networks, bringing in out-of-state solar companies and associations. Spurred on by policy feedback in other states, primarily California, these advocates had crossed over into Arizona to try to defend the net metering law. Here, we see an example of a policy feedback spillover. But even these groups were not powerful enough to contest the utility opponents, who could rely on regulator-guaranteed profits. These advocates were less organized, with fewer resources to devote to the conflict. The solar companies also had to contest the issue in every relevant utility proceeding at the commission and even at the board of an independent utility. Their resources were spread thin across several venues. While the clean energy advocates attempted to use the power of ideas to counter the utilities' rhetoric by framing it as a right-wing issue of public choice and freedom, they were ultimately unsuccessful. The solar advocates had far less political influence over the commission. In Arizona, clean energy opponents were able to capture their regulator and eliminate key policies supporting the state's clean energy industry.

When a renewed effort was made to increase the state's clean energy targets through a 2018 ballot initiative (Proposition 127), this measure failed by a wide margin, with 31% in favor to 69% opposed. Partially, advocates were outspent: opposition political action committees spent around $40 million, while advocates spent $26 million, around two-thirds as much. In addition, the opponents likely influenced a politician they had funded—Attorney General Mark Brnovich—to change the ballot initiative's language to highlight the program's costs for voters.[3] The language was very similar to the language that APS used in its advertisements against the measure.[4] Hence, the opponents used campaign contributions, relationships and ideas to undermine the clean energy ballot initiative.

As a result of the opponents' longstanding stranglehold over Arizonan clean energy policy, the state has consistently fallen behind on its own targets. Although the state had 39% clean electricity in 2018, most came from nuclear and hydropower—a mere 5% came from wind or solar power, putting it way below average nationally.[5] The state lacks any plan to supply 100% clean electricity by 2050. Instead, the electric utilities continue to propose building more fossil fuel infrastructure through new natural gas plants. In Arizona, the opponents have maintained a tight grip over the political system and have used their influence to hold back progress on clean energy to the detriment of our collective ability to address climate change.

After Continuous Failure to Implement Early Clean Energy Targets, Arizona Enacts an Ambitious Policy

Unlike the other cases in this book, understanding renewable energy policy in Arizona requires a primary focus on the state regulator.[6] This is because Arizona is one of only 13 states that elects its public utility commission (PUC). The ACC was established through the state's constitution in 1912 at the height of the Progressive Era (Leshy 1988). In Article 15, the commissioners were described as elected officials who would oversee "public service corporations."[7] In this way, electricity was framed as a public service, with monopolies requiring strong oversight. Correspondingly, the ACC was centered on popular control of private monopoly utilities through elected commissioners. The fact that the ACC is embedded in the state's constitution and its commissioners are elected makes the commission largely independent, rather than an agent of the governor or the legislature. Some even consider the ACC to be the "fourth branch of [Arizona] government."[8] As a result, the commission has not relied heavily on other branches for policy direction. Unfortunately—and quite contrary to the framers' intentions—Arizona's PUC has developed into an institution suffering from significant regulatory capture from interest groups.

Initially, the commission did little to push the utilities to clean up their energy supply. Instead, Arizona has had a long history of dependence on fossil fuels. In 2018, 61% of the state's electricity was still generated from fossil fuels.[9] Arizona's three large utilities—APS, Salt River Project (SRP), and Tucson Electric Power (TEP)—pushed for this polluting energy supply. Arizona Public Service, the largest private utility in the state, is headquartered in Phoenix. Tucson Electric Power is the second largest private utility in the state and operates in Tucson. Both of these private utilities have built their businesses on the back of coal, their primary fuel source.

Salt River Project is the largest public utility in the state, operating in the half of Phoenix that APS does not control. As one of the biggest public utilities in the United States, SRP serves around one-third of the state's generation. Although this public utility was first established for farming purposes, it evolved into an electricity provider through hydropower dams. In recent years, though, the utility has relied on natural gas as its primary fuel.[10] The commission does not regulate SRP because it was established in 1903, prior to the Arizona Constitution. Consequently, it operates independently, with its own board. The SRP board election process resembles a feudal institution: many current board members descended from the founders, and only landowners can vote, in proportion to the number of acres they own.[11]

Given its abundant sun, Arizonan politicians believed early on that the state could be a leader in solar. In 1975, Democratic Governor Raul Castro created the Solar Energy Commission that financed research and development for the technology. The state also benefited from federal tax credits, which lasted from 1978 until 1985. In the 1980s, Arizona was a pioneer nationally in clean energy policy when it enacted a small proto-renewable portfolio standard (RPS). This policy required that all the utilities obtain a small amount of their power from renewable energy sources.[12] But only TEP met this requirement, by building a landfill gas project. Thus, this state's first RPS policy was not successfully implemented.

In 1994, Arizona made a second attempt at requiring more clean energy through a policy called "Renewable Resource Goals for Affected Utilities." Enacted through the ACC, these were non-binding directives for utilities to procure more renewables. At the time, APS invested in some solar projects, mostly for demonstration purposes. But, again, this policy was ineffective. Without a binding target, utilities made it clear they would not change their investments.

In 1996, the commission tried a third time to increase clean energy in the state. The ACC passed a binding solar-specific portfolio standard as part of electricity restructuring. This was the first time a portfolio standard was successfully linked with restructuring in the United States. Bureaucrats within the PUC played an important role, convincing a Democrat, Commissioner Renz Jennings, to champion the idea.[13] At the time, solar was still a niche technology, and the issue was not yet salient with the utilities or the public. Consequently, bureaucrats had greater autonomy and ability to influence policy (Rabe 2004).

The policy aimed to have solar supply 0.5% of electricity by 1999 and 1% by 2001. While these were small numbers on paper, they were ambitious in practice. Installed solar projects were almost nonexistent at the time. Given the technology's immaturity, the policy costs would also be significant. Commission staff estimated the program would raise the state's generation costs around 4.5% (Berry & Williamson 1997). Unfortunately, implementation once again proved the stumbling block for progress. In 1999, the policy was ended before it was ever implemented when deregulation was frozen due to ongoing conflict between the commission, APS, and TEP over stranded cost settlements.[14] Thus, while some research lists Arizona's RPS enactment as 1996, this is perhaps unwarranted since the policy never led to a single solar project being built.

In 2000, the commission expanded from three to five elected commissioners. Shortly thereafter, Arizona tried a fourth time to enact an RPS in 2001.[15] At the time, the renewable energy leaders on the commission were both Republicans— Chairman Carl J. Kunasek and Commissioner William A. Mundell. In this version of the RPS, eligible technologies were expanded beyond solar to include wind, landfill gas, and biomass. Still, solar was to supply half the target. The policy had annual benchmarks, with a goal of 1% by 2005 and flat lining from 2007 onwards at 1.1%. These were more modest targets than the bureaucrats' earlier proposal. The policy also included "multipliers" for specific project characteristics: early projects, in-state projects, and in-state manufacturing.[16] It also included a distributed generation credit multiplier, another idea from a bureaucrat at the ACC.[17] All of these provisions had the perhaps unintended consequence of weakening the policy's overall ambition. But if the policy were actually implemented, it would have the potential to grow new advocates within the state.

However, the commission struggled to implement even this unambitious policy. The utilities for their part did not respond as if the policy were binding. They clearly did not see the regulator as capable of directing their behavior. Arizona also lacked a broader policy framework to encourage uptake of residential solar, including a net metering policy that applied to all the utilities. This made it difficult for individuals to install solar. At the time, the utilities did not encourage any residential or small-scale projects. Instead, they built a few of their own large, utility-scale solar plants. Consequently, few renewables were built in these early years, and Arizona consistently missed its RPS targets from 2002 to 2007.

By 2004, the commission was aware of the implementation failure and took up the issue again. This time, it spent several years redesigning the policy to increase its effectiveness. In its fifth iteration, Arizona's clean energy target was renamed the "renewable energy standard and tariff" (REST). The commission proposed a more ambitious goal of 15% clean energy by 2025. The policy took almost 2 years to finalize, with the final rules adopted at the end of 2006.[18] At the time, all five commissioners were Republicans, and only one member opposed the plan.[19] This broad support from Republicans shows that polarization had not occurred. With hindsight, it is surprising that the utilities did not try to block the policy more forcefully. This latest iteration included a provision that would ultimately undermine utilities' interests: a distributed generation carve-out, requiring smaller-scale systems that the utility was unlikely to finance or own.

Instead, it was advocates who had a stronger grasp of the policy proposal. The Arizona Solar Energy Industries Association (AriSEIA) championed the idea. This network of interest groups convinced one of the commissioners that a distributed generation requirement would allow the public to participate.[20]

They crafted a narrative that the policy would be more "fair" if the ratepayers could also take part, since they were paying for the program through electricity bills. Through working with the commissioners and using a compelling narrative, advocates were able to get the carve-out passed. The distributed generation target started out small, at 5% of the 2007 REST target. But it grew rapidly to 30% of the target by 2011, making it a sizable portion of the overall clean energy mix in the state. In fact, Arizona had the highest distributed generation target in the country at the time.[21] The advocates may have been looking to the future when they pushed this policy. Allowing the public to benefit from the policy might help advocates lock in the program through policy feedback. Perhaps they knew that citizens who participated in and profited from clean energy would want to keep the policy in place.

However, after implementation, APS became opposed to this ambitious distributed generation plan. Before this policy was enacted, the utility had been financially supporting AriSEIA. Given the solar industry was small at that time, these utility contributions were significant to the network. Initially, the trade association primarily had solar hot water heating companies—a technology that displaces natural gas—and therefore it posed little threat to an electric utility. But when the association lobbied for the distributed generation requirement that would spur solar PV, this angered APS. At this point, the relationship between the clean energy industry and the utility turned hostile. As an individual involved with the association put it, "Things kind of changed. We never had the same perspective as the utilities."[22] This policy marked a turning point for the utilities. As more groups and individuals got involved in renewable energy, they would have to increase their resistance. Still: it was not the last clean energy policy that the utilities would regret letting pass at the commission.

Utilities Agree to a Policy They Later Regret: Net Metering and the Fog of Enactment

Beginning in 2007, the commission aimed to improve its latest clean energy target's lagging implementation. Once again, the utilities were failing to comply. They were missing their goals and were doing particularly poorly at meeting the distributed generation requirements. To improve the policy's implementation, the commission began developing a comprehensive net energy metering (NEM) and interconnection policy.[23] This would allow homeowners and companies to invest in solar more easily. The commission also took up the idea because the federal Energy Policy Act of 2005 compelled states to consider net metering and interconnection standards.

Previously, Arizona's utilities had the option of voluntarily setting up net metering. Given the asymmetry in bargaining power between a ratepayer and a utility, this approach yielded poor outcomes for early solar adopters. For example, during the 1990s, SRP was hostile to homeowners installing solar panels on their roofs (Johnstone 2011). The utility only paid solar customers 2.4 cents per kilowatt hour (¢/kWh), even though it sold power for almost four times that price. The accounting system was also poor. Many customers had conflicts with the utility over whether they were being paid for *all* the power they had provided. This was not unique to SRP. Overall, Arizona utilities paid low rates to the few customers who had installed solar. They were not "net" metering policies: customers were not paid the same, retail rate for the electricity that they bought and sold. And they likely weren't getting paid for all their extra energy. Unsurprisingly, this arrangement led to little participation from customers. By the end of 2005, only 350 APS customers and 160 SRP customers had ever installed solar PV.[24]

The net metering policy was less controversial than the state's latest renewable energy target, according to a commission employee involved in both proceedings.[25] Several advocates working through associations intervened in the rulemaking, including AriSEIA, Americans for Solar Power, the Distributed Energy Association of Arizona, and the California-based Vote Solar. These groups argued for generous terms that would enable the solar industry: large systems should be eligible, there should not be a cap on participation, and fixed fees should not be used. Together, these rules would amplify the policy's ability to shift the political landscape by growing the advocates faster.

Surprisingly, the utilities did not have major objections to the policy.[26] In the NEM proceeding, APS said it supported the policy, provided only renewable energy and not combined heat and power projects could participate. APS went so far as to point out that NEM customers may actually provide *benefits* to the grid, including "voltage support, reliability, lower losses, power quality improvements, and in selective instances, the possible deferral or even avoidance of distribution investment."[27] Indeed, in January 2009, APS would publish a report that valued distributed generation solar between 7 and 14 ¢/kWh in 2025; at that time, electricity in Arizona cost less than 11 ¢/kWh.[28] That said, APS also requested additional charges to cover grid costs. The ACC responded that other states had not approved such charges. As the commission pointed out, the goal was to encourage uptake of distributed generation, and utility charges for solar power would undermine adoption.[29] Consequently, the commission did not approve additional charges in 2008. The utility also wanted projects to have a maximum size of 100% of the connected facility's peak load. In a compromise, the rule passed with a maximum of 125%. But overall, the policy's most likely opponents requested only minor changes.

Without opposition from the utilities, there was broad support for the net metering policy. By this point, the only commissioner to oppose the state's latest RPS, Republican Commissioner Mike Gleason, had become Chairman. He also voted against the net metering rule, but the other four Republican commissioners supported it. As then commissioner Kris Mayes described it in October 2008, "Arizona's net metering rules are already being viewed as ground breaking by other states around the country. For the first time, Arizonans are going to receive the full, fair value of the electricity they produce from their solar panels and sell back to the state's utilities."[30] The narrative of fairness that advocates were advancing had stuck. They had managed to influence the regulator. When the final net metering rule was issued in October 2008, many believed that Arizona would lead the country in solar energy.

Given the controversy that would follow, how can we understand this absence of conflict during enactment? This issue is all the more puzzling given the regulatory capture shown in Arizona before and after this time. In part, opponents did not show up for the fight because they were unable to predict the future. Utilities could not forecast how solar technology's costs would decline over the coming decade. Nor could they foresee how federal and state policies would interact. Companies were only just learning to combine federal tax credits with state net metering policies through an innovative business model called "solar leasing."[31] This approach was not yet widely in use, particularly not outside of California, where SolarCity was founded in 2006 and Sunrun in 2007.

In short, we see the fog of enactment operating here, in this case quelling opposition from utilities. If utilities had been acting in their best interest from the start, we would have expected them to weaken net metering in Arizona. But the utilities did not believe there was pent-up demand for citizens to own solar, given their ability to suppress the sector's growth up to that point. Cost declines would also prove important. California was in the process of bringing down solar's costs through policies driving deployment. Thus, the consequences of clean energy policy were spilling across states through technological innovation. The opponents could not foresee the trends that were aligning to boost solar's prospects.

Further underscoring the utilities' inability to predict net metering's consequences, SRP followed the commission's lead, independently expanding its policy. Before it adopted this new net metering policy, customers interested in installing solar and selling excess electricity to SRP had to sign complex bilateral agreements.[32] Few customers did this. Beginning in 2004, SRP created the "Earthwise" program that allowed small solar projects, up to 10 kW, to participate. Under this program, customers could carry forward bill credits for excess electricity. They would be paid "an average market price" for excess energy at the end of the year. This policy was not true retail net metering since the utility was paying customers less than the price that the customers paid for electricity, and the payout would only happen once a year. It was not a good incentive for homeowners to invest in solar technology. In 2008, SRP changed this value to "an average *annual* market price" bringing the policy closer to net metering, and increased the maximum project size to 20 kW. It's clear that utilities could not anticipate net metering's consequences—why would a utility choose autonomously to adopt the policy if it knew in advance how it would affect profits? And why would it continuously expand the program if it did not believe that solar development was in its interest? Clearly, the fog of enactment was at work, blocking utilities' ability to understand policies' consequences.

Together, these changes at both the commission and SRP, along with rapid cost declines from other states' policies, led to strong growth in residential solar adoption in Arizona. Both net metering and the RPS distributed generation carve-out led to a boom in small-scale solar. In response, solar companies grew in the state. Initially, they organized through their existing industry network, AriSEIA. But by 2008, out-of-state companies had crossed into Arizona. California-based companies, including Sunrun, SolarCity, Clean Power Finance, Sungevity, SunEdison, and SunPower, began installing more of the state's solar power. As a result of Californian policy, these solar leasing companies had developed and implemented a successful third-party ownership model. In 2010, solar leasing became even more accessible when customers could sign leases with SolarCity without any upfront capital and without having to maintain the systems themselves.[33] Many residential and commercial customers were taking advantage of significant solar incentives from their utilities, further reducing their costs.

It took six policies and three decades to kick-start the solar revolution in Arizona. But the net metering program and distributed generation target finally began propelling small-scale solar. In January 2009, APS had just 900 net metering customers. By 2012, growth was approaching 500 systems a month.[34] By the end of 2012, SRP had 3,500 customers with net metering, TEP had 2,600, and APS was approaching 16,000.[35] But by 2012, this rapid uptick in residential solar energy adoption created a significant backlash from Arizona's utilities, particularly APS. The opponents had learned through implementation. They now understood what the stakes were. And they were ready to fight back.

Opponent Interest Groups Use an Election to Capture Their Regulator

After the net metering policy was implemented in Arizona, the utilities learned more about its consequences. Across the country, individuals started using state and federal incentives in greater numbers to install small-scale solar on their homes. As a result, utility revenues started slipping. Customers with solar reduced their payments to the utilities. With high fixed costs, utilities became concerned that they would need to increase their rates to cover these lost revenues. High rates, in turn, would incent more customers to turn to solar. And the cycle would continue, ending with utilities stuck with expensive assets and inadequate revenues to cover their operating costs given their dwindling customer base. This dynamic, termed "the death spiral," became a major issue at utility conferences (Blackburn et al. 2014; Kassakian & Schmalensee 2011). As a result, by 2011 many utilities across the country had become hostile toward net metering policies and distributed generation customers. The same was true in Arizona, particularly in the case of the private utility APS. Opponents were beginning to organize to attack these laws.

In Arizona, opponents moved to try to weaken the net metering policy by influencing their regulator. They aimed to change *who* was in charge of making decisions by intervening in the 2012 elections for the ACC. Given that the commission's main job is to regulate monopoly utilities, APS had a policy at the time not to participate in its regulator's elections. The company claimed it abstained from making campaign contributions. Since the commission race has low turnout and poor visibility among the public, if utilities did intervene in the electoral process, they would likely have an outsized influence (Anzia 2011).

In the fall election, two Democratic incumbents on the commission, Paul Newman and Sandra Kennedy, narrowly lost re-election. Instead, three Republican commissioners were elected: Bob Stump, Robert Burns, and Susan Bitter Smith. As a result, all five commissioners were Republican in 2013. In principle, this might not have been a problem for renewable energy. Arizonan Republicans had often championed renewable energy broadly and solar energy specifically. But the kind of Republican being elected had changed—utilities were driving partisan polarization on the issue. This election would mark a turning point for the ACC's position on clean energy.

Afterward, journalists from *The Arizona Republic* uncovered that APS *had* intervened in the 2012 election, against the company's official policy and against good governance norms. Two of the three Republican candidates that year— Bob Stump and Bob Burns—were affiliated with the American Legislative Exchange Council (ALEC), with one holding a senior position in the conservative network.[36] As we will see in the Ohio case, ALEC began promoting an anti-renewables agenda in 2011. Similarly, APS's holding company—Pinnacle West—was at that time a member of ALEC. Given its shared links to this interest group network,[37] APS likely believed that these ALEC affiliated candidates would support its objectives, including rolling back clean energy policy.[38]

During the election, APS funded mailers in support of these Republican candidates, despite the company's official position not to participate.[39] In the aftermath, and only after being contacted by journalists, utility officials said that these mailers were not sent under their direction, claiming that the nonprofit that sent the mailers did not consult with them. They blamed the Arizona Chamber of Commerce and Industry's president, Glenn Hamer, for acting unilaterally. However, APS had donated money to Hamer's nonprofit the Arizona Business Coalition, after which $7,500 was funneled to the Taxpayers' Voice Fund, which supported the Republican candidates.[40] While both APS and Hamer maintained that he acted unilaterally and sidestepped the rest of the coalition, the fact that the $7,500 was one of the group's largest expenditures in 2012 and that an APS official was on the board of this group casts doubt on this claim. It is conceivable that in a low-turnout election where candidates run on modest public funds, these independent expenditures may have proven decisive. Compared to higher-profile races, influencing a low-profile race is easier—it costs less money.[41]

With these newly elected commissioners, changes began to take place at the ACC. The incoming cohort of regulators started out the New Year by firing their executive director and replacing him with a Republican political staffer and former chief of staff to a Speaker of the Arizona House of Representatives.[42] Typically, executive directors at a commission are closer to bureaucrats than political operatives. In short, this was a starkly divergent choice for the agency's chief administrator.

Next, the commission accepted the utilities' proposal to eliminate long-standing incentives for solar. The two private utilities, APS and TEP, had run programs to fund commercial and residential solar using revenue from a $4 monthly charge on customers' bills. In early 2013, APS proposed to quickly reduce and then eliminate this incentive. There was tension at the commission between the elected officials and their staff on the best response to the utility's proposal.[43] The ACC staff opposed these sudden changes, arguing that the programs should be phased out to maintain the state's solar industry.[44] But the commissioners disagreed—rather than phasing out the commercial incentives, the commission *eliminated them entirely*, with APS and Commissioner Gary Pierce proposing these changes. The utilities also reduced their residential incentives by more than 50%.[45] Overall, the commission allowed the utilities to immediately cut $40 million in annual funding for solar energy.[46] The opponents were breaking the feedback cycle by cutting off advocates' resources.

These unanticipated cuts had a dramatic effect on Arizona's solar industry. Large, commercial projects were canceled overnight. Solar companies closed shop. The solar association's membership shrank, dramatically reducing the network's effectiveness. As resources dried up, the solar advocates fragmented. Rather than cooperating, the few remaining companies reacted to this scarcity by splintering into ever more associations: a solar hot water association, a distributed solar association, and what was left of the original group. This lack of unity undermined the industry's ability to influence policy. They were no longer pooling resources for lobbying or coordinating on messaging or strategy. The utilities had managed to repeal a policy and through it quell its rival by cutting off crucial revenues from the advocates. As renewable energy advocates weakened, it would be easier for the opponents to make further changes to policy. Here we see dramatic changes in the political clout of advocates as a result of swift policy changes—the kind of dynamics we would expect to see with undermining policy feedback.

After these incentives were removed, Commissioner Gary Pierce floated a proposal to reduce the clean energy target for APS to 13.35% rather than 15% by 2025.[47] This proposal was made despite the fact that APS was *ahead* of schedule in meeting its target. It is unusual to propose a reduction in an RPS for just one utility. But the chair had a particularly close relationship with APS. It would later become clear that Pierce was holding regular ex parte meetings with APS's chief executive officer (CEO), Don Brandt, at that time—perhaps seven meetings on this topic specifically. Meeting privately with regulated entities during public rate cases violates the commission's rules. It is clear that APS had the ear of at least one commissioner.

Pierce justified his proposal on the grounds that the RPS could be eliminated for large industrial users, a group that accounted for around 10% of APS's electricity sales. This would allow industrial entities to free-ride and not pay for addressing the energy system's negative externalities. It is a common initial strategy to weaken clean energy laws—this same approach was passed in Texas and Ohio. However, such a clientelistic retrenchment attempt proved unpalatable with the other commissioners and the public. Advocates organized a large protest and a letter-writing campaign, with more than 7,000 signatures on a petition and a flurry of calls and emails sent to the commission.[48] Consequently, Pierce withdrew his proposal and instead turned to less overt retrenchment tactics.

In January 2013, APS requested that the commission consider additional charges for net metering customers due to a supposed "cost shift" between solar and non-solar customers. This was not an argument unique to Arizona. By 2013, private utilities across the country were trying to retrench net metering policies. They were working together, through their networks, to understand the issue, protect their interests, and develop effective strategies. That same month, the Edison Electric Institute (EEI)—the national private utility association—published a widely read and critical study on net metering.[49] In Arizona, APS also prepared a report to justify its position, hiring Navigant Consulting. It strategically released this report just after the commission election, in December 2012.[50] In this way, the public would not be privy to its plans until it was too late.

This report set the framework for the utility's attack on the policy. It argued that non-solar customers increasingly had to pay for grid costs that solar customers were forgoing. As a result, APS alleged it would need to raise rates unfairly on non-solar customers. It framed the issue around "neighbor-to-neighbor fairness," arguing that non-solar customers were subsidizing solar customers. Promoting the idea that net metering was an unfair policy was key to the opponents' campaign.

Of course, such a notion of a cost shift between industrial and residential customers was never raised when APS tried to exempt industrial customers from paying for the clean energy policy entirely or proposed building unnecessary natural gas plants.[51] And the Navigant report did not consider the way that APS was imposing costs on the public through air pollution and climate change, in its failure to transition away from fossil fuels. The utility's report did not include these costs, stating it "excludes other societal benefits not directly reflected in utility rates, such as environmental or health impacts."[52] The utility was advancing a narrow, self-serving view that focused on its own interests more than the public interest.

Unfortunately, the regulators were increasingly reluctant to serve in their role as independent and evidence-based decision makers who push utilities to serve the public interest. Instead, the commission directed APS to gather further information on the question before it would open a regulatory proceeding on the topic.[53] This was an unusual decision. Typically, the ACC would run a process to gather evidence at the commission, in some cases holding a formal evidentiary hearing.[54] Instead, the commission delegated its regulatory responsibilities to an interest group, directing APS to hold a series of technical workshops on the value of distributed generation solar. This was a sign of growing regulatory capture in Arizona.

With these workshops proceeding, it was clear to both the advocates and opponents that a serious conflict would occur in 2013. They were gearing up for a fight, with a likely decision on net metering at the commission later that year. Both sets of interest groups had a lot to lose if the decision did not go their way. But the private utility was much better prepared for this conflict. It had significant influence over the regulator. It held the power to set the agenda since it was holding the technical meetings in its own offices. And these meetings were crucial—they would decide what to count and what not to count when adjudicating the question of a cost shift. The utility also had a large staff working on the issue—a staff, it should be noted, that was paid for from utility revenues from monopoly customer rates.

By contrast, the advocates were in disarray. The inability of the commission to implement the first four renewable energy policies meant that the solar industry was slow to develop. Once the final RPS was successfully implemented, advocates lost a few important policy battles, eroding their resources. This policy retrenchment cut the solar industry's major funding sources. With funding drying up, the advocates' industry associations began to fracture. At the time, Arizona had the second most solar installed of any state; yet its solar industry was underfunded, and most of the advocacy groups were semiprofessionalized, with only one staff member. Given implementation resistance and retrenchment from opponents, the industry was never able to gather momentum, build coalitions, or organize.[55] When opponents put net metering retrenchment on the agenda in 2013, the advocates were not mobilizing the public. They were not planning their strategy for intervening and blocking the policy at the commission. They were not even updating their websites. The advocates were ill prepared for the coming policy fight.

Expanding the Scope of Conflict: Interest Groups Bring in the Public and Wield Competing Ideas

As the Arizonan advocates splintered, California-based clean energy advocates stepped in to counter the opposition. By 2013, the solar leasing companies had organized through The Alliance for Solar Choice (TASC), a coalition of six companies that together installed the majority of the country's rooftop solar.[56] TASC began its Arizona campaign by hiring a local lawyer to represent the industry at the commission proceedings. Next, it hired an Arizonan public relations firm to design an advertising and public outreach campaign. The firm created a public-facing organization: Tell Utilities Solar Won't Be Killed (TUSK). They recruited Barry Goldwater, Jr., a longtime solar supporter and well-known Arizonan conservative, to be the face of the campaign. The goal was to market solar to Republicans. The out-of-state advocates, enabled by policy feedback elsewhere, had crossed into Arizona. They had more resources and were trying to bring the public into the conflict, in an attempt to influence the regulator.

In response, APS funneled millions of dollars into two conservative groups—Prosper Inc. and 60 Plus—to run a counter campaign. The 60 Plus Association is a national group founded in 1992 that has operated across state lines, representing conservative seniors, with more than 167,000 supporters in Arizona.[57] Prosper Inc. was a new organization, founded by a former Speaker of Arizona's House of Representatives. As "dark money" organizations, these groups took funds from APS and Koch affiliates, masking their attempts to rollback clean energy laws.[58] They quickly got to work launching a website criticizing "corporate welfare" for solar energy in 2013. They also funded several television ads that aimed to convince people that solar customers ought to pay fixed charges because it was "unfair" if solar customers did not pay for grid costs. Initially, APS lied and denied that it was behind this advertising. However, investigative journalists uncovered the utility had supported these organizations, and APS eventually admitted to its role.[59] The opponents spent far more than the advocates on these public campaigns. One estimate put APS's spending at $3.7 million compared to TASC's $436,000.[60] Opponents also drew on their networks for support—the national private utility association, EEI, spent an additional $520,000 on 10 days of television ads in support of APS.[61] While the advocates tried to counter their opponents, they did not have the benefit of guaranteed profits to underwrite their campaigns.

The groups did not just use the public to try to influence the regulators—they also wielded ideas. Both sides invested in studies that estimated the costs and benefits of distributed solar energy for Arizona's electricity system. These reports were not aimed at the public but at influencing the commissioners. In early May 2013, the solar industry issued its report, written by a consulting firm, Crossborder Energy. This report argued that for every $1 APS invested in solar, it would save its customers $1.54. These results framed the technology as a net positive for the state. Two days later, APS released its own report, an update of its earlier study.[62] Rather than arguing that solar was worth the 7–14 ¢/kWh as it had estimated in 2009, this new report said it was only worth 4 ¢/kWh. That estimate put solar well below the 12 ¢/kWh retail rate for residential customers, undercutting the justification for net metering.

Of course, the studies used different assumptions to estimate the costs and benefits of solar for the grid, making them apples to oranges comparisons. The APS report looked at the issue in a given year, with varying levels of solar penetration. It also did not include the environmental and societal benefits of solar beyond briefly considering CO_2 emissions. In contrast, the Crossborder study considered the benefits and costs of solar over the potential lifetime of installations. It included far more benefits, estimating the avoided cost of air pollution. This study also considered the combined effect of solar with demand-side energy efficiency programs at reducing the need for supply-side investments. Thus, these reports were more a function of organized combat between interest groups than reflections of facts per se. As one former commissioner put it,

> Here's the problem with the way we do analyses of the costs and benefits of distributed solar: all we end up with is dueling studies. And you don't really have an independent entity that both sides trust doing the analysis—because at the end of the day somebody is paying for each one of those studies. If the commission had commissioned that study and paid for it, then you could have come up with something that both

sides would have agreed with. But, with budget cuts at PUCs, then each side is docketing their own study.[63]

It is not surprising that interest groups would advocate their interests in studies that they funded—it is a common pattern across the country.[64] Instead, the fault lies with the commission, which abdicated its responsibility to investigate the issue independently and never held an evidentiary hearing for the case. Many observers suggested that the lack of an evidentiary hearing showed that the ACC's eventual decision was more political than technical.

Instead of the commission holding a hearing, in late May, the Residential Utility Consumer Office (RUCO)—the state's ratepayer-funded advocate—intervened to hold its own workshop. Both advocates and opponents were invited to present their views, with time for public comments. Solar advocates argued for greater customer choice; opponents focused on costs being shifted onto nonparticipants. After this meeting, RUCO concluded that a cost shift was occurring and recommended the ACC open a docket to address the issue.[65] The opponents were succeeding in making their voices heard.[66]

Regulatory Capture Leads to Further Policy Retrenchment

APS put forward its net metering proposal in July 2013 after holding its own workshops to investigate the issue. In response, the ACC opened a docket to make a decision on the issue of whether cost shifting was occurring between solar and non-solar customers.[67] It was quite unusual for a utility to request that the commission approve new charges outside of a rate case—the normal way that new charges are levied. Given this unorthodox approach, bureaucrats at the commission intervened, arguing against proceeding. They stated that these changes should be dealt with in a rate case. Indeed, APS had finished a rate case the year before, in May 2012, when two Democrats were still on the commission. They did not bring up net metering or solar incentives at that time. After APS intervened in the 2012 elections, however, it had managed to elect a slate of commissioners that it could more easily influence. Clearly, APS saw an opportunity with the current commission and did not want to wait until its next rate case in 2015 since the commission's composition would change in the 2014 election.

APS's filing was nearly 400 pages. The utility requested changes to how new net metering customers would be compensated. Rather than being paid the retail rate, APS proposed that net metering customers be paid a rate equal to the cost of producing electricity from the Palo Verde nuclear plant: 4¢/kWh.

This was the same value that the consulting report it had funded had estimated solar was worth. This change would amount to $50–$100 a month of additional charges for solar net metering customers. Using this number, APS was using a negotiation tactic called "anchoring"—starting at an extreme and unrealistic point to stretch the window of what was considered reasonable. The utility no doubt knew it would not get a charge this large when its average customer's bills were $120–$150 a month.[68]

APS also requested that these changes go into effect almost immediately, starting in October 2013. However, its proposal would grandfather existing customers. This strategy was likely chosen to push through a speedy decision while quelling opposition from the easiest citizens to mobilize: existing net metering customers.[69] If in the future individuals wanted to transfer the ownership of their solar installation, were they to sell their house, then these additional charges would not apply for the new owner. The policy thus protected existing customers' assets. In short, APS's proposal was politically savvy—it aimed to keep the scope of conflict narrow.

At the end of September 2013, the commission staff responded to the APS proposal, arguing that the matter should wait until APS's next rate case because the question of a cost shift was fundamentally an issue of electricity rate design. If the commissioners decided to proceed nevertheless, the staff presented two alternative options: either a small flat fee for new NEM customers of around $2/month; or a cap on APS's payments.[70] If a fixed fee was imposed, the staff proposed an amount that was a mere 2% of APS's top number. Of course, neither of these solutions was in the utility's interests. Ideally, the utility wanted to stop citizens from owning solar installations. It had realized that it wanted to maintain its monopoly over owning and profiting from the electricity system's assets.

The interest group opponents proved more influential than the bureaucrats. The commissioners largely ignored the staff recommendations, siding with the utility. This suggests that bureaucratic autonomy on clean energy policy in Arizona had weakened as the issue became more salient with interest groups. Opponents maintained a near monopoly over the policymaking agenda. That said, Commissioner Pierce asked that parties respond to the staff recommendations on which scenarios would be most appropriate.

Advocates rejected the premise of the proposal, however, and argued that the utility had violated procedure by seeking this change outside of a rate case. They called on the commission to ignore APS's plan and conduct another rate case if new charges were going to be imposed. They argued that a cost shift was not yet happening and, as such, stated a monthly fee was unnecessary. They also claimed that existing policy was sufficient to address any alleged issues.[71] Taken together, these were attempts to resist APS's plan and keep the commission from implementing an unfavorable policy.

Eventually, a third party intervened. Purporting to be neutral, the state's rate-payer advocate once again tried to mediate. In October 2013, RUCO created a model to analyze the question, coming up with a $1/kW proposal. This would amount to around $7 a month per customer, depending on the size of the homeowner's solar panels. Notably, the number fell between APS's plan and the commission staff's proposal. Since the commission did not conduct its own evidentiary hearing or commission its own report on the issue, the RUCO estimates were the only source of information that was independent from the interest groups.[72] Momentum began to grow around this compromise. *The Arizona Republic*, the newspaper of record in the state, argued that while the decision should ultimately be taken through a rate case, this was a fair interim step.[73]

The final decision was scheduled to take place after 2 days of hearings on November 13 and 14, 2013. Advocates, including the solar industry through TASC and environmental groups like the Sierra Club and Vote Solar, organized a public demonstration at the commission for these days. On the first day of the hearings, around 500 people turned up outside the commission to protest APS's proposal. This was by far the largest protest in the regulator's 100-year history.[74] The advocates were using the public in their conflict, attempting to raise an obscure regulatory body's salience and visibility. In this way, they were also trying to influence the elected body through outside lobbying. One of the advocates involved in the protest described its importance this way,

> It set the tone for the day. There were hundreds of people. And around 100 people gave public comments inside the building. It was a large enough event that TV crews came out to cover it and it became a prime time news story. It elevated the decision so that the commissioners knew that whatever they decided, it would be very well publicized.[75]

The advocates believed that increasing the commissioners' sense that the public was watching would reduce the costs opponents would be able to impose on clean energy. The strategy likely worked, particularly because Arizona's PUC is an elected body. One of the commissioners at the time confirmed that the public protest was notable: "We were all cognizant that lots of people were interested and watching what we were doing. It had to be defensible for the docket. People are always worried about the next election."[76] That said, the commissioner went on to state that they were unconvinced that the public was united in its opposition or understood the ultimate decision: "But the communication I was getting was about 50/50. It was such confusion. I had talked to 50 groups since that decision—nobody knows what we did." In this way, the elected commissioner was discounting the public, claiming it was ignorant. It is difficult to hold a regulatory body accountable when its elected members do not even believe that the public *can* understand its decisions.

On the second day of the hearings, TASC and RUCO came to a compromise position of $0.70/kW, somewhat lower than RUCO's initial proposal of $1/kW. This would amount to a charge of around $5 a month on most solar customers' bills. As is similarly seen in the Kansas case, after relentless attacks, eventually the advocates decided to compromise and accept some weakening of the policy. The advocates were less politically influential than the incumbent opponents who had captured their regulator. The earlier policy retrenchments had also left the industry weakened, with far fewer resources than the utilities, who had millions in guaranteed profits they could use to fund their lobbying and campaigns every year.

At the end of the last day of the public hearings, the commissioners made their decision. They largely conformed to the compromise RUCO and TASC had brokered. The commissioners voted 3 to 2 to charge future APS customers on a monthly basis for installing rooftop solar, with the two dissenters arguing that the charge was not large enough. The charge would apply to customers installing new solar on or after January 1, 2014, on an interim basis, until the next APS rate case. Importantly, the ACC decided that the current net metering policy *did* create a cost shift that caused non-solar customers to pay higher rates. This finding created a precedent across the country that would prove more important than the specific costs imposed that day. This policy would spillover to other states, establishing the grounds necessary for other utilities to ask for higher charges on solar in the future. On the one hand, advocates heralded the 2013 decision as a success—it was a charge of $5 rather than $50–$100. On the other hand, it set a clear precedent, not only for Arizona but for other states. The consequences for this policy feedback were not confined to Arizona.

As a further indication of APS's interests, after these charges were imposed on citizens owning solar, in July 2014, APS proposed its own solar leasing program. They planned to start by building 20 MW—a large amount for residential solar. Since the utility would fund, install, own, and maintain these systems, APS could profit off of them, just as they did with other assets. APS could leverage their monopoly status keep out competition from third-party rooftop installers. They planned to compensate customers who put APS-owned panels on their property with a $30 monthly bill credit for 20 years. Customers themselves could not control their electricity bills, and in essence, the program and compensation functioned as APS renting out customers' real estate.[77] This was much lower than compensation under solar leasing from independent companies. After collaborating with the commission on this proposal, the utility moved forward with the program, with an estimated participation of around 1,500 customers.[78] The solar leasing companies responded, arguing this was anticompetitive behavior on the part of a monopoly utility. But the commission wouldn't hear these arguments. The utility's program proceeded, with little resistance from the commissioners.

Opponents Work the Primaries to Drive Polarization

Following this policy decision, two seats on the commission were up for election in 2014. The advocates and opponents geared up for another big fight. Gary Pierce, who had proven himself APS's closest ally, had termed out and would no longer be eligible for re-election. Given this turnover in a key utility ally, both APS and the solar companies through TASC organized for a significant election year. The utility was interested in maintaining its influence over the regulator, while the solar companies sought to undermine this tight relationship.

APS began its intervention early, working first in the Republican primary. The utility knew that if its candidates were elected, they would not be like past Republicans who had championed solar. The utility financially supported two candidates who would go on to win seats on the commission: Tom Forese and Doug Little. Both of these candidates were sympathetic to APS's views. Their two primary opponents, Vernon Parker and Lucy Mason, were both pro-solar and backed by TUSK, the front group for the solar leasing industry. TUSK ran email campaigns attempting to raise grassroots funds for Parker and Mason.[79] However, both of the utility-backed candidates won the primary in August, with likely more than $1 million spent supporting them.[80] Although Arizona law does not require disclosure and APS refused to admit to spending the money on Forese and Little via third-party groups, journalists believed that the majority of these funds came from APS, a fact which APS would only confirm years later.[81] By contrast, the solar industry spent less than a quarter of the amount, around $240,000, supporting candidates during the Republican primary.

Opponents also outspent advocates during the general election. APS contributed to independent groups that supported the Republican candidates, Forese and Little.[82] Through dark money groups, such as Save Our Future Now, journalists estimated at the time that APS likely spent about $1.4 million in negative ads against Democrat Sandra Kennedy and others, spending more than $3 million total over the course of the race. However, years later, after several commissioners called for more disclosure, APS would admit that it spent about $11 million on the 2014 ACC elections.[83] Estimating solar companies' contributions is also challenging, but they likely spent much less. TUSK likely spent a total of $556,000, with only $315,000 spent in the general election.[84]

Thus, the utility likely outspent the solar companies by about 20 times. The 2014 race for the Corporation Commission was then the second most expensive race in the state's history, only behind the 2014 Arizona governor's race.[85] For such a typically low-profile election, this spending was remarkable. It points to the utility's need to maintain its near monopoly on influence at its regulator. The advocates could not match this heft.

The utility's spending during these elections likely translated into significant influence over policymaking.[86] After the 2014 race, a whistleblower at the commission released information that showed that APS had interfered with its regulatory body.[87] According to this former commission employee, Commissioner Gary Pierce had held at least 14 ex parte meetings with APS's CEO between 2007 and 2015. Eventually, both the FBI and the Arizona attorney general's office would investigate these issues. The FBI has taken a particular interest in the way the 2014 ACC election was funded. Apart from the fact that APS spent $11 million on the race under other organizations' names, there were other abnormalities in that election. For example, the Sunlight Foundation uncovered that APS may have funneled money to the commission race via a university foundation, at Arizona State University (ASU).[88] Adding to the controversy, Bill Post—the former chair and CEO of APS's corporate parent Pinnacle West and a then board member, who had worked at APS for 38 years—chaired the ASU Foundation board at the time.[89] APS and the ASU Foundation officials deny any direct link. But given APS's past behavior in denying election spending until journalists or federal investigators uncover the truth, it would be understandable to believe they are lying.

Opponents Continue to Attack Solar, Causing the Industry to Shrink and Undermining Policy Feedback

The commission's 2013 decision only applied to one utility, APS. On the heels of the 2014 election, Arizona's two other utilities acted in early 2015 to impose fees on *their* net metering customers. Salt River Project, which is not regulated through the ACC, proposed a new monthly charge for solar customers in December 2014. Their board of directors scheduled a vote on February 26, 2015, to decide the issue. Like APS's first proposal, SRP suggested very large charges—raising rates by an average of $50 for new net metering customers.[90] Following a series of contentious public hearings, the charges were approved on February 26, with 12 of the 14 directors voting in favor. Although SRP made other changes, these costs were primarily imposed on new customers installing solar after December 8, 2014. In this way, SRP backdated the changes to solar customers who acted after they announced their plan to shift the policy. The rate changes would take effect almost immediately, starting in April 2015.

The advocates tried to resist this policy change using the courts. SolarCity, one of the members of TASC and the then largest solar leasing company in the country, filed an antitrust lawsuit for anticompetitive behavior in Arizona's federal court on March 3, 2015. This was a bread-and-butter issue for the company—SolarCity had around 46% of the customers with solar installed in SRP's service territory.[91] Salt River Project argued before a district court to dismiss the suit on the basis of the state action immunity doctrine—in other words, suggesting that antitrust lawsuits do not apply because SRP is a state-regulated agency. The motion was dismissed, with the decision appealed to a federal court. The Supreme Court announced in December 2017 that it would hear the case. Weeks before oral arguments, SRP and SolarCity settled. Here, we see advocates strategically using an indirect route through the courts to gain advantage in policy combat, when other more direct strategies were either not feasible or not likely to lead to success.

One month after the SRP decision, on March 25, 2015, TEP applied to the ACC for a rate change for new net metering customers. It used the same playbook APS had pioneered in 2013: proposing paying new solar customers the same price for electricity as it would pay to buy power from a commercial solar power plant. The change would amount to around a $22/month charge for new solar customers. TEP argued that solar customers would still save an average of $80 a month relative to the typical customer.[92] The next week, on April 2, 2015, APS mirrored TEP's proposal, similarly requesting a charge of around $21/month, through an increased grid charge. This would amount to multiplying the charge approved just 18 months prior by a factor of four.[93] Once again, to limit solar companies' ability to organize the public in opposition to these proposed rate hikes, existing solar customers would be grandfathered in and could keep their current rates. APS requested that the ACC move forward and increase the charge, with an aggressive timeline of August 2015 to approve and implement the proposal. Initially, TEP's proposition was dismissed. However, at the end of 2018, the ACC approved a new monthly fee for new TEP solar customers.[94]

The advocates organized through their networks to block these proposals. But with so many utilities targeting net metering, solar companies struggled to resist retrenchment. With each new proposal moving in parallel, in a different venue or proceeding, the advocates were fighting a battle on multiple fronts. Further, these changes were not just happening in Arizona: they were happening across the country. Since these solar companies operated across state lines, they were facing attacks in many other PUCs. The utilities, by contrast, were well funded and they only had to work in one state. As monopolies with guaranteed revenues, they had millions to spend on these policy conflicts. Winning these conflicts paid them back: when new charges were approved, it increased their profits. By contrast, for each new charge the solar companies failed to resist, their profits and thereby their ability to influence policy decreased. This is policy feedback in a nutshell. But in this case, policy changes were strengthening the opponents and weakening the advocates.

The consequences of these monthly charges were quickly reflected in solar installation rates. Since APS's first charge was approved in late 2013, installations in its service territory reduced dramatically. As Figure 7.1 shows, in 2014 solar installations in APS's service territory fell 5% compared to 2013. The decline in growth is particularly dramatic compared to SRP's trajectory, where installations grew more than 800% over the same period. Since the utilities both operate in Phoenix, in very close geographic proximity, the reductions in APS's service territory are likely causally attributable to the $5/month average grid charge implemented at the end of 2013.

Once SRP imposed monthly fees in 2015, installations in their area dropped precipitously—an abrupt quarter-over-quarter reduction of over 75%. Immediately after the policy was implemented, SolarCity saw a sharp 96% decline in installations.[95] These results show the material consequences of the

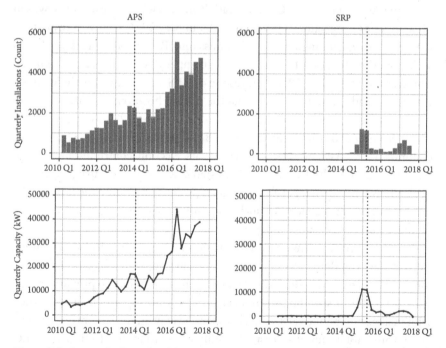

Figure 7.1 Quarterly Growth in Net Metering Capacity in Arizona Public Service (APS) versus Salt River Project (SRP). *Dashed line shows policy retrenchment.* (Source: http:// arizonagoessolar.org/.)

policy change. Through these fees, utilities managed to cut off resources from clean energy advocates, shrinking the solar industry in Arizona and quelling the main dissenters to their proposals. With each victory, it was easier for opponents to win the next battle.

Regulatory Capture Is Uncovered, but Arizona's Net Metering Policy Is Repealed

While opponents were able to retrench clean energy policy in Arizona, it was not costless. Through taking their conflict public, APS exposed the extent to which it had captured its regulator. This did not go unnoticed by journalists, the public, nor even the commission itself. Beginning in 2015, Commissioner Bob Burns began to ask APS questions about its election expenditures. Burns was a Republican who received campaign contributions from APS when he was running for election in 2012. He also served as an ALEC state chair when he was president of the Arizona Senate in 2011 and had even been a member of ALEC's board. Initially, Burns supported APS in its attacks on net metering. He was an unlikely person to take on the solar opponents.

But something changed in 2015, and Burns became a dogged regulator. He asked the Arizona Attorney General Mark Brnovich whether it would be within his abilities as a regulator to subpoena APS. In May 2016, Brnovich responded that he could; and in August 2016, Commissioner Robert Burns filed subpoenas seeking information on APS and its parent company's expenditures on commission races from 2011 to 2016.[96] In response, APS sued Burns. The judge ruled that Burns had the right to subpoena the utility; however, because the other regulators did not agree with him, he could not force APS to comply.[97] With the re-election of Sandra Kennedy in 2018 and subsequent backing from other commissioners, APS eventually disclosed its election contributions, though questions remain. The fact that APS resisted disclosing its campaign spending in elections for its own regulator for years is problematic.[98] And the fact that the utility has gone to such lengths, including suing a regulator, shows clear efforts to undermine its regulator's independence.

In 2016, three positions on the commission were up for re-election, including Burns's seat. The Republican primary was contested, with five people running for the three open slots. Burns made it through the Republican primary, in part with $700,000 in spending from solar groups, who supported his campaign with mailers and phone calls. APS also spent heavily on the commission race in 2016, with a total sum of at least $4.2 million.[99] During the election, the CEO of APS, Don Brandt, sent an email to his employees, urging them to vote for the Republican candidates, including Burns. Clearly, APS would rather have a known Republican adversary than any Democrats on the commission.

Burns is not the only person to raise concerns about corruption and regulatory capture at the commission.[100] Pinnacle West, the holding company for APS, received two grand-jury subpoenas from the US attorney's office in Arizona in June 2016 for election spending related to the commission. In addition, the FBI investigated whether Gary Pierce leveraged his position to support his son Justin's bid for Arizona Secretary of State; the Arizona Free Enterprise Club, one of the groups that APS has used as an intermediary, contributed $733,000 to Justin Pierce's campaign.[101] Eventually, Gary Pierce was charged federally with bribery and conspiracy, with evidence unearthed as part of the larger probe into the ACC elections. Although the bribe was unrelated to the electricity case, it may simply have been the easier way to charge Pierce, given the evidence.[102] Eventually, federal prosecutors dropped the bribery case and called it a mistrial. Given all these developments, the public began to view the ACC as a captured regulator. For example, a September 2017 poll found that two-thirds of Arizonans believed the commission is corrupt.[103] Notably, similar levels of Republicans, Democrats, and Independents shared this view.

Given the ongoing investigations and controversy, in March 2017, APS said it would disclose its campaign contributions. It maintained that intervening in the election of its own regulator was legal and ethical given that the First Amendment allows freedom of speech and citing the Supreme Court decision on Citizens United.[104] APS claimed that only profits were used to fund its election spending and that it did not charge customers for these costs. This is a rather weak argument given that private utilities make profits through regulatory decisions at the commission. Further, APS is a monopoly, so its customers cannot leave. Ultimately, the money that APS or Pinnacle West uses in campaigns is derived from its customers, who cannot choose to buy from another company, if, for example, they disagree with its political stances.

After these stinging losses, the advocates tried a new, public tactic in 2016, when they fielded a ballot initiative: the Arizona Solar Energy Freedom Act. They even had a credible former ACC Republican commissioner, Kris Mayes, lead the proposal. However, the utilities' dominance was not easily challenged. A counterinitiative was soon filed. The same thing occurred in Florida that year, when utilities and the public applied for dueling ballot initiatives. In that state, the utilities successfully fended off the solar advocates' initiative.[105] In Florida, the solar coalition realized it would not have enough political influence to beat a counterinitiative, which if adopted could further undermine its weak position. In this way the opponents reshaped the negotiation landscape, getting the advocates to retreat.

In Arizona, APS asked for a full rate case in mid-2016, before the election was concluded. Their request included numerous strategies to retrench solar energy. As occurred in Kansas (Chapter 6), the advocates sat down to negotiate with their opponents after years of endless attacks. APS and SolarCity came together to work out the compromise, with the solar companies conceding ground, given their lack of influence at the commission.[106] In the August 2017 decision, the commission eliminated net metering. The decision was only a modest 8% reduction in the price solar customers would be paid for each unit of energy supplied. However, the bigger decision was that the rate could be recalculated in the future. In other words, this change allowed APS to continuously reduce how much it paid for solar energy. In such an asymmetric bargaining situation—wherein the utilities have all the information—solar customers' payments will likely continue to decrease, barring electoral shifts at the commission. Unsurprisingly, the changes applied almost immediately, giving the solar industry little time to adapt. By this point, solar leasing companies had already begun pulling out of the state—in 2015, SolarCity relocated 10% of its workers out of Arizona.[107]

But repealing net metering was only one way that APS targeted solar in its rate case. The utility also requested other under-the-radar changes, including dramatic increases in *all* customers' fixed monthly fees. This change made solar less profitable. It was a new strategy utilities were using to reduce solar energy across the country. Once again, APS asked for very high charges, starting the negotiation at $24/month—almost three times as large as the existing fixed charges. Eventually, the commission approved a charge of $15/month, representing an increase of almost 75%. In addition, APS requested changes to the definition of peak times, shifting them away from the hours where the sun is shining toward the evening when the sun has gone down. The commission also approved this change. In these subtle ways, APS further undermined solar in the state. Meanwhile, the utility engaged in greenwashing, claiming it was pro-solar and focused on equity by promising to expand its own solar program to low-income households. In truth, such a program allowed APS to make greater profits while giving these low-income households minimal breaks on their electricity bills.

Throughout this case, we have seen how a utility's ability to capture its regulator has undermined citizens' ability to invest in clean energy. While some individuals and even a commissioner have contested these rate changes, without big shifts in Arizona's politics and the extent of APS's power, it is unlikely they will be reversed. After many years, the opponents succeeded in cutting off resources from their advocates. From 2016 to 2019, installations plummeted, and job losses in the solar industry were dramatic, falling 10% in 2018. With no substantial solar energy policies left in Arizona, some solar companies left the state entirely.

Conclusion

Arizona's clean energy laws are a clear case of regulatory capture undermining policy feedback. By 2017, Arizona had retrenched its solar energy policies: it had eliminated net metering, cut incentives, and raised fixed fees on customers. Retrenchment occurred in Arizona because interest group opponents held greater influence over the regulator than advocates. The state was leading a trend that has since played out nationally, with steady increases in the number of fixed monthly charges since 2015.[108] In many cases, opponents only apply policy changes to future adopters of solar energy, quelling opposition from the easiest citizens to mobilize: current solar owners. For example, in both Indiana and Nevada, opponents reduced compensation rates. However, Nevada did not initially grandfather existing customers into the prior rate structure. This difference likely explained the extensive backlash that forced the return to net metering in 2017.[109] In other states utilities were smart to grandfather existing customers and keep the scope of conflict smaller.

In Arizona, policy retrenchment weakened solar growth, which saw a 57% drop in installations from 2013 to 2014 and similarly low numbers in 2015. While APS numbers increased after 2016, this was likely because the utility's customers wanted to act before the net metering program ended for new projects in 2017.[110] After that point, APS installations again plummeted.[111] The market in SRP's territory took even longer to recover. At SRP, rate changes caused steep declines in the number of applications. In response to the rate hikes, advocates launched protests and ran candidates for the SRP board in 2016.[112] Advocates successfully elected two pro-solar board members in both 2016 and 2018, building their influence on that board. Still, with 14 seats, the advocates were outnumbered. At both utilities, solar adoption has been successfully weakened.

Given their long-term struggle to rollback these policies and the extent of their influence with their regulator and boards, it is puzzling why APS and SRP did not block net metering policies from passing in the first place. This is where the fog of enactment is key. In some cases, potential opponents may not initially know what their interests are vis-à-vis a policy. In those cases, even when regulatory capture is operating, policies that are counter to an influential opponent's interests can be enacted and implemented. When these opponents update their beliefs about the policy, in part learning through interest group networks that cross state lines, they will begin to attack the policy. With sufficient power, reversals will begin to occur.

In Arizona, solar's success began to threaten the incumbent utilities' ability to build and profit from new infrastructure. In 2012, APS forecasted that it would add 3.7 gigawatts (GW) of natural gas in the next 15 years—and only 0.7 GW of renewables. In 2014, they *increased* their forecast for natural gas. Likewise, in 2017, they called for 5.4 GW of natural gas additions by 2032 yet kept their renewable target a mere 0.7 GW—never raising that goal in 5 years.[113] These plans show that the utility does not want to build clean energy—it wants to build and profit off of fossil fuels in the coming decades.

In sharp contrast with the utilities' plans, 100% of new-generation capacity in Arizona in 2014 came from solar energy. It is clear that this growth in clean energy threatened the incumbents since the three big utilities in the state attacked the net metering policies beginning around that time. These opponents were successful, even though new advocates had emerged that vigorously defended the policy. These advocates, who in part were enabled through policy feedback in earlier acting jurisdictions, simply had not developed sufficient political influence to overcome the opponents' attacks and convince politicians to hold the policy in place.

This case also provides an interesting example of how campaign contributions can lead to regulatory capture at low-visibility and low-salience elected institutions. With few members of the public paying attention, regulated entities battle for which individuals will make it through the primary and eventually win the election. This can lead to partisan polarization, if interest groups back candidates that agree with their interests. The same dynamic has occured in Michigan, where the private utility Consumers Energy spent $43 million on political donations in recent years.[114] Similarly to APS, this utility was able to unseat a vocal critic by spending heavily in a primary race.

In Arizona, the commission became increasingly captured over time, as a result of interest groups intervening in elections. When interest groups play a central role in getting a politician elected, that person may feel a debt. Many commissioners were interested in implementing the utility's vision. For example, the chair of the commission violated rules, meeting one-on-one with APS's CEO in periods when major decisions were being made on clean energy. Overall, the ACC largely abdicated its responsibility to investigate the proposed policy changes, outsourcing the workshops to the utility and to ratepayer advocates and never undertaking an evidentiary hearing on the issue themselves. Overall, the regulator did not fulfill its constitutional role.

Although solar companies attempted to counteract the utilities' influence, they were outmatched in money spent on elections, on advertising, and on campaigns. The in-state solar groups were fractured and poorly organized, in part because their main sources of revenue—solar incentives—were eliminated in 2013. APS would drive further wedges into the solar advocates' coalition by casting California billionaires and out-of-state solar companies as trying to impose their policies on Arizona.[115]

The case also shows how policy feedback can spillover into other jurisdictions. Out-of-state solar groups, bolstered through laws in early acting states like California, had resources to spend in Arizona to defend solar policy. They were able to hire experienced lawyers and public relations firms to craft a public and regulatory campaign to resist net metering fees. They attempted to expand the scope of conflict, bringing the public into a debate before and after key elections. Still: they were outspent by the utilities, perhaps as much as 20 times in the 2014 election. After this pivotal year, the advocates had lost the war.

Since this time, utilities' resistance to clean energy has continued. In 2018, Californian billionaire Tom Steyer saw an opportunity to push for increased renewable energy in the state.[116] Steyer's group, NextGen Climate Action, led a ballot initiative to fast-track both the amount of renewables and the timeline for the state's RPS. Proposition 127 would have required utilities to generate 50% of their electricity from renewable sources by 2030. Raising more than $26 million to pass the measure, NextGen Climate attempted to marshal support in Arizona. As usual, the advocates were outspent. Pinnacle West, APS's parent corporation, contributed nearly $40 million to the opposition campaign. Yet funding was not the only challenge that advocates faced. The Arizona Attorney General's office added language to the measure that highlighted the proposal's costs. These actions "raised eyebrows" among officials with the Secretary of State's office.[117] Here, again, we could reasonably believe that APS had influenced this decision. As advocates noted, in 2014 APS had spent millions in ads against Attorney General Brnovich's opponent.[118] With this language and with the greater spending by opponents, the measure failed by a wide margin of nearly 70% to 30%.[119] In addition to having more financial resources, APS continues to have influential allies across the Arizona government.

In the future, Arizona will likely continue to build solar capacity because the costs have now declined to the point that it is economically competitive with other energy sources. However, the utilities are more likely to build this technology at grid scale or take over from solar leasing companies as residential customers' solar brokers. As Chapter 3 demonstrated, utilities are very slow to change and are poor innovators. Empowering these opponents to lead the development of solar energy is unlikely to create significant innovation, speedy deployment, or dispersed assets. It is notable that APS has millions of dollars to run ads against solar but not enough money to pay for the costs of solar. Instead, the utilities will continue to concentrate wealth as monopolistic rent-seekers and will likely deploy far less capacity than solar leasing companies would. Further, given all the ways APS has attempted to influence its regulator to cut renewable energy requirements, it would be naive to suppose that the utility would prove the best pathway to Arizona's clean energy future.

8

When the Fog of Enactment Lifts

Utilities Drive Rapid Retrenchment of Ohio's Renewable Energy Laws

In some cases, opponents can stymie policy with the potential for feedback before it has had an opportunity to grow advocates. Ohio's clean energy laws represent a case where opponents drove policy retrenchment so rapidly that feedback never strengthened advocates. As one of the last states to enact a clean energy target, Ohio's legislature was slow to act. While advocates had pushed for a renewable portfolio standard (RPS) for several years, it was only when a new Democratic governor took office in 2007 that they found success. Advocates packaged a clean energy goal as part of a large electricity restructuring law—as also occurred in Texas and many other states. This law should have driven growth in clean energy companies. But unlike Texas, there was concerted resistance to the policy from the beginning.

By the time Ohio acted, opponents had seen these laws' consequences in other states. They had learned that it was in their interest to resist clean energy targets more forcefully—and sooner. Consequently, there was much less uncertainty among opponents that an RPS would harm their bottom line. During the enactment process, utilities and large energy consumers worked to strip the policy of its teeth, removing binding targets and timetables. In this form, the bill passed the Senate. Without interim targets, advocates opposed the bill, and it seemed poised to fail. However, the Republican House Speaker took up the issue. In a broad negotiation, he reinserted a timetable for binding renewable energy targets and added a cost cap to the policy. In addition to passing an RPS, Ohio's law created significant targets for energy efficiency as well as nuclear and clean coal technologies. The fact that the clean energy target included coal showed the clout the opponents maintained—very few states counted fossil fuels in their RPS goals. Still, in 2008, Ohio looked like it was ready to begin the transition away from coal.

Short Circuiting Policy. Leah Cardamore Stokes, Oxford University Press (2020). © Oxford University Press.
DOI: 10.1093/oso/9780190074265.001.0001

However, when the clean energy targets were implemented, opponents continued to resist. At the Public Utility Commission of Ohio (PUCO), they argued that the cost cap should be interpreted in a way that would require no new renewable energy to be built.[1] The opponents were weaponizing ambiguity, arguing that legislators intended a much stricter cost limitation for the policy. This tactic was similar to the strategy used in Texas to resist solar energy targets' implementation (Chapter 5). However, because Ohio held broader negotiations over the bill—including advocates and executive branch staff in the process—there was much less uncertainty about legislative intent. Thus, this tactic to resist implementation failed. Instead, the policy went into effect with binding targets, and renewable energy began to grow in the state.

However, opponents—including utilities and industrial energy users—continued attacking the law. By 2010, a mere two years after Ohio passed its first goal, renewable energy rollbacks were on the national agenda. Conservative anti-environment groups leading the effort included the American Legislative Exchange Council (ALEC) and the Energy & Environment Legal Institute.[2] These groups, which act through networks that cross state borders, decided to target Ohio. They issued anti-renewables reports and tried to pass a model bill that would repeal the RPS.

By 2011, retrenchment was firmly on the agenda in Ohio's legislature. Both the House and Senate were Republican-controlled, and John Kasich (R) had begun his first term as governor. While the first two repeal efforts failed, in 2014 the Republican leadership decided the rollback was a priority. The opponents had succeeded in polarizing the issue along partisan lines.[3] The repeal bill (SB 310) proposed freezing the targets, which would render the policy useless.

Both advocates and opponents tried to strategically shape and communicate public opinion to the legislature. But, in this case, the opponents were more effective. Without sufficient time for the first bill to catalyze new actors, the advocates remained politically much weaker than the incumbent opponents. While advocates tried to oppose the bill through a public campaign, they were outmatched. The opponents, by contrast, brought in out-of-state groups to make hundreds of thousands of phone calls right before a crucial vote and to field biased public opinion polls. In addition to the direct policy retrenchment, opponents succeeded in passing another, under the radar change that dramatically undermined wind energy in Ohio. In a budget bill rider, the legislature increased the necessary distance between wind energy projects and property lines. This low-profile change all but halted the wind industry in the state.

When the policy went back into effect, after the two year freeze was over, the opponents continued attacking the law. They passed another bill in 2016 that would have extended the freeze for two more years, but the Governor vetoed it. Meanwhile, the utilities began to seek bailouts for their struggling coal and nuclear plants. While the PUCO approved this funding, its decisions were overturned through the courts and the Federal Energy Regulatory Commission (FERC). But this did not dissuade the opponents. The utilities invested millions in the 2018 elections to get the bailouts and the clean energy repeal through the legislature.

In 2019, Ohio passed a bill (HB 6) that bailed out several coal and nuclear plants while gutting the state's RPS and efficiency policies. Ohio's clean energy and energy efficiency laws had saved the state billions, and helped to clean up the state's dirty air (Dimanchev et al. 2019). But these benefits were cast aside in favor of the utilities' financial interests. While the advocates attempted to overturn the bill through a referendum, the opponents mounted a significant and potentially illegal counter campaign. Ultimately, the advocates were unsuccessful in keeping Ohio's clean energy laws in place. Consequently, Ohio's grid has barely begun the transition away from fossil fuels—in 2018, the state was forty-eighth in the nation for renewable energy, with only 2% of its grid from renewables.

The Ohio case shows that opponent interest groups, working through conservative and business networks across the states, can stymie feedback before it has a chance to take hold. Given that interest groups learn from other states, they are more certain about policy consequences in late-acting states. In cases where policies undermine their interests, opponents will attack quickly. Apart from directly lobbying and building influence with legislators, opponents can also drive polarization. In Ohio, fossil fuel–dependent utilities and industries worked over several years to erode Republican support for clean energy. These long-standing industries maintained a large lobbying staff and much greater influence than the newly formed and poorly resourced advocates. In these ways, interest group opponents can block progress on clean energy.

Ohio's Coal-dominated Energy History

While Ohio may not be the first state that comes to mind for fossil fuel dependence, it has a long history with coal. Until the early 1970s, coal dominated Ohio's electricity system because of the state's large reserves.[4] Today, it relies heavily on imports from West Virginia, consuming twice as much coal as it produces.[5] The four large private utilities in the state are all wedded to coal: American Electric Power (AEP) Ohio, Duke Energy, FirstEnergy (later FirstEnergy Solutions and Energy Harbor), and Dayton Power & Light Company (DP&L). Unsurprisingly, these fossil fuel–dependent utilities are hostile to renewable energy technologies. Abundant and cheap fossil fuels also helped grow heavy industry and manufacturing in Ohio.[6] As is the case in Texas (Chapter 5), these companies that consume large amounts of energy have similarly proven important clean energy opponents.[7] Although Ohio has begun to move away from fossil fuels, it is a slow transition with significant resistance from the utilities and large energy consumers. Even in 2015, 8 of the 10 largest power plants in Ohio were coal.[8]

This significant reliance on coal has led to environmental and health problems in the state. In the early 1970s, efforts to reduce air pollution focused on switching from coal to natural gas in the electricity sector. However, during the energy crisis natural gas prices rose and little fuel switching occurred (Hirsh 1999a). Given the state's ongoing reliance on coal, federal environmental policies have been particularly challenging for Ohio. Since 1990, when the federal Clean Air Act Amendments passed, urban areas in the state have struggled to meet national air quality standards.[9] Over the years, Environmental Protection Agency (EPA) rules and regulations have forced many coal-fired power plants in Ohio to retire. As a result of federal regulations, by 2014, Ohio had the most coal plant retirements planned or finished of any state—14% of the total US retirements.[10] Proposed changes to regulations on ozone and carbon under the Obama administration would have resulted in even more closures. Environmental policy had finally started to catch up with Ohio's polluting industries. By 2014, utilities in the state were hostile to government interventions that could further undermine their facilities' profitability.

In addition to a heavy reliance on coal, the state has two nuclear plants. Both of these plants were expensive to construct, with significant cost overruns. Built in the 1970s and 1980s, the Perry Nuclear Generating Station is one of the most expensive nuclear power plants ever built—costing $6 billion.[11] The other nuclear project, the Davis-Besse plant, suffered significant incidents and near accidents. By the 2000s, Ohio had begun investing in natural gas.[12] With the growth in hydraulic fracturing after 2011, natural gas usage grew dramatically.[13] The state's resources include the Marcellus Shale, which stretches from New York through Ohio and West Virginia, and the recently discovered Utica Shale (Gold 2014). Located in eastern Ohio, Utica was hailed as one of the "biggest discoveries in US history" in 2011, with an estimated worth between $15 and $20 billion (Gold 2014). In 2008, natural gas provided only around 2% of the state's supply; but by 2013, it jumped to 15%, and by 2018, it was up to 34%.[14] As fracking continues to expand, natural gas will likely contribute a growing share of the state's energy mix. This is a problematic trend: while natural gas is cleaner than coal, it still exacerbates climate change. Hence, Ohio has simply switched from one fossil fuel to another, rather than beginning the transition to clean energy.

Ohio Narrowly Enacts a Clean Energy Law

Compared to many other states, even those with a similar reliance on fossil fuels, Ohio was a late actor on clean energy policy. With a significant manufacturing sector, there were already renewable energy companies operating in the state before any clean energy law passed. These companies, like Toledo-based First Solar, were supplying technology to earlier-acting states. In 2005, a loose coalition called "Ohio Advanced Energy" began pushing for a renewable energy target. The group included First Solar as well as wind companies from Ohio's northeast and the Cleveland Foundation. Soon, out-of-state interest group networks, that had grown from earlier policies passed elsewhere, joined the growing coalition—including the American Wind Energy Association (AWEA) and the Solar Energy Industries Association (SEIA).[15] However, Republican governor Bob Taft was in office. Despite the significant renewable energy jobs that already existed in Ohio, he did not have any interest in advancing renewable energy policy. During his tenure, the coalition made little progress in getting the issue onto the agenda. The House and Senate were also Republican-controlled and disinterested. This is somewhat surprising since many Republicans were champions of clean energy at that time. But in Ohio, coal was the fuel of choice, and this long-standing industry retained strong relationships with policymakers.

When then Democratic congressional representative Ted Strickland ran for governor in 2006, the advocates saw an opportunity. Strickland had worked on energy issues while serving on the House Energy and Commerce Committee in Congress. The coalition approached his campaign, and he was receptive to the idea of an RPS. Far from an empty campaign promise, once elected, Governor Strickland appointed Mark Shanahan to lead his energy portfolio in 2007. Shanahan was a bureaucrat with a history of working on environmental policy. He had served as director of the Ohio Air Quality Development Authority since 1989. He was also a vocal critic of Ohio's coal-centric utility sector. In his new role in the administration, Shanahan began work on passing an RPS.

The administration's efforts were bolstered by ongoing conflict over how to deregulate the electricity sector. Ohio had struggled to transition to a competitive electricity market. In 2008, the law required new legislation on the issue, before utilities' plans expired at the PUCO. This pressure on the legislature to enact landmark energy legislation provided an opportunity for the governor to articulate a new vision for Ohio's coal-dominated electricity system. On August 29, 2007, Governor Strickland gave a speech at the Toledo Chamber of Commerce where he outlined his "Energy, Jobs, and Progress" plan. He was interested in promoting clean energy but in a cost-effective way and with a broader definition than just "renewables." Concerned that wind and solar could raise rates, given the experience of early-acting states, the governor made it clear that he did not want this outcome because it would harm the state's manufacturing sector. He also argued that new job creation in Ohio could come from supporting renewable and "advanced" energy sources. The latter included clean coal, advanced nuclear, and co-generation. In this way, the governor showed some deference to the incumbent coal industry and the utilities. The speech also emphasized the need for reinvestment in Ohio's electricity infrastructure, an energy efficiency target, and net metering. Given the staid nature of Ohio's electricity sector over the prior 100 years, his ambition to radically alter the system cannot be overstated. Governor Strickland even called on Ohio to address global warming through emissions reporting and to work on carbon sequestration and clean coal. He was clearly signaling to the coal-wedded utilities that change was coming.

The legislature responded to this broad agenda by introducing a bill in late 2007 (SB 221). At the time, both the House and Senate were Republican-controlled. Senator Bob Schuler, a Republican from Cincinnati, sponsored the bill. He was a long-serving politician and a former chair of the Senate's Energy & Public Utilities Committee. He had received his largest corporate campaign contributions from FirstEnergy, Ohio's third-largest utility, in the last election.[16] Thus, it was perhaps unexpected that he would champion renewables and energy efficiency. But this would be his last term in office, meaning the repeated game of donor and candidate was over for Senator Schuler (Powell 2012). The fact that he would not have to seek campaign contributions again likely reduced the utilities' influence with the senior senator.

While the bill focused on restructuring, it also addressed the governor's priorities. It contained a clean energy goal, reforms to net metering, and a unique energy efficiency goal. The energy efficiency resource standard (EERS) was modeled after an RPS. Each year, it required a percentage increase in efficiency. Private utilities would have to comply by modestly increasing their energy savings by 0.3% in the first year and 2% in the final year. The clean energy portion of the bill was called the "alternative energy portfolio standard," with a target of 25% by 2025. It was modeled off of Pennsylvania's RPS—a policy that included a fossil fuel as a "renewable" resource. As a member of the coalition pushing renewable energy policies at that time put it,

> When we looked at other states we profiled more like Pennsylvania. We're not Colorado, we're not Vermont. There was a prevailing sense that clean coal was going to be an important part of the energy mix and fracking hadn't hit yet. And people said nuclear is emissions free and we have a couple nuke plants and maybe we want to continue to do that. So the governor's office said we want a two-tiered system.[17]

Thus, the policy split the clean energy target in two: half would come from re-newable energy resources and the other half from advanced energy resources, including clean coal and nuclear. Initially, the legislation directed the PUCO to determine the specific interim targets. As often occurs when administrative dis-cretion is granted, this strategy was likely chosen to provide the legislature with political cover (Huber & Shipan 2002). It would also allow administrators, who understood the policy in greater detail, to design the specifics.

However, opponent utilities were wise to take note of the risk in this ap-proach. They knew that granting discretion to the bureaucrats could open them up to stronger targets if they had less influence at the PUCO compared to the legislature. The opponents pushed to rewrite the bill to eliminate the bureau-cratic discretion. In response, the Senate removed the bill's language directing the PUCO to create interim targets and only left the final RPS target of 25% by 2025. This change increased the ambiguity of the bill's consequences consid-erably. Here we see opponents strategically trying to create a fog during enact-ment, giving them leverage to try to undermine the law's implementation.

From the advocates' perspective, the lack of interim targets would render the bill voluntary, allowing the utilities to delay procuring renewables. The opponents could later lobby the legislature to change the bill, claiming the targets were impossible to meet. In such a future negotiation, there would be fewer crit-ical issues like restructuring on the table to provide leverage for advocates. And the policy's lack of effectiveness would mean that policy feedback had not begun to nurture new advocates.

The governor and his staff asked the advocates to continue supporting the bill, despite the loss of interim targets; but the coalition refused. According to one renewables lobbyist, "Eliminating the language all together was a problem because it basically made it voluntary. Strickland and Shanahan encouraged us to support that bill and we didn't. So we had a tension where we said you guys, we recognize politically you're doing the best [you can] but we're not going to endorse."[18] Regardless of the lack of support from the clean energy advocates, the bill passed the Senate unanimously, 32 to 0, on October 31, 2007.

At this point, the advocates believed the proposed RPS would do very little for Ohio. In response, Republican representative Jim McGregor introduced a new stand-alone RPS bill in February 2008 (HB 487). McGregor had an avid in-terest in the environment, having worked for a decade at the Ohio Department of Natural Resources before serving as a mayor for nearly two decades. He was also very concerned about energy independence. Given his record, he was assigned the chair of a new and ultimately short-lived committee, the Committee on Alternative Energy. But, Representative McGregor's bill was assigned to a different and less sympathetic committee—the House Public Utilities' Committee—where it made little progress. The RPS seemed doomed to failure, with the advocates struggling to influence the legislature to pass a binding, ambitious target.

Early in 2008, however, Republican House Speaker Jon A. Husted decided to strengthen SB 221's renewable energy provisions. With Husted's leadership, the House put the interim benchmarks back into the bill. It also added a solar carve-out of 0.5% by 2025, with interim targets. Finally, to boost job creation in Ohio, the bill included a requirement that at least half of the renewable energy target be met with in-state resources. All of these provisions strengthened the bill's ambition and its likely impact. As the Texas case showed (Chapter 5), without a solar-specific target, the bill would not drive any new solar investment. Including the in-state requirement would help ensure that Ohio gained some of the benefits from job creation. These provisions would also help with policy feedback: creating new jobs in the state could strengthen the clean energy advocates, helping to guard against future retrenchment attempts. With these changes, advocates changed their position and supported the bill.[19]

Likely, Speaker Husted had several motivations for strengthening the bill's renewable energy provisions. Some actors involved in the negotiations believe that Husted was interested in running for higher, statewide office. Husted would go on to run for and win a position in the state Senate and later become secretary of state—a position he won narrowly.[20] In 2019, he became the lieutenant governor. As House Speaker, he was looking to prepare a résumé to bolster his chances in these races. Given that Ohio is a swing state, appearing bipartisan would help his case. He may have been interested in being able to claim he was a "job creator." As one advocate said,

> I think [Husted] was intrigued by the possibilities this new industry could bring. And he accepted that renewable energy costs were a little more, but falling. And I think he liked the politics. There was this chess match and he triangulated and got to [Democratic governor] Strickland's left on renewables and so he had us as an industry saying, "This is awesome." And all the environmental groups thought "We love Husted."[21]

Of course, Husted would face opposition from the utilities if he tried to strengthen the bill's renewable energy targets. But in the complex negotiation with the utilities over restructuring, these groups were more focused on other provisions. As was the case with other major electricity reforms, such as Texas's 1999 restructuring law (SB 7), the utilities and large industrial consumers were more focused on other parts of the package. This provided an opportunity to get renewable energy onto the agenda in exchange for making other concessions to electric utilities. Some argue that Husted used the RPS as a tool in the negotiations over the restructuring bill, particularly given FirstEnergy's interests. As one political staffer involved in the negotiations put it,

> My own perspective is that Husted very craftily used his support for renewables and the RPS benchmarks as a negotiating tool to win things the utilities wanted on the rate structure side. For example, how much power the PUCO would have to review the utilities' plans and whether they would have the option to go with either market rates or standard purchase offers. And the reality of that became that all of the green energy folks went along with the RPS agreement. I don't think they ever understood that we were giving up things to FirstEnergy to protect renewables.[22]

Here we see one way the fog of enactment can operate. While advocates and opponents negotiated with politicians on the bill, it was not always clear what provisions were implicitly being exchanged during bargaining. In this case, the quote suggests that the actors with greater political influence—the utilities—had a fuller sense of the negotiation than those with less influence—the renewable energy advocates.

Not all the changes made to the bill in the House improved the clean energy policy's likely efficacy. Although the advocates succeeded in reinstating the interim targets, the House Public Utilities Committee also amended the bill to include a cost cap. A cost cap allows companies to not comply with targets if the policy costs greater than a given amount. If the provision kicks in, it halts the policy's implementation. Cost caps are one way that opponents have tried to weaken a policy, creating a mechanism that can be used during implementation to undermine a law.

Opponents put cost caps on the agenda through their influence with the legislature. Specifically, the private utility FirstEnergy, and an industry association, the Industrial Energy Users of Ohio (IEU-Ohio), pushed for this provision.[23] FirstEnergy Corporation, through its various subsidiaries served around a fifth of Ohio's electricity at the time, primarily through coal and nuclear energy. After bankruptcy, parts of the company would change its name to FirstEnergy Solutions and Energy Habor. The IEU-Ohio was established in 2003 as a network of large industrial companies that spends $3 billion on electricity and natural gas annually.[24] Its members include fossil fuel and other petrochemical companies, with some overlap with the Texas Industrial Energy Consumers, discussed in Chapter 5. The largest members include Air Liquide, Airgas, Marathon Petroleum, and TimkenSteel. The association is influential in part because of these companies' strong roles in the state's economy—collectively, the members employed more than 250,000 people, around 4% of the state's workforce in 2018. IEU-Ohio's then lobbyist, Sam Randazzo, maintained close ties with many Republican legislators working on energy issues. The association would go on to vocally oppose Ohio's energy efficiency standards and argue that they were poorly implemented government mandates. FirstEnergy and IEU-Ohio would prove particularly adept opponents of renewable energy and energy efficiency.

In addition to the cost cap, FirstEnergy was able to convince Ohio legislators that interim targets would be inappropriate for the advanced energy target—the goal for nuclear and clean coal. They argued that it was not possible to incrementally grow the energy supply from nuclear or a carbon capture and sequestration (CCS) plant because these projects were too large, with longer planning horizons. Nuclear could take a decade to permit and build. And clean coal technology did not yet work commercially. The opponents used these facts to successfully argue that advanced resources should only be required by the final policy deadline in 2024. They claimed a long-term target would allow the utilities the time necessary to plan. But it could also create compliance problems if utilities delayed. This change greatly increased ambiguity in the law: with a policy set so far in the future, it was unlikely to bind utilities' short-term behavior. This made the policy's likely consequences much harder to predict. Eventually, this long time horizon would help opponents retrench the clean energy target.

With the compromise reached between the interest group advocates and opponents, the bill made progress. Underscoring the environmental nature of the reform, the bill passed the Ohio House unanimously on Earth Day—April 22, 2008. Clearly, Republican Speaker Husted was aiming to make an environmental statement. In its modified form, when the bill went to a floor vote the next day in the Senate, it passed unanimously. Ohio had successfully adopted a landmark clean energy goal. What this law meant, however, was not yet clear.

Implementing Ohio's Energy Targets

Once enacted, the law went to the PUCO for implementation. As commonly occurs, ambiguity gave the regulatory agency significant latitude in how to interpret the law. Interest groups would get another opportunity to battle over clean energy policy. Both the advocates and opponents intervened extensively at PUCO on the renewable energy target. Significant conflict occurred over the cost cap—the provision added in the House in response to pressure from electric utilities and large energy consumers. The language in the law stated that utilities need not comply if the "reasonably expected cost of that compliance exceeds its reasonably expected cost of otherwise producing or acquiring the requisite electricity by three per cent or more." It was not clear how this provision would be interpreted during implementation.

Opponents wanted the law interpreted in a way that would undermine clean energy. The utilities and large energy consumers argued that if renewables cost 3% more than conventional sources, utilities need not comply. This interpretation would mean that *zero* renewable energy projects would be built for the forseeable future—the technologies were still declining in cost and just starting to become competitive with polluting fossil fuels that did not have to pay for their externalities. In effect, the opponents were arguing that it was the legal intent of the legislators to create a *voluntary* policy. Given voluntary clean energy goals' effectiveness in other states, this would have resulted in no progress on renewables. A very similar argument was used by the same kind of opponents in Texas to block their solar law's implementation.

However, advocates, including the renewable energy coalition and the governor's staff, argued that the clause meant that renewables procurement could not raise the *total* cost of the utilities' electricity supply by more than 3%. They argued that the lawmakers' intent was to spur new investments into renewables.[25] Eventually, the PUCO decided in the advocates' favor—they agreed that the legislature had intended to create a binding clean energy goal. It likely helped that a PUCO staff member was present at the final bill negotiations. According to the staffer involved in interpreting the language at the commission, "Ohio doesn't have a cap on a technology basis or utility or system wide basis. . . . That is in the original statute. [We looked at] primarily the intended language. And that was used in other states as well."[26] That staffer's direct involvement in the bill negotiations undermined the opponents' ability to create uncertainty about the enactment process and thereby weaken the policy during implementation. Additionally, the state residential utility consumer advocate, the Ohio Consumers' Counsel, backed up the advocates. According to someone who worked there at that time, "When I was [at the Ohio Consumers' Counsel], we were a strong advocate for our clients and we fought hard for them and part of what we brought was 221 and we advocated that very strongly and the utility companies did not like that."[27] By contrast, in Texas, no advocates or regulators were involved when the final bill with the solar carve-out was negotiated.

The advocates won this implementation fight. The law now had the potential to create positive policy feedback. New industries and projects could develop in Ohio, as had occurred with other states after they implemented their clean energy targets. These industries would bring in revenues for rural, conservative districts. And Republicans might find themselves supporting renewable energy policy expansion in Ohio—just as Texas Republicans did in 2005, when they invested heavily in wind energy infrastructure and doubled down on their clean energy target.

In Ohio, the first attempt to expand the state's goal came in 2010 when a bill was proposed to create property tax exemptions for advanced and renewable energy projects (SB 232).[28] Legislators hoped these tax benefits would help spur new energy projects. The law passed. With these supportive policies in place, new renewable energy capacity started to develop in Ohio. In 2010, the utilities met their first target of 0.5% of the electricity mix from renewable energy sources. The state had doubled its renewable energy installed capacity in a mere 2 years.[29] Policy feedback was starting to take hold.

However, other indicators suggested that there was growing resistance to the state's clean energy laws. While the utilities made the overall renewable energy target in 2010, they missed the solar energy requirements by 10%.[30] Solar, while more popular, remained very expensive—particularly in this northern state. In addition, some members of the public began to push back against wind energy. Wind is the most viable renewable energy resource in Ohio (Jacobson et al. 2014). However, wind was not built as fast as in Ohio as in comparable states, like Kansas, because of local resistance from homeowners and citizens. To give a sense of scale, in 2014 there were 11 anti-wind groups in Ohio compared to 5 in Kansas.[31] These anti-wind activists began to work closely with legislators, most notably Senate Republican William "Bill" Seitz, to try to make wind energy even harder to build.[32] For example, Tom Stacy and his group Save Western Ohio have been influential with politicians. His organization has also received funding from fossil fuel organizations.[33] As a consultant with the fossil fuel–funded think tank the Institute for Energy Research, Stacy drafted a number of studies on the cost of wind that have since been challenged yet were lauded by Seitz.[34] By allying with fossil fuel interests, these anti-wind groups were strengthening their resources and ties to Ohio politicians.

Meanwhile, the utilities delayed planning for their long-term, advanced energy targets. This other half of the state's energy goals required nuclear and coal with CCS to supply 12.5% of the grid by 2024. Unsurprisingly, given national trends, it was difficult for the state to develop either technology. Since 2008, no new coal plants were being built anywhere in the United States—let alone expensive CCS plants. Cheap natural gas had made coal uneconomic. By 2009, one of Ohio's main utilities, AEP Ohio, had started a CCS experiment at a West Virginian plant on the Ohio border.[35] But the results showed how difficult and expensive the technology would be, and the utility halted the project unexpectedly in July 2011. Nuclear power also remained very difficult to site, permit, and build across the United States. Building nuclear would likely be even more difficult in Ohio, given the state's history with the technology being both expensive and accident-prone (Ghosh & Apostolakis 2005).[36] Overall, the advanced energy targets were proving difficult.

The law's energy efficiency requirements also hit implementation snags, bolstering policy opponents' arguments. Not only did the utilities loathe the PUCO telling them what to do but large industrial consumers who were less familiar with such government oversight resented their mandated efficiency targets. To comply, industrial consumers had to either pay the utility or fund efficiency projects themselves. These opponents believed these requirements should be eliminated for a number of reasons: they were unnecessary or impossible; projects were not ideal for their business needs; and, paying the utility would help their competitors. Their frustration increased once the *easy* energy efficiency savings were exhausted. Adding to their complaints, the policy was implemented in a complex way that struck the opponents as unfair. Rather than counting how much energy was saved—kilowatt hours (kWh) reduced—the PUCO created benchmarks, and only reductions *below* these levels would count. As one representative for the industrial energy users put it,

> The[re were] lunatic decisions that were made on how to count things on energy efficiency. Instead of counting the actual amount of kWh reduction they created a hypothetical benchmark and then [reductions] counted below that. This convention is nowhere in the law, and in fact, it violates the law. And the effect was to elevate the compliance obligation.[37]

Here, we see clearly an opponent arguing that there was a difference in how the law was written and how it was later interpreted. As a result of this implementation decision, electric utilities found it difficult to comply with and profit off of the energy efficiency standards. Consequently, they wanted to eliminate the targets altogether. By contrast, smaller industrial and manufacturing companies, affiliated through the Ohio Manufacturers' Association (OMA), supported the policies because it provided funds to reduce their costs from upgrading to efficient technology.[38] These companies had less capital to invest without government support. Thus, the way the law was implemented created some advocates—those benefiting financially from the program—but also strong opponents. By the end of 2010, resistance to all three clean energy targets was growing.

Networked Opponents Target Ohio's Clean Energy Laws for Retrenchment

Ohio's renewable energy, energy efficiency, and advanced energy targets were all facing significant implementation resistance. These policies threatened the coal industry and found opposition from industrial energy users. The backlash also occurred more swiftly because Ohio was a later actor in clean energy. By 2010, opponents had learned from clean energy laws implemented in other states. Across the country, electric utilities, large industrial corporations, and other fossil fuel companies began to strategize on how to resist these policies. Through ALEC, model bills were developed to repeal RPS policies in 2011, with the first bill circulated in 2012.

When these groups began targeting Ohio, they drew on ideas from ALEC and other right-wing networks. In 2011, the American Tradition Institute—now called the Energy & Environment Legal Institute (E&E Legal)—commissioned an anti-RPS report. E&E Legal is an anti-environment organization best known for harassing climate scientists. It received funding from fossil fuel corporations, including prominent coal companies like Peabody Energy and Arch Coal. This organization works across state lines, issuing reports attacking clean energy targets, and was involved in the legal challenge to Colorado's RPS law. In the Ohio case, the Beacon Hill Institute—a right-wing think tank—wrote the E&E Legal–funded report.[39] The report argued that the state's clean energy targets would cost ratepayers several billion dollars and result in job losses.[40] Of course, this report did not consider the health or climate costs of continuing to burn poisonous coal energy (Dimanchev et al. 2019). Instead, it considered the costs of climate action. Importantly, ALEC sent this report to all of the members of the Ohio legislature in April 2011, seeding the idea of repealing the law. There is some indication it worked. Reports that overstate the costs of renewable energy have led to significant misunderstanding among politicians. For example, in one interview in late 2014, an Ohio politician stated that wind energy would cost 22 ¢/kWh in the state.[41] In fact, Ohio wind projects were built around 4.3 ¢/kWh in 2013 (Wiser & Bolinger 2014)—five times cheaper than this politician estimated. These opponents were working through their networks to try to directly influence legislators with ideas—and their message was getting through.

Just 5 months later, in late 2011, efforts began in the Ohio legislature to retrench the state's clean energy targets. It was an attempt to stop the state from transitioning away from fossil fuels, which supplied 89% of the electricity sector that year.[42] Senator Kris Jordan, a relatively junior member from central Ohio, introduced the first repeal bill (SB 216). In 2010, Senator Jordan was listed as a member of ALEC's Energy, Environment and Agriculture Task Force. Unsurprisingly, the bill closely resembled ALEC's model legislation, "The Electricity Freedom Act."[43] This is in line with what Alexander Hertel-Fernandez (2014) has found—it is often junior members who lack capacity for independent policy generation who introduce ALEC model bills. But this first bill did not pass or even make it to the floor for a vote.[44]

Instead, Ohio seemed poised to expand its clean energy laws, through positive feedback. In September 2011, the newly elected Republican Governor

John Kasich held an energy summit where he discussed tweaking the advanced energy targets to focus on co-generation—an easier technology to build than clean coal or nuclear. Essentially, co-generation involves large industrial companies hosting power generation on site and using the steam byproduct for other purposes like heating. This method saves significant cost and energy, and through it, reduces pollution. Governor Kasich also made several statements at the summit signaling his support for wind and solar, saying that working on these technologies is "the pursuit of the future" and "our commitment to them shouldn't waiver despite the fact that their costs aren't yet where we want them to be."[45] The clean energy industry expected policy expansion or at least stability.

In response to the Governor's speech, in 2012, the legislature passed a new bill that made co-generation an eligible technology for the advanced energy target (SB 315). While there were ample opportunities during this policy revision to change or rollback the renewables requirements, the bill left those provisions intact. The bill passed both the House and the Senate easily, with wide margins, and the Governor signed it into law. This decision looked like a re-endorsement of the clean energy law in Ohio under a new Republican governor. According to one person working in the clean energy industry, "There was a sense that Kasich wouldn't change the policy going forward and people got into the market in a bigger way at that point in time."[46]

Despite this positive change to Ohio's clean energy policies, the retrenchment attempts continued in 2013. This time, the opponents had a far more seasoned and persistent political champion: Republican Senator Bill Seitz, a member of the board of ALEC, chair of the Senate Public Utilities Committee, and friend to anti-wind groups. In February 2013, Senator Seitz introduced a repeal bill (SB 58). Despite voting for the 2008 bill that established the clean energy targets, by 2011 Seitz had become the most vocal opponent of renewables in the legislature. He now worked diligently to get rid of Ohio's renewable energy "mandates."[47] Seitz, who would build up a reputation as a staunch opponent of renewables, once suggested, "We're not prepared to continue our march up State Mandate Mountain."[48] He also had strong ties to the utilities, having received significant campaign contributions from FirstEnergy and AEP from 2006 onward.[49] AEP's support for Seitz jumped sevenfold from 2008 to 2012, over the same time when he began working on the repeal effort.[50] More broadly, all the utilities increased their contributions to politicians after 2008. According to Innovation Ohio, Ohio's four electric utilities made about $2.7 million in political contributions between 2008 and 2013.[51]

Much like in Texas, this tight relationship between the legislature and interest group opponents gave electric utilities and fossil fuel corporations a direct line to legislators. In Ohio, the opponents gained a seat at a private table where the plan to repeal the RPS was being drafted. Specifically, in the summer of 2013, Senator

Seitz held several private meetings with opponents at his law office, offsite from the Capitol.[52] IEU-Ohio and several utilities—most likely FirstEnergy and AEP—were present at this meeting to develop the specific provisions for a bill that would rollback the clean energy laws. At that time, the utilities wanted to eliminate the energy efficiency standards and gut the RPS. New renewable energy capacity would undercut their ability to argue at the PUCO for long-term power purchase agreements for their uneconomic coal plants, which they had sunk large amounts of debt into. By contrast, advocates had no seat in the negotiations—Seitz did not meet with renewable energy companies or other advocates.

Unlike Senator Jordan's proposal, Senator Seitz's bill (SB 58) was stealthy and smart. It proposed to revise rather than outright repeal the policy. It would also phase out the in-state renewable energy requirement by the end of 2018. Seitz claimed to target this requirement for repeal on two grounds: first, higher costs and, second, concerns over the provision being unconstitutional under the Commerce Clause. As a lawyer, Seitz was particularly adamant that any in-state requirement could be challenged in the courts. Although, in fact, no utility or other party had attempted to do that in Ohio. Importantly, eliminating the in-state requirement would weaken the clean energy advocates growing inside Ohio, breaking the feedback cycle.

In addition, Seitz's bill would allow industrial consumers to opt out of paying for the renewable energy requirements. This move was very similar to what occurred in Texas, allowing big companies to free ride off the public during an expensive energy transition. That said, this first bill was not exclusively hostile to renewables. It also included some provisions that would strengthen or maintain clean energy: it would allow renewables to make up any shortfalls in the 2024 advanced energy target and keep intact the renewables interim targets.

The bill made some progress in the legislature, with significant hearings in the Senate Public Utilities Committee, where Seitz was the chair. Notably, none of the utilities testified, perhaps because they had made their views known to the bill sponsor and committee chair in prior, private meetings.[53] The utilities united to support the bill behind the scenes. By contrast, industrial corporations in the state remained split on the issue. Some heavy industry, organized through the IEU-Ohio and the Ohio Energy Group, supported the bill. But, the OMA opposed it because of the proposed changes to the energy efficiency requirements.[54] The OMA's membership included smaller businesses that supported these programs they provided financial incentives to help them use less energy. This split in the industrial companies likely contributed to the bill's failure—the opponents were not presenting a united front. Further, the renewable energy advocates actively opposed the bill, drumming up significant press. Eventually, the Republicans caucused and decided not to move forward with the it. The advocates had won this battle—but the war would continue.

Opponents Drive Partisan Polarization on Clean Energy and Succeed in Retrenching Ohio's Law

The advocates' success was short-lived, however. The next year, opponents continue to attack Ohio's clean energy laws. They were chipping away, slowly succeeding at driving partisan polarization. In February 2014, the Senate leadership decided that Republican senator Troy Balderson would lead the new bill (SB 310) rather than Senator Seitz. Senator Balderson was from eastern Ohio, where there are significant coal resources. He was also the chair of the Energy and Natural Resources Committee and vice chair of the Public Utilities Committee. Still, Senator Seitz was very involved in the process. Email records show that Senator Seitz continued to work closely on the bill with several utilities, then lobbyist Sam Randazzo at IEU-Ohio, and anti-wind activists.[55]

The opponents ensured that a number of provisions were written into the new bill that would undercut path dependence. The in-state requirement would be eliminated immediately, rather than at the end of 2018. The advanced energy target would also be cut, rather than letting renewables make up for any shortfall, as the prior bill had allowed. The bill proposed specific line items for renewables and energy efficiency on customers' bill, making the costs more visible to the public. This was an effort to expand the scope of conflict. Opponents likely thought they could use these line items to encourage customers to blame renewables for their rising electricity bills, sowing the seeds for retrenchment. Most importantly, the initial bill drafts proposed permanently freezing the policy, meaning that unless another vote occurred to restart the policy, it would stay repealed.[56] Such a change would stop policy feedback in its tracks, choking Ohio's nascent renewable energy industry. But in more subtle ways, the other proposed changes would disrupt feedback—without a requirement for in-state generation, there would likely be fewer in-state advocates pushing to keep the policy in the future.

In the lead-up to the vote in the legislature, interest group advocates and opponents both brought the public into the policy conflict. One astroturfing group calling itself "Ohioans for Sustainable Jobs," supported rolling back the RPS. This strategy of naming groups to intentionally mislead citizens on the nature of the campaign is increasingly common (Walker 2014). Utilities used the same approach in Florida to block a solar energy ballot initiative, through the astroturf group, "Consumers for Smart Solar."[57] In Ohio, the group's members included the Ohio Chamber of Commerce, IEU-Ohio, and the Ohio Energy Group.[58] They commissioned a swiftboating-style poll that asked citizens a leading and vague question on whether the legislature should change its policy given the large shifts in energy and the economy since 2008.[59] With this wording, unsurprisingly, the vast majority of citizens supported the legislature changing the law. Grover Norquist's organization, Americans for Tax Reform, also called over 100,000 Ohioans in the 2 days leading up to the final vote, telling them to support the repeal.[60] Clearly, the opponents believed it was important to bring the public into the conflict over clean energy, to increase their influence with the legislature.

But the advocates also understood the value of drawing the public into the policy conflict as they tried to block the bill. Rather than fielding their own polls, the clean energy advocates highlighted findings from the Yale Project on Climate Change Communication, which showed that majorities of Ohioans wanted the governor, politicians, and businesses to do more on climate change, including strong support for clean energy targets. As this Ohio-specific poll found, "A majority (59%) supports requiring electric utilities to produce at least 20% of their electricity from wind, solar, or other renewable energy sources—even if it costs the average household an extra $100 a year. Comparatively few (35%) would oppose this policy" (Leiserowitz et al., 2013, 7). In this way, the advocates used research to try to demonstrate that there was strong public support for keeping Ohio's clean energy policy.[61]

But in 2013, the Senate leadership decided retrenching the state's clean energy laws was a priority. Senate President Keith Faber likely championed the bill behind the scenes. His district was in rural, western Ohio, and he became the Senate president in January 2013. He maintained strong ties with FirstEnergy and AEP, having received significant campaign funds from these utilities for over a decade.[62] The opponents had the ear of a powerful politician, and he decided to put repeal on the agenda. However, Governor Kasich still supported clean energy. He met with Senate President Keith Faber and requested changes to the bill, including modifying the renewable energy target from a *repeal* to a *freeze*, with an automatic restart after two years. The governor likely implied he would veto the bill if these changes were not made.[63] After this meeting, SB 310 was amended to create a 2-year policy freeze rather than a repeal. During this period, a study committee would investigate the issue and draft new legislation.[64] But this modification hardly reassured the advocates. A study committee would likely be made up of the same politicians who passed the bill. Meanwhile, given policy uncertainty, clean energy businesses in the state would shrink. This would make it easier to repeal the clean energy law two years later, when the freeze concluded.

Arguing that a similar bill had involved significant hearings the year prior, Republicans quickly moved this new bill through the committee *without any testimony*, sending it directly to the Senate floor. This is the same tactic seen federally in 2017 when Republicans rushed bills on healthcare and tax reform to floor votes without hearings. In Ohio, clean energy advocates argued that the lack of hearings on a new bill was unfair. Despite the opposition, SB 310 passed the Senate in early May 2014 by a margin of 21 to 12.

By this point, partisan polarization had grown substantially: only three Republicans voted against the repeal bill. Given that Ohio had struggled to build renewable energy in the state, few rural Republicans saw the benefits it could bring their communities in terms of jobs and local revenue. Several individuals inside and outside of the legislature suggested that the Republican leadership in the Senate leaned heavily on their members to support the bill. As one former political staffer stated, "the Republican caucus used campaign money to get the vote. They threatened to not support them in primaries. Faber said if you don't vote for this bill we will not support your campaign."[65] Why did the Republican leadership do an about-face in a few short years? Likely, interest group opponents had persuaded them to make clean energy retrenchment a high priority. They were using campaign funding to drive polarization on the issue, as similarly occurred in Kansas. But in this case, there was no established renewable energy industry available to field its own political action committee (PAC) to support Republicans willing to break ranks with the party.

After the bill cleared the Senate, there did not initially appear to be enough votes in the House to pass the bill, with the Republican caucus coming up short. A coalition of renewable energy advocates—including the Ohio Advanced Energy Economy along with several consumer advocacy groups—attempted to change the 2-year freeze to a 1-year freeze. The advocates tried a number of strategies to block the bill: fielding a television ad, issuing a report, and getting mayors across the state to sign letters asking the legislature to keep the standards.[66] Businesses represented another prominent coalitional partner, with manufacturers such as Honda and Honeywell fighting for the energy efficiency policies.[67] The wind energy association AWEA, which had a lot to lose from this law, focused its lobbying on changing the legislation to a 1-year freeze.[68] But these efforts failed.

Eventually, the bill passed the House at the end of May 2014, just after the state primary elections were over, by a narrower vote of 55 to 42. Although the vote was largely along party lines, six Republicans opposed the bill and three Democrats supported it. Thus, while partisan polarization had grown, it was not a perfectly sorted issue. But the fact remained that the opponents won. When the bill passed, Senator Seitz was quick to point out to the advocates in a public memo that by failing to support his bill the year prior (SB 58), they had ended up with a worse outcome (SB 310).[69] Advocates lobbied the governor to veto the legislation. For example, the national Evangelical Environmental Network delivered a petition with more than 14,000 signatures.[70] But the advocates did not succeed in influencing Kasich's decision. He signed the law in June 2014 with a spokesperson from his office stating that it was a "balanced" approach. Ohio was the first state to directly repeal its clean energy policy, through this freeze. After SB 310 passed, Kansas would go on to repeal its binding RPS, and West Virginia its voluntary RPS in 2015. Other states, like North Carolina, New Hampshire, and Colorado fended off retrenchment attempts during the same time period.

But the opponents did not rest satisfied with this result. They came back to attack the policy in another, less overt way. That same year, Ohio made a second, lower-profile change to its clean energy policy through a House budget bill (HB 483). As is typically the case, it covered a variety of topics. Unusually, the bill included a provision that changed the required distance from a wind turbine to a property line—the so-called setback rule. A setback is a zoning requirement that defines how far a wind turbine has to be from a property line or building. In Ohio, before 2014 the setback rule was 1.1 times the height of the wind turbine to the nearest property line, averaging 550 feet. The 2014 budget bill changed the setback to 1,125 feet from the turbine to the property line. In practice, this would almost triple the distance required, often requiring 1,300 feet from the property line. Under this new policy, almost all of the existing wind projects *could not have been built*. For example, AWEA estimated that under these new rules, the largest wind project in Ohio would only have 12 turbines rather than 152.[71]

Why would a politician add this poison pill to a budget bill? Some believe that Senate President Keith Faber introduced this amendment because of anti-wind protestors in his district.[72] Alternatively, Senator Faber may have seen an opportunity to build his relationship with the utilities and receive greater campaign contributions from FirstEnergy and AEP in future elections.[73] Regardless of the reasons for the Senate president pushing this policy, it was another significant blow to the clean energy advocates. Governor Kasich could have line-item vetoed this provision in the budget bill, as he did with other items that year—but he signed the wind setback into law in June 2014. Signing these two bills suggested that Governor Kasich was not nearly as pro-renewables as he had first appeared. It is possible that utility and industrial interest groups had increased their influence over his office. Utility contributions to Governor Kasich increased from the 2010 elections to the 2014 elections.[74] David Koch himself even gave $12,155 to support Kasich's re-election, just 6 weeks prior to the governor's approval of these bills.[75]

Unsurprisingly, since this law was enacted, wind projects in Ohio have halted. Existing projects with prior approval still moved forward, but they had to proceed more slowly since any project changes would put them under the new rules. According to an AWEA report, this policy has cost the state over $4.2 billion in lost economic activity.[76] This estimate is credible, given that neighboring states like Indiana and Michigan have invested three to four times as much in wind energy. By 2018, only around 1% of Ohio's electricity supply was from wind energy.[77] Short of a new law to change these setback rules, wind energy will remain undeveloped in Ohio.[78] Given that this is likely the best renewable energy resource the state has, this law is extremely problematic for decarbonization.

Together, these two changes to Ohio's renewable energy policies represented a significant policy retrenchment. The interest group opponents had managed to influence legislators, weakening the advocates by directly attacking their industry. As one renewable energy advocate put it at the time, "It's getting close to being death by a thousand cuts. If the RPS resumes [after the study committee] and we can get something on setbacks, which we're working on, we all survive. But, whatever happens on this has to be the end. They've got to leave us alone. You can't keep changing the market rules."[79] The renewable energy industry has suffered job losses since these changes in 2014. By one estimate, more than 1,400 jobs were lost in the wind energy industry between 2015 and 2016, a change attributed to increasing uncertainty in the state's legal framework for renewable energy.[80] Utilities also did little to invest in renewable energy projects in the state, instead buying renewable energy certificates (RECs) from out of state. This meant that few renewables were built. Clearly, policy feedback had failed in Ohio.[81] And unfortunately, the opponents did not leave the advocates alone. The attacks on clean energy only continued.

Utilities Gut Ohio's Clean Energy Laws to Bailout Coal Plants

After the latest law was implemented, the Energy Mandates Study Committee was formed to evaluate Ohio's clean energy laws. Most of the politicians on the committee had voted for the rollback, including senators Seitz and Balderson. The committee members also had strong ties to the opponents, having received over $800,000 in campaign contributions from utilities, and coal, oil and gas companies.[82] As he had done when drafting the repeal bills, Seitz worked closely with industry lobbyists, writing that "[lobbyists and he] should be meeting as a small group to figure out what that [EMSC] report is going to say."[83] He also suggested the report include misinformation on climate science.[84] Unsurprisingly, the final report, delivered in 2015, recommended an indefinite extension of the RPS freeze. The report also exaggerated the costs associated with renewables and omitted many benefits, leaning heavily on research from Koch Industries-funded organizations.[85]

This report fueled further attacks on Ohio's clean energy laws. In 2016, two bills (SB 320 and HB 554) aimed to eliminate or weaken the state's clean energy goals. The usual suspects sponsored these bills, including senators Seitz, Balderson and Faber. Both AEP and FirstEnergy advocated for these bills.[86] Although one bill passed, Governor Kasich vetoed it. In 2017, a bill that would make the renewable targets voluntary passed the House easily (HB 114). The Senate version of that bill compromised with the advocates: it reduced the RPS to 8.5% by 2022, and agreed to reverse some of the wind energy setback restrictions. However, Seitz, who had now become the majority leader in the House, opposed this bill that would have kick-started the wind energy industry.[87] The bill failed to pass out of committee.

While these debates over the state's clean energy laws raged on, utilities began a campaign to bailout their failing coal and nuclear plants. Cheap natural gas had caused wholesale power prices to fall in Ohio's power markets. This made it difficult for some of the utilities' plants to compete. A few coal plants in particular were struggling: the Ohio Valley Electrical Corporation (OVEC) plants, and FirstEnergy's Sammis plant. Originally constructed in the 1950s, OVEC now manages two coal plants in Ohio and Indiana—Kyger Creek and Clifty Creek—with a combined 2.3 gigawatts (GW) of capacity. In 2006, the plants underwent large retrofits so that they could continue operating, taking on $820 million in new debt. This was a common decision at that time, leading many utilities—private and rural electric cooperatives alike—to take on coal debt. Given this investment in the OVEC plants, the utility co-owner signed a contract in 2011 that would keep the plants open until 2040. The contract stipulated that no owner could exit the agreement unless all parties chose to shut down the plants. This created a bind for the owners—the principal owner, AEP, as well as FirstEnergy, which had a smaller stake—when the plant began losing money. These weren't the only plants struggling to turn a profit as cheap natural gas flooded the market. FirstEnergy also operated the 2.2 GW Sammis coal plant and the states' two nuclear plants, which were also losing money.

After making these bad investments, the utilities were stuck with a problem: how would they pay for the debt they had in these plants, while the plants were losing money? Beginning in 2014, both FirstEnergy and AEP requested PUCO approve additional charges for ratepayers to cover their investments that were no longer market-competitive. The IEU-Ohio and the Ohio Consumers' Counsel opposed these efforts.[88] Environmental groups, including the Sierra Club, launched a "No Coal Bailouts" campaign that involved running ads and collecting petition signatures.[89]

Meanwhile, the clean energy opponents began negotiating directly with the advocates, to try to find a deal that the PUCO could approve under a 2008 FERC waiver. FirstEnergy reached an eight-year deal in late 2015 with some stakeholders that would bailout its nuclear plants, and the OVEC and Sammis coal plants. Clean energy advocates opposed this deal, since it would subsidize polluting sources. Around the same time, AEP reached an eight year agreement with the Sierra Club and PUCO staff to exchange a bailout for eventual conversion or closure of the coal plants, and building 900 MW of renewable energy.[90] These agreements worked their way through the PUCO process, and were both approved in early 2016. Many groups opposed these decisions, including other environmental groups and the OMA. Rival generators who wanted to compete in the Ohio market challenged these decisions, requesting that FERC rescind its waiver that allowed these agreements. In April 2016, FERC rescinded the waiver, rejecting these deals on the grounds that they distorted competitive markets.[91]

Instead, in late 2016, PUCO approved a $600 million "distribution modernization rider" for FirstEnergy. While this was funding ostensibly for upgrading the grid, the PUCO imposed no requirements or oversight. The advocates were concerned the money would be used to bailout the utility's coal plants. In response to this decision, environmental and consumer groups took the PUCO to court. In June 2019, the Ohio Supreme Court ruled that FirstEnergy did not have specific plans to modernize the grid and rejected PUCO's decision. Yet the court did not force FirstEnergy to pay back the $440 million in subsidies it had already collected from ratepayers.[92] During this period, FirstEnergy also sought Trump administration support; however, FERC rejected a DOE coal bailout plan in 2018 that would have benefited the utility.[93] Meanwhile, AEP secured a limited bailout through the PUCO for part of the OVEC plants.

With the advocates using the courts and FERC to block or limit the coal bailouts, the utilities continued to try to work with the legislature to secure money for their stranded costs. In 2017, a bill was introduced that would subsidize the OVEC plants (HB 239). The bill's sponsors had received significant campaign contributions from utilities. Further, the sponsors' written testimony to the House Public Utilities Committee matched the content provided by the utilities, suggesting strong influence from the opponents.[94] As usual, Seitz supported the bill. Representatives from AEP, DP&L, Duke Energy, and the Ohio Electric Cooperatives, all testified in support throughout 2017. The advocates, including EDF and the Sierra Club, testified in opposition.[95] This narrow bill, which would only bailout the OVEC plants, failed. Other similar bills also did not make progress. After failing to secure these bailouts, on March 31, 2018, FirstEnergy Solutions, a subsidiary of FirstEnergy that managed its unprofitable generation plants, filed for bankruptcy.

But the clean energy opponents did not stop trying to pass these bailouts. To gain greater influence with the legislature, the utilities worked over many years to build up their relationships with Republican politicians and to change the makeup of the legislature and governor's office. In the lead up to the 2018 election, FirstEnergy Solutions spent at least $2.7 million on lobbyists and PR firms.[96] As part of this effort, the company hired groups with close ties to Mike DeWine, who was running for governor at the time—a position he would win. In the 2018 election, FirstEnergy Solutions gave large campaign contributions to both the Democratic and Republican gubernatorial candidates, spending almost $350,000 on this race alone.[97] Given it was a tight election—only 3.7 points separated the candidates—the company was hedging its bets.

The opponents' bets quickly paid off. Once Governor Mike DeWine took office, he appointed Sam Randazzo—who had worked as a lobbyist for IEU-Ohio for many years to undermine the state's clean energy laws—to be chairman of the PUCO. This role also made him the chair of the Ohio Power Siting Board, which made decisions on wind farms. Previously, Randazzo had represented groups attempting to block wind farms in front of this board.[98] While advocates argued this represented a clear conflict of interest in his nomination, Randazzo nevertheless assumed the role. While Randazzo would be unlikely to approve coal plant bailouts, given his history of advocating for industrial energy consumers, he would no doubt work to undermine the clean energy laws, which he had worked for many years to rollback.

Even more importantly, FirstEnergy Solutions backed Larry Householder in the 2018 elections.[99] At the time, he was a state representative vying for the role of House speaker in a tight race. Here, the utility took an unusual approach to secure their preferred outcome: not only did they support Householder, they also backed all the other House candidates who would support him. It total, the utility gave over $184,000 to more than a dozen representatives who supported his candidacy.[100] The bankrupt company wanted to be sure that they would have the votes necessary to finally pass a bailout for their ailing plants in 2019. And private equity played a role here as well. The hedge funds that had bought these distressed assets likely wanted to ensure they made a profit, regardless of the cost to the climate. As one advocate put it, "the real owners of FirstEnergy Solutions are hedge funds, who are gamblers. They see distressed assets and they put in $60 million into lobbying to get a return for $1 billion [if they get their bailout bill passed.]"[101] This bet would pay off.

After Householder secured the speakership in 2019, the opponents finally found success in gutting the RPS and energy efficiency policies through a new bill (HB 6). This bill took a much broader tack: it would weaken the RPS, eliminate the efficiency standard, make wind energy even harder to build, and bailout the state's ailing nuclear plants. Notably, the nuclear bailouts required no transparency on the part of FirstEnergy Solutions, in terms of what they would be doing with these new ratepayer funds. The company's requested funding and timelines fluctuated continuously, suggesting that perhaps not all the nuclear bailout funds were as necessary as FirstEnergy Solutions claimed. Yet, the legislature showed no interest in ensuring the utility would use the bailout funds for their nuclear plants alone.

Rhetorically, clean energy opponents in the legislature, such as Representative Seitz, argued that they *had to eliminate* the RPS and energy efficiency laws alongside the bailout in order to keep rates the same. It did not matter to the opponents that the efficiency law had likely saved ratepayers $5.1 billion in less that an decade. Since industrial energy consumers opposed it, it had to go.[102] The bill also planned to eliminate the RPS solar carve-out the next year, in 2020. This would kill what little incentive was left to build in-state generation, given that the setback laws had decimated the wind industry. It would choke off the renewable energy companies' funding, breaking the small momentum for renewables in Ohio. The bill also proposed lowering the RPS targets while eliminating any clean energy requirement after 2026. Without an ongoing RPS target, the utilities would not need to build new renewables through long-term contracts: they could just buy cheap RECs to comply for the coming years, and stop after 2026. And in a more subtle way, the bill changed what part of the system had to comply. As one advocate put it: "It is not just that the RPS is reduced from 12.5% to 8.5%. The bill also removes the industrial load from calculating the RPS. With the industrial load comprising about 33% of the load, this means an 8.5% RPS is more like a 5.5% RPS."[103] This was the same approach we saw in Texas (Chapter 5)—industrial energy users were not going to pay their fair share in the energy transition.

The initial bill did not include any funding to bailout the OVEC or Sammis coal plants. With all the benefits flowing to FirstEnergy Solutions, AEP did not support this plan. However, likely because of AEP's lobbying, a new version was introduced that gave generous funding to bailout the OVEC plants. As one journalist put it: "they put in the coal bailout to get AEP, Duke, and DP&L on board. Because AEP when that bill was first filed, their press person said that they were really sort of in opposition to the bill. . . . There's no doubt that this was to bring the utilities on board."[104] With all the utilities in support, the bill began to make swift progress. To make matters worse, the advocates struggled to secure their own lobbyists, even those who had previously worked for them. FirstEnergy Solutions had put them on retainers, even if they were not doing any work.[105] The opponents' goal was to keep the state's best lobbyists tied up, so that they couldn't support the advocates' efforts to kill the coal bailout.

Throughout the process, the clean energy opponents tried to spin the bill as a boon for clean energy. In a truly Orwellian doublespeak, the bill was called the

"Clean Air Program," even while it bailed out coal plants and gutted the RPS and energy efficiency laws. To give themselves cover, the bill contained $140 million for solar—but this modest sum was for plants that had *already been approved*. The funding would drive no additional clean energy. The $1.1 billion for FirstEnergy Solutions' existing nuclear plants was an order of magnitude bigger. How did the coal bailout stack up by comparison? The language made this difficult to esti-mate, because the bill deferred to the PUCO to set the amount that would cover the utilities' losses each year. This ambiguity was no doubt intentional on the part of the legislators and utilities, providing them cover. It was not clear to an-yone how large the coal plant subsidies would end up being—as usual, the fog of enactment was operating.

What is my best estimate for the coal bailout? Notably, the residential monthly charge for the coal plants was almost twice as large as the charge for nuclear and solar. Some analysts argued these coal plant would lose $50–60 million a year, putting the total coal plant subsidies around $600 million by 2030.[106] However, the bill allowed the utilities to carry forward losses and get compensated later. Given the losses that FirstEnergy Solutions was projecting from the OVEC plants in its bankruptcy proceedings, the costs for these two plants could be much higher: around $1.7 billion.[107] And that figure is only for the Ohio private utilities out to 2030. Overall, the OVEC coal plants could lose an estimated $5.3 billion if they continued to operate until their planned retire-ment in 2040.[108] And these figures do not take into consideration the large neg-ative externalities from the plant, through air pollution related deaths or climate impacts (Dimanchev et al. 2019). This bill gave a billion dollar lifeline to an eco-nomic and environmental loser. It was trying to hide a lump of coal inside a giant legislative package that was thinly wrapped in clean energy.

With the coal bailouts in the bill, the House passed it 53 to 43 in a bipartisan vote. However, the utilities had less influence in the Senate, which was not as willing to fund the bailout or support further attacks on wind energy. The Senate lowered the amount that the utilities could collect for their ailing coal plants, and delayed the subsidies for a year. They also rejected the plan to allow townships to block wind energy. With these changes, the bill passed in the Senate by a vote of 19 to 12, again with a bipartisan split on either side.

This version was returned to the House, where Householder scheduled a last minute vote. The bill passed by a narrower margin of 51 to 38 in July 2019. Notably, it would not have become law without support from Democrats. The nine Democrats who voted for the bill in the House included members with ties to FirstEnergy Solutions, from districts near the Sammis coal plant or the nuclear plants. Other supportive Democrats were from districts near AEP's headquar-ters in Akron, Ohio. Further, several unions lobbied in support of the bill, given the existing workforce at the nuclear and coal plants. After a decade of attacks on the clean energy laws, there were few clean energy advocates or jobs in the state to contest these opponents. These Democrats would rather side with the utilities and the unions than nurture a new clean economy, even if it meant subsidies for coal. Just six days after the bill was passed, Governor DeWine signed it into law.

Despite claiming that they would maintain the union contracts at their plants, FirstEnergy Solutions filed a scheduled update to the bankruptcy proceedings just 12 hours after the final bill passed. In this update, the utility walked back their commitment to union contracts, including pensions. Given how closely he was working with FirstEnergy Solutions, it's possible that Speaker Householder rushed the vote, knowing that this bankruptcy update could cost him votes in the House. Union workers such as the International Brotherhood of Electrical Workers and the Teamsters, who supported the bailout bill, were blindsided. As one advocate put it, "The unions got duped, because after they supported the legislation, [FirstEnergy Solutions] said we are going to gut the pensions. So I think the Democrats and the labor unions were duped."[109]

Days after the law was signed, FirstEnergy Solutions also revealed they had cancelled plans to close the Sammis coal plant slated to retire in 2022. While they claimed this was not because of funds from the nuclear bailout, a representative from their company also said, "House Bill Six is really designed to support our nuclear plants, and all the money from that would go to those nuclear plants. . . . But at the same time, it would make our company economically healthy enough that we would be able to look at other investments like investing in the Sammis Plant."[110] Given that the law does not require FirstEnergy Solutions to open up its books to the PUC, to ensure that all the funds from the bailout are necessary to keep the nuclear plants operating, this is hardly reassuring. The timing of these decisions suggest that the bailout was not just helping keep the OVEC coal plants open, but the Sammis coal plant as well. It was a bill to save three large coal plants from closing.

After this crushing loss, the clean energy advocates organized to try to stop the law from going into effect. Under Ohio law, within 90 days of a governor signing a bill into law, signatures can be collected to put a referendum on the ballot to reverse that law. The advocates were trying to bring the public into the debate, giving ratepayers a chance to stop the new charges and the gutting of the state's RPS and energy efficiency laws. But the opponents did not rest. Dark-money groups—including Protect Ohio Clean Energy Jobs, Generation Now, and Ohioans for Energy Security—tried a range of tactics to stop the referendum, such as targeting Facebook users to withdraw their signatures.[111] While the groups aiming to block signature collection have not disclosed their funding sources, evidence points clearly to an affiliation with FirstEnergy Solutions.[112] These groups used highly questionable tactics, including lying to the public. Some ads implied that the Chinese government was attempting to control

Ohio's electricity.[113] This falsehood was repeated by senior legislators, including Speaker Householder. The fight became so contentious that petition collectors experienced violence and intimidation, allegedly from Generation Now-backed "petition blockers."[114] In the wake of this fervent opposition, by the time the deadline came, the advocates had failed to gather enough signatures. While there was a lawsuit pending at the time of this writing, it did not look good for the advocates. The billion dollar coal bailout would likely proceed as planned. After using such questionable tactics to secure this bill, in late 2019, FirstEnergy Solutions announced it would rebrand as Energy Harbor—perhaps a move to strip itself of all that bad publicity.

Conclusion

Ohio was a late actor on renewable energy policy—so late that networked utilities and other fossil fuel interest groups had begun resisting these policies by the time the state passed its first law. Unlike Texas in the late 1990s, there was no longer high uncertainty about clean energy policy or technologies. By 2008, it was clear that renewables threatened coal and natural gas. For this reason, fossil fuel–dependent companies—including utilities and industrial energy users—began to resist renewables more quickly in Ohio. There was no fog of enactment operating in the Ohio case. During negotiations over the enabling legislation, opponents tried to weaken the policy. When this failed, they tried to resist the law during implementation, arguing that the provision that the opponents had ensured was in the law—a cost cap—should be interpreted to slow down renewables. Again, they failed. Initially, there was broad, bipartisan support for clean energy in the Buckeye state.

To make progress on retrenchment, opponents began strengthening their relationships with politicians. They gave significant campaign contributions to key legislators like the Senate president and the chair of the Senate Public Utilities Committee. They also wrote reports that claimed the law was expensive, sending these documents to all the legislators. By this time, opponents had mobilized across the country through ALEC and other right wing networks to undermine clean energy, drafting model bills. These strategies paid off, increasing the opponents' political influence. When it came time to craft the retrenchment legislation, these actors met with the lead opponent in the legislature in private meetings off-site, where they discussed specific bill language. Members of the public who resisted wind turbines in their backyards similarly cultivated tight relationships with legislators, including the Senate president.

By contrast, the advocates struggled to mobilize the public against retrenchment or resist partisan sorting in the Republican Party. As a result, two significant bills passed in 2014 that dramatically undermined Ohio's support for clean energy. These legal changes stymied the budding renewable energy industry by freezing the policy, eliminating the in-state requirement, and changing setback rules for wind turbines. All these changes undermined the momentum the Ohio clean energy industry was gaining, and significant job losses followed. Instead of building new renewable energy projects in the state—as was required before the rollback—utilities simply bought RECs, a practice which drove little new investment. Since then, Ohio has continued to fuel its electricity system with fossil fuels, increasing natural gas while stalling clean energy development.

After these laws passed, utilities began lobbying state and federal policymakers to bail out their failing coal plants. While they managed to secure some funding for coal through the PUCO, clean energy advocates successfully challenged these decisions through the courts and FERC. Meanwhile, attacks on the clean energy laws continued. After the RPS freeze ended, Seitz worked to extend it again. While the opponents did not publicly take positions, a number of lobbyists with AEP and FirstEnergy advocated for weakening Ohios' clean energy policies behind closed doors.[115] Eventually, in 2016 the legislature passed a bill that extended the freeze for another two years (HB 554), but Governor Kasich vetoed it. These constant attacks created significant uncertainty for the renewable energy industry. Why invest in renewables if there will be no requirements in a year?

The attacks continued in 2019, when the Ohio House passed a bill (HB 6) that subsidized coal and nuclear plants while eliminating the renewable energy and energy efficiency requirements. While the Senate version kept some of the RPS on paper, in practice it gutted the program: eliminating the solar energy carve-out, not requiring ongoing renewables after the program's last year, and not requiring industrial users to comply.

One of the darkest parts of this story is that the politicians and lobbyists leading these climate delay efforts rose in power over time. Balderson went on to be a Congressman. Seitz became the majority leader in the House. Randazzo became the Chair of PUCO. And Faber became Ohio's state auditor. Everyone involved in the effort to pass the worst energy policy in the country got promotions.

This case underscores that policies must catalyze enough advocates to challenge incumbent opponents. In Ohio, the initial RPS policy failed to grow a renewable energy industry large enough to rival the political influence of long-standing opponents. Instead, the industry was small and poorly organized when the retrenchment bills were proposed. As a lobbyist for the industry put it,

There are a lot of Republican legislators, who when 58 [the first repeal bill] crashed, said they would be fine with that. You have a whole bunch of legislators who are in the middle and two or three who have a real agenda. [Those legislators] have close ties to ALEC and FirstEnergy and AEP and that's their job to have close ties with them. The wind industry is a cottage industry of lobbying. There's 3 or 4 of us. There's like 18 lobbyists for FirstEnergy and that's one utility. We feel like we're holding this together with a thread. We have two wind farms in Ohio and we have great ties to legislators from those areas. But FirstEnergy has transmission and distribution over the top one-third of the state, and AEP on the southern and eastern side. Why would they listen to us when AEP says we have employees in your district and an office and we have issues? And we say there's a company called Iberdrola based in Spain and they have a wind farm in NW Ohio. They're kind of like, who? I don't have a problem with you. But I don't know who you are.[116]

As this quotation clearly illustrates, the policy feedback process takes time. Relationships with legislators do not happen overnight. Advocates must grow large enough to wield sufficient political influence. Opponents in Ohio ensured that there would not be enough time for this shift in power to occur—they moved swiftly to retrench the clean energy law.

Thus, timing is a crucial element for feedback. Early-actor jurisdictions are more likely to create path dependence in policy because the fog of enactment is likely to be operating. When a policy is new, opponents are less likely to understand its consequences. But when late states follow leaders, they can see the effects from policies implemented elsewhere. In the Ohio case, the utilities and industrial energy users had watched other states pass renewable energy laws. They understood the stakes and resisted these policies more forcefully from the beginning. We can see that if opponents move swiftly to retrench laws, they can interrupt policy feedback. When laws are quickly reversed, not enough time has passed to redistribute political resources. In such a case, incumbent opponents will remain disproportionately empowered compared to advocates. Under these conditions, policy feedback and path dependence are unlikely. Incumbent opponents can crush advocates before they have had time to establish the political influence necessary to fight back.

Conclusion

We must admit that we are losing this battle . . . Yes, we are failing, but there is still time to turn everything around.

—Greta Thunberg[1]

If you drive east from Los Angeles towards Palm Springs, you will pass through the humble beginnings of the clean energy revolution. Lining the highway are decades-old wind turbines quietly turning their blades, like ghosts from the not-so-distant past. Where did these strange creatures come from? Like all clean energy technology, policy drove their creation. In 1977, the Carter administration called for 20% of the nation's power to come from renewable energy sources by the year 2000. President Carter signed into law large tax credits for the nascent renewable energy industry. The next year, California enacted a landmark law that set a goal for wind energy to supply 1% of the state's electricity in a decade (Righter 1996a).[2] These were the first clean energy targets in the country, and they drove unprecedented growth in renewables.

Combined with state tax incentives and the federal Public Utility Regulatory Policies Act (PURPA), these policies kicked off a veritable gold rush in wind energy in California. By 1985, more than 12,000 wind turbines had been built, equivalent to about one and a half coal plants.[3] The California experiment was the biggest in the world at the time, representing 96% of global wind energy with total investments over $2 billion (Righter 1996a; Starrs 1988). By 1987, California met its first goal, and wind supplied 1% of the state's electricity (Starrs 1988). And it wasn't just wind energy that was booming in the Golden State: policies drove utility-scale solar, biomass, and geothermal plants.[4] By the late 1980s, 90% of all of the solar power generated in the world was made in California.[5] New clean energy companies grew in the state, in theory creating interest group advocates who could push for more ambitious policy.[6]

But the California case—like the others in this book—is not a simple story of path dependence. The Reagan administration was far less supportive of clean energy than the Carter administration. At the end of 1988, federal tax incentives

Short Circuiting Policy. Leah Cardamore Stokes, Oxford University Press (2020). © Oxford University Press.
DOI: 10.1093/oso/9780190074265.001.0001

expired for all types of renewable energy projects. That same year, the California government suspended important clean energy policies (Smith 2013). This policy retrenchment was devastating for the advocates that early clean energy laws had incubated. With lost revenue and insurance companies failing to pay out claims, many renewable energy projects were abandoned rather than repaired (Morris 2000; Righter 1996a). Little new capacity in wind, solar, biomass, or geothermal was added after 1988. By the 1990s, large clean energy companies were going bankrupt.[7]

In the wake of this devastation for the nascent renewable energy industry, utility companies began lobbying to further weaken clean energy laws. Existing policies forced utilities to buy power from independent companies rather than relying on their own carbon-intensive power plants. As monopolies, electric utilities resented being told what to do and they resisted these rules. For example, in 1995 PG&E tried to create specific surcharges on customers' bills for California's renewables programs and make the legislature approve the clean energy policy each year.[8] This change would have made the costs more visible to the public and retrenchment more likely since the policy would have to be renewed annually. When California's electricity system was restructured in the late 1990s, clean energy advocates failed to get a renewable portfolio standard (RPS) embedded in the law, due to utility opposition, lack of support from the California Public Utilities Commission (CPUC), and fragmented advocate support. In the 1990s, California lost its global lead in clean energy. It would take almost two decades for the state to get back on track.

This pattern does not just hold for California. Over the past three decades, conflict over the energy system has played out across the United States between advocates for a clean energy future and incumbent utility opponents holding onto a fossil fuel past. These utilities promoted climate denial as they successfully delayed the transition to clean energy. The 1990s and the beginning of the 2000s were lost decades for preventing global climate disaster. If we look only at California's landmark 2018 law—requiring 100% clean energy by 2045—it is easy to believe this is a triumphant story of advocates winning through positive feedback. *But this law came 40 years after the first clean energy target was passed in that state.* As the climate crisis grows worse, we do not have 40 years to wait for every other state to move their goals from 1% to 100% clean energy.

Decarbonizing the US electricity system is the first linchpin globally for mitigating climate change and achieving net zero emissions. Unfortunately, the pace of change in the electricity system across the American states is paltry. After a decade of strong growth, jobs in the solar sector have been falling since 2016. In 2018, only 36% of the US electricity supply came from clean energy sources, including nuclear. Between 2009 and 2018, annual growth in renewable energy was a mere 0.7 percentage points (p.p.). Even in the best years—2016 and

2017—renewable energy only grew by 1.3 p.p. If we assume that new nuclear will continue to struggle, then renewable energy must increase by at least 2 p.p. annually just to keep pace with decarbonizing the existing electricity system by 2050.[9] Meeting even this modest target at this pace requires all existing nuclear to stay open. If we want to move faster, and decarbonize the grid by 2035, then we need renewables to grow by 3.7 p.p. annually—more than five times faster than they have been growing over the past decade.

That pace ignores two critical factors: the need to expand the grid to electrify other sectors and the need to replace retiring nuclear capacity. First, we must grow the entire electricity system by 50%–120% to electrify other sectors (Iyer et al. 2017; Jenkins et al. 2018; Williams et al. 2014).[10] To keep pace with the decarbonization demands of transportation, buildings and industry means that clean energy needs to grow 5 p.p. and 9.6 p.p. annually for a 2050 and 2035 target, respectively. This would represent a 7–14 times increase over the historic average deployment rates. That said, these targets would be easier to meet with a big push on energy efficiency. If we can power our societies with less energy, it will be much easier to decarbonize the grid and electrify new sectors over the necessary timelines because we will not need to build as much new infrastructure.

Second, we must keep in mind that large amounts of clean energy will be going offline in the coming decades as nuclear plants retire. By 2040, 60% of the existing nuclear plants in the United States are slated for retirement.[11] If we assume that only a handful of the existing nuclear plants are still operating in 2050, then this capacity must also be replaced. Since nuclear currently supplies 20% of the grid, and 55% of clean energy, we need growth rates for renewables around 5.7 p.p. annually for a 2050 target. Given that nuclear provides around-the-clock, emissions-free power, this electricity source will be particularly challenging to replace.

In short, if we are targeting 100% clean energy by 2050, we are talking about at least a 8-fold increase in the annual pace of renewable energy deployment. To accomplish 100% clean energy by 2035, if we keep the existing nuclear fleet operating, we will require at least a 12-fold increase over the best years for renewables growth. If nuclear plants are shutdown and little progress is made on energy efficiency, then meeting a 2035 target requires building more than one-tenth of the entire, existing grid infrastructure every year until the deadline. That would mean moving 15 times faster than we have in the past decade. To say this would be a heroic pace is an understatement. Moving at this speed will strain environmental assessment processes and will likely lead to significant resistance at the local level (Stokes 2016). And these dramatic transformations will take place all while we build out transmission and storage across the country at an unprecedented scale. While many believe that the electricity sector will be easy to decarbonize, these facts speak for themselves—it will not be simple (Davis et al. 2018). Speed and scale are not secondary issues, but the fundamental challenge.

The earth's climate has already warmed by more than 1 °C. Record-breaking hurricanes are now an annual occurrence in the United States. Droughts last longer. Across the world, unprecedented fires rage. How did we get into this mess, as a country and as a planet? One common answer is we are all to blame, through our everyday choices: whether to drive, bike or walk, to take a flight, to buy stuff made of plastic. But this answer is ahistorical and ignorant of how institutions shape the choices we *can* make. No one can unilaterally choose to live in a low-carbon economy. When we fail to take an institutional view, we obscure the role of power in our daily lives. Some actors in society have more power than others to shape how our economy is fueled. We are not all equally to blame.

We must direct our attention to the historical and institutional roots of our current dependence on fossil fuels. In this book, I have shown that our failure to address the growing climate crisis is a result of opposition from electric utilities and fossil fuel companies. These companies have resisted innovation (Hirsh 1999a; Hughes 2004). They have lied about climate science (Anderson et al. 2017; Oreskes & Conway 2010). And they have attacked climate policies. By bending the political system to their will, these companies have created the climate crisis. Until policies are in place that effectively challenge fossil fuel companies and electric utilities' political dominance, the lives of billions of people, communities, species, and ecosystems are in grave danger.

In this conclusion, I begin by reassessing the evidence for interest group influence in American politics, examining its implications for theories of policy feedback and path dependence. I then turn to the specific case of clean energy laws, examining how this book's cases generalize more broadly across the American states. I end the chapter with some practical thoughts on how to make progress on clean energy policies given the entrenched nature of organized combat between interest groups. To address climate change, policy advocates need to win policy conflicts more often. Clean energy advocates must learn from their opponents' playbook.

There are still reasons to hope: in 2019, the Green New Deal and substantial climate plans from all the major Democratic presidential candidates pushed climate policy back onto the national energy agenda. For the first time in a decade, politicians began talking seriously about a national clean energy standard (CES). At the state level, there is also exciting, renewed action. California, Hawaii, New Mexico, New York, Washington State, Colorado, Maine, and Nevada have all passed laws that target 100% clean energy on necessary and feasible timelines.[12] At the time of writing, Maryland and New Jersey have passed bills to get half of their electricity from renewables by 2030. Illinois, New Jersey, and Massachusetts are similarly considering bills to get to 100% carbon-free energy.[13] Cities have also joined in.

These laws are not enough to avert the climate crisis, but they are a start. Without the actions of laggard states and with all the inevitable implementation challenges, we would be unwise to rest easily. Ultimately, we must have a federal law to drive renewable energy adoption across all 50 states. The battle for clean energy is not yet over. We have not yet lost the war against climate change. But we must remain clear-eyed about what we are up against: interest groups that profit from and promote pollution. Opponents who seek to keep the status quo. Defeating climate change is, at its core, a political battle over policy. We must be ready to fight.

The Case for Organized Combat and the Limits of Path Dependence

Interest group conflict is at the core of policy change in America. Conflict over policy continues after enactment. In fact, it may increase after implementation as actors learn about policies' effects in practice. When policies are first drafted and passed, there is significant ambiguity and uncertainty. I call this dynamic the "fog of enactment." As I have argued, the fog is more likely under a number of conditions: when policies are new, during major reforms, in technical policy domains, and in cases where policies interact across scales of government.

When policies are novel—and haven't been passed or implemented widely in other jurisdictions—politicians, regulators, and interest groups all struggle to understand their potential implications. In cases of complex, omnibus bills, provisions may be buried deep in proposals that stretch hundreds of pages. In technical policy domains, politicians and interest groups alike may struggle to forecast outcomes. And policy effects can be particularly difficult to anticipate when states and the federal government share jurisdiction. In these cases, actors may creatively combine rules from different levels of government in ways that are difficult to predict in advance. While actors often claim to understand legislation's consequences if passed, in practice this is challenging to do. As the survey data I presented in Chapter 2 shows, it is the norm for politicians and their staff to struggle to anticipate policy outcomes.

However, ambiguity and uncertainty declines over time. After implementation, policy effects become clearer. In part this occurs through networks of interest groups that cross state lines—including national associations and federated groups. Networks play three important roles: they help interest groups learn to anticipate policies' consequences, they help interest groups disseminate effective political strategies, and they facilitate collective action. Interest groups enabled through policy feedback in early acting jurisdictions can move to other places, driving policy change. In this way, policy feedback can spillover from state to state.

Early on, advocates used networks to successfully push clean energy laws. In part, these networks grew out of earlier policies. For example, many advocates emerged from California after its renewable energy experimentation in the 1980s, and these groups moved into other states. The Energy Foundation also cultivated a national network of advocates in the early 1990s to develop policy ideas, share political strategies, and facilitate collective action. These advocates watched early policies and learned about how they would work in the next state. We know that states can act as a laboratory for ideas, exporting policy ideas to other states. But those ideas do not just move because they are "good" or "successful." Advocates work to move policy ideas that serve their interests across state lines.

Networks of policy opponents, however, often counter advocates' efforts. Business and conservative groups that work across state lines have been central to pushing for clean energy laws' retrenchment. Like advocates' networks, these groups facilitate collective action, helping opponents learn and disseminate political strategies. For example, the American Legislative Exchange Council (ALEC) created model bills designed to repeal RPS and net metering laws. Conservative think tanks and advocacy groups including Americans for Prosperity (AFP), Americans for Tax Reform, the Beacon Hill Institute, the Cato Institute, the Goldwater Institute, and the Texas Public Policy Foundation have similarly worked to retrench clean energy laws. These groups have strong ties to oil and gas industries as well as electric utilities—when they attack clean energy laws, they are acting in their own interest.

In addition to relying on networks, there are a number of other strategies interest groups use in their battles over policy. When feedback has not yet empowered advocates, opponents work directly with legislators or regulators to weaken laws. Opponents can use lobbying, campaign contributions, relationships, and ideas to try to erode policy and stop path dependence. Often, policy changes unfold with little public visibility, through a kind of "quiet politics" wherein interest groups capture political institutions (Culpepper 2010). However, when positive feedback has begun to take hold and advocates have increased their political influence, opponents may be forced to work indirectly to undermine laws. In these cases, they can expand the scope of conflict by working through the parties, the public, and the courts. While I have focused primarily on how opponents have used these strategies, advocates can also learn to apply them.

Interest Group Battles Through the Parties, the Public, and the Courts

After policy feedback has begun to take hold, and advocates have more political influence, opponents must work indirectly to achieve policy retrenchment. As I have shown in this book, there are three main pathways for indirect influence: the parties, the public and the courts. First, interest groups can work through political parties to promote policy change. On the right, networks of conservative politicians and interest groups, such as ALEC and AFP, try to influence the parties. As interest groups drag the parties further apart, partisan polarization develops. To date and across most policy issues, Republicans have moved farther to the right while Democrats have stayed fairly stable—a trend called asymmetric polarization (Hacker & Pierson 2006). The same is true for climate policy. Climate change is has been found to be the most polarized policy domain (Guber 2012). Clean energy is becoming almost as polarized as climate policy along partisan lines. Why has this occurred? I argue it is driven by interest groups. Utilities and other fossil fuel corporations have worked hard to undermine support for clean energy among Republicans.

When working through the political parties to change policy, primaries are particularly important. Opponents can financially back politicians who support their point of view in an attempt to influence policy (Powell 2012). Although utilities often claim that they do not intervene in political races, in practice they do. As was shown in Chapter 7, the private utility Arizona Public Service (APS) spent at least $55 million over several years supporting anti-solar candidates in Republican Party primaries and general elections for positions on the Arizona Corporation Commission (ACC).[14] In contrast, the solar companies likely spent half as much.[15] The elections resulted in the opponents' preferred politicians winning office, and these commissioners went on to dramatically rollback solar energy laws.

In the 2010s, the climate movement began to use the same strategies to try to drive action that fossil fuel companies have used to stall it. For example, in 2013 the billionaire Tom Steyer founded a political action committee (PAC), NextGen America. This organization has focused on targeting both Democrats and Republicans if they are not sufficiently pro-climate. Since 2017, the group Justice Democrats has used the primary system to push the Democratic Party to the left on climate change. It helped recruit and elect Representative Alexandria Ocasio-Cortez, who went on to champion the Green New Deal when she took office in 2019. Groups like Future Now are also popping up to contest right-wing, anti-climate networks. The use of primaries to shift party positions on climate is not just available to the right—increasingly, environmental advocates on the left are using this strategy.

Partisan polarization on climate is not inevitable—support could shift back to the bipartisanship we saw before 2008 (Figure 1.1). In the past, Republican lawmakers have backed clean energy laws. Since renewables are popular with the public, ambitious state politicians interested in seeking higher office often champion clean energy laws. This is particularly the case with Republicans, who use these policies as a feather in their cap to show concern for the environment and bipartisanship. Governor George W. Bush did in Texas, before he launched his presidential bid; Speaker Jon A. Husted did this in Ohio, before he campaigned for secretary of state. And both Governor John Kasich of Ohio and Governor Sam Brownback of Kansas were wary of signing laws that would make them seem anti-renewables. There is also a growing cadre of right-wing think tanks and grassroots groups that support climate action: the Niskanen Center; republicEN; the Green Tea Coalition, an alliance between the Tea Party and the Sierra Club; Florida's Conservatives for Energy Freedom and Floridians for Solar Choice; and Michigan's Conservative Energy Forum.

In addition to the parties, interest groups can use the public in their policy campaigns. Political science research has demonstrated that policy change tends to follow public opinion (Erikson et al. 1993; Lax & Phillips 2009; Stimson 2004; Stimson et al. 1995). Studies examining mass feedback effects have also shown how specific entitlements can create new identities among the public, leading to policy stability (Mettler 2002; Mettler & Soss 2004). However, in obscure, low-salience policy domains—a description that applies to many areas— interest groups play a critical role as self-appointed translators for the public (Smith 2000). When turnout is low, organized interest groups have greater sway over the electorate (Anzia 2011).

In a technical policy area that average citizens do not understand, I argue that interest groups and to a lesser extent politicians—construct public preferences. Building on the idea of outside lobbying, this book has examined the ways that interest groups create public opinion for politicians (Kollman 1998). For example, interest groups commonly run public opinion surveys. Question wording on these surveys may not adhere to accepted scholarly standards, instead falling into the category of a "push poll," where leading questions all but guarantee certain findings. With the desired results in hand, groups communicate "public preferences" through the media or to politicians directly.

Interest groups may also try to influence public opinion by making the costs of a policy salient to the public. We see this in Ohio, where the 2014 retrenchment bill included a requirement to place a line item for renewables on citizens' electricity bills. By calling out renewables' costs, opponents were trying to increase the likelihood of further retrenchment by raising the salience of the policy with the public. Similarly in Arizona in 2018, the attorney general— who had received significant campaign funding from the utility APS's parent company—added language to a ballot initiative that highlighted clean energy's costs. The utility's parent company went on to use the same language in its advertisements opposing the measure.[16] By highlighting costs, opponents can try to undermine public support for climate action. Of course, these opponents neglect to communicate the massive and irreversible costs of climate instability.

Even more nefariously, interest groups can run fake campaigns, rather than going to the trouble of actually organizing or polling the public. For example, in New Orleans, Entergy ran an astroturf campaign in 2017, in which they paid actors to deliver speeches in support of a proposed gas plant. For 10 public speakers and 75 demonstrators in front of the City Council, Entergy New Orleans's chief executive officer (CEO) paid $29,000—a meager investment if the gas plant was approved.[17] Astroturf campaigns are increasingly common in American politics and are used to try to influence politicians and their staff. It is often up to journalists to communicate the true origins of these campaigns through investigative reporting.

These tools to construct and communicate public preferences are not just available to opponents. Overall, support for clean energy policy is quite high—much higher than support for a carbon price, for example (Howe et al. 2015). Hence, these laws start from a place of significant popularity in most states (Stokes & Warshaw 2017). Clean energy advocates have tried to increase public support by highlighting jobs, health benefits from improved air quality, and the dangers fossil fuels pose to the climate. Apart from job creation and air pollution, however, these benefits can often seem intangible to the public, making advocates' task of communicating renewables' benefits difficult. Climate change, in particular, is so polarized that it is usually ineffective as a messaging strategy for clean energy (Stokes & Warshaw 2017).

Despite polarization, advocates can still use public support to campaign for clean energy laws. The Yale Project on Climate Change Communication, for example, creates maps that show what the public thinks in each congressional district—key information that advocates can use to communicate public preferences to politicians (Howe et al. 2015; Mildenberger et al. 2017). Data for Progress, a think tank, similarly creates downscaled public opinion estimates to argue that public policy is often not in line with the majority's preferences. As they show, many left-leaning policies are wildly popular with the public. Using this kind of high-resolution data can help groups communicate public preferences when specific climate policies are proposed, for example, the Green New Deal.[18]

The courts are the third pathway interest groups can use in their conflict over policy. If opponents are not able to change the law directly, they seek to resolve their grievances through the legal system. On balance, interest groups prefer using other channels to challenge policy as there is significant uncertainty with court cases' outcomes. In Colorado, for instance, opponents mounted an unsuccessful Commerce Clause challenge against the state's clean energy law. That said, even when cases are ultimately unsuccessful, legal threats can be powerful. The fear of a court challenge has the potential to shift policy. For example, several clean energy laws that had local content requirements, to encourage local job creation in the state, have since been modified due to fears of a legal challenge (Carley et al. 2018). At the federal level, opponents have pursued cases against climate policy like the Clean Power Plan. This also occurs internationally: in 2019, major challenges to Canada's national carbon price were launched though the legal system. Future work should examine in greater detail the role of the courts in short-circuiting policy feedback.

While opponents have tried to use the legal system to block progress on clean energy, advocates have also taken to the courts for their own ends. In Arizona, SolarCity challenged the legality of net metering charges. More broadly, the legal system is becoming an increasingly important venue for battles over climate policy. Significant investigative reporting and academic work revealed that ExxonMobil knew the science of climate change in the 1970s and 1980s (Supran & Oreskes 2017). Yet, ExxonMobil launched a denial campaign and lied to the public for decades (Oreskes & Conway 2010). In response, the attorney generals of New York and Massachusetts opened legal investigations into the company in 2015 and 2016, respectively.[19] While the New York case was unsuccessful, that does not mean that other challenges will not prevail. States, cities, and counties have similarly instigated suits against several fossil fuel companies, including for compensation from climate damages. This strategy mirrors efforts to hold tobacco companies accountable for fraudulent behavior—an effort that, after decades, eventually succeeded.

Of course, these three indirect pathways to political influence and policy change do not capture all the critical actors, institutions, or interest group strategies in American politics. For example, interest groups often use the media to try to influence policy. To date, the media has done a poor job of communicating the stakes in climate policy battles. But this book also rests on the dedicated work of dozens of journalists who have uncovered electric utilities and fossil fuel companies' lies and political strategies. I will leave it to other scholars to investigate the role the media plays in organized combat more fully.

In this book, I have made a case for focusing on organized combat between interest groups to understand policy. How does putting interest group conflict at the center of a theory of policy change alter our expectations about policy feedback, path dependence, and lock-in? When we remember that opponents retain significant power after enactment, policy feedback appears much less likely than the preponderance of the literature suggests. From the empirical cases examined in this book, we can see a number of reasons why path dependence can fail.

Time is an important variable in any policy study (Pierson 2004). For policy feedback to work, laws must be in place long enough to grow advocates' political power. It is notable that most of the clean energy policies that opponents have aggressively targeted were passed quite late—in 2008 or later. In these cases, there was insufficient time for clean energy advocates to establish themselves as a counterbalancing force to their opponents.

Reassessing the Evidence for Interest Group Influence in American Politics

While I have laid out a theory that places interest groups at the center of policy change, it is notable that this runs counter to important scholarship in American politics. Interest groups' role in influencing public policy is controversial.[20] A substantial amount of research argues that campaign contributions and lobbying largely do not influence policy outcomes (Ansolabehere et al. 2003; Gerber 2004; Huber & Arceneaux 2007). For example, Frank Baumgartner and colleagues looked at a range of different policies at the federal level, examining the relationship between lobbying and policy. They concluded that lobbying resources are not strongly correlated with policy change, finding instead that defenders of the status quo typically win policymaking conflicts (Baumgartner et al. 2009). Using correlations between roll-call votes and campaign contributions, scholars have argued that money in politics is mere consumption (Ansolabehere et al. 2003).

However, my qualitative research at the state level shows that examining the details of policy fights unfolding over decades may reveal a different story. In this book, I have built a model of policy change that places networked interest groups at the center, bridging both mass and elite feedback theories. Using this more complex model of how policy can reshape politics allows for a better understanding of the conditions under which policy retrenchment is likely. Such a model, which by its nature is endogenous and reliant on feedback, does not lend itself easily to quantitative testing. It instead requires qualitative evidence of interest groups' and politicians' political behavior over time.

One reason that studies that put campaign contributions into a regression are unlikely to find effects is because of the complex ways that corporations cover their tracks. For example, Koch Industries supported the Kansas Republican Party and its members in numerous ways—directly with donations to specific candidates; and indirectly via the Republican House Campaign Committee, through its platinum membership with the Kansas Chamber of Commerce, and by its participation in ALEC.[21] When individual Republican politicians receive campaign funds, the money need not come directly from Koch Industries; it can be funneled through diverse channels, often several steps removed (Leonard 2019). In other states, such as Arizona, tracing these contributions is even more difficult because groups that are not formally affiliated with campaigns are not required to disclose their funding. This fact allowed the private utility APS to significantly influence its regulator's primary and general elections without having to disclose its involvement. Similarly, it is difficult to track lobbying's influence in contexts where groups refuse to publicly testify, instead holding secret meetings. We see this happening across all the cases. We should be asking: how much lobbying is happening in public, and how much is happening out of view?

Money and lobbying are not the only vehicles for interest groups' influence. Interest groups can also shape policy by wielding ideas (Layzer 2012). This strategy further complicates the process of identifying interest group influence as it can be subtle, accomplished via agenda-setting and framing. For instance, corporations have reframed RPS policies as "mandates" and net metering as a "subsidy" or a "cost shift." Conservative think tanks and utilities drove this change in language in all the states where they pushed for retrenchment. Examining the ways that interest groups shape ideas, and through it the sense of what is possible, is a challenging task (Layzer 2012).

Despite these identification challenges, a growing literature illustrates the complex and indirect levers interest groups pull to shape policy. As Alexander Hertel-Fernandez (2018) has shown, corporations can mobilize their employees into politics and, through it, shape policy. In a brilliant experiment, Joshua Kalla and David Broockman (2016) demonstrate that campaign contributions can facilitate access to congressional representatives' offices. Building on this work, I have shown with Matto Mildenberger and Alexander Hertel-Fernandez that these contributors can then shape policy. We asked congressional chiefs of staff and legislative directors whether they had ever changed their mind about a policy after meeting with a campaign contributor. Using a list experiment, a technique that can estimate sensitive issues, 45% of senior staff admitted donors had influenced them (Hertel-Fernandez et al. 2019).

In addition to finding a substantial role for interest group influence in policy change, the findings from this book call into question a prevalent view that positive feedback and path dependence are the norm. Instead, I show that small changes at the margin may not cascade into dramatic transformations in policy. As Kathy Thelen puts it, "The losers do not necessarily disappear, and their adaptation can mean something very different from embracing and reproducing the institution" (1999, 385). Path dependence in policy change is far from guaranteed.

Clean Energy Trajectories Across the United States

The theory developed in this book was built by examining clean energy laws across the American states over the past several decades. Renewable energy began as a niche policy area. In the 1980s and 1990s, advocates and bureaucrats dreamed up new policy instruments with esoteric terms like "renewable portfolio standard" and "net metering." Groups of like-minded advocates met through cross-state networks to debate policy ideas and political strategies. When an energy crisis occurred or when electricity restructuring was put on the agenda, these groups seized the opportunity to get their ideas onto the agenda—and they were often successful. At the time, private utilities were distracted—restructuring represented an existential threat to their organizations and business model. They believed renewables were unworkable at scale and therefore posed little threat to their survival. Limited by their own paradigm and distracted by restructuring, they could not see through the fog of enactment. They failed to predict the changes that renewable energy policies would bring. It was these conditions that allowed the first clean energy laws to pass across a majority of the states. However, once these laws were implemented and renewable energy technologies grew, utilities and other fossil fuel companies learned. The energy transition has morphed into a political battle over who will profit off of the electricity system. The era of quiet politics in climate policy has ended.

Over the decades, a gulf has opened up across the states on policy and the amount of clean energy in each state's grid (Table 9.1). This variation is a function of interest group political power. In many states, fossil fuel energy incumbents have retained power and used their influence to drive policy retrenchment or block policy enactment. A dozen states have failed to enact any clean energy goal—even a voluntary one—and seven states have never passed net metering. For example, in 2018 Florida lacked any clean energy target, given fierce opposition from electric utilities, who spent tens of millions on politics to block progress.[22] As a result, this sunny state had only 15% clean energy in 2018. In other states, clean energy laws were passed but remained very weak. This has resulted in policy drift, where some states no longer have any clean energy laws driving progress. In states like Utah, stringent cost caps mean that utilities may not have to comply. Other states have defined clean energy in ways that weaken the policy. Under Pennsylvania's clean energy law, even fossil fuels are eligible.[23] Other states, like Ohio and Texas, have exempted their industrial energy consumers from having to comply with the RPS. Hence, retrenchment is unfolding in a number of under-the-radar ways.

These battles are not just taking place at the state level. Federally, a number of decisions have unfolded that imperil clean energy's progress. In Congress,

Table 9.1 Cases of RPS Policy Change in US States

Retrenchment and Inaction			Positive Feedback	
Policy Inaction	**Policy Drift**	**Successful Policy Retrenchment**	**Successful Policy Expansion**	**Failed Policy Retrenchment**
Alabama (RPS, NEM)	Iowa (RPS)	Arizona (NEM)	Texas (RPS wind)	Colorado (NEM, RPS)
Alaska (RPS)	North Dakota (VRPS)	Kansas (RPS)	Arizona (RPS)	Connecticut (NEM)
Arkansas (RPS)	Oklahoma (VRPS)	Ohio (RPS)	California (RPS)	Iowa (NEM)
Florida (RPS)	South Carolina (VRPS)	Texas (RPS solar)	Colorado (RPS)	Maine (RPS, NEM)
Georgia (RPS, NEM)	South Dakota (VRPS)	Hawaii (NEM)	Connecticut (RPS)	Minnesota (RPS)
Idaho (RPS, NEM)	Wisconsin (RPS)	Indiana (NEM)	Delaware (RPS, NEM)	New Hampshire (RPS)
Kentucky (RPS)		Kentucky (NEM)	Hawaii (RPS)	North Carolina (RPS)
Louisiana (RPS)		Maine (NEM)	Illinois (RPS)	Florida (NEM)
Mississippi (RPS, NEM)		Michigan (NEM)	Maine (RPS)	Pennsylvania (RPS)
Nebraska (RPS)		Minnesota (NEM)	Maryland (RPS)	Washington (RPS, NEM)
South Dakota (NEM)		New York (NEM)	Massachusetts (RPS)	Wisconsin (RPS)
Tennessee (RPS, NEM)		Nevada (NEM)	Michigan (RPS)	
Texas (NEM)		Oklahoma (NEM) Utah (NEM)	Minnesota (RPS)	
Wyoming (RPS)		West Virginia (RPS)	Nevada (RPS, NEM)	
		Wisconsin (NEM)	New Jersey (RPS)	
			New Mexico (RPS)	
			New York (RPS)	
			Oregon (RPS)	
			Rhode Island (RPS)	
			Vermont (RPS)	
			Wisconsin (RPS)	
			Washington (RPS)	

VRPS, voluntary RPS.

Republicans have been trying to cut research and development funding for clean energy, while increasing funding for fossil fuels.[24] In addition, Congress has decided to phase out key deployment support for renewables: the production tax credit (PTC) expires on January 1, 2021, and the investment tax credit (ITC) will begin phasing out in 2020. Notably, the ITC will be phased out entirely for residential customers in 2022—creating significant challenges for rooftop solar companies and altering citizens' ability to participate in solar production. The Trump administration has also levied hefty import taxes on solar panels from China, harming the US domestic industry that installs this technology.[25] Taken together, these actions are raising clean energy's costs in the United States.

Despite these problematic developments federally, clean energy companies are challenging utilities' dominance in state legislatures and public utility commissions. These advocates are using a number of strategies to try to expand clean energy policies: increasing the target or bringing the timetable forward; reducing taxes on projects; expanding the entities required to meet the target; financing supportive infrastructure; and modifying laws to make them less vulnerable to legal challenges. These strategies will all make it easier to address climate change.

In many states, successful policy expansion has occurred and advocates have thwarted efforts to weaken clean energy laws. For example, in California, clean energy advocates—including clean energy companies, consumer advocates, and environmental groups—exerted greater political influence than their opponents. They were able to expand the state's policies over time—in 2018, the state set a goal of 100% clean energy by 2045. And these bold targets are not just happening at the state level. As of July 2019, 130 cities had set goals for 100% of their electricity to come from clean energy sources, in part through the America's Pledge Initiative.[26]

What happens to a clean energy law in one state or city does not just matter for that jurisdiction. Innovation spills across state lines—and even international borders. When one place decides to invest heavily in clean technology, it brings down costs for others. As technology costs decline, the camel's proverbial nose is under the tent. As one advocate argued,

> The biggest mistake of the Koch brothers' networks was the belief that renewables would be a niche market. Had they started 5 years ago [in 2010] with these attacks, we would be screwed. Because utility opponents are everywhere—but they are just one constituency with more than one interest amongst them. . . . There was no serious non-utility opposition to renewables and now there is. But now renewables are cheap enough. All the initial RPS policies were in jurisdictions where there was restructuring and they thought if they could get rid of

the environmentalists [in the negotiations by giving them an] RPS or this system benefits charge thing, that would make it easier.[27]

That said, even while innovation drives cost reductions in clean energy, cost competitiveness does not make the clean energy transition inevitable. Navigating the retirement of existing fossil fuel infrastructure and ensuring that no new plants are built will remain central challenges. Over the past decade, many utilities sunk billions into retrofits to keep old coal plants operating. These debts make these plants difficult to retire. Even today utilities are still proposing vast amounts of new natural gas plants,[28] which research demonstrates is not compatible with climate stability (Tong et al. 2019). Both these new and retrofitted plants will become "stranded costs" as they face early retirement—and someone must pick up the tab. Who will pay for these costs: the public, through increased electricity rates, or private utilities and their shareholders?

Currently, many utilities are being paid to retire their coal plants through accelerated depreciation or securitization payments. These policies allow utilities to retire their plants but still receive payments from ratepayers for their stranded costs. For example, in 2019, New Mexico passed a clean energy law that included payments to the private utility PNM to shut down the final units at its coal plant. These payments were 50% higher than past payments for retiring coal assets.[29] In this case, ratepayers will pay these costs.

Stranded cost payments represent a kind of bailout for utilities that acted negligently. Since the 1980s, utilities knew that climate change would make further investments in fossil fuel infrastructure untenable (Anderson et al. 2017). Yet, they continued to finance dirty technologies and retrofit plants they should have retired. One way of interpreting stranded cost payments is as a reward for corporations who continued to invest in polluting plants long after they knew these projects were making the climate unstable. Stranded cost payments may therefore create a moral hazard. If electric utilities know they will be paid for continuing to invest in fossil fuels, why should they change their corporate strategy and stop proposing new natural gas plants? On the other hand, utilities may be particularly interested in being partners in the transition if they can both secure funds for their existing assets and make profits off of new clean energy infrastructure.[30] Hence, securitization may buy laggard utilities' cooperation. These thorny questions will only get more challenging in the coming years.

Ultimately, we should not be naive that slow progress in a handful of states will get us where we need to go. If anything, the challenge has only become harder as the hour grows short. Two-thirds of the American electricity system is still fueled by dirty power. Vast amounts of new infrastructure must be built in a very short window of time. And fossil fuel companies and electric utilities have grown wiser. Clean energy policy has exited a period of ambiguity and entered a stage when opponents understand the stakes. These opponents have expanded the scope of conflict over clean energy, bringing the fight to politicians, regulators, the parties, the public, and the courts.

If anything, fossil fuel companies and electric utilities' tactics have become more extreme as the climate movement has gained momentum. South Dakota, Louisiana, Oklahoma, Texas, and other states have outlawed protests against energy infrastructure, like pipelines. While advocates are successfully challenging these laws in court, at least 18 states have considered bills that ban anti-pipeline activism.[31] Like other anti-environment strategies documented in this book, opponents have passed this idea through their networks. After the first anti-protest bill passed in Oklahoma in 2017, ALEC developed a model bill that many other states have taken up.[32] The goal with this legislation is to further delay the energy transition. Fossil fuel companies have also begun attacking electric vehicles (EVs), in an attempt to delay their growth. For example, there is evidence that Koch Industries is spending millions to attack EVs, launching new organizations for this purpose.[33] If anything, the opponents have broadened their attacks on the energy transition.

Given the dire situation we find ourselves in, what is the path forward? There are a number of options to make rapid progress on clean energy in the United States, helping the world avert catastrophic climate change. Federal legislation is particularly important, given the growing gulf between leader and laggard states. The federal government could pass a national clean electricity standard. Such a policy would prevent state level rollbacks by setting a minimum standard for progress. The federal government could also put hundreds of billions annually into deploying clean energy and rebooting America's research and development ecosystem. This spending could be packaged in an omnibus energy bill—like the Energy Policy Acts of 1992 and 2005—or a big climate bill, like the failed Waxman-Markey.

Taxing polluters to ensure that they pay the full costs of the harms they create is an often favored approach. This can be done through carbon pricing: either a carbon tax or a cap-and-trade system. But given that fossil fuel subsidies are still prevalent (Ross et al. 2017), and carbon taxes have continuously failed to pass, the polluter-pays principle has to date proven challenging to implement. Many fossil fuel companies and electric utilities do not pay any federal taxes and instead receive federal tax rates that are, in effect, negative.[34] Further, carbon pricing has shown serious limitations in terms of changing corporate and consumer behavior (Mildenberger 2020).

Linking climate policy with social and economic policy through a package like a Green New Deal may be one promising way to build public support climate action. Research I have conducted with Parrish Bergquist and Matto Mildenberger shows that a climate policy bill that includes social and economic policy is more popular than a standalone carbon pricing bill (Bergquist et al. 2019). If carbon pricing is used, addressing income inequality is likely essential to ensuring policy durability since raising the costs of fossil fuels will make it harder for everyday Americans to pay their bills.

Moving away from dangerous fossil fuels will require a strategy to reduce political opponents' power and stranglehold over energy policy. Hence, these bills must contain provisions that pay companies, unions, and the parts of the public that will bear the costs of the transition to clean energy. Dealing with utilities' and fossil fuel companies' stranded assets is likely to be a difficult sticking point. Should these negligent corporations be paid to write down fossil fuel infrastructure and reserves? It may be necessary to get powerful opponents to stand down. Yet, paying off large corporations that committed fraud and harm through decades of climate denial and delay may sit poorly with many. The federal government could also pursue legal action against fossil fuel companies and electric utilities through the Department of Justice, as occurred with tobacco companies under the Clinton administration.

It is difficult to predict how clean energy will develop in the United States over the next decade. Policies could remain stable or even expand, helping to accelerate the deployment of carbon-free technologies. This outcome would help the world address climate change, particularly since the US is the engine of global innovation. Alternatively, opponents could continue to drive climate delay: weakening and rolling back laws or preventing their passage. If these attacks are successful, they will slow down the pace of renewable energy deployment, as happened in the 1980s and 1990s. The shift away from polluting energy sources is far from inevitable. Regardless of the approach taken, it is clear that state actions will prove insufficient to drive climate action at the speed we need. The federal government must step up.

Some Practical Advice for Clean Energy Advocates

Given that the fog of enactment is no longer operating for the clean energy laws I focus on in this book, advocates must find a new strategy to succeed in expanding climate action and thwarting retrenchment. Here I provide some practical ideas for how to design policies to be more durable to withstand attacks from organized, opponent interest groups aiming to short-circuit progress. Advocates must borrow from their opponents' playbook. Key strategies include: reforming institutions; focusing less on ownership; strengthening advocates' networks while concentrating opponents; and, expanding the scope of conflict through the parties, the public, and the courts. Expanding the scope of conflict includes bolstering clean energy advocates' links to the parties, emphasizing the benefits of clean energy for the public, addressing income inequality, and pursuing legal challenges against electric utilities and other fossil fuel companies. Ultimately, the goal is to increase advocates' political influence to drive climate action.

Reform Institutions

Clean energy advocates must take on the difficult task of reforming institutions, most prominently public utility commissions (PUCs). The electricity system, both before and after restructuring, was not built for renewable energy technologies. Its rate structure, rules, and technologies were developed to serve centralized plants, primarily fossil fuels but also nuclear and hydropower. Consequently, when renewable energy technologies interface with this system, problems arise.

Given that the institutional arrangements set up in the early 1900s are still largely in place today, reforming electricity regulation is no small challenge. For one, private utilities retain significant power in shaping the electricity policy agenda. They are seen as the "experts" on the topic, leading many regulators to defer to them. Utilities also receive government-guaranteed profits, giving them lots of funds to spend on lobbying regulators. We know that low-salience institutions, that the public pays little attention to, combined with weak advocates makes regulatory capture far more likely (Mullin 2009). Hence, PUC reforms must bolster advocates' power and raise the salience of the institution with the public.

There are a number of institutional reforms that would bolster advocates' influence. First, many more states could adopt an Intervenor Compensation Program. First enacted in California in 1981, this program pays public interest advocates who intervene in PUC proceedings for the costs of their participation if they meet specific criteria.[35] The fee awards are paid by the investor-owned utilities and collected in customer rates. The California program was evaluated in 2013 by an independent audit, which found it was well managed and effective. It cost an average of $6.25 million annually—equivalent to about 17 cents per resident.[36] This is a very small price for a program that has built a robust group of advocates in California—including The Utility Reform Network (TURN)— who have acted as effective advocates for consumers and the environment. From a cost–benefit perspective, this program saves California customers hundreds of millions annually by providing a check on utilities' dominance.[37] A few other states, including Wisconsin and Oregon, compensate public interest intervenors. While Hawaii's legislature tried to enact a program in 2017, the bill failed to pass the legislature. Overall, many other states would be wise to adopt this program as it would drive a policy feedback process: enabling advocates who could shift policy and undermine utilities' stranglehold over PUCs.

In addition to informal intervenors, offices of ratepayer advocates—which exist in many states—could play an important role in advocating for clean energy. In the early 1980s, as utilities were coming under increasing criticism for rising rates, many states established ratepayer advocates. These offices intervene in PUC proceedings, theoretically in the public interest. However, unlike an Intervenor Compensation Program, these advocates are often selected for political reasons and can be removed from their positions at any time. For example, in many states the governor or the legislature appoints the head of these offices. This can lead to ratepayer advocates who are ineffective or even counter-productive to clean energy. For example, Kansas's ratepayer advocate opposed the initial clean energy standard and later stood by silently when opponents attacked the law.[38] In Arizona, the ratepayer advocate brokered a deal to put fixed charges onto net metering customers for the first time. Hence, in some states, ratepayer advocates tend to focus on protecting the public interest in a narrow sense—keeping electricity bills low—without considering costs from environmental harms, including air pollution and climate change. Broadening ratepayer advocates' mandates to include environmental issues is essential to increasing their ability to support a transition to clean energy.

Providing more resources to PUCs may also help with accountability, oversight and stakeholder engagement. Given that research suggests that professionalized state legislatures and bureaucracies are less likely to suffer from interest group capture, we might expect the same is true for professionalized PUCs (Hertel-Fernandez 2019; McCarty 2014). With greater resources, PUCs should be able to conduct evidentiary hearings when there are issues in question, such as estimating the value of distributed generation. If the regulators do not have in-house expertise, they will tend to defer to the utilities, who have their own interests. Greater funding can help thwart regulatory capture.

The PUC planning process also needs to reform to make it more transparent. Currently, most states use proprietary models project into the future how much electricity will be used and which technologies can meet this demand. These models were designed for a centralized, fossil fuel–dominated electricity system. In many states, these models consistently overforecast the amount of electricity needed (Carvallo et al. 2018) and favor fossil fuel sources, most notably natural gas.[39] While in some cases advocates can buy licenses to use these models, the cost is prohibitive for many groups. In addition, many of the inputs into these models—such as the assumed cost of renewable energy power—are redacted. To scrutinize the assumptions that utilities are making typically requires advocates to sign nondisclosure agreements. This arrangement makes it difficult to understand or criticize utilities' unrealistic assumptions when they deliver plans that dramatically favor natural gas over clean energy alternatives.

Some states, like Hawaii and California, have started to require more public oversight of electricity planning models.[40] In these cases, advocates can open up the black box and question the assumptions that utilities are making. Another way to bring greater independence into the planning process is to use ratepayer funds to hire third-party consultants to determine key assumptions, such as the load forecast and the future technology mix. Ensuring that advocates can shape the evidence brought to bear in utility proceedings is essential. The alternative is the dynamic we saw in Arizona, where the private utility was asked to hold research meetings at its own offices. PUCs have a responsibility to make the evidence they use in decision-making transparent—reforms that require this would greatly bolster clean energy advocates.

More broadly, shifting the incentives for utilities in PUC rate cases is essential to driving clean energy adoption. Performance-based regulation is one solution that several states have adopted, including New York. Under this approach, PUCs set goals for utilities to achieve, establish measures for how to reach those goals, and then tie utility revenue, executive compensation, and investor returns to meeting these goals. This kind of regulation can be particularly useful for areas that traditional utility regulation has struggled to address: driving reductions in greenhouse gas emissions; increasing distributed generation including solar; and increasing electric vehicle charging infrastructure (Littel et al. 2017). Of course, like any other regulation, it must be designed and implemented effectively to achieve the desired outcomes. Solutions that ignore political power and focus only on technical fixes may run into problems.

In addition to regulatory reforms that bolster clean energy advocates, increasing these institutions' salience is important. The Energy and Policy Institute, a utility watchdog group, is particularly adept at investigating utilities and holding them accountable through the media, bringing crucial attention to an obscure policy area. While it may seem that electing commissioners would be one way to ensure that PUCs represent the public interest, in practice the opposite is often true (Besley & Coate 2003). As the Arizona case shows, electing regulators does not prevent the problem of regulatory capture—it may instead exacerbate it. In a low-salience area like energy policy, electing commissioners may allow well-financed interest groups to sway elections, potentially amplifying regulatory capture. Utilities and industrial consumers are far more likely to be well organized and able to support specific candidates. Campaigns to drive public attention to PUC elections may result in these institutions being more accountable to the public, as was seen recently in New Mexico and Mississippi. In cases when the PUC becomes a captured and broken institution, the salience of the institution will likely rise. This gives advocates the opportunity to elect stronger, public-minded commissioners. However, most of the time, PUCs remain obscure institutions. Hence, it is likely unwise to push for elections at more utility commissions.

Ethics changes may help nibble at the edges of regulatory capture. In 2017, Governor Jerry Brown of California signed legislation to reform the CPUC. The law banned utility executives from serving on the PUC if they had just left a utility, created an ethics officer, and codified the role of auditors.[41] In Arizona, responding to public backlash against APS's interference in commissioner elections, the ACC has changed its code of ethics. Some observers, including the utility watchdog the Energy and Policy Institute, note that these ethics rules are unlikely to prove effective, particularly given APS's vast amount of spending on ACC elections.[42] Of course, enforcing these ethics rules also requires dogged journalists to drive up the salience of the institution for the public. Ethics changes alone are insufficient.

There is also a need to improve rules around corporate donations in the states. Given their monopoly status, utilities are fundamentally different from other groups in terms of their "right" to spend money on politics—including their regulators' elections. It is particularly nefarious when utilities use profits from their monopoly businesses to influence commission elections because ratepayers cannot choose to exit. There is a need to address corporate contributions to politicians and elected regulators, as the campaign to undo the Citizens United case is attempting to do.

Changing interest groups' ability to directly influence PUC elections is crucial, albeit difficult. Regulators may have the ability to ban entities that contribute to campaigns from participating in proceedings. However, many utilities—like APS—have parent companies, and it is these groups that spend money on campaigns. Could these companies that use profits to capture their regulators, leading to higher rates, be held accountable in rate cases? It is possible that commissioners could audit spending and disallow these expenditures. Commissions could also try to levy fines against utilities that spend funds on elections. Election spending by monopoly utilities could also be banned outright by commissions or state legislatures—although such decisions would likely face court challenges. Even if changes to rules and laws prove unsuccessful after legal challenges, advocates can also take their fight to the public, eroding utilities' social license. Campaigns could focus on pressuring politicians and Commissioners to pledge not to take money from electric utilities and fossil fuel companies. For example in Virginia, activists have successfully pressured Democrats to not take money from the utility Dominion Energy.[43]

Campaigners could also focus on public disclosure of money in politics. Absent limitations on corporate campaign contributions, sunlight laws would ensure that donations to legislators and regulators are at least traceable, shedding light on the extent of regulated utilities' influence. For example, Colorado requires extensive disclosure from PUC members.[44] In Illinois, institutions such as the Sunshine Project have attempted to build a culture of disclosure across government agencies.[45] Taken together, these reforms would provide important checks and balances on utilities' ability to capture their regulators. Ideally, they would help accelerate the clean energy transition.

Focus Less on Ownership

Many states now have grassroots campaigns in progressive cities that aim to convert private monopoly utilities into public utilities, or secure greater customer choice programs. The campaigns are laudable for many reasons: they raise awareness about harms from the electricity system; aim to hold accountable unethical private utilities; and mobilize citizens to take action on the climate crisis. However, these campaigns may struggle to generate their desired outcomes for several reasons. First, it is not clear that ownership structure is the critical variable for clean energy. Second, fragmenting the electricity system into smaller energy providers may have unintended consequences. And third, advocates may find it difficult to win.

It is not clear that a utility's ownership structure is the key variable to making progress on clean energy. If it was, we should expect that publicly owned utilities (POUs) and rural electric cooperatives would have a cleaner electricity mix than investor-owned utilities (IOUs). Unfortunately, this is not the case. For one thing, rural electric cooperatives have built a dirtier electricity mix. Both their generation assets and their retail electricity mix have a higher fraction of fossil fuels than the national average.[46] In 2016, coops' assets were 92% fossil fuels, while IOUs' assets were 78% fossil fuels.[47] While it is more difficult to estimate POUs' mix, it does not appear it is cleaner than IOUs. In part, these utilities may have struggled to decarbonize because it is harder for POUs and cooperatives to access federal tax credits for wind and solar. And RPS policies often do not apply to them, since they are not under PUC jurisdiction.

While IOUs are likely the worst offenders in terms of spending on climate denial and delay, unfortunately POUs and cooperatives have often taken a similar approach. The national associations for the POUs and the cooperatives have both funded climate denial.[48] For example, the National Rural Electric Cooperative Association was a member the Global Climate Coalition, a climate denial organization that operated throughout the 1990s. In 2018, a group of rural electric cooperatives in Colorado spent almost $500,000 supporting Republicans to avoid having regulatory oversight that would push them to adopt more clean energy.[49] The same thing has occurred with rural electric cooperatives in Alabama.[50] Generally, cooperatives have little public participation, making them far from democratic organizations (Spinak 2014). In three out of four races, turnout in elections for these boards is less than 10%.[51] Although some cooperatives may be climate champions, many are not. Even in this book, which does not focus on rural electric cooperatives, I have documented these organizations seeking permits to expand their coal plant (Sunflower Electric in Kansas), supporting coal plant bailouts (Ohio Electric Cooperatives), and supporting climate denial (National Rural Electric Cooperatives Association).

In many states, POUs resist clean energy targets. In California, for example, advocates were not able to impose an RPS policy on the POUs until years after the IOUs had one in place. Even in 2018 and 2019, there were POUs in California aiming to weaken the state's RPS law. These municipal utilities worked to delay closing gas plants and proposed that existing hydropower should count under the RPS—a change that would have gutted the targets.[52] Similarly, the Florida Municipal Power Agency proposed large monthly fees on customers in 2019 to squash residential solar energy growth. As the CEO put it, this would make solar customers "go away."[53] Municipal utilities and rural electric cooperatives have proven successful at avoiding clean energy targets and net metering laws. In more than one-third of states with a binding RPS, POUs or cooperatives are exempt from complying with the law. Two-thirds of states with net metering laws similarly exempt these utilities from complying.[54] These facts raise questions about public ownership as a solution to speed up clean energy adoption. At the federal level, the Tennessee Valley Authority (TVA) has enacted policies that block renewable energy development. It has put limits on customer owned clean energy assets and pressured utilities that work with the TVA to sign long-term contracts that would lock them into buying dirty power.[55] Utilities of all types act in their fiduciary interest to protect their existing assets against newer, low carbon projects. Regardless of the utility ownership structure, most are working to keep their fossil fuel infrastructure online. It is not just the profit motive that causes utilities to fight renewables.

In general, these public power campaigns are playing out in progressive cities, where activists are trying to pressure municipal governments to take over a part of an existing private utility or to create customer choice programs. Unfortunately, fragmenting the electricity system may have unintended consequences. Small community choice energy programs across the country have struggled to sign long-term power purchase agreements to drive new investments in renewables. Instead, these programs often buy renewable energy certificates (RECs), which are largely ineffective at driving additional clean energy projects.[56] The clean energy transition will require an enormous amount of investment in big projects, such as offshore wind, battery storage, pumped-storage hydroelectricity and transmission lines. These projects will require significant capital and coordination. Breaking the electricity system up into smaller and smaller utilities will likely make these projects harder to build, not easier. It could also make it harder for advocates to win, as they will have to organize to hold utilities accountable across more venues.

Finally, advocates for public power may find it very hard for their campaigns to succeed. As Chapter 3 showed, economists worked over many decades to try to restructure the electricity system. While they won in some states, their reform project proved a mixed success, and many of their desired outcomes were not achieved. Public power campaigns represent existential threats to private utilities. Unsurprisingly, these companies have fiercely resisted municipalization and community choice aggregation campaigns. Between 2006 and 2016, only 13 places converted from an IOU to a POU—and they were primarily small towns of less than 10,000 people.[57] For more than a decade, citizens in Boulder have tried to take over a part of Xcel's territory. Yet they still have not won. And while many parts of California are aiming to set up consumer choice programs, many are struggling to get off the ground given the costs of exiting the existing system. In 2019, there was an offer for San Francisco to buy a piece of the private utility PG&E's territory—a move that was opposed by the unions within that utility.[58] The costs of municipalization are also quite high. Overall, these campaigns are very long and difficult to win.

All this said, there are some benefits to public power campaigns. Even when reformers fail, they may shift utilities' incentives to act. Xcel has become far more willing to transition its assets to clean energy in the wake of the Boulder campaign. Were similar campaigns to play out in blue cities within red laggard states, such as a campaign in Atlanta, we might expect similar outcomes. Unfortunately, most of these campaigns are in blue cities in blue states. To my knowledge, there are no campaigns to turn some of the worst IOUs into POUs, such as APS, AEP, FirstEnergy Solutions (now Energy Harbor) or Southern Company. That said, it may be true that in progressive states it is easier to hold a public utility accountable than a private utility. Perhaps if we were starting from a blank slate, that institutional structure would be preferable. And there may be ways to create or adapt existing public institutions to rapidly deploy renewables, whether at the local, state or federal level.

The question is: are these campaigns the best use of environmental advocates' time? Advocates can choose to focus attention on improving the existing regulatory structure and on passing new clean energy laws. Or they can fight life-or-death battles with private utilities. With the hour running short and with limited resources, my own view is that advocates should focus more on reforming existing institutions. Private monopoly utilities are already a kind of public-private partnership. These corporations are accountable to the government through PUCs, which approve spending, rates, and resource plans. While PUC proceedings are rather dry and technical, they are available for advocates to participate in, to hold utilities' accountable. Were advocates to focus on passing Intervenor Compensation Programs, they could even find themselves with funding to work to reform these institutions. As my book has shown, these processes can be captured by utilities. But the oversight institutions for POUs and cooperatives—city councils and boards—can similarly be weak and captured.

The fundamental issues in the clean energy transition are contesting utilities' entrenched power, creating incentives for renewables, and dealing with stranded assets. While "regulatory reform," "new laws," and "better PUC oversight" may sound boring, they could prove the shortest path to victory. For example, were Arizonans able to elect just two commissioners that supported renewables, they would have the mandate to impose a 100% clean energy target on the state's private utilities *overnight*. They could also block new natural gas plants and negotiate deals to shut down existing fossil fuel assets. We know that this is the case because it is what is happening in Michigan. Since taking office in 2019, Governor Gretchen Whitmer has appointed two environmental advocates to that state's PUC. Already, there are signs that the state will begin moving faster to transition its electricity grid to clean power. The fact is that private utilities are not unregulated corporations. By using and strengthening our existing state regulatory bodies, we can make serious progress on decarbonization.

Strengthen Advocates' Networks

Across policy domains, the right has proven far more successful at building and maintaining robust cross-state networks than the left (Hertel-Fernandez 2019). The same is true for climate and energy policy. Clean energy opponents working through ALEC, the Edison Electric Institute (EEI), AFP, and other networks have become capable of blocking new laws, stalling progress, and even rolling back policies. These opponents have succeeded despite widespread public support and the urgency of the climate threat. When advocates lack similarly strong networks, they struggle to contest their opponents' dominance. Hence, advocates must work to strengthen coalitions, avoid fragmentation, and concentrate their opponents in laggard jurisdictions to make federal action easier.

It is much easier for the opponents to organize. Electric utilities receive guaranteed profits from their regulators, which they can use to invest in political action. They have dozens of full-time staff working on regulatory proceedings. With this asymmetry in resources, utilities can attend and contribute to multiple dockets at the PUC without an issue. By contrast, advocates often fracture when scarcity hits, struggling to intervene across multiple cases. Given this structural disadvantage for advocates, coordination and cohesion are crucial. Foundations should continue the work started by the Energy Foundation in the early 1990s and invest in cross-state networks. These networks need to have a blend of insider groups, which can build relationships with legislators and negotiate over bill provisions; and outsider groups, which can push policy ambition through grassroots activism and organizing. The US Climate Action Network is one example of an important cross-state network that works to organize the climate movement.

Avoiding coalition fragmentation is particularly crucial. Given that the term "renewable energy" is a big tent, it is easy for groups to fracture when resources become scarce. This fracturing renders groups less politically influential, as was seen in Arizona. As one funder of clean energy advocacy put it,

> At the beginning there were few groups. Now there are a lot of groups and debate and disagreement about the right approach. And the industry has gotten more complex—SEIA and AWEA and the factions. They're all powerful. And the factions, they hurt themselves by not thinking more broadly about the industry good. All they think about is paragraph 3, section 2, and how that will affect their industry.[59]

When advocates lose policy battles, the consequences are swift. As policy resources are cut off, companies may close up business altogether. For NGO advocates, losses require resilience and a commitment to continue the work, as locking in a policy often takes a decade or more.

In these moments, the clean energy coalition may need to seek outside or unexpected partners. It is important to remember that interest groups' relationships are not bounded and static but open and in flux. Over time, some utilities may even become allies, if they are able to pioneer business models that allow them to profit more readily from clean energy. We are seeing the beginnings of this dynamic with a few utilities that are leading on clean energy, including Xcel Energy (Colorado, Minnesota), Consumers Energy (Michigan), and NIPSCO (Indiana). In Minnesota, Xcel Energy agreed to retire existing coal plants and invest heavily in clean energy after working with labor and environmental groups, including the Sierra Club.[60] In Colorado, Xcel has committed to reduce carbon emissions 80% by 2030—a target now codified in state law. Consumers Energy has shut down seven of its 12 coal plants, reducing carbon emissions by 38%, and has committed to phasing out all coal energy by 2040.[61] In Indiana, the utility NIPSCO took on a big fight with the coal industry to shut down its uneconomic coal plants—a far cry from the Ohio utilities seeking coal plant bailouts.[62] While these utilities are currently rare birds, we can hope that others in the industry will begin to follow their lead. Over time, more utilities may become advocates for climate policy as their clean energy holdings grow (Kim et al. 2015).

In addition to building their advocacy coalition, groups can work to isolate their opponents. California now boasts a 100% clean energy target. Why did positive feedback occur in that case? In part, a strong alliance between consumer advocates, labor and environmental groups drove this policy expansion. But the decline in opponents was also crucial. Between the first RPS policy in 2002 and the most recent expansion 16 years later, California's economy deindustrialized. Several fossil fuel companies—including the petrochemical company Occidental Petroleum (Oxy) and the natural gas generator Calpine—moved their headquarters from California to Texas. Over this time period, many of the early opponents to California's ambitious clean energy laws—manufacturers, industrial energy users, and fossil fuel companies—waned in political influence in Sacramento. Apart from the utilities and the shrinking oil industry, the opponents have largely left town.

Of course, this makes policy expansion more difficult in Texas—and retrenchment more likely. However, if California continues to invest in clean energy, it will create positive spillovers for other states for two reasons. First, as technology is deployed the costs tend to fall—a relationship called a "learning curve" (Arrow 1962). When these leading states build technology, they bring down the costs for laggard states. Second, by creating new industries, California has helped birth new advocates for clean energy that move into other states to defend against retrenchment. These actors crossing state lines are an example of a policy feedback spillover. While we often think of a state's policy experimentation as happening within its borders, this is not strictly true. Political and policy changes in one state affect other states.

Concentrating opponents in one area also makes the passage of federal climate policy more likely if it increases the number of senators and representatives who would support a bill in Congress. Were such a law enacted, this would also weaken the importance of policy retrenchment in any given state. Unfortunately, under the Trump administration, we are seeing federal environmental policy being rolled back. Clean energy and environmental policy are being weakened, opening up a gulf between Democratic- and Republican-controlled states. But there are still reasons to hope that laws passed in a given state will eventually unlock progress across the country and, ultimately, the world.

Expand the Scope of Conflict

To date, opponents have successfully expanded the scope of conflict on clean energy and climate policy, driving polarization in the parties, the public and, in some cases, contesting policy through the courts. Advocates must use these same levers to drive progress. Working through the parties, clean energy advocates must attempt to undermine polarization by backing candidates—including Republicans—who support climate action. Advocates must also take the public seriously, which means ensuring support for clean energy at the local level and reducing income inequality so that ratepayers can afford rising energy costs. Finally, advocates should pursue cases through the courts to hold electric utilities and fossil fuel companies accountable for climate denial and delay.

First, advocates must engage with the parties to support and elect sympathetic politicians. In an age of policy retrenchment, clean energy advocates must become more politically savvy and invest more money in politics, including PACs. Engaging in primaries and general elections puts pressure on politicians to support climate policy. In addition, it provides politicians an alternative source of campaign finance if opponents target them for breaking rank. For example, the Tom Steyer–backed group NextGen America has developed an extensive political strategy to advance climate action. It has organized clean energy ballot initiatives in three states,[63] tied climate with other issues like immigration to bolster a progressive coalition, and registered thousands of voters in toss-up states like Arizona.[64] The group also built a significant super PAC that backs pro-climate candidates, spending $96 million and $16 million in the 2016 and 2018 elections, respectively.[65] This kind of political action is a crucial counterweight to incumbent fossil fuel interest groups that back politicians who favor further delay on climate policy.

Employees are another important lever that opponents, including electric utilities, have used in policy conflicts (Hertel-Fernandez 2018). Renewable energy companies should mobilize their own employees, as their closest public allies, to support renewable energy policies. In both Kansas and Texas, many conservatives saw that the wind industries brought new jobs and economic development to rural parts of the states. There are already some examples of wind and solar companies mobilizing their workers to support federal tax credits (Hertel-Fernandez 2018). Increasing unionization rates in the clean energy industry may be particularly important to mobilizing workers effectively. At present the fossil fuel industry maintains much higher unionization rates.

More broadly, advocates must work with the public. Interest group capture is more likely when policy is obscure (Lowi 1972; Wilson 1989). As Andrea Campbell (2010) argues, if interest groups explain citizens' interests, make policy easier to understand, and raise a policy's salience, the public may be able to act as a counterweight to business influence. One way to do this is to create drama around the policy, as late-night television host John Oliver did for "net neutrality"—a term that is just as obscure as "net metering." We can similarly see this play out in immigration policy. When lawmakers attempted to retrench immigration laws in Arizona and Texas, public outcry followed. Immigration is a complex issue without obvious impacts on many people's daily lives. Why did the public pay attention? Activists successfully mobilized people, called for boycotts on visits to these states, and persuaded celebrities to join the movement.

Clean energy advocates must learn to make climate policy more interesting to the average American. As it stands, most people know very little about energy policy (Ansolabehere & Konisky 2014). These issues can feel abstract and distant from everyday experience. As Rebecca Solnit has eloquently put it, "Addressing climate means fixing the way we produce energy. But maybe it also means addressing the problems with the way we produce stories. And so we should seek out new kinds of stories—stories that make us more alarmed about our conventional energy sources than the alternatives, that provide context, that show us the future as well as the past."[66] The narrative around climate change has finally begun to shift in this direction. With the election of Representative Alexandria Ocasio-Cortez in 2018, and activism from groups like the Sunrise Movement and Greta Thunberg's Fridays for Future strikes, climate change is in the public discourse again for the first time in a decade. Clearly, politicians are beginning to feel pressure to act—all the major candidates in the Democratic Presidential primary developed climate plans in 2019, and even a few Republicans in Congress began floating climate bills. Advocates must build on this momentum, finding new ways to increase media coverage of energy and climate issues, bringing in more prominent advocates, and getting the public involved.

Climate policy will also need to address inequality. In the United States, income inequality has been rising since the 1970s.[67] Already, one in three Americans struggle to pay their energy bills.[68] We should expect energy prices to rise in the coming years for a number of reasons. If a price is put on carbon pollution, Americans' energy costs will go up. Renewable energy is also slightly more expensive than conventional sources. In addition, the entire electricity system must expand while it goes through critical upgrades that have been deferred for decades. As coal plants retire, regulators may push stranded costs onto ratepayers. Many Americans will struggle to pay for the additional costs of decarbonizing, upgrading, and expanding the electricity system. Rising electricity costs will be a particularly hard burden for low-income Americans.

However, there are a number of ways to solve this challenge. First, the federal government can reduce the costs of renewables by investing in energy innovation. Important areas for research, development and deployment include low-carbon flexible electricity sources and storage technologies—both of which are needed for high levels of renewable energy penetration. Second, more progressive electricity payment structures could be enacted so that corporations bear more of the electricity system's costs. This is the opposite of the current electricity rate structure, which requires individuals to pay higher rates than industrial or commercial customers. The electricity system has never fully aligned costs with customer classes, and recent decisions have only worsened this dynamic. Policies that allow large, polluting industrial companies to *opt out* of paying for renewables—passed in both Ohio and Texas—are highly problematic. *The polluters are paying less.* Of course, ensuring that fossil fuel corporations and other industrial energy users pay their fair share will be very difficult politically since corporations suffer from far fewer collective action challenges than individuals (Olson 1965). But consumer advocates bolstered through Intervenor Compensation Programs, alongside clean energy companies, may be well placed to overcome these challenges.

Raising the minimum wage and ensuring basic a social safety net would also aid the energy transition. If people were paid a living wage, they would have more money to pay for electricity that does not pollute or impose costs on future generations. Reducing income inequality can help more progressive environmental and energy policies be passed, implemented, and expanded. This theory has gained traction with the Green New Deal, which packages climate and social policy together (Bergquist et al. 2019). Rather than just raising the cost of energy, the federal government can spend money to help low income Americans manage the transition, for example by paying them to trade their cars in for electric vehicles. Inequality is tightly linked to climate policy—if we do not understand this, we are likely to find policies are rolled back when people struggle to pay for increasing energy costs.

Ensuring that the public is willing to bear the costs of infrastructure in their communities is also critical to transforming the electricity system. In some cases, very fast build-outs of wind energy have led to public backlash, stopping policy in its tracks (Stokes 2016). We cannot afford to have communities block large numbers of wind projects or transmission lines—we simply do not have enough time for further delay. How can we ensure local acceptance of clean energy? Bringing communities into local decision-making and using community benefits agreements may be particularly important to ensuring local acceptance (Schenk & Stokes 2013). If all community members see financial benefits—not just the ones whose property hosts the project—onshore wind may find greater local acceptance.

Equity should also be at the center of energy transition policy. To date, public participation in energy generation has largely happened through wealthy citizens adopting residential solar (Sunter et al. 2019). But this dynamic is shifting with community solar and policies designed to target low-income customers. Ultimately, we must ensure that a diverse cross section of the public is able to participate in and benefit from the energy transition—not just monopoly corporations.[69] Across income and racial lines, the public must be a partner and must see benefits.

In addition to working through the parties and the public, clean energy and climate advocates would be wise to use the courts to advance their cause. In the last several years, the courts have become a key battleground for climate policy (Adler 2019; Burger & Wentz 2018). In 2015 and 2016, in response to investigative journalism, the attorney generals in New York and Massachusetts launched investigations of ExxonMobil.[70] Although the oil giant attempted to thwart these probes, both states pursued cases. In late 2018, the New York attorney general sued the company for a fraud against investors, naming former CEO Rex Tillerson as a knowing participant in the scheme. In late 2019, the trial took place and ExxonMobil prevailed. But this is only the first case and it was pursued on relatively narrow grounds. The Massachusetts case, which likely will take a different approach, has yet to begin. Under a future federal administration, the Department of Justice could also pursue further claims in this area. We could expect the government to pursue cases similar to the lawsuits launched against the tobacco industry in the late 1990s, potentially resulting in large settlements. A second legal strategy involves cities making public nuisance claims against fossil fuel companies. Cities in California, Colorado, and Washington State, alongside Rhode Island, Baltimore, and New York City, have all alleged that these corporations knew about climate science for decades. Yet, instead of reducing the harms their products caused, fossil fuel companies promoted climate denial and worked to stall government action. These cities and states seek billions in damages to pay for adaptation costs, such as building sea walls. A third set of legal cases involves children suing the federal government for inaction on climate change.

To date, these lawsuits have targeted oil and gas companies rather than electric utilities. One exception is an earlier lawsuit, *Connecticut v. American Electric Power (AEP)*, which several states and New York City brought against electric utilities in an attempt to require them to reduce their greenhouse gas emissions (Burger & Wentz 2018). In 2011, the Supreme Court dismissed this case on the grounds that the emissions were already regulated under the Clean Air Act. Given the growing evidence that private utilities were active in climate denial— including Southern Company, AEP, as well as the EEI and the Electric Power Research Institute—we might expect these corporations to be face legal action in the future. Electric utilities could be challenged under state common law, to avoid some of the federal preemption issues that came up in *Connecticut v. AEP*.

Whether or not any given court case is successful, advocates would be wise to pursue legal challenges against electric utilities and other fossil fuel companies. At a minimum, these cases could undermine corporate-funded denial campaigns, which have continued to the present day. More optimistically, legal action may shape corporate and government behavior, driving clean energy adoption and other climate action (Setzer & Byrnes 2019). If these companies continue to promote climate denial and delay, they must be challenged directly. Given the billions of dollars that electric utilities and other fossil fuel companies make annually in profits and the very small sums that they spend on clean energy, lawsuits may be one critical tool to speed up the energy transition. We must erode polluters' social license to operate.

Final Thoughts

Optimistically, there are 30 years remaining to transition the economy away from carbon-pollution towards 100% low-carbon energy technologies to avoid warming the planet by more than 1.5° C (Intergovernmental Panel on Climate Change 2018; Trancik et al. 2014). Thomas Edison had a vision for this transition over 100 years ago. But the utility executives who inherited his project betrayed their industry's roots in radical innovation. The idea that fossil fuels are somehow the endpoint of energy innovation is ahistorical: humans have gone through several energy transitions over the past several hundred years: from wood to coal, from coal to oil, from oil to electricity. These transitions typically take many decades to a century and are never fully complete (Smil 2010). But a dramatic change in the energy sources we rely on is both possible and necessary. We have done this before, and we must do it again. Whether the clean energy transition occurs fast enough to address climate change remains an open question. Smart companies should realize the massive economic opportunity available in this transition. With electrification of the transportation sector and other parts of the economy, electric utilities have the biggest chance in more than 50 years to expand their market. Instead of seizing this opportunity, most electric utilities and other fossil fuel companies are continuing to delay.

Still: there are reasons to feel hopeful. Over the past several decades, some states have made significant progress on clean energy. California has followed a promising path, with its expanding targets and significant investments in energy storage and grid expansion. So have New Mexico, Washington state, New York, Hawaii, and Iowa. In these cases, policies have empowered new actors who have pushed to expand laws and defend them from attack. The key to success may lie in growing clean energy advocates, their networks, and their coalitions, to ensure there is sufficient support to counter opposition along the difficult road to decarbonizing our economy. Scaling these policies up to the federal level will be particularly important to ensure that action does not remain uneven across the states.

For too long, a small set of interest groups have captured legislative and regulatory processes around the world. They have used their power to imperil the health and well-being of all people on the planet. These organized interest groups have knowingly filled our air with pollution, have knowingly poisoned people, have knowingly denied climate science and delayed action (Oreskes & Conway 2010). Fossil fuel companies and electric utilities did all this while lining their investors' pockets with guaranteed profits. We must change the ending of this story and hold polluters accountable. The fossil fuel era must end.

Appendix

LIST OF INTERVIEWS

Interview Number	Description	Date	Case(s)
1	Political staffer	6-Sep-13	California
2	Renewable energy advocate at an NGO	11-Sep-13	California
3	Bureaucrat	20-Sep-13	California
4	Committee staff	3-Oct-13	California
5	Utility employee	4-Oct-13	California
6	Bureaucrat	10-Oct-13	California
7	Renewable energy advocate at an NGO	10-Oct-13	California
8	Committee staff	13-Oct-13	California
9	Political staffer; former bureaucrat	13-Oct-13	California
10	Political staffer	14-Oct-13	California
11	Bureaucrat	14-Oct-13	California
12	Renewables association employee	15-Oct-13	California
13	Commissioner	15-Oct-13	California
14	Lobbyist for renewables industry	15-Oct-13	California
15	Renewable energy advocate at an NGO	16-Oct-13	California
16	Academic	18-Oct-13	California
17	Utility employee	13-Jan-14	California
18	Renewables association employee	14-Jan-14	California
19	Renewables association employee	16-Jan-14	Arizona

Interview Number	Description	Date	Case(s)
20	Renewable energy advocate at an NGO	17-Jan-14	Arizona
21	Renewables association employee	17-Jan-14	Arizona
22	Think tank employee	20-Jan-14	Arizona
23	Utility employee	21-Jan-14	Arizona
24	Renewables association employee	22-Jan-14	Arizona
25	Renewable energy advocate at an NGO	22-Jan-14	Arizona
26	Former commission employee	22-Jan-14	Arizona
27	Lobbyist for renewables industry	23-Jan-14	Arizona
28	Commission staffer	24-Jan-14	Arizona
29	Public relations for renewables industry	24-Jan-14	Arizona
30	Renewable energy advocate at an NGO	24-Jan-14	Arizona
31	Renewable energy advocate at an NGO	27-Jan-14	Arizona
32	Former commissioner	27-Jan-14	Arizona
33	Renewable energy advocate at an NGO	28-Jan-14	Arizona
34	Former renewables association employee	30-Jan-14	Arizona
35	Utility employee	30-Jan-14	Arizona
36	Academic	31-Jan-14	Texas
37	Renewables association employee	3-Feb-14	Texas
38	Academic	4-Feb-14	Texas
39	Lobbyist for renewables industry	6-Feb-14	Texas
40	Former politician	6-Feb-14	Texas
41	Renewables association employee	10-Feb-14	Texas
42	Renewable energy advocate at an NGO	10-Feb-14	Texas
43	Renewable energy advocate at an NGO	10-Feb-14	Texas
44	Commissioner	10-Feb-14	Texas
45	Renewable energy advocate at an NGO	11-Feb-14	Texas
46	Renewables association employee	11-Feb-14	Texas
47	Renewable energy advocate at an NGO	12-Feb-14	Texas
48	Renewable energy advocate at an NGO	12-Feb-14	Texas
49	Political staffer	13-Feb-14	Texas
50	Political staffer	13-Feb-14	Texas

Interview Number	Description	Date	Case(s)
51	Clean energy company employee	14-Feb-14	Texas
52	Commissioner	17-Feb-14	Arizona
53	Former commissioner	18-Feb-14	Texas
54	Lobbyist for renewables industry	18-Feb-14	Texas
55	Renewable energy opponent at an NGO	18-Feb-14	Texas
56	Former commissioner	20-Feb-14	Texas
57	Former commissioner staffer	20-Feb-14	Texas
58	Lobbyist for oil and gas industry	21-Feb-14	Texas
59	Utility employee	24-Feb-14	California
60	Renewable energy advocate at an NGO	25-Feb-14	California
61	Renewable energy advocate at an NGO	25-Feb-14	California
62	Renewables company employee	26-Feb-14	Arizona
63	Renewables company employee	26-Feb-14	Multiple
64	Renewables association employee	26-Feb-14	California
65	Bureaucrat	26-Feb-14	California
66	Renewables company employee	26-Feb-14	California
67	Bureaucrat	27-Feb-14	California
68	Academic	8-Apr-14	California
69	Foundation employee	15-Apr-14	Multiple
70	Renewable energy advocate at an NGO	31-Jul-14	Ohio
71	Consultant	25-Sep-14	California
72	Foundation employee	25-Sep-14	Multiple
73	Renewables association employee	26-Sep-14	California
74	Renewable energy advocate at an NGO	1-Oct-14	California
75	Renewable energy advocate at an NGO	3-Nov-14	Ohio
76	Commission staffer	3-Nov-14	Ohio
77	Lobbyist for heavy industry	3-Nov-14	Ohio
78	Lobbyist for renewables industry	4-Nov-14	Ohio
79	Politician	4-Nov-14	Ohio
80	Renewable energy advocate at an NGO	4-Nov-14	Ohio
81	Journalist	4-Nov-14	Ohio

Interview Number	Description	Date	Case(s)
82	Utility employee	5-Nov-14	Ohio
83	Former politician	5-Nov-14	Ohio
84	Political staffer	5-Nov-14	Ohio
85	Renewable energy advocate at an NGO	10-Nov-14	Kansas
86	Renewable energy advocate at an NGO	10-Nov-14	Kansas
87	Lobbyist for renewables industry	10-Nov-14	Kansas
88	Politician	11-Nov-14	Kansas
89	Renewable energy advocate at an NGO	11-Nov-14	Kansas
90	Politician	11-Nov-14	Kansas
91	Bureaucrat	12-Nov-14	Kansas
92	Utility employee	12-Nov-14	Kansas
93	Renewable energy advocate at an NGO	13-Nov-14	Kansas
94	Renewable energy advocate at an NGO	13-Nov-14	Kansas
95	Politician	8-Dec-14	Ohio
96	Renewable energy advocate at an NGO	12-Feb-15	California
97	Renewable energy advocate at an NGO	19-Mar-15	Multiple
98	Renewable energy advocate at an NGO	3-Mar-16	California
99	Foundation employee	27-Sep-17	Multiple
100	Foundation employee	31-Oct-18	Multiple
101	Renewable energy advocate at an NGO	1-Mar-19	Texas
102	Lobbyist for renewables industry	8-Mar-19	Texas
103	Think tank employees	8-May-19	Multiple
104	Journalist	18-Jul-19	Ohio
105	Renewable energy advocate at an NGO	19-Jul-19	Ohio
106	Journalist	22-Jul-19	Ohio
107	Renewable energy advocate at an NGO	14-Aug-19	Ohio
108	Renewable energy advocate at an NGO	23-Aug-19	Ohio

NGO, nongovernmental organization.

NOTES

Chapter 1

1. In 2009, the state had installed over 9,000 megawatts (MW) of wind energy and got 12% of its electricity from wind energy.
2. Solar Energy Industries Association, Solar State by State, Q3 2018.
3. In 2016, carbon emissions from the Texas electric power sector totaled 207.5 million metric tons of carbon dioxide compared to 219.6 million metric tons in 1999. US EIA, Energy-Related Carbon Dioxide, Emissions by State, 2005–2016, February 2019; World Resources Institute, CAIT—US States Greenhouse Gas Emissions, 2014.
4. Juliet Eilperin, "Climate skeptic group works to reverse renewable energy mandates," *The Washington Post*, November 24, 2012.
5. Gabe Elsner, "The Campaign Against Net Metering: ALEC and Utility Interests' Next Attack on Clean Energy Surfaces in Arizona," Energy and Policy Institute, November 18, 2013.
6. Of course, interest groups are not the only causes behind polarization. Scholars examining this issue closely have shown evidence for a number of other factors. Explanations can be external to the legislature, for example, an increasingly polarized electorate, growing money in politics or growing income inequality; or the causes may be internal to a given legislature, for example, institutional rule changes (Roberts & Smith 2003; Theriault 2008; Barber & McCarty 2016). Some suggest that southern realignment, wherein white southerners sorted into the Republican Party due to racial policy, is an important driver (Abramowitz & Saunders 1998; Valentino & Sears 2005). Other explanations are also emerging. For instance, research tackles the role of partisan media in polarization (DellaVigna & Kaplan 2007; Gerber et al. 2008; Hopkins & Ladd 2012; Prior 2013). And some scholars argue convincingly that growing economic inequality is a key driver of polarization (McCarty et al. 2006; Gelman 2009). Still, many of these issues interact with interest group behavior. Thus, interest groups should be understood as a key part of contemporary polarization.
7. US Energy Information Administration, "Annual Energy Review—Total Energy," 2012; International Energy Agency, "Data and statistics—Total primary energy supply by source," 2019.
8. International Energy Agency, "Global Energy Demand Grew by 2.1% in 2017, and Carbon Emissions Rose for the First Time Since 2014," March 22, 2018; International Energy Agency, "Global Energy Demand Rose by 2.3% in 2018, Its Fastest Pace in the Last Decade," March 26, 2019.
9. "The Use of Energy in the United States Explained: Energy Use for Transportation," US EIA, May 10, 2019; "Frequently Asked Questions," US EIA, March 1, 2019.
10. REN21, "Renewables 2018 Global Status Report," June 14, 2019.
11. "Electricity Explained: Electricity in the United States," US EIA, April 19, 2019.

12. Congressional Research Service, "The Value of Energy Tax Incentives for Different Types of Energy Resources," March 19, 2019.
13. David Coady, Ian Parry, Nghia-Piotr Le, and Baoping Shang, "Global Fossil Fuel Subsidies Remain Large: An Update Based on Country-Level Estimates," International Monetary Fund, May 2019.
14. Corrie Clark, "Renewable Energy R&D Funding History: A Comparison With Funding for Nuclear Energy, Fossil Energy, Energy Efficiency, and Electric Systems R&D," Congressional Research Service, June 18, 2018.
15. Ibid.
16. ARPA-E, "ARPA-E Budget," https://arpa-e.energy.gov/?q=arpa-e-site-page/arpa-e-budget; Erin Smith and Addison Stark, "ARPA-E at 10," Bipartisan Policy Center blog, April 8, 2019.
17. There was a smaller 10% investment tax credit that preceded the 2005 law.
18. Congressional Research Service, "The Value of Energy Tax Incentives for Different Types of Energy Resources," March 19, 2019.
19. RPS policies are usually implemented with a trading mechanism. Companies that produce electricity from renewable energy sources may receive a Renewable Energy Credit that can be traded to utilities that need to comply with the standard. Through trading, lower-cost technologies and projects should theoretically prevail.
20. Some of these policies are voluntary goals rather than binding policies; see Figure 1.2.
21. Ohio, however, still enacted its RPS as part of a later restructuring reform in 2008.
22. North Carolina Clean Energy Technology Center, "The 50 States of Solar: 2018 Policy Review and Q4 2018 Quarterly Report," January 2019.
23. Small-scale, distributed solar is more accepted than large-scale projects.
24. Kathryne Cleary, Karen Palmer, and Kevin Rennert, "Clean Energy Standards," *Resources for the Future*, January 2019.
25. Steve Clemmer, Jeremy Richardson, Sandra Sattler, Dave Lochbaum, "The Nuclear Power Dilemma," Union of Concerned Scientists, November 2019.
26. Michael Scott, "Nuclear Power Outlook," US EIA, May 7, 2018.
27. According to one study, around 60% of the potential hydropower resources in the United States are already developed. M. Bowman, "EIA Projections Show Hydro Growth Limited by Economics not Resources," http://www.eia.gov/todayinenergy/detail.cfm?id=17051.
28. US EIA Annual Energy Outlook 2019 Projections and the Oak Ridge National Laboratory New Stream-Reach Development Resource Assessment (NSD).
29. In some parts of the United States, such as the Northeast, imports of Canadian hydropower may be important. That said, Canada may also want to use these resources to decarbonize its own grid.
30. Letter from the Secretary of Energy Steven Chu, October 12, 2009.
31. US Government Accountability Office, "Advanced Fossil Energy: Information on DOE Provided Funding for Research and Development Projects Started from Fiscal Years 2010 through 2017," report to the ranking member, Subcommittee on Energy, Committee on Energy and Natural Resources, US Senate. GAO-18-619. September 2018.
32. "Natural Gas: Natural Gas Prices," US EIA, June 28, 2019.
33. These estimates are in part a function of assumptions about methane versus carbon dioxide global warming potentials (Edwards & Trancik 2014).
34. This simple benchmark is broadly in line with more detailed targets developed by others. For example, one study suggests we need 37.3% clean energy by 2017 (Williams et al. 2014). Hence, if anything, my metric provides a marginally easier target for states to meet.
35. "Frequently Asked Questions: What Is U.S. Electricity Generation by Energy Source?," US EIA, March 1, 2019.
36. Ray Chen, "Natural Gas and Renewables Make Up Most of 2018 Electric Capacity Additions," US EIA, May 7, 2018.
37. Paul Hockenos, "Carbon Crossroads: Can Germany Revive Its Stalled Energy Transition?" YaleEnvironment360, December 13, 2018.
38. "Electricity: Detailed State Data," US EIA, June 28, 2019.
39. Ibid.
40. Ibid.

41. Ibid.
42. Counting behind the meter solar put Arizona's renewables closer to 7%. EIA "Arizona Profile Analysis," January 17, 2019.
43. Between 2016 and 2017, renewables grew by an average 1.2 p.p. If we extrapolate this rate outward, we find 39% renewable energy sources by 2045 when the nuclear plant begins shutting down.
44. "Electricity: Detailed State Data."
45. Ibid.
46. Ibid.
47. Bloomberg New Energy Finance, "New Investment in Clean Energy."
48. Wind Europe, "Wind Energy in Europe in 2018," https://windeurope.org/about-wind/statistics/european/wind-energy-in-europe-in-2018/; World Wind Energy Association, "Wind Power Capacity Worldwide Reaches 600 GW, 53,9 GW Added in 2018," February 25, 2019, https://wwindea.org/blog/2019/02/25/wind-power-capacity-worldwide-reaches-600-gw-539-gw-added-in-2018/.

Chapter 2

1. This chapter benefited enormously from previous research on policy feedback I undertook with Alex Hertel-Fernandez and Matto Mildenberger.
2. A third mode, of policy stability without change, could also be identified. However, since I am considering policy change, I do not examine these cases. In addition, the notion of policy drift problematizes the idea that policy can be considered stable since the nature of the problem the policy is addressing is usually in continuous flux.
3. For an example of research that does examine when policy feedback ends, see Mettler (2011), which examines federal aid for education that ended during the financial crisis despite support.
4. "Vital Statistics on Congress: Data on the U.S. Congress, Updated March 2019," Brookings Institution, March 4, 2019.
5. Michelle Singer, "Under the Influence," CBS, *60 Minutes*, March 29, 2007.
6. Jennifer Pahlka, "Fixing Government: Bottom Up and Outside In," The Long Now Foundation, February 1, 2017.
7. Interview 97, renewable energy advocate at a nongovernmental organization, March 19, 2015, multiple cases.
8. According to sexual harassment expert Marty Langelan, "Title IX turned out to be the legislative equivalent of a Swiss Army knife. . . . It opened up opportunities in so many areas we didn't foresee." Change was also slower than predicted, "Dr. Sandler said later that she had been naive in guessing how quickly change would come." She initially thought, she said, that "it would only take a year or two for all the inequities based on sex to be eliminated." Over time, she kept lengthening that prediction, until, she said, she finally realized that true change "would take more than my lifetime to accomplish." Katharine Seelye, "Bernice Sandler, 'Godmother of Title IX,' Dies at 90," *New York Times*, January 9, 2019.
9. Z. Bryon Wolf, "The Senate Voted on a Tax Bill Pretty Much Nobody Had Read," CNN, December 2, 2017.
10. Jim Tankersley, "Tucked Into the Tax Bill, a Plan to Help Distressed America," *New York Times*, January 29, 2018.
11. Matthew Gardner, Steve Wamhoff, Mary Martellotta, and Lorena Roque, "Corporate Tax Avoidance Remains Rampant Under New Tax Law," Institute on Taxation and Economic Policy, April 2019.
12. Ibid.
13. Ibid.
14. Still, perceptions remain crucial in this stage. If actors anticipate that regulation will be implemented and shift their resources or create new incentives and information, they may act before it is implemented (Rittenhouse & Zaragoza-watkins 2017). But if interest groups believe they can block implementation, then they will not respond to these potential changes.
15. Code for America, "2017 Impact Report"; Code for America, "2018 Impact Report; Code for America, "Healthy Communities." Nonetheless, the number of total people receiving benefits

from these programs has slightly declined since 2015: California Department of Social Services, "CalFresh Data Dashboard," May 2, 2019, https://www.cdss.ca.gov/inforesources/Data-Portal/Research-and-Data/CalFresh-Data-Dashboard

16. Michael Isaac Stein, "The Energy Industry's Secret Campaign to Get Us to Build More Power Plants," *The Nation*, May 14, 2019.

Chapter 3

1. As quoted in Hubbard (1916, 339).
2. Matthew Wald, "Pro-Coal Ad Campaign Disputes Warming Idea," *New York Times*, July 8, 1991.
3. Matthew Belvedere, "Like the New EPA Chief, Southern Company's CEO Doesn't See CO_2 as Main Reason for Climate Change," CNBC, March 28, 2017.
4. Notably, the New York attorney general's case against Exxon for climate denial names Rex Tillerson. Anecdotally, when I sat next to a utility executive at a dinner in 2013, he was still claiming that mercury did not really affect human health. Heck, he used to play with that mercury as a kid—clearly that hadn't affected his IQ.
5. Agis Salpukas, "70's Dreams, 90's Realities; Renewable Energy: A Luxury Now. A Necessity Later?," *New York Times*, April 11, 1995; "National Debate Topic 1997–98: Renewable Energy: Are Renewable Energy Sources Viable Alternatives to Fossil Fuels?" *Issues & Controversies*, Infobase, August 29, 1997.
6. Steven L. Clemmer, Alan Nogee, Michael C. Brower, & Paul Jefferiss, "A Powerful Opportunity Making Renewable Electricity the Standard," Union of Concerned Scientists, January 1999.
7. Note, this figure excludes hydropower. Technically, hydropower projects built after 1992 were eligible for the program, but in practice almost all of the US hydropower is much older, so very little would have counted toward the targets. US EIA, "Hydroelectric Generators Are Among the United States' Oldest Power Plants," March 13, 2017; "Electricity: Detailed State Data," US EIA, June 28, 2019.
8. Tom Kenworthy, "A Renewable Energy Standard: The Proof Is in the States," Center for American Progress, May 19, 2009; David Roberts, "The Faint Silver Lining of the Waxman-Markey Clean-Energy-Mandates Cloud," Grist, June 17, 2009.
9. The trend toward large, centralized plants was further amplified during World War I (Hughes, 1983).
10. Some argue this story may not be exactly true, but it still captures the move away from flat charges toward volumetric charges (Yakubovich et al. 2005).
11. NELA became the EEI in 1933 (Bradley 1996). The EEI remains an extremely influential industry association for private utilities. In the 1890s there was also a smaller association called the Association of Edison Illuminating Companies, which involved a group of utility executives from Edison-related companies (Yakubovich et al. 2005).
12. US EIA, "Average Retail Price of Electricity to Ultimate Customers by End-Use Sector," *Electric Power Monthly*, July 24, 2018.
13. US EIA, "U.S. Economy and Electricity Demand Growth Are Linked, but Relationship Is Changing," http://www.eia.gov/todayinenergy/detail.cfm?id=10491
14. International Energy Agency & Organisation for Economic Co-operation and Development, *Worldwide Trends in Energy Use and Efficiency*, 2008.
15. This structure still exists to some extent today, through rate differences across classes of customers. Large industrial consumers consistently pay lower rates for electricity than commercial customers, who pay less than residential customers.
16. Technically, the reference was made to a secret nuclear fusion project, not fission technology. But it was said without explaining its context, leading most to interpret it as a reference to conventional nuclear fission.
17. With the second oil crisis in 1979, the Carter administration also worked on synthetic fuels (Breetz, 2013). However, this chapter focuses on efforts before the crisis.
18. Co-generators, however, could use any fuel source such as natural gas.
19. One year earlier, in 1977, the Federal Power Commission was renamed the Federal Energy Regulatory Commission, and its powers and mandate were both expanded significantly.

20. With this decision, they ignored the risk of arbitrage, wherein QFs would have an incentive to draw excess power from the grid so that they could sell it at a higher price, for a profit.

21. However, 14 states actually had higher average rates (Devine et al. 1987). As Chapter 5 explains, other factors helped to explain the renewables boom in California.

22. I use the terms "deregulation" and "restructuring" interchangeably in this chapter. Critics tend to prefer the term "deregulation," while proponents prefer "restructuring." Of course, the use of each term is a political choice, which seeks to emphasize a particular point of view. And even after so-called deregulation, there is still in truth a regulated market overseen by government—albeit a different type of regulation.

23. The law required large wholesale wheeling (using utility transmission lines for sales) but not smaller, retail wheeling. However, states could set up retail wheeling if they wanted to. Hirsh (1999a, 243–244) has an extensive discussion on the topic.

24. In part, the US Navy drove nuclear investments (Cowan 1990). Overall, the military has been an important incubator for new energy technologies (Velandy 2014).

25. Steven Mufson and Lisa Rein, "Maryland Adopts Plan for Energy Efficiency," *Washington Post*, July 21, 2007.

26. Center for Climate and Energy Solutions, "Decoupling Policies," March 2019, https://www.c2es.org/document/decoupling-policies/

27. While the Renewable Energy and Energy Efficiency Technology Competitiveness Act was passed in 1989, this law set broad targets for energy technology innovation without specific incentives or mandates.

28. It is clear that environmental constraints are more important than supply constraints for fossil fuels. There are enough fuels on the planet for many centuries, but the climatic consequences of continuing to burn these fuels would be disastrous for human civilization.

29. This trend was also present in natural gas prices before the shale gas boom.

30. Biomass is one renewable source that does require fuel and creates carbon emissions. New hydropower can also release methane. The construction of steel for wind turbines also produces greenhouse gases.

31. *EPRI Journal*, September 1977, Issue 7, https://www.documentcloud.org/documents/3540308-EPRI-1977-Journal-No-7.html#document/p15/a353329

32. Matthew Wald, "Pro-Coal Ad Campaign Disputes Warming Idea," *New York Times*, July 8, 1991.

33. 1991 Information Council on the Environment Climate Denial Ad Campaign, http://www.climatefiles.com/denial-groups/ice-ad-campaign/

34. Global Climate Coalition Membership, circa 1993. http://www.climatefiles.com/denial-groups/global-climate-coalition-collection/membership-lists/.

35. Intermountain Rural Electric Association (IREA) Internal Memo, July 17 2006.

36. The Energy Policy Act of 1992 also created the Renewable Energy Production Incentive, which was very similar to the PTC but applied to nonprofit entities, such as municipal utilities and rural electric cooperatives, rather than for-profit companies. The law also made a 10% investment tax credit for solar and geothermal permanent.

37. The Energy Foundation was created by Pew, Rockefeller, and Hewlett. While these large funders did not constrain the EF's funding decisions, regional funders did constrain the funding geographically. Interview 100, foundation employee, October 31, 2018, multiple cases.

38. Interview 100, foundation employee, October 31, 2018, multiple cases.

39. This policy is also called a "public goods charge." Interview 64, renewables association employee, February 26, 2014, California.

40. Interview 100, foundation employee, October 31, 2018, multiple cases.

41. Interview 98, renewable energy advocate at an NGO, March 6, 2016, California; interview 100, foundation employee, October 31, 2018, multiple cases.

42. However, the advocates built in a trading mechanism in an attempt to have it fit more easily with the restructuring agenda.

43. Interview 97, renewable energy advocate at an NGO, March 19, 2015, multiple cases.

44. Interview 97, renewable energy advocate at an NGO, March 19, 2015, multiple cases.

45. Tom Starrs. Washington State University, "A Presentation by Keynote Speaker Thomas J. Starrs."

46. This law also required state PUCs to consider net metering and interconnection rules, creating a PURPA interconnection standard.

47. US Department of the Treasury, "Overview and Status Update of the §1603 Program," April 1 2017.

48. S. Kan et al., *U.S. Solar Market Insight Report*, 2014.

49. Juliet Eilperin, "Climate skeptic group works to reverse renewable energy mandates," *The Washington Post*, November 24, 2012.

50. Tom Stanton, "Status Report on Distributed Energy Resources and Evaluating Proposals and Practices," National Regulatory Research Institute, September 2015.

51. From $3.80/W in 2008 to $0.86/W in 2012 (Kind 2013).

52. Gabe Elsner, "The Campaign Against Net Metering: ALEC and Utility Interests' Next Attack on Clean Energy Surfaces in Arizona," Energy and Policy Institute, November 18, 2013.

53. ICF, "Review of Recent Cost-Benefit Studies Related to Net Metering and Distributed Solar," May 2018.

54. North Carolina Clean Energy Technology Center, "The 50 States of Solar: 2015 Policy Review and Q4 2015 Quarterly Report," February 2016; North Carolina Clean Energy Technology Center, "The 50 States of Solar: 2018 Policy Review and Q4 2018 Quarterly Report," January 2019.

55. Tom Stanton, "Review of State Net Energy Metering and Successor Rate Designs," National Regulatory Research Institute, May 2019.

56. North Carolina Clean Energy Technology Center, "The 50 States of Solar: 2018 Policy Review."

57. Although, changes in who controls the government could still undermine publicly owned assets ability to promote renewables.

58. EEI had total operating revenues of $364 million in 2017 compared to AWEA's $21 million of revenue in 2016 and the Solar Energy Industries Association's $7.5 million of membership dues revenue in 2017.

59. Author's own research based on publicly available information.

Chapter 4

1. Interview 47, renewable energy advocate at a nongovernmental organization (NGO), February 12, 2014, Texas.

2. Bureau of Economic Analysis, "Regional Data: GDP and Personal Income."

3. The American Council for an Energy-Efficient Economy scored Texas twenty-fifth on its 2018 score sheet despite the Department of Energy's evaluation that Texas has the potential for 87.3 megawatt (MW) hours in electricity savings by 2035—the largest sum in the United States (https://www.energy.gov/eere/slsc/us-energy-efficiency-potential-maps).

4. Interview 53, former commissioner, February 18, 2014, Texas.

5. The Public Utilities Regulatory Act was amended through SB 373. At the time, companies like Enron were pushing for transmission access so that they could profit off of the new electricity market. This law began the transition to a competitive wholesale generation market and required utilities to allow generators to use their transmission infrastructure at a fair cost (Dyer 2009).

6. The process actually started prior to 1995 but was put on pause several times as the PUC awaited direction from the legislature.

7. In practice, the IRP events were planned from 1996 until 1999, suggesting that not all utilities held these public opinion exercises before the IRP process was abandoned due to SB 7 and impending deregulation.

8. Interview 47, renewable energy advocate at an NGO, February 12, 2014, Texas.

9. Interview 53, former commissioner, February 18, 2014, Texas.

10. Interview 58, lobbyist for oil and gas industry, February 21, 2014, Texas.

11. In late 1996, the PUCT also transformed the Electric Reliability Council of Texas (ERCOT) into an independent system operator, further shifting the system toward competition. In an

attempt to resist state regulation, the electric utilities' themselves established ERCOT in 1970, and today the ERCOT system covers about 75% of the Texas grid (Dyer, 2011).

12. Interview 56, former commissioner, February 20, 2014; interview 58, lobbyist for oil and gas industry, February 21, 2014, Texas.

13. Interview 58, lobbyist for oil and gas industry, February 21, 2014, Texas.

14. Interview 49, political staff, February 13, 2014, Texas.

15. Initially, the PUCT regulated rural electric cooperatives as well as investor-owned utilities; but after deregulation, cooperatives stopped being subject to PUC rules.

16. Interview 58, lobbyist for oil and gas industry, February 21, 2014, Texas.

17. Interview 53, former commissioner, February 18, 2014, Texas.

18. Interview 41, renewables association employee, February 10, 2014; interview 57, former commissioner, February 20, 2014, Texas.

19. Bloomberg News, "Enron Acquires Zond, a Major Wind Power Company," *New York Times*, January 7, 1997.

20. Interview 45, renewable energy advocate at an NGO, February 11, 2014, Texas.

21. Interview 41, former politician, February 6, 2014, Texas.

22. The final provisions required cuts of 50% from 1997 by 2003 for nitrous oxide and 25% over the same period for sulfur dioxide. These provisions applied to grandfathered plants, built before the Texas Clean Air Act was passed, particularly in the Dallas area (Hudson & Rowe 2005).

23. Interview 58, lobbyist for oil and gas industry, February 21, 2014, Texas.

24. For more on the Energy Foundation, see https://www.ef.org/about-us/

25. Interview 47, renewable energy advocate at an NGO, February 12, 2014, Texas.

26. According to the Energy Foundation's 1998 990-PF form, in 1998, EDF was given $110,000 to work on renewables and conservation advocacy and $150,000 to work on air pollution.

27. Interview 45, renewable energy advocate at an NGO, February 11, 2014, Texas.

28. Interview 45, renewable energy advocate at an NGO, February 11, 2014, Texas.

29. Interview 45, renewable energy advocate at an NGO, February 11, 2014; interview 58, lobbyist for oil and gas industry, February 21, 2014, Texas.

30. Given the conflicts over how to calculate a baseline for the percentage of renewables, the RPS was changed to a capacity, rather than a generation, target. A capacity target requires a certain amount of infrastructure to be built; for example, if each wind turbine is 1 MW, 3,000 turbines would need to be built for a 3,000-MW target. In contrast, most RPS policies use a generation target, which requires a certain percentage of electricity to be *produced* from renewable energy sources. The move toward a capacity target suggests opponent interest groups' influence in watering down the proposal.

31. The amendment read, "Each retail electric provider, municipally owned utility, and electric cooperative operating in the state shall obtain a minimum of 1.65 percent of its annual capacity requirements from renewable energy technologies by January 1, 2003, 2.15 percent of its annual capacity requirements from renewable energy technologies by January 1, 2005, 2.75 percent of its annual capacity requirements from renewable energy technologies by January 1, 2007, and 3 percent of its annual capacity requirements from renewable energy technologies by January 1, 2009."

32. Interview 45, renewable energy advocate at an NGO, February 11, 2014, Texas.

33. Interview 53, former commissioner, February 18, 2014, Texas.

34. According to the Energy Foundation's 1998 990-PF form, in 1998 Public Citizen was granted $100,000 to work on its "Cleaner Air Comes From Cleaner Energy Campaign."

35. Interview 47, renewable energy advocate at an NGO, February 12, 2014, Texas.

36. Ibid.

37. Ibid.

38. TREIA Membership Directory, November 1999.

39. For example, in the TREIA spring 1997 newsletter, the chief executive officer of BP indicated his support for action on climate change; however, he still maintained some skepticism toward policy solutions and drew a contrast to environmentalist policy preferences.

40. Interview 47, renewable energy advocate at an NGO, February 12, 2014, Texas.

41. The TREIA Newsletter, spring 1997, p. 5.

42. EDF, "Clean Energy for the Energy Capital of the United States: Houston Light & Power Customers Voice Strong Opinions in Deliberative Poll," February 4, 1998, https://www.edf.org/news/clean-energy-energy-capital-united-states-houston-light-power-customers-voice-strong-opinions-d

43. TREIA newsletter, winter 1996–7, p. 3.

44. Interview 47, renewable energy advocate at an NGO, February 12, 2014, Texas.

45. These efforts included corresponding with Rabe, who did not disclose sufficient detail on the bureaucrat for legitimate reasons of confidentiality, 24 interviews with Texan advocates and opponents involved with the RPS, and archival research on hundreds of documents.

46. US Department of Energy, WINDExchange, "U.S. Installed and Potential Wind Power Capacity and Generation," https://windexchange.energy.gov/maps-data/321

47. A number of other factors also helped enable Texas's large transmission investment. Gas prices were rising throughout 2004 and 2005, reaching $7.30/mcf in July 2005, when the RPS expansion bill passed. There was a concern at the time over increasing electricity supply diversity, given the almost exclusive reliance on coal and gas. Both poor air quality in the large cities and high gas prices made additional wind investment, including in transmission capacity, welcome. And given that Texas's electricity grid is largely isolated likely helped spur the competitive renewable energy zone (CREZ) investment. With few interconnections, it would be difficult for Texas to export its wind energy (Rabe 2004). To balance the system, then, Texas would have to increase its own ability to absorb the intermittent wind energy. In addition, the isolated grid insured that most of the benefits, for example, reduced transmission congestion, would go to Texas companies. This reduced coordination problems since transmission investments can have geographically dispersed benefactors and beneficiaries (Baldick & Kahn 1993). For these reasons, a large transmission bill was easier to pass in Texas than other states.

48. The Steering Committee of Cities Served by Oncor and the Texas Coalition for Affordable Energy, "The Story of ERCOT," February 2011.

49. Electric Reliability Council of Texas, "Transmission Issues Associated With Renewable Energy in Texas; Informal White Paper for the Texas Legislature, 2005," March 28, 2005.

50. Senator Fraser's letter to the PUCT, December 6, 2006.

51. US Department of Energy, WINDExchange, "U.S. Installed and Potential Wind Power Capacity and Generation."

52. In early 2009, FPL changed its name to NextEra Energy Resources. In 2014, it was the largest owner and operator of renewable energy projects (wind and solar) in North America. The wind farm implied in this passage is Horse Hollow.

53. The project is located in Taylor County and Nolan County. All of Taylor County was in Senate District 24 in 2005; around one-quarter has been redistricted out of that district since then.

54. While this initial bill did not pass, in a special session it was revised as SB 20 and successfully passed.

55. For one example, see John Smithee, Comments on Project 31852, February 16, 2006.

56. J. Malewitz, "$7 Billion CREZ Project Nears Finish, Aiding Wind Power," *Texas Tribune*, October 14, 2013.

57. Interview 58, lobbyist for oil and gas industry, February 21, 2014, Texas.

Chapter 5

1. Interview 51, clean energy company employee, February 14, 2014, Texas.

2. Dave Levitan, "Picking Winners: Obama Budget Shifts Tax Incentives Toward Renewables," *InsideClimate News*, April 15, 2010.

3. The exception was small municipal utilities' service areas that operated outside of the deregulated market and RPS policy.

4. Interview 45, renewable energy advocate at a nongovernmental organization (NGO), February 11, 2014, Texas.

5. Interview 47, renewable energy advocate at an NGO, February 12, 2014, Texas.

6. Ibid.

7. In part, this may be because the renewable energy groups were poorly engaged with the process surrounding SB 20 and SB 533, often neglecting to testify on the bill at all.
8. Interview 58, lobbyist for oil and gas industry, February 21, 2014, Texas.
9. Interview 58, lobbyist for oil and gas industry, February 21, 2014, Texas.
10. Texas Association of Manufacturers, press release "Manufacturing Veteran Tony Bennett Named President of Texas Association of Manufacturing," August 27, 2012, https://manufacturetexas.org/press/manufacturing-veteran-tony-bennett-named-president-of-texas-association-of-manufacturing
11. The TIEC has also previously used the name "Texas Industrial Consumers."
12. This list comes from the fact that if the TIEC participates in a PUC rate case, it must list the members it is representing for the case.
13. Interview 58, lobbyist for oil and gas industry, February 21, 2014, Texas.
14. Interview 51, clean energy company employee, February 14, 2014, Texas.
15. Ibid.
16. Interview 55, lobbyist for renewables industry, February 18, 2014, Texas.
17. Interview 47, renewable energy advocate at an NGO, February 12, 2014, Texas.
18. Interview 102, lobbyist for renewables industry, March 8, 2019, Texas.
19. Interview 45, renewable energy advocate at an NGO, February 12, 2014, Texas; interview 49, political staff, February 13, 2014, Texas; interview 50, political staff, February 13, 2014, Texas; interview 54, lobbyist for renewables industry, February 18, 2014, Texas; interview 58, lobbyist for oil and gas industry, February 21, 2014, Texas.
20. Interview 58, lobbyist for oil and gas industry, February 21, 2014, Texas.
21. The TAM lobbyist also represents the TIEC before the PUCT.
22. In the Texas Renewable Energy Industries Association's (TREIA's) August 2005 newsletter, the renewable advocates celebrated the passage of SB 20. Their only concern focused on how to count renewable energy credits and not the far more consequential use of "target" versus "goal."
23. In the case of Representative Blake, there was a proposed biomass facility in his district.
24. Compliance premiums for non-wind technologies, which would essentially grant solar projects additional renewable energy certificates (RECs).
25. Interview 57, former commissioner staffer, February 20, 2014, Texas.
26. Interview 43, renewable energy advocate at an NGO, February 11, 2014, Texas.
27. T. Evilsizer, *Industries Storm States Over Climate Change*, National Institute on Money in State Politics, 2009.
28. The commission's incentives included allowing small generators to aggregate to meet the 10-MW minimum for RECs and fossil fuel generators to repower with renewable fuel and receive RECs. Neither of these rules would spur solar development.
29. Interview 58, lobbyist for oil and gas industry, February 21, 2014, Texas.
30. An updated list can be found on the PUCT website under Filings for Case 35113.
31. Solar Energy Industries Association, "Texas Solar," 2019, https://www.seia.org/state-solar-policy/texas-solar
32. Interview 50, political staff, February 13, 2014, Texas.
33. Interview 57, former commissioner staffer, February 20, 2014, Texas.
34. Instead, two small renewable energy–related bills passed: a property-assessed clean energy law and a small bill which clarified that solar installations would not raise a building's tax valuation. While these laws would remove some barriers, they were not the critical enabling legislation necessary to build a solar industry in Texas. They were incremental, status-quo policies that did not require the legislature or administration to take action to transform the electricity system.
35. Interview 54, lobbyist for renewables industry, February 14, 2014, Texas.
36. M. J. Bradley, "Benchmarking Air Emissions of the 100 Largest Electric Power Producers in the United States," June 2019.
37. Interview 47, renewable energy advocate at an NGO, February 12, 2014, Texas.
38. Interview 54, lobbyist for renewables industry, February 18, 2014, Texas.
39. The exception to the rule is the municipal utilities in San Antonio and Austin, which have both created their own policies to drive solar uptake in their service territories.

40. For an explanation of the current state of Texas net metering and distributed generation policy, see the National Renewable Energy Laboratory's website: https://www.nrel.gov/solar/rps/tx.html

41. Adam Burke, "In Sunny Nevada, a Defeat for the Solar Industry," *Marketplace*, February 23, 2016; Nichola Groom, "Nevada Reinstates Key Solar Energy Policy," *Reuters*, June 15, 2017.

42. According to the Solar Energy Industries Association, Texas was fourth in 2017 and sixth in 2018.

43. Tim Sylvia, "Five Texas Munis Partner to Add 500 MW of Solar," *PV Magazine*, September 20, 2018.

44. Titiaan Palazzi and Dan Seif, "Why Distributed Solar Is Winning in Texas," *GreenBiz*, February 28, 2018.

Chapter 6

1. Coral Davenport and Eric Lipton, "How G.O.P. Leaders Came to View Climate Change as Fake Science," *New York Times*, June 3, 2017; Jane Mayer, "Covert Operations," *New Yorker*, August 23, 2010.

2. Interview 86, renewable energy advocate at a nongovernmental organization (NGO), November 10, 2014, Kansas.

3. Koch Industries and the Kansas Chamber of Commerce were at the forefront of funding a far-right wave in the 2010s. Governor Brownback and his political allies solicited their funding to primary moderate Republicans. Mark Binelli, "Rogue State: How Far-Right Fanatics Hijacked Kansas," *Rolling Stone*, June 12, 2013.

4. According to the Department of Energy, Kansas had installed 113 megawatts (MW) of wind power capacity in 2001.

5. Interview 92, utility employee, November 12, 2014, Kansas.

6. Westar Press Release, "Westar Launches Kansas' Largest Wind Energy Program," October 1, 2007.

7. One of the bills was HB 2479.

8. Interview 87, lobbyist for the renewables industry, November 10, 2014, Kansas.

9. Specifically, Governor Sebelius suggested that wind farms should not be developed in the area through a voluntary ban in the area bounded by the roads US-24, US-77, US-400, K-99, and K-4.

10. Kansas Energy Council Staff, "KCC Staff Wind Study: A Benefit Cost Study of the Governor's 2015 Wind Challenge (1,000 MW by 2015)," October 2008.

11. Interview 94, renewable energy advocate at an NGO, November 13, 2014, Kansas.

12. Sarah Kessinger, "Sebelius Calls for Renewable Energy Mandates," *Salina Journal*, February 2, 2008.

13. One version of the bill, SB 148, passed in 2007, included an RPS.

14. Interview 94, renewable energy advocate at an NGO, November 13, 2014, Kansas.

15. Interview 92, utility employee, November 12, 2014, Kansas.

16. Originally, Sunflower wanted to build two 700-MW plants, so this represented a reduction. Sunflower also agreed to take on new energy efficiency programs and to increase its renewables faster than other utilities (20% by 2016) as part of the settlement agreement.

17. Siemens also likely relocated in Kansas because of a secondary bill, SB 108, also passed in 2009. This bill amended the Economic Revitalization and Reinvestment Act to allow wind and solar manufacturing companies to apply for up to $5 million in bonds.

18. Interview 92, utility employee, November 12, 2014, Kansas.

19. Interview 92, utility employee, November 13, 2014, Kansas.

20. Interview 87, lobbyist for renewables industry, November 11, 2014, Kansas.

21. Earthjustice, "Groups Ask Kansas Supreme Court to Overturn Sunflower Coal Plant Permit," August 15, 2011.

22. The last new coal plant to come online occurred in Virginia in 2012. T. Cormons, "A Sad Day for VA — Wise County Coal Plant Fires Up," *Appalachian Voices*, August 11, 2012.

23. The Kansas legislature passed another bill in the 2013/2014 session to attempt to ease the plant's permitting process in Kansas. Whether it will proceed remains to be seen, particularly

given the federal Clean Power Plan. In 2017, the company's board suggested a "remote" chance that the Holcomb plant would be built. P. Hancock, "Holcomb Power Plant Unlikely to Be Built, Company Says; $93 Million Already Spent," *Lawrence Journal-World*, September 18, 2017.

24. In 2005, he voted for an amendment to the Energy Policy Act of 2005, to create a federal RPS. In 2007, along with 32 other senators, he co-sponsored S.CON.RES.3, which created a target of 25% renewable energy by 2025.

25. Governor Sam Brownback, Kansas State of the State, January 12 2011.

26. Governors' Wind Energy Coalition, Letter to Congress, November 15, 2011.

27. Rick Plumlee, "Deal Limits Flint Hills Wind Farm Expansion," *Wichita Eagle*, May 7, 2011.

28. US EIA, https://www.eia.gov/electricity/monthly/epm_table_grapher.php?t=epmt_5_6_a

29. D. G. Tuerck, P. Bachman, and M. Head, *The Economic Impact of the Kansas Renewable Portfolio Standard*, 2012.

30. G. Elsner, *Heartland Institute Pushes Flawed Analysis Attacking Kansas RPS*, Energy & Policy Institute, March 26, 2014.

31. In June 2013, Dennis Hedke wrote an editorial in the *Wichita Eagle* entitled "Climate Science Isn't Settled."

32. The Heritage Foundation is a conservative think tank that has been a major actor in the climate denial movement (Oreskes & Conway 2010).

33. Andy Marso, "Koch works behind scenes on renewable energy bill." *The Topeka Capital-Journal*, February 26, 2013.

34. Ibid.

35. Interview 88, politician, November 11, 2014, Kansas.

36. Interview 92, utility employee, November 13, 2014, Kansas.

37. This wind energy PAC also gave money to Governor Sam Brownback's campaign. Governmental Ethics Commission, "Campaign Finance Receipts & Expenditure Report," January 10, 2014, http://ethics.ks.gov/CFAScanned/House/2014ElecCycle/201401/H122JJ_201401.pdf

38. Compared to the Kansas Chamber of Commerce's $360,000 in contributions, the Kansas New Energy Economy PAC had just over $45,000 in 2013 according to the Kansas Governmental Ethics Commission.

39. Since the Kansas legislative session runs for 2 years, the bill only died in committee in May 2014, along with the other anti-RPS bill.

40. National Institute on Money in State Politics.

41. Dennis Hedke and Forrest Knox, "Rep. Dennis Hedke and Sen. Forrest Knox: Renewable Mandate Driving up Energy Costs," *Wichita Eagle*, May 20, 2014.

42. Senate Bill No. 82, Amended, p. 1, February 28, 2013.

43. Kimberly Svaty, "Wind Energy in Kansas: House Energy & Environment Committee," The Wind Coalition, January 21, 2015.

44. Interview 94, renewable energy advocate at an NGO, November 12, 2014, Kansas.

45. Bryan Lowry, "Brownback's Office Clarifies His Position on Renewable Energy Standards," *Wichita Eagle*, July 23, 2014.

46. Kansas Corporation Commission, Retail Rate Impact Report 2014, March 1, 2014.

47. James M. Taylor, "Kansas Renewable Mandates Causing Skyrocketing Electricity Prices," The Heartland Institute, January 24, 2014.

48. Interview 92, utility employee, November 12, 2014, Kansas.

49. Suzanne Goldberg, "Leak Exposes how Heartland Institute Works to Undermine Climate Science," *The Guardian*, February 15, 2012.

50. Elliot Negin, "Unreliable Sources: How the Media Help the Kochs and ExxonMobil Spread Climate Disinformation," *Huffington Post*, June 3, 2013.

51. Interview 93, renewable energy advocate at an NGO, November 13, 2014, Kansas; interview 94, renewable energy advocate at an NGO, November 13, 2014, Kansas.

52. Interview 94, renewable energy advocate at an NGO, November 12, 2014, Kansas.

53. Judy L. Thomas and Bryan Lowry, "How Kansas Lawmakers Keep You From Finding out What They're Doing — Until It's Too Late," *Kansas City Star*, December 1, 2017.

54. Ibid.

55. Interview 86, renewable energy advocate at an NGO, November 10, 2014, Kansas.

56. The question wording was, "In 2009 the Kansas Legislature passed a comprehensive energy bill that requires Kansas utility companies to generate 20 percent of their electricity from renewable sources by the year 2020. Do you support or oppose that law?" Support was even higher when citizens were asked in general if they supported renewables: 91% indicated support.

57. Support from Democrats was even higher, at 82%.

58. Most people said that it would have no effect, rather than that it would decrease their likelihood of voting for the candidate.

59. Initially, this bill was unrelated to renewable energy policies, but it was gutted and amended in March 2014, becoming a substitute bill in the Senate. The Senate Committee on Utilities, where Senator Apple remained the chair, sponsored the new version of the bill.

60. In Kansas, Speaker of the House Ray Merrick has served on the ALEC board and chaired Kansas's chapter. Similarly, Senate president Susan Wagle, current board member, has served as a national chair. In Ohio, Speaker of the House William Batchelder and Senate president Keith Faber had ALEC membership.

61. Interview 88, politician, November 11, 2014, Kansas.

62. The Koch-affiliated group AFP also funded a television ad encouraging Kansas residents to oppose the RPS and contact their legislators or Governor Brownback. Americans for Prosperity, "AFP-Kansas RPS Repeal Ad: Details and Sources," January 29, 2014.

63. Koch Industries, http://www.followthemoney.org/entity-details?eid=1457&default=contributor

64. Kansas 2012, Election Overview, http://www.followthemoney.org/election-overview?s=KS&y=2012

65. Bryan Lowry, "Kansas AFP Director Acknowledges Informal Contact With Group Behind Energy Mailings," Wichita Eagle, May 9, 2014.

66. Andy Marso, "AFP State Leader Admits Link to Group Opposing Renewable Energy Law: Americans for Prosperity State Director Says His Role Was Personal, Not Connected to AFP," Topeka Capital-Journal, May 8, 2014.

67. Ibid.

68. Estimates suggest AFP spent $387,000, the Kansas Senior Consumer Alliance spent $40,000, and the Chamber of Commerce spent $18,000. The Wind Coalition and the Wind Works for Kansas campaign spent around $60,000. See Wichita Business Journal, "Top List of Lobbyists 2014"; Government of Kansas, "Summary of Expenditures Reported by Registered Lobbyists," April 2014; "Wind war's total: Nearly half a million dollars," Topeka Capital-Journal, May 24, 2014.

69. Interview 94, renewable energy advocate at an NGO, November 12, 2014, Kansas.

70. Interview 93, renewable energy advocate at an NGO, November 12, 2014, Kansas.

71. Ibid.

72. Republican representatives Russ Jennings and Tom Sloan were both targeted for not supporting the repeal efforts. Scott Rothschild, "Fight Over Renewable Energy Continues in GOP Primary," Lawrence Journal-World, June 15, 2014.

73. Andy Marso, "Rep: Koch Using Kansas Chamber to Retaliate on Renewable Energy," Topeka Capital-Journal, June 16, 2014.

74. Email correspondence from Representative Scott Schwab, June 12, 2014, to "Kansas Chamber of Commerce Friends." Full text available at http://www.dailykos.com/story/2014/06/16/1307511/-KS-House-Republican-Kochs-Lobby-Unfairly-Has-Questionable-Lobbying-Practices

75. According to the Kansas Governmental Ethics Commission.

76. Koch Industries gave $3,400 directly to Apple. The Kansas Chamber of Commerce gave him $4,148, and the Kansas Republican Senatorial Committee gave him $16,850, https://www.followthemoney.org/entity-details?eid=13011941

77. This estimate was for a 100-MW farm, http://www.kansas.com/news/politics-government/article20465616.html

78. KS 79-201, http://www.ksrevisor.org/statutes/chapters/ch79/079_002_0001.html

79. Interview 86, renewable energy advocate at an NGO, November 10, 2014, Kansas.
80. Bryan Lowry, "Compromise Reached for Softened Kansas Renewable Energy Standards," *Kansas City Star*, May 4, 2015.
81. Ibid.
82. Ibid.
83. Andy Marso, "Property Tax Change Part of Largely Symbolic Renewable Energy Bill," Kansas Health Institute, May 12, 2015.
84. *Hutchinson News*, "Siemens Gamesa Announces Mass Layoff at Hutchinson Plant," August 18 2017, http://www.hutchnews.com/news/20170818/siemens-gamesa-announces-mass-layoff-at-hutchinson-plant
85. Center for Public Integrity analysis based on National Renewable Energy Laboratory and US Energy Information Administration (EIA) data, https://publicintegrity.org/environment/statehouses-not-the-sun-drive-solar-energy-gaps/
86. US EIA, "Electricity: Electricity Data Browser," https://www.eia.gov/electricity/data/browser/

Chapter 7

1. My best estimate of the solar industry's political spending during the period covered in this chapter is $28 million, which is 50% smaller than APS's estimated spending of $55 million.
2. James R. Wrathall and Elias B. Hinckley, "Arizona Update: Solar Controversies Causing Market Upheaval," Association of Corporate Counsel, March 4, 2015.
3. APS contributed an estimated $425,000 to elect Mark Brnovich.
4. Terry Tang, "Arizona AG Accused of Bias Against Clean Energy Initiative," Associated Press, September 18, 2018.
5. APS generated 7.7% renewable energy in 2018. Pinnacle West Capital Corporation, "2018 Annual Report." Tucson Electric Power has been more compliant and generated 14% from renewables in 2018. Tucson Electric Power, "Green (Energy) Acres," https://www.tep.com/renewable-resources-2/
6. APS also devotes resources to lobbying the Arizona legislature, some portion of its $350,000 to $700,000 annual lobbying expenditure. It also focuses on the executive branch more broadly. Most recently, APS has seen favorable outcomes under Governor Ducey. He appointed two commissioners aligned with APS earlier in his tenure and, in June 2019, selected another commissioner who has ties with APS. Peter Aleshire, "APS Finally Discloses Massive Political Spending," *Payson Roundup*, April 5, 2019; Iulia Gheorghiu, "Arizona Commissioner Tobin Resigns, Following Frustrations With Staff as 'Sixth Commissioner,' " *Utility Dive*, May 31, 2019.
7. As Article 15, Section 3, outlines, "The corporation commission shall have full power to, and shall, prescribe just and reasonable classifications to be used and just and reasonable rates and charges to be made and collected, by public service corporations within the state."
8. Lou Gum, "ACC Ethics in Question, Says Former Commissioner," KAWC News, August 16, 2018.
9. US Energy Information Administration, "Arizona: State Profiles and Energy Estimates," https://www.eia.gov/state/?sid=AZ#tabs-4.
10. Salt River Project, "Facts About SRP," https://www.srpnet.com/about/facts.aspx
11. Ryan Randazzo, "Solar Advocates Hope to Oust SRP Board Members," *The Arizona Republic*, March 1, 2016; Ryan Randazzo, "SRP System for Electing Leaders Criticized as Unfair and Undemocratic," *The Arizona Republic*, June 6, 2019; SRP, "SRP Governance and Elections," https://www.srpnet.com/elections/Default.aspx
12. This occurred through the integrated resource planning process. The total target was 17 megawatts (MW). According to a bureaucrat involved in the program, the target was 10 MW for APS, 5 MW for TEP, and 2 MW for other smaller utilities. Interview 28, commission staffer, January 24, 2014, Arizona.
13. Several interview subjects noted the importance of Commissioner Jennings in passing the standard. At that time, the commission consisted of two Democrats and one Republican, with Jennings able to marshal votes from his colleagues. Democratic commissioner Weeks was

also supportive. Interview 25, renewable energy advocate at a nongovernmental organization (NGO), January 22, 2014, Arizona; interview 28, commission staffer, January 24, 2014, Arizona; interview 34, former renewables association employee, January 30, 2014, Arizona.

14. "Arizona Restructuring Suspended," http://www.eia.gov/electricity/policies/restructuring/arizona.html

15. The policy was first proposed in April 1999 as the "environmentally-friendly portfolio standard" and later renamed the "environmental portfolio standard." The rulemaking process began in May 2000.

16. ACC decision number 62506, May 4, 2000.

17. Interview 28, commission staffer, January 24, 2014, Arizona.

18. Arizona Corporation Commission, Decision number 69127, November 14, 2006.

19. Arizona Corporation Commission, *Commissioners Approve Rules Requiring 15 Percent of Energy From Renewables by 2025*, November 1, 2006.

20. AriSEIA worked with Commissioner Kris Mayes and a supportive staffer. Interview 34, former renewables association employee, January 30, 2014, Arizona.

21. National Conference of State Legislatures, "State Renewable Portfolio Standards and Goals," February 1, 2019.

22. Interview 34, former renewables association employee, January 30, 2014, Arizona.

23. The proceeding started earlier, as part of electricity restructuring in 1999, with support from several new, competitive energy companies including Enron and New Energy Ventures and the Distributed Energy Association of Arizona. It also developed while the REST was being developed, in April 2005. Part of the impetus for action was the Energy Policy Act of 2005, which included an NEM standard that states could either adopt as is or modify.

24. Ed Taylor, "Valley Businesses See Sunnier Days for Solar," *East Valley Tribune*, March 8, 2006.

25. Interview 28, commission staffer, January 24, 2014, Arizona. Additionally, a former commissioner involved in both policies noted that the NEM received far less debate. Interview 32, former commissioner at ACC, January 27, 2014, Arizona.

26. Notably, even SRP followed the docket, likely because it realized any NEM decision would also likely affect its plans.

27. Arizona Public Service Company's Comments to Staff's Request for Written Comments to Proposed Net Metering Rules, January 4, 2008.

28. R.W. Beck Inc., *Distributed Renewable Energy Operating Impacts and Valuation Study*, prepared for Arizona Public Service, 2009.

29. ACC Meeting Minutes, "Net Metering Workshop," September 7, 2006.

30. Arizona Corporation Commission, "ACC Approves 'Net Metering' to Offset Consumer Costs for Renewable Energy," October 20, 2008.

31. Some customers with tax liability could already combine the state and federal policies. But in practice, solar leasing made this arrangement accessible to far more people.

32. See Chapter 3 for an explanation of electricity wheeling.

33. By 2014, SolarCity provided 34% of installations—the clear market leader. Daniel Gross, "The Miracle of SolarCity," *Slate*, July 31, 2015.

34. APS application to open NEM docket, July 12, 2013.

35. EIA Form 826 detailed data. APS data are for 2013 because no data are available for it in 2012.

36. According to one news report and the Center for American Democracy, ACC chair Bob Stump participated in ALEC. Commissioner Bob Burns is a former Arizona ALEC state chair. In addition, another commissioner who was elected before 2012, Brenda Burns, was on ALEC's board for 9 years and was national chair in 1999. D. A. Barber, "The Battle for a Solar Arizona: Arizona Is Being Sucked Into a War Over Residential Solar Energy," *Tucson Weekly*, September 26, 2013.

37. APS also knew that former ALEC-affiliated commissioners such as Bob Stump were more favorable to their policies. Energy and Policy Institute, "Attacks on Renewable Energy Policy by Fossil Fuel Interests 2013–2014," May 2014.

38. An APS spokesperson asserted that the company was a proud member of ALEC due to its pro-business stances. Luige del Puerto, "Months After Publicly Leaving ALEC in 2012, APS Quietly Rejoined," *Arizona Capital Times*, November 7, 2013. Moreover, APS has historically supported ALEC-affiliated legislators because of their anti-solar stances. The trend is no

different for the ACC candidates. Lee Fang, "Arizona GOP Candidate Debbie Lesko Copied and Pasted Bills Written by Lobbyists," *The Intercept*, April 19, 2018.

39. Robert Anglen and Ryan Randazzo, "2 Utilities' Cash Went to 3 ACC Campaigns," *The Arizona Republic*, November 5, 2013.

40. Ibid.

41. Some researchers suggest that public financing reduces the influence of money in elections and the influence of interest groups (Malhotra 2008). Even a small contribution could undo the intent of public financing laws.

42. Commissioner Gary Pierce was formerly a representative in the House. Arizona Corporation Commission, "Commission Names Jodi Jerich as Executive Director," January 3, 2013.

43. While the ACC staff appeared to act more in line with the public interest prior to 2014, the staff now appears to be aligned with the utilities, at times being at odds even with commissioners. Gheorghiu, "Arizona Commissioner Tobin Resigns."

44. ACC Decision number 73636.

45. Despite eliminating support for new solar projects, APS made it clear that it still wanted the renewable energy credits for use in compliance with the RPS target. In other words, while it wasn't paying for the renewables anymore, it still wanted to own them to meet requirements under the renewable energy policy.

46. Herman K. Trabish, "A Sneak Attack on Commercial Solar in Arizona," *Greentech Media*, February 25, 2013.

47. Ryan Randazzo, "Officials Consider Altering Renewable Mandate," *The Arizona Republic*, February 7, 2013.

48. Ibid.

49. Edison Electric Institute, *Disruptive Challenges: Financial Implications and Strategic Responses to a Changing Retail Electric Business*, January, 2013.

50. Navigant Consulting report prepared for APS, *Net Metering Bill Impacts and Distributed Energy Subsidies*, December 2012.

51. A report from the Lawrence Berkeley National Laboratory suggests that unnecessary infrastructure for natural gas shifts costs to customers. Galen Barbose, *Putting the Potential Rate Impacts of Distributed Solar Into Context*, January 2017.

52. Navigant Consulting report prepared for APS, *Net Metering Bill Impacts*, 1.

53. This discussion occurred in APS's docket on its renewable energy charges on customer's bills, E-01345A-12-0290. The decision number is 73636.

54. Interview 32, former commissioner, January 27, 2014, Arizona.

55. Interview 34, former renewables association employee, January 30, 2014, Arizona.

56. The founding members of TASC were SolarCity, Sungevity, Sunrun, Verengo, Solar Universe, and REC solar.

57. 60 Plus Association, *Seniors Group Releases TV Ad Highlighting Terry Goddard's Devotion to Obama Agenda*, October 24, 2014.

58. Rachel Finkel, "60 Plus Association," FactCheck.org, June 23, 2014, https://www.factcheck.org/2014/04/60-plus-association-2; Miriam Wasser, "Koch Brothers Help Fund Anti-Grand Canyon Monument, Pro-Uranium Mining Efforts in Arizona, Tax Documents Show," *Phoenix New Times*, April 18, 2016.

59. Rod Kuckro, "APS Admits to Bankrolling Anti-solar TV ads," *Utility Dive*, October 22, 2013.

60. Ryan Randazzo, "Expense of Solar Battle in Millions," *The Arizona Republic*, November 6, 2013.

61. Ibid.

62. SAIC report prepared for APS, *2013 Updated Solar PV Value Report*, May 2013.

63. Interview 32, former commissioner, January 27, 2014, Arizona.

64. The trend of disparate results from NEM cost and benefit studies is common across the country. A study commissioned by the Department of Energy outlined how many studies use different value categories and different "classes" such as utilities or consumers or society at large as the main unit of analysis: ICF, "Review of Recent Cost–Benefit Studies Related to Net Metering and Distributed Solar," May 2018.

65. The governor appoints RUCO directors, and thus, depending on the governor's relationship with APS, the RUCO is not immune to capture.

66. Indeed, the next director of the RUCO would have a texting relationship with APS employees: Ryan Randazzo, "Texts Show Close Ties Between Arizona Consumer Advocate, APS," *The Arizona Republic*, September 8, 2016.

67. ACC Docket number E-01345A-13-0248.

68. According to APS at that time, average bills were $150.91 in the summer and $121.72 in the winter, https://www.aps.com/en/residential/accountservices/serviceplans/Pages/standard.aspx

69. The original proposal included a provision for leased systems to be non-transferable after a home is sold. Fearing continued backlash, APS moved its position to grandfathering all existing customers. Interview 31, renewable energy advocate at an NGO, January 27, 2014, Arizona.

70. The cap on APS's payments would be per unit of power such that the cost of power would be the same as or lower than that purchased from a solar power purchase agreement.

71. They argued that the Lost Fixed Cost Recovery program covered this issue.

72. Several interview subjects argued that the RUCO intervened because the advocates were able to leverage support for rooftop solar among some conservatives. Interview 30, renewable energy advocate at an NGO, January 27, 2014, Arizona; interview 32, former commissioner, January 27, 2014, Arizona.

73. Editorial Board, "Finally, a Fair Way to Resolve Arizona's Solar Squabble," *The Arizona Republic*, October 30, 2013.

74. Sandy Bahr and Refugio Mata, "New Charges on Rooftop Solar Approved Today by AZ Corporation Commission Will Threaten Arizona's Clean Energy Freedom Economy," The Sierra Club, November 14, 2013.

75. Interview 31, renewable energy advocate at an NGO, January 27, 2014, Arizona.

76. Interview 52, commissioner, February 17, 2014, Arizona.

77. APS, "APS Solar Communities," https://www.aps.com/en/ourcompany/aboutus/investmentinrenewableenergy/Pages/aps-solar-communities.aspx?src=solarcommunities

78. Peter Fairley, "Utilities and Solar Companies Fight Over Arizona's Rooftops," *IEEE Spectrum*, June 19, 2015.

79. Ryan Randazzo, "Candidates for Corporation Commission Differ on Corporate Support," *The Arizona Republic*, June 30, 2014.

80. Ryan Randazzo, "Little–Forese Team Wins Corp. Commission Republican Primary," *The Arizona Republic*, August 26, 2014.

81. Howard Fisher, "Arizona Public Service Details how It Spent $10 Million on Elections," Tucson.com, May 19, 2017.

82. Howard Fisher, "APS Admits Spending Millions in 2014 Election of Energy Regulators," *Arizona Capitol Times*, March 29, 2019.

83. ACC Docket number E-01345A-19-0043.

84. TUSK Campaign Finance Report, *2014 Post-General Election Report*, December 4, 2015.

85. Under prior estimates, in 2014 the commission election was the seventh most expensive race in the state's history. Mary Jo Pitzl and Rob O'Dell, "Outside Money Played Huge Role in Arizona Elections," *The Arizona Republic*, November 8, 2014.

86. APS spends between $350,000 and $700,000 annually on lobbying costs. Email records also show extensive policy correspondence between APS lobbyists and the ACC. See ACC Docket number E-01345A-19-0043; David Pomerantz, "Arizona Commissioner Andy Tobin Texted APS Lobbyists Frequently, Including About Open Rate Case," Energy and Policy Institute, October 29, 2018; David Pomerantz, "Arizona Commissioner Justin Olson Answered Questions About Arizona's Energy Policy by Copying Parts of an APS Memo Verbatim, Emails Show," Energy and Policy Institute, October 18, 2018.

87. The whistleblower alleged that he was offered a promotion in exchange for his silence. Brahm Resnik, "Whistleblower Alleges Wrongdoing at Arizona Agency," *12News*, February 20, 2015.

88. Specifically, the APS Foundation donated $180,000 to ASU in 2013. Subsequently, the ASU Foundation gave $100,000 to Save Our Future Now, one of the major groups that paid for ACC election advertisements. This was an odd donation: it was the only grant that the ASU Foundation gave out that year that was not to the university or a charity. Jacob Fenton, "ASU Foundation Links Utility Funds to Anti-solar Push," Sunlight Foundation, March 10, 2015.

89. "Bill Post to Retire at Pinnacle West, Don Brandt to Step In," *Phoenix Business Journal,* January 21, 2009.

90. Customers could minimize their charge by reducing how much peak-demand power they took from the grid.

91. Ryan Randazzo, "SolarCity Sues SRP for Antitrust Violations," *The Arizona Republic,* March 3, 2015.

92. Joseph Barrios, "TEP Proposes More Equitable Credits for New Solar Power System Users," Tucson Electric Power, March 25, 2015.

93. Under the current policy, APS net metering customers were paying $0.70/kW, and this new request would in effect increase that to $3/kW for future customers.

94. Residential customers have to pay a $2.23 monthly meter fee, which has increased from the previous $2 fee. TEP had proposed an increase to $3.50. David Wichner, "New Tucson Electric Power Solar Customers to Get Lower Credits for Excess Electricity," *Arizona Daily Star,* September 12, 2018.

95. Jeff St. John, "Salt River Project Asks Supreme Court to Take Up SolarCity Antitrust Case," GreenTechMedia, September 13, 2017.

96. Ryan Randazzo, "Arizona Corporation Commission's Robert Burns Subpoenas APS, Pinnacle West," *The Arizona Republic,* August 25, 2016.

97. Robert Walton, "Newly-Elected Arizona Commissioner Prepares to Subpoena APS Over Political Spending," *Utility Dive,* February 28, 2019.

98. Ryan Randazzo, "APS Refuses Request to Disclose Political Contributions," *The Arizona Republic,* December 31, 2015.

99. ACC Docket number E-01345A-19-0043.

100. The election of Democrat Sandra Kennedy in 2018 and more support from Republican Body Dunn, elected in 2016, has meant that the majority of commissioners are in favor of APS campaign contribution disclosure. Howard Fisher, "APS Admits Spending Millions in 2014 Election of Energy Regulators," *Arizona Capitol Times,* March 29, 2019.

101. Jeremy Duda, "APS Docs Reveal It Funded 2014 'Dark Money' Effort Supporting Commissioner's Son," *AZMirror,* April 2, 2019.

102. The public record reveals that there were a number of emails related to the deal and co-conspirators willing to testify for the government. Pierce was accused of accepting a bribe and real estate deal from a water company in exchange for a more favorable rate case. At that point, APS had not been named as being under investigation. Jacques Billeaud, "Prosecutor: Gary Pierce Bribery Case Grew From Larger Probe," Associated Press, July 5, 2017.

103. Ryan Randazzo, "Poll: Arizona Voters Say Utility Regulators Have Been 'Corrupted,'" *The Arizona Republic,* September 8, 2017.

104. Donald E. Brandt, CEO of APS, "September 8, 2015 Letter Concerning Campaign Contributions to ACC Candidates," ACC Docket number AU-00000A-15-0309.

105. David Roberts, "Florida's Outrageously Deceptive Solar Ballot Initiative, Explained," *Vox,* November 8, 2016.

106. Krysti Shallenberger, "The Art of the Compromise: Inside the APS Solar Rate Design Settlement," *Utility Dive,* March 10, 2017.

107. Ryan Randazzo, "SolarCity Relocating 85 Arizona Workers, Cites Solar Fees," *The Arizona Republic,* April 30, 2015.

108. North Carolina Clean Energy Technology Center, *The 50 States of Solar: 2018 Policy Review and Q4 2018 Quarterly Report,* January 2019.

109. Julia Pyper, "Does Nevada's Controversial Net Metering Decision Set a Precedent for the Nation?" GreenTechMedia, February 4, 2016; Robert Walton, "Indiana Will Phase Out Retail Rate Net Metering," *Utility Dive,* May 4, 2017; John Weaver, "Net Metering Drives Rooftop Solar Resurgence in Nevada," *PV Magazine,* May 7, 2018.

110. Jason Berry, "Phoenix-Area Homeowners Rush to Install Solar Before APS Changes Rates," *AZ Family,* June 15, 2017.

111. Pinnacle West, "Powering Growth, Delivering Value," slide 30, September 26, 2018.

112. Ryan Randazzo, "SRP Elections: 2 Solar Candidates Unseat Incumbents," *The Arizona Republic,* April 4, 2018.

113. APS, "2012 Integrated Resource Plan: Filed in Compliance With A.A.C. R14-2-703," March 2012; Paul Smith, "2014 Integrated Resource Plan: Arizona Department of Environmental Quality Stakeholder Meeting," June 2, 2015; APS, "2017 Integrated Resource Plan: Filed in Compliance With A.A.C. R14-2-703," April 2017.
114. Jonathan Oosting, "Consumers Energy: Settlement Won't Stop Political Spending by Parent Company," *The Detroit News*, February 26, 2019.
115. Carolyn Kormann, "The Battle for Solar Energy in the Country's Sunniest State," *The New Yorker*, October 24, 2018.
116. At the same time of the ballot initiative, Commissioner Andrew Tobin drafted an energy modernization plan that would increase the RPS to 80% renewables and nuclear energy by 2050. Ultimately, Tobin was, however, not able to garner support from enough commissioners for his proposal. Steven Mufson, "The Hottest Fight in American Politics? Arizona's Smackdown Over Solar Power," *The Washington Post*, November 2, 2018; Julia Pyper, "The Battle Over Arizona's Clean Energy Mix," GreenTechMedia, September 23, 2018.
117. Ryan Randazzo, "Arizona Clean-Energy Ballot Measure Supporters Say Attorney General Undermined Proposal," *The Arizona Republic*, September 18, 2018.
118. Ibid.
119. Ballotpedia, "Arizona Proposition 127, Renewable Energy Standards Initiative (2018)," https://ballotpedia.org/Arizona_Proposition_127,_Renewable_Energy_Standards_Initiative_(2018)

Chapter 8

1. Interview 76, commission staffer, November 3, 2014, Ohio.
2. At the time this group was called the American Tradition Institute.
3. Whereas the national party had already begun polarizing on renewable energy, some states were slower. GOP state party control across the nation on opposing renewable energy gradually increased. Clare Foran and National Journal, "The Koch Brothers' Next Frontier," *The Atlantic*, November 21, 2014.
4. Southeastern Ohio is part of the Northern Appalachian basin, with significant deposits of high-quality, bituminous coal as well as coal-bed methane. Mining began in the state in the early nineteenth century. However, Ohio's coal tends to be higher in sulfur content, and therefore mining declined to about half of its peak production in 1970. D. L. Crowell, *History of Coal Mining in Ohio*, 2005.
5. US Energy Information Administration (EIA), "Ohio: State Profile and Energy Estimates— Profile Analysis"; US EIA, "Weekly U.S. Coal Production," http://www.eia.gov/coal/production/weekly/tables/weekly_production.cfm
6. For example, a 266-megawatt (MW) coal plant in Niles, Ohio, operated from 1954 until 2012, and several steel manufacturing plants were co-located in the town to access cheap energy. Many coal, steel, and iron manufacturing plants were also located along the Ohio River.
7. That said, coal consumption in the industrial sector has declined. In 2016, the sector consumed 112.3 trillion Btu, compared to 248.2 trillion Btu in 1990. US EIA, "State Energy Consumption Estimates 1960 Through 2016," Table CT6, Ohio.
8. US EIA, "Ohio Electricity Profile 2015," https://www.eia.gov/electricity/state/archive/2015/ohio/
9. J. Koncelik, "EPA's Long Anticipated Ozone Decision," *Ohio Environmental Law Blog*, December 1, 2014.
10. J. Koncelik, "Retirement of Coal Power Plants Accelerates," *Ohio Environmental Law Blog*, October 2, 2014.
11. US EIA, "State Nuclear Profiles," https://www.eia.gov/nuclear/state/archive/2010/ohio/
12. US Nuclear Regulatory Commission, "NRC Issues Preliminary Risk Analysis of the Combined Safety Issues at Davis-Besse," September 20, 2004, https://web.archive.org/web/20061003054919/http://www.nrc.gov/reading-rm/doc-collections/news/2004/04-117.html
13. E. W. Hill, K. Kinahan, and A. Immonen, *Ohio Utica Shale Region Monitor*, Cleveland, 2014.

14. US EIA, "Ohio State Energy Profile," Available online at: https://www.eia.gov/state/print.php?sid=OH

15. At the time, SEIA was called the Solar Alliance.

16. Realtors were also large contributors. National Institute on Money in State Politics, information via followthemoney.org.

17. Interview 78, lobbyist for renewables industry, November 4, 2014, Ohio.

18. Interview 78, lobbyist for renewables industry, November 4, 2014, Ohio.

19. Ibid.

20. Secretary of State 2010 election results, http://www.sos.state.oh.us/sos/elections/Research/electResultsMain/2010results/20101102sos.aspx

21. Interview 78, lobbyist for renewables industry, November 4, 2014, Ohio.

22. Interview 84, political staff, November 5, 2014, Ohio.

23. Interview 77, lobbyist for heavy industry, November 3, 2014, Ohio; interview 84, political staff, November 5, 2014, Ohio.

24. "About IEU-Ohio," http://www.ieu-ohio.org/about_us.aspx

25. Interview 75, renewable energy advocate at an NGO, November 3, 2014, Ohio.

26. Interview 76, commission staffer, November 3, 2014, Ohio.

27. Interview 75, renewable energy advocate at a nongovernmental organization (NGO), November 3, 2014, Ohio.

28. These payments in lieu of taxes would apply to advanced energy projects built before 2017 and large renewable energy projects built between 2009 and 2011.

29. In 2007, before the RPS was passed, there were 112 MW installed; by 2010 there were 231 MW installed. US EIA, "Ohio: State Profile and Energy Estimates," http://www.eia.gov/state/data.cfm?sid=OH

30. LBNL RPS compliance data, Ohio 2009.

31. "Wind Energy Opposition and Action Groups," https://www.wind-watch.org/allies.php

32. There is extensive email correspondence between Senator Seitz and several anti-wind activists. As he says at one point in June 2014, "Who would ever have believed that when the two of you wandered into my Senate office some seven years ago as complete strangers, we would have come to this point in our efforts?!"

33. Tom Stacy and other anti-wind groups have been directly linked with fossil fuel interests, including the Koch Brothers and Americans for Prosperity. Energy and Policy Institute, "Analysis: Americans for Prosperity Anti-Wind Letter, June 2014," June 16, 2014.

34. Dave Anderson, "Tom Stacy: A Top Anti-Wind Activist Who Got Paid by a Fossil Fuel Funded Group," Energy and Policy Institute, April 2, 2018.

35. Christa Marshall and Evan Lehmann, "AEP Move to Stop Carbon Capture and Sequestration Project Shocks Utilities, Miners," New York Times, July 15, 2011.

36. Moreover, nuclear energy has met a powerful enemy in oil and gas companies that seek to preserve natural gas's strong hold on the market. The American Petroleum Institute has opposed state subsidies for nuclear energy and sent mailers for Ohioans to contact their legislators. Russell Gold, "Oil-Gas Lobby Opposes State Subsidies for Nuclear Power Producers," Wall Street Journal, April 25, 2017.

37. Interview 77, lobbyist for heavy industry, November 3, 2014, Ohio.

38. Ohio Manufacturers' Association, "OMA Supporting Common Sense Energy Efficiency Rules," May 22, 2009, http://www.ohiomfg.com/communities/energy/oma-supporting-common/

39. In addition, the Mercatus Center, a right-leaning think tank affiliated with George Mason University and known for market-based and deregulatory stances, wrote a report attacking Ohio's energy efficiency targets in 2014.

40. American Tradition Institute and the Beacon Hill Institute, "The Cost and Economic Impact of Ohio's Alternative Energy Portfolio Standard," 2011.

41. Interview 79, politician, November 4, 2014, Ohio.

42. US EIA, "Ohio's Fuel Mix for Power Generation Is Changing," https://www.eia.gov/todayinenergy/detail.php?id=5030

43. While the model legislation was finalized in 2012, it was developed in the years prior and likely influenced Senator Jordan between 2010 and 2011.

44. Senator Jordan would reintroduce this bill in subsequent years, and it would again make no progress.

45. Governor John Kasich letter to Energy Summit participants, September 2011.

46. Interview 80, renewable energy advocate at an NGO, November 4, 2014, Ohio.

47. Bill Seitz, "Seitz: The Case Against Clean Energy Mandates," *The Enquirer*, January 9, 2017.

48. Tom Knox, "Seitz on Renewable-Energy Freeze: 'I Don't Think We're Likely to Resume Our March up Mandate Mountain,'" *Columbus Business First*, September 10, 2015.

49. "William Seitz's Campaign Finances," Vote Smart, https://votesmart.org/candidate/campaign-finance/45594/william-seitz#.XK5QxZhKg2w

50. AEP gave $2,500 in 2009 and $19,000 in 2012. "Electric Utilities Contributions to Seitz, William J (Bill)," National Institute on Money in State Politics, information via followthemoney.org.

51. Innovation Ohio, "Rate of Return: What Will Ohio's Electric Utilities Get for Campaign Cash?" December 3, 2013.

52. Matt Kasper, "The Repeated Effort by Ohio ALEC Members to End the State's Clean Energy Law," Energy and Policy Institute, September 17, 2015; interview 80, renewable energy advocate at an NGO, November 4, 2014, Ohio; interview 95, politician, December 8, 2014, Ohio.

53. Interview 82, utility employee, November 5, 2014, Ohio.

54. Ohio Manufacturers' Association, "Senate Bill 58—Increases Electricity Costs: Bad for Ohio Manufacturers," http://www.ohiomfg.com/senate-bill-58/

55. Tom Knox, "Bill Seitz on His Opposition to Energy Mandates, and His Work With ALEC," *Columbus Business First*, September 12, 2014.

56. In addition to changing the renewable energy and advanced energy targets, the bill would decrease the onus for utilities to meet efficiency targets. Efforts taken by customers to increase energy efficiency that met federal requirements count, even if the utility did not initiate the work. Infrastructure fixes to transmission and distribution would also count if they cut how much energy the lines lost. As such, any further work would likely be in excess of requirements and could more easily be used to meet future targets.

57. Utilities such as Duke Energy and Florida Power and Light Company teamed up with Koch-funded groups to oppose the initiative. Energy and Policy Institute, "Special Interests Behind Anti-Solar Ballot Initiative Consumers for Smart Solar," November 16, 2015.

58. Tom Knox, "Business Group Poll Says Ohio Voters Want Energy Efficiency Mandates Changed," *Columbus Business First*, April 28, 2014.

59. "Six years ago, when the Ohio legislature passed the law mandating reductions in electricity consumed, certain assumptions were used to justify the law, many of which were wrong. For example, legislators assumed electricity would be in short supply and new electric generation would be expensive. But today, there's ample low-cost electricity and will be for years to come. Knowing this . . . should the Ohio state legislature, taking into account the new information, go back and change the law?" Knox, "Business Group Poll Says"; 72% agreed.

60. Email correspondence between Chris Prandoni at Americans for Tax Reform and Senator Seitz, Thursday May 8, 2014.

61. As another example, the Ohio Advanced Energy Economy released research on the cost savings from the renewable standard. Tom Knox, "Energy-Efficiency Mandates Would Save $4B by 2025, Group Says," *Columbus Business First*, April 24, 2014.

62. "Show Me Electric Utilities Contributions to Faber, Keith Lloyd," National Institute on Money in State Politics, information via followthemoney.org.

63. Joe Vardon and Dan Gearino, "Kasich Urges Changes in 'Green Energy' Bill," *The Columbus Dispatch*, May 3, 2014.

64. The bill treated the energy efficiency targets in the same way—a 2-year freeze and reconsideration by the committee.

65. Interview 84, political staff, November 5, 2014, Ohio.

66. John Funk, "TV and YouTube Spot by Opponents of Ohio SB 310 Claims Energy Efficiency and Renewable Freeze Would Threaten Jobs, Raise Bills," Cleveland.com, May 20, 2014; interview 75, renewable energy advocate at an NGO, November 3, 2014, Ohio.

67. Tom Knox, "Big Manufacturers Urging Lawmakers to Keep Energy-Efficiency Benchmarks," *Columbus Business First*, April 8, 2014.

68. John Funk, "Ohio Senate Bill 310 Derailed; Coalition Favoring Efficiency and Renewable Energy Proposes Another Compromise," Cleveland.com, May 21, 2014.

69. Memo from Senator Seitz, "Thoughts on Energy Reform Legislation and Next Steps," May 30, 2014.

70. Joanna Foster, "Ohio Churches Fight to Save Renewables and Energy Efficiency," *ThinkProgress*, May 22, 2014.

71. AWEA Press Release, "Gov. Kasich Should Veto Wind Energy-Killing Provision of H.B. 483 That Jeopardizes $2.5 Billion Investment in Ohio," June 9, 2014.

72. Interview 78, lobbyist for renewables industry, November 4, 2014, Ohio. A number of other respondents named Julie Johnson as an influential anti-wind advocate. Interview 84, political staff, November 5, 2014, Ohio; interview 95, politician, December 8, 2014, Ohio. See as well, Holly Zachariah, "Wind-Farm Operator Upset With Energy Law," *Columbus Dispatch*, June 15, 2014.

73. Those involved suggest that bills favorable to utilities, when timed during campaign season, act as a signal to indicate shared alignments. Interview 84, political staff, November 5, 2014, Ohio. AEP gave Faber about $25,000 in 2012, $18,500 in 2016; FirstEnergy gave $23,000 in 2012 and then $31,500 in 2016. National Institute on Money in State Politics, information via followthemoney.org.

74. FirstEnergy gave about $11,000 in 2010 and $24,000 in 2014, and AEP gave $8,500 in 2010 and $24,000 in 2014 to Governor Kasich's campaigns.

75. National Institute on Money in State Politics, information via followthemoney.org.

76. AWEA, Wind Energy Foundation and Renewable America Report, *Blowing in the Wind: Ohio's Overly Restrictive Wind Setback Law Is Putting Billions in New In-State Investment at Risk*, 2017.

77. Ohio Public Utilities Commission, "How Does Ohio Generate Electricity?" 2019.

78. Efforts in 2017 to change the wind setback rules were blocked. Randazzo and Seitz's relationship remained close, with Seitz calling on Randazzo for detailed talking points and a push to influence the House Speaker. For more, Scott Peterson, "Powerful Lobbyist Steered Seitz Effort to Block Ohio Wind Power Jobs," April 16, 2018.

79. Interview 78, lobbyist for renewables industry, November 4, 2014, Ohio.

80. Clean Jobs Midwest, 2016, Report.

81. HB 114 in 2017 and 2018 attempted to make the EERS freeze indefinite, an effort again led by Seitz. Anti-wind astroturf advocates like the Consumer Energy Alliance, backed by fossil fuel companies, were influential in shaping the language of the bill. While the bill sped through the House, it was ultimately stalled in the Senate. For more, Nick Hromalik, "Victory in Ohio: Energy Efficiency Rollback Bill Stalls Without Action," MEEA, February 12, 2019; Brad Wieners and David Hasemyer, "Killing Clean: The Playbook to Destroy Clean Energy," InsideClimate News and the Weather Channel, December 29, 2017.

82. Connor Gibson, "Ohio Politicians on Energy Mandates Study Committee Took $830,000 From Dirty Energy Companies," *HuffPost*, October 16, 2016.

83. Dave Anderson, "Insider Emails: Polluter Lobbyists Behind Clean Energy Standards Freeze in Ohio," *Energy and Policy Institute*, December 9, 2016.

84. Ibid.

85. Gabe Elsner, "Ohio Energy Study Committee Relied Upon Flawed Testimony," September 30, 2015, Energy and Policy Institute; Brian Maffly, "USU business school courts billionaire ideologue," *The Salt Lake Tribune*, September 8, 2010.

86. "Follow the money behind attacks on clean energy in Ohio," *Energy and Policy Institute*, December 28, 2016.

87. Kathiann M. Kowalski, "Ohio bill would relax wind setbacks — and clean energy standards," *Energy News*, June 26, 2018.

88. John Funk, "PUCO rejects deal to have ratepayers subsidize a coal-fired power plant," *The Plain Dealer*, January 12, 2019.

89. David Roberts, "This Ohio utility has an innovative plan to save coal power: force customers to buy it," September 3, 2015, *Vox*; Neil Waggoner, "Don't Bail Out Dirty Coal Plants," August 28, 2014, *The Sierra Club*; Kathiann M. Kowalski, "FirstEnergy touts benefits of plan critics decry as 'bailout'," August 14, 2014, *Energy News*.

90. Darren Sweeney, "AEP Ohio, Sierra Club defend settlement in Ohio PPA plan," December 22, 2015, *SNL Generation Markets Week.*

91. John Finnigan, "Ohio Failed to Protect Customers and Markets – So Federal Regulators Came to the Rescue," May 2, 2016, EDF.

92. Laura Hancock, "Ohio Supreme Court nixes FirstEnergy electric grid charge," June 19, 2019, *Cleveland.com*; Kathiann M. Kowalski and John Funk, "How affiliate arrangements, subsidies and riders led to higher electric bills in Ohio — even as power prices declined," September 20, 2019, *Energy News.*

93. Dave Anderson, "FirstEnergy's Wall Street investors lobbied for bailout bill in Ohio," August 26, 2019, Energy and Policy Institute; Jeff St. John, "FERC Rejects Energy Secretary Rick Perry's Coal and Nuclear Energy Market Bailout Plan," January 8, 2018, *GreenTechMedia.*

94. Dave Anderson, "Top candidates for Ohio House speaker back bailouts for utilities that back their campaigns," May 10, 2018, Energy and Policy Institute.

95. Ohio Environmental Council, Environmental Defense Fund, and Environmental Law and Policy Center, "Appellants' merit brief of Ohio Environmental Council, Environmental Defense Fund, and Environmental Law and Policy Center," February 2, 2018.

96. Andrew Tobias, "FirstEnergy and its allies, seeking nuclear plant bailout, have spent millions on influence campaign," *Cleveland.com*, April 17, 2019.

97. Andrew Tobias, "Nuclear bailout bill shows how big money can be put to work in the Ohio Statehouse," *Cleveland.com*, May 2019.

98. Kathiann Kowalski, "State lawmaker part of effort to stop Ohio wind project," *EnergyNews*, April 27, 2015.

99. The relationship between Householder and FirstEnergy did not start in 2018—FirstEnergy flew both Householder and his son to Trump's inauguration: Jeremy Pelzer, "FirstEnergy PAC writes big checks to House speaker hopeful Larry Householder, campaign allies," *Cleveland.com*, January 30, 2019.

100. Jeremy Pelzer, "FirstEnergy PAC writes big checks to House speaker hopeful Larry Householder, campaign allies," *Cleveland.com*, January 30, 2019.

101. Interview 107, Renewable energy advocate at an NGO, August 14, 2019, Ohio.

102. Midwest Energy Efficiency Alliance, "Energy efficiency in Ohio: Energy & bill savings for customers, 2009–2017," April 21, 2019.

103. Interview 105, Renewable energy advocate at an NGO, July 19, 2019, Ohio.

104. Interview 106, Journalist, July 22, 2019, Ohio.

105. Interview 107, Renewable energy advocate at an NGO, August 14, 2019, Ohio.

106. Liam Denning, "Ohio's Nuke and Coal Bailout: Throwback Mountain," *Bloomberg*, July 24, 2019.

107. In its bankruptcy filings, FirstEnergy Solutions claimed it would lose $12 million a year on the OVEC plants. Given its 5% ownership stake, this translates into an estimated loss of $240 million per year for the plants. Given the 66% ownership stake that Ohio's private utilities held in OVEC, over the 11 years the bill covered, this would translate into $1.735 billion.

108. Jeffrey Tomich, "Money pit or fuel hedge? In Midwest, it depends who's paying," *E&E News*, May 25, 2018.

109. Interview 107, Renewable energy advocate at an NGO, August 14, 2019, Ohio.

110. Dave Anderson, "FirstEnergy's Wall Street investors lobbied for bailout bill in Ohio," *Energy and Policy Institute*, August 26, 2019.

111. Rebecca Leber, "Dark Money Is Pouring in to Protect the 'Worst Energy Policy in the Country'," *MotherJones*, October 10, 2019.

112. Dave Anderson, "Who's behind Ohioans for Energy Security's ad campaign to scare voters?" *Energy and Policy Institute*, August 28, 2019.

113. Kathiann M. Kowalski, " Who's behind the Chinese conspiracy ads against Ohio's nuclear referendum?" *Energy News Network*, September 23, 2019.

114. Andy Chow, "Nuclear Bailout Supporters Clashing With Referendum Petitioners In The Field," *Statehouse News Bureau*, October 1, 2019.

115. Christine Bowen Wright, *Agent Activity & Expenditure Report*, September 20, 2016, https://www2.jlec-olig.state.oh.us/olac/Reports/AERView_Legislative.aspx?id=496368; FirstEnergy, *Agent Activity & Expenditure Report*, September 29, 2016, https://www.documentcloud.org/documents/3232515-First-Energy-2016-Lobbying-Disclosure-Ohio-SB.html

116. Interview 78, lobbyist for renewables industry, November 4, 2014, Ohio.

Chapter 9

1. Lyrics from "The 1975" by The 1975. Adapted from Greta Thunberg, "Our House is on Fire," Speech at World Economic Forum, Davos, January 25, 2019.

2. California's goal was 1% by 1987 and 10% by 2000, although the latter goal would not be met (Righter, 1996a).

3. These were small turbines: 0.07 megawatts (MW) on average, compared to the 1.5-MW turbines that are routinely installed today.

4. With the tax credits and PURPA avoided cost rates in place, ARCO Solar built solar photovoltaic projects several megawatts in size. Large solar thermal technologies were also pioneered in California at this time, most notably the Solar Energy Generating Stations projects which began construction in 1984 in the Mojave Desert. By 1990, these projects grew to be 350 MW in scale, and they continue to operate today. In addition, the first distributed generation solar projects were built in California in 1993, at Pacific Gas & Electric Company's (PG&E's) 500-kW, grid-connected Kerman plant. US Energy Information Administration, "Renewable Energy Annual 1996," 1997.

5. Michael J. Weiss. "Everybody Loves Solar Energy, but ..." *New York Times*, September 24, 1989.

6. Most notably, Kenetech, then U.S. Windpower, moved its operations to California from Massachusetts in the early 1980s to capitalize on the booming wind industry (Righter 1996a).

7. Luz International, an important early solar company, went bankrupt in 1991. Kenetech, an important early wind company, went bankrupt in 1996.

8. PG&E Draft Memo, "Proposal: To Remove Non-Utility Programs From Electric Rates and to Fund These From Electricity Surcharges," April 5, 1995.

9. In 2009, clean energy supplied 31% of the nation's grid; in 2018, it supplied 37%. BloombergNEF and the Business Council for Sustainable Energy, *2019 Sustainable Energy in America Factbook*.

10. Given that renewable energy is intermittent, this figure may actually be much higher in terms of installed capacity if a high renewables scenario is used when the grid is grown.

11. Without successful nuclear license extensions, 59 of the 97 US reactors are slated for retirement before 2040. In the short term, 11 reactors are slated to retire by 2025. Data from US Nuclear Regulatory Commission.

12. The first five states listed have binding RPS goals, while the next three have voluntary goals.

13. Nathanael Johnson, "Breathe Easier: States Are Passing a Buttload of Clean Energy Bills," *Grist*, June 10, 2019.

14. APS's parent company Pinnacle West spent this money. Notably, APS is the holding company's only entity. Part of the money was funneled through two 501(c)4 organizations: Save Our Future Now and the Arizona Free Enterprise Club. Bob Christie and Jacques Billeaud, "APS Finally Comes Clean About Political Spending," Associated Press, April 26, 2019

15. Christian Roselund, "APS, Pro-Solar Group Together Spend $6 Million on Arizona Corporation Commission Races," *PV Magazine*, November 6, 2016.

16. Ryan Randazzo, "Arizona Clean-Energy Ballot Measure Supporters Say Attorney General Undermined Proposal," *Arizona Republic*, September 18, 2018.

17. Michael Isaac Stein, "The Energy Industry's Secret Campaign to Get Us to Build More Power Plants," *The Nation*, May 14, 2019.

18. Sean McElwee, "People Actually Like the Green New Deal," *The New York Times*, March 27, 2019.

19. David Hasemyer, "Fossil Fuels on Trial: Where the Major Climate Change Lawsuits Stand Today," *InsideClimate News*, January 6, 2019.

20. Instead, many American political scientists have increasingly focused on the role of public opinion in influencing policy change (Erikson et al. 1993; Lax & Phillips 2009; Stimson 2004; Stimson et al. 1995).

21. FollowTheMoney.org, "American Legislative Exchange Council," accessed July 10, 2019, https://www.followthemoney.org/entity-details?eid=3596644

22. Ivan Penn, "Florida's utilities keep homeowners from making the most of solar power," *The New York Times*, July 7, 2019.

23. Under Pennsylvania's RPS, coal-bed methane, coal gasification, and coal waste are eligible.

24. Christian Roselund, "House Committee Calls for Cuts in Renewable Energy R&D, More Money for Fossil Fuels," *PV Magazine*, May 18, 2018.

25. Zeeshan Aleem, "Donald Trump Has Finally Dealt His First Blow to China's Economy," *Vox*, January 23, 2018.

26. Sierra Club, "100% Commitments in Cities, Counties, & States," https://www.sierraclub.org/ready-for-100/commitments; Rocky Mountain Institute, America's Pledge, https://rmi.org/americas-pledge/

27. Interview 97, renewable energy advocate at a nongovernmental organization (NGO), March 19, 2015, multiple cases.

28. David Pomerantz, "Utility Carbon Targets Reflect Decarbonization Slowdown In Crucial Next Decade," Energy and Policy Institute, June 25, 2019.

29. New Mexico Legislature, *Fiscal Impact Report on Energy Transition Act*, March 7, 2019.

30. Interview 106, journalist, July 22 2019, Ohio.

31. Susie Cagle, "'Protesters as Terrorists': Growing Number of States Turn Anti-Pipeline Activism Into a Crime," *The Guardian*, July 8, 2019.

32. Ibid.

33. Peter Stone, "The Kochs Are Plotting A Multimillion-Dollar Assault On Electric Vehicles," *The Huffington Post*, February 18, 2016.

34. Matthew Gardner, Steve Wamhoff, Mary Martellotta, and Lorena Roque, "Corporate Tax Avoidance Remains Rampant Under New Tax Law," *Institute on Taxation and Economic Policy*, April 2019.

35. Intervenors must demonstrate significant financial hardship and a "substantial contribution" to the outcome of a commission decision. These groups are chartered to represent the interests of residential or small business customers.

36. California State Auditor, *California Public Utilities Commission. Despite Administrative Weaknesses, It Has Generally Awarded Compensation to Intervenors in Accordance With State Law*, Report 2012-118, July 2013.

37. As the California state auditor found in 2013, in several cases intervenors paid less than $1 million resulted in savings for ratepayers between $130 and $354 million. Ibid.

38. Interview 91, bureaucrat, November 12, 2014, Kansas.

39. David Pomerantz, "Decarbonization Slowdown in Crucial Next Decade," Energy and Policy Institute, June 25, 2019.

40. In many states, groups have access to proprietary models under nondisclosure agreements, but these terms of these agreements may limit their ability to intervene.

41. Office of State Senator Jerry Hill, "Governor Brown Signs CPUC Reform Legislation by Senator Hill," October 2, 2017.

42. Matt Kasper, "'Code of Ethics' Has Not Increased Trust in Arizona Corporation Commission, as APS Seems Poised to Continue Spending on Races," Energy and Policy Institute, October 12, 2018.

43. Graham Moomaw, "More than 50 Democrats running for Virginia House pledge to refuse Dominion money," *Richmond Times-Dispatch*, April 18, 2017.

44. Article 6 Colorado Sunshine Law, Part 2 Public official disclosure law, Sections 202 & 203, https://www.sos.state.co.us/pubs/info_center/laws/Title24/Title24Article6Part2.html

45. Illinois Commerce Commission, "Sunshine Project," https://www.icc.illinois.gov/about/sunshine-project

46. Joseph Goodenberry et al., "Electric industry generation, capacity, and market outlook." Resource Adequacy and Markets Working Group, National Rural Electric Cooperative Association, July 2019.

47. American Public Power Association. Public Power: 2018 Statistical Report. A Supplement of Public Power Magazine.

48. Matt Kasper, "As utilities flee newly scandalous UARG, remaining members make dishonest claims about its purpose," Energy and Policy Institute, April 23, 2019; Rod Kuckro, "Coal-heavy electric cooperatives take hard line on EPA Clean Power Plan," E&E News Energywire, December 15, 2014.

49. Joe Smyth, "Colorado Rural Electric Association spent electric cooperatives' money supporting Republican politicians," Energy and Policy Institute, October 23, 2019.

50. Daniel Tait, "Alabama cooperative customers unknowingly funding political candidates," Energy and Policy Institute, March 27, 2018.

51. Matt Grimley, "Just how Democratic are rural electric cooperatives?" Institute for Local Self-Reliance, January 13, 2016.

52. Sammy Roth, "Hydropower bill would sabotage California's clean energy mandate, critics say," Los Angeles Times, April 30, 2019; American Public Power Association, "California moves a step closer to 100% RPS," August 29, 2018.

53. Alissa Schfer, "FMPA coordinating statewide campaign to raise Florida municipal utilities' fixed fees, block solar," Energy and Policy Institute, 22 August 2019.

54. Author's research based on examining state laws.

55. Daniel Tait and Joe Smyth, "TVA attempts to chain local power companies to longer contracts in effort to prevent defection risk," Energy and Policy Institute, September 22, 2019.

56. Herman K. Trabish, "As CCAs take over utility customers, local renewable generation emerges as the next big growth driver," Utility Dive, October 8, 2019.

57. Larry Miloshevich, "A Strategy and Six Ways to Address Community Energy Goals," Energy Freedom Colorado, November 2018.

58. J. D. Morris, "PG&E union mounts formidable opposition to SF takeover attempt," San Francisco Chronicle, September 27, 2019.

59. Interview 72, foundation employee, September 25, 2014, multiple cases.

60. Rebecca Kling and Jessica Tritsch, "Xcel Energy Agrees to Coal Plant Retirements, Historic Clean Energy Commitment in Agreement With Clean Energy Groups and Labor," Sierra Club, May 20, 2019.

61. Leonard N. Fleming, "Consumers Energy Pledges 80% Emissions Cut by 2040," Detroit News, February 19, 2018.

62. Dan Gearino, "Close Coal Plants, Save Money: That's an Indiana Utility's Plan. The Coal Industry Wants to Stop It," Inside Climate News, April 26, 2019.

63. Mark Hand, "Ballot Box Battle Over Clean Energy Is Brewing in Three States," ThinkProgress, February 14, 2018.

64. Rachel Leingang, "In Arizona, an Effort to Register Young People to Vote Was a Success. But Will It Matter?" The Arizona Republic, October 24, 2018.

65. Mark Shtrakhman, "NextGen Climate Action Committee," FactCheck.org, April 20, 2018.

66. Rebecca Solnit, "Are We Missing the Big Picture on Climate Change?" New York Times Magazine, December 2, 2014.

67. Chad Stone, Danilo Trisi, Arloc Sherman, & Roderick Taylor, "A Guide to Statistics on Historical Trends in Income Inequality," Center on Budget and Policy Priorities, December 11, 2018.

68. US Energy Information Administration, "One in three U.S. households faced challenges in paying energy bills in 2015," https://www.eia.gov/consumption/residential/reports/2015/energybills/

69. L. Stokes and M. Mildenberger, "The Politics of Equitable Climate Policy," Scholars Strategy Network Forum on Building Democratic Support for Equitable Carbon Pricing, 2016.

70. David Hasemyer, "Fossil Fuels on Trial: Where the Major Climate Change Lawsuits Stand Today," InsideClimate News, January 6, 2019.

REFERENCES

Abramowitz, A., & Saunders, K. (1998). "Ideological Realignment in the U.S. Electorate," *Journal of Politics*, 60/3: 634–52.

Adler, D. P. (2019). *U.S. Climate Change Litigation in the Age of Trump: Year Two*. New York: Sabin Center for Climate Change, Columbia Law School.

Aklin, M., & Urpelainen, J. (2013). "Political Competition, Path Dependence, and the Strategy of Sustainable Energy Transitions," *American Journal of Political Science*, 57/3: 643–58. DOI: 10.1111/ajps.12002

Aklin, M., & Urpelainen, J. (2018). *Renewables: The Politics of a Global Energy Transition*. Cambridge, MA: MIT Press.

Aldrich, D. P. (2008). *Site Fights: Divisive Facilities and Civil Society in Japan and the West*. Ithaca, NY: Cornell University Press.

Aldy, J. E., Gerarden, T. D., & Sweeney, R. L. (2018). "Investment Versus Output Subsidies: Implications of Alternative Incentives for Wind Energy." NBER Working Paper Series 24378, National Bureau of Economic Research, Cambridge, MA.

Alvarez, R. A., Pacala, S. W., Winebrake, J. J., Chameides, W. L., & Hamburg, S. P. (2012). "Greater Focus Needed on Methane Leakage From Natural Gas Infrastructure," *Proceedings of the National Academy of Sciences*, 109/17: 6435–40. DOI: 10.1073/pnas.1202407109

Alvarez, R. A., Zavala Araiza, D., Lyon, D. R., Allen, D. T., Barkley, Z. R., Brandt, A. R., Davis, K. J., et al. (2018). "Assessment of Methane Emissions from the U.S. Oil and Gas Supply Chain," *Science*, 361/6398: 186–8. DOI: 10.1126/science.aar7204

Anadon, L. D., Bunn, M., Chan, G., Chan, M., Jones, C., Kempener, R., Lee, A., et al. (2011). *Transforming U.S. Energy Innovation*. Cambridge, MA: Belfer Center for Science and International Affairs, Harvard Kennedy School.

Anderson, D. D. (1981). *Regulatory Politics and Electric Utilities: A Case Study in Political Economy*. Boston: Auburn House Publishing.

Anderson, D., Kasper, M., & Pomerantz, D. (2017). *Utilities Knew: Documenting Electric Utilities' Early Knowledge and Ongoing Deception on Climate Change From 1968–2017*. San Francisco: Energy and Policy Institute.

Anderson, K., & Peters, G. (2016). "The Trouble With Negative Emissions," *Science*, 354/6309: 182–3. DOI: 10.1126/science.aah4567

Ansolabehere, S., De Figueiredo, J. M., & Snyder, J. M. (2003). "Why Is There so Little Money in U.S. Politics?" *Journal of Economic Perspectives*, 17/1: 105–30.

Ansolabehere, S., & Konisky, D. M. (2009). "Public Attitudes Toward Construction of New Power Plants," *Public Opinion Quarterly*, 73/3: 566–77. DOI: 10.1093/poq/nfp041

Ansolabehere, S., & Konisky, D. M. (2014). *Cheap and Clean: How Americans Think About Energy in the Age of Global Warming*. Cambridge, MA: MIT Press.

Anzia, S. F. (2011). "Election Timing and the Electoral Influence of Interest Groups," *Journal of Politics*, 73/2: 412–27. DOI: 10.1017/s0022381611000028

Anzia, S. F. (2018). "Looking for Influence in All the Wrong Places: How Studying Subnational Policy Can Revive Research on Interest Groups," *Journal of Politics*, 81/1: 343–51. DOI: 10.1086/700726

Anzia, S. F., & Moe, T. M. (2016). "Do Politicians Use Policy to Make Politics? The Case of Public-Sector Labor Laws," *American Political Science Review*, 110/4: 763–77. DOI: 10.1017/S0003055416000484

Arnold, R. D. (1992). *The Logic of Congressional Action*. New Haven, CT: Yale University Press.

Arrow, K. J. (1962). "The Economic Learning Implications of Learning by Doing," *Review of Economic Studies*, 29/3: 155–73.

Averch, H., & Johnson, L. (2017). "Behavior of the Firm Under Regulatory Constraint," *American Economic Association*, 52/5: 1052–69.

Baldick, R., & Kahn, E. (1993). "Transmission Planning Issues in a Competitive Economic Environment," *IEEE Transactions on Power Systems*, 8/4: 1497–503.

Ballew, M. T., Leiserowitz, A., Roser-Renouf, C., Rosenthal, S. A., Kotcher, J. E., Marlon, J. R., Lyon, E., et al. (2019). "Climate Change in the American Mind: Data, Tools, and Trends," *Environment*, 61/3: 4–18. DOI: 10.1080/00139157.2019.1589300

Barber, M. J., & McCarty, N. (2016). "Causes and Consequences of Polarization." Mansbridge, J., & Martin, C. J. (eds) *Political Negotiation: A Handbook*, pp. 37–89. Washington, DC: Brookings Institution.

Barbera, P., Casas A., Nagler, J., Egan, P. J., Bonneau, R., Jost, J. T., & Tucker J. A. (2012). "Who Leads? Who Follows? Measuring Issue Attention and Agenda Setting by Legislators and the Mass Public Using Social Media Data," *American Political Science Review*, 25: 363–80. DOI: 10.107/S0003055419000352

Barbose, G. (2018). *U.S. Renewable Portfolio Standards: 2018 Annual Status Report*. Berkeley, CA: Lawrence Berkeley National Laboratory.

Baughman, M. L., Joskow, P. L., & Kamat, D. P. (1979). *Electric Power in the United States: Models and Policy Analysis*. Cambridge, MA: MIT Press.

Baumgartner, F. R., Berry, J. M., Hojnacki, M., Kimball, D. C., & Leech, B. L. (2009). *Lobbying and Policy Change: Who Wins, Who Loses, and Why*. Chicago: University of Chicago Press.

Baumgartner, F. R., & Jones, B. D. (2002). *Policy Dynamics*. Chicago: University of Chicago Press.

Baumgartner, F. R., & Jones, B. D. (2009). *Agendas and Instability in American Politics*, 2nd ed. Chicago: University of Chicago Press.

Baumgartner, F. R., & Leech, B. L. (1998). *Basic Interests: The Importance of Groups in Politics and in Political Science*. Princeton, NJ: Princeton University Press.

Bawn, K., Cohen, M., Karol, D., Masket, S., Noel, H., & Zaller, J. (2012). "A Theory of Political Parties: Groups, Policy Demands and Nominations in American Politics," *Perspectives on Politics*, 10/3: 571–97. DOI: 10.1017/S1537592712001624

Béland, D. (2010). "Reconsidering Policy Feedback: How Policies Affect Politics," *Administration and Society*, 42/5: 568–90. DOI: 10.1177/0095399710377444

Bell, S. E., & York, R. (2010). "Community Economic Identity: The Coal Industry and Ideology Construction in West Virginia," *Rural Sociology*, 75/1: 111–43. DOI: 10.1111/j.1549-0831.2009.00004.x

Benson, S. M., & Orr, F. M. J. (2008). "Carbon Dioxide Capture and Storage," *MRS Bulletin*, 33/4: 303–5.

Bergquist, P. (2018). "Congress as Theatre: How Advocates Use Ambiguity for Political Advantage," *Journal of Public Policy*. 1–37. DOI: 10.1017/S0143814X18000284

Berry, C. R., Burden, B. C., & Howell, W. G. (2010). "After Enactment: The Lives and Deaths of Federal Programs," *American Journal of Political Science*, 54/1: 1–17.

Berry, D., & Williamson, R. (1997). "Solar Power and Retail Electric Competition in Arizona." *Solar Today*, 11/2: 34–7.

Besley, T., & Coate, S. (2003). "Elected Versus Appointed Regulators: Theory and Evidence," *Journal of the European Economic Association*, 1/5: 1176–206.

Binder, S. A. (2008). "Consequences for the Courts: Polarized Politics and the Judicial Branch." Nivola, P. S., & Brady, D. W. (eds) *Red and Blue Nation*, pp. 107–33. Washington, DC: Brookings Institution.

Binder, S. A., & Lee, F. E. (2015). "Making Deals in Congress." Mansbridge, J., & Martin, C. J. (eds) *Political Negotiation: A Handbook*, pp. 91–120. Washington, DC: Brookings Institution.

Bird, L., Bolinger, M., Gagliano, T., Wiser, R., Brown, M., & Parsons, B. (2005). "Policies and Market Factors Driving Wind Power Development in the United States," *Energy Policy*, 33/11: 1397–407. DOI: 10.1016/j.enpol.2003.12.018

Blackburn, G., Magee, C., & Rai, V. (2014). "Solar Valuation and the Modern Utility's Expansion Into Distributed Generation," *Electricity Journal*, 26/11: 1–15. DOI: 10.1016/j.tej.2013.12.002

Bodansky, D. (2008). *Nuclear Energy: Principles, Practices, and Prospects*, 2nd ed. New York: Springer-Verlag.

Bonica, A. (2014). "Mapping the Ideological Marketplace," *American Journal of Political Science*, 58/2: 367–86. DOI: 10.1111/ajps.12062

Bonvillian, W. B., & van Atta, R. (2011). "ARPA-E and DARPA: Applying the DARPA Model to Energy Innovation," *Journal of Technology Transfer*, 36/5: 469–513. DOI: 10.1007/s10961-011-9223-x

Borenstein, S. (2002). "The Trouble With Electricity Markets: Understanding California's Restructuring Disaster," *Journal of Economic Perspectives*, 16/1: 191–211.

Boyes, W. J. (1976). "An Empirical Examination of the Averch-Johnson Effect," *Economic Inquiry*, 14: 25–35.

Bradley, R. L., Jr. (1996). "The Origins of Political Electricity: Market Failure or Political Opportunism," *Energy Law Journal*, 17: 59–102.

Breetz, H. L. (2013). *Fueled by Crisis: U.S. Alternative Fuel Policy, 1975–2007*. PhD dissertation, Massachusetts Institute of Technology.

Breetz, H., Mildenberger, M., & Stokes, L. (2018). "The Political Logics of Clean Energy Transitions," *Business and Politics*, 20/4: 492–522. DOI: 10.1017/bap.2018.14

Broockman, D. E., & Skovron, C. (2018). "Bias in Perceptions of Public Opinion Among Political Elites," *American Political Science Review*, 112/3: 542–63. DOI: 10.1017/S0003055418000011

Bruch, S. K., Ferree, M. M., & Soss, J. (2010). "From Policy to Polity: Democracy, Paternalism, and the Incorporation of Disadvantaged Citizens," *American Sociological Review*, 75/2: 205–26. DOI: 10.1177/0003122410363563

Brulle, R. J. (2018). "The Climate Lobby: A Sectoral Analysis of Lobbying Spending on Climate Change in the USA, 2000 to 2016," *Climatic Change*, 149/3–4: 289–303. DOI: 10.1007/s10584-018-2241-z

Brysse, K., Oreskes, N., O'Reilly, J., & Oppenheimer, M. (2013). "Climate Change Prediction: Erring on the Side of Least Drama?," *Global Environmental Change*, 23/1: 327–37. DOI: 10.1016/j.gloenvcha.2012.10.008

Burger, M., & Wentz, J. (2018). "Holding Fossil Fuel Companies Accountable for Their Contribution to Climate Change: Where Does the Law Stand?" *Bulletin of the Atomic Scientists*, 74/6: 397–403. DOI: 10.1080/00963402.2018.1533217

Burke, M., Davis, W. M., & Diffenbaugh, N. S. (2018). "Large Potential Reduction in Economic Damages Under UN Mitigation Targets," *Nature*, 557/7706: 549–53. DOI: 10.1038/s41586-018-0071-9

Campbell, A. L. (2003). *How Policies Make Citizens: Senior Political Activism and the American Welfare State*. Princeton, NJ: Princeton University Press.

Campbell, A. L. (2010). "The Public's Role in Winner-Take-All Politics," *Politics & Society*, 38/2: 227–32. DOI: 10.1177/0032329210365046

Campbell, A. L. (2012). "Policy Makes Mass Politics," *Annual Review of Political Science*, 15/1: 333–51. DOI: 10.1146/annurev-polisci-01e2610-135202

Candelise, C., Gross, R., & Leach, M. a. (2010). "Conditions for Photovoltaics Deployment in the UK: The Role of Policy and Technical Developments," *Proceedings of the Institution of Mechanical Engineers, Part A: Journal of Power and Energy*, 224/2: 153–66. DOI: 10.1243/09576509JPE768

Carley, S. (2009). "Distributed Generation: An Empirical Analysis of Primary Motivators," *Energy Policy*, 37/5: 1648–59. DOI: 10.1016/j.enpol.2009.01.003

Carley, S. (2011). "The Era of State Energy Policy Innovation: A Review of Policy Instruments," *Review of Policy Research*, 28/3: 265–94.

Carley, S., Davies, L. L., Spence, D. B., & Zirogiannis, N. (2018). "Empirical Evaluation of the Stringency and Design of Renewable Portfolio Standards," *Nature Energy*, 3: 754–763. DOI: 10.1038/s41560-018-0202-4

Carlisle, J. E., Feezell, J. T., Michaud, K. E. H., & Smith, E. R. A. N. (2016). *The Politics of Energy Crises*. Oxford: Oxford University Press.

Carpenter, D. (2010). "Institutional Strangulation: Bureaucratic Politics and Financial Reform in the Obama Administration," *Perspectives on Politics*, 8/3: 825–46.

Carpenter, D., & Moss, D. A. (2014). "Introduction." Carpenter, D., & Moss, D. A. (eds) *Preventing Regulatory Capture—Special Interest Influence and How to Limit It*, pp. 1–22. New York: Cambridge University Press.

Carvallo, J. P., Larsen, P. H., Sanstad, A. H., & Goldman, C. A. (2018). "Long Term Load Forecasting Accuracy in Electric Utility Integrated Resource Planning," *Energy Policy*, 119: 410–22. DOI: 10.1016/j.enpol.2018.04.060

Caughey, D., Warshaw, C., & Xu, Y. (2017). "Incremental Democracy: The Policy Effects of Partisan Control of State Government," *Journal of Politics*, 79/4: 1342–58. DOI: 10.1086/692669

Charles, D. (2009). "Leaping the Efficiency Gap," *Science*, 325/5942: 804–11.

Chick, M. (2007). *Electricity and Energy Policy in Britain, France and the United States Since 1945*. Northampton, MA: Edward Elgar Publishing.

Christensen, N. S., Wood, A. W., Voisin, N., Lettenmaier, D. P., & Palmer, R. N. (2004). "The Effects of Climate Change on the Hydrology and Water Resources of the Colorado River Basin," *Climatic Change*, 62/1–3: 337–63. DOI: 10.1023/B:CLIM.0000013684.13621.1f

Clack, C. T. M., Qvist, S. A., Apt, J., Bazilian, M., Brandt, A. R., Caldeira, K., Davis, S. J., et al. (2017). "Evaluation of a Proposal for Reliable Low-Cost Grid Power With 100% Wind, Water, and Solar," *Proceedings of the National Academy of Sciences*, 114/26: 6722–7. DOI: 10.1073/pnas.1610381114

Clemmer, S., Richardson, J., Sattler, S., & Lochbaum, D. (2018). *The Nuclear Power Dilemma*. Cambridge, MA: Union of Concerned Scientists.

Cohen, M., Karol, D., Noel, H., & Zaller, J. (2009). *The Party Decides: Presidential Nominations Before and After Reform*. Chicago: University of Chicago Press.

Cohen, M. D., March, J., & Olsen, J. (1972). "A Garbage Can Model of Organizational Choice," *Administrative Science Quarterly*, 17/1: 1–25.

Cowan, R. (1990). "Nuclear Power Reactors: A Study in Technological Lock-in," *Journal of Economic History*, 50/3: 541–67.

Crenson, M. (1971). *The Un-politics of Air Pollution: A Study of Non-Decisionmaking in the Cities*. Baltimore, MD: Johns Hopkins Press.

Culpepper, P. D. (2010). *Quiet Politics and Business Power: Corporate Control in Europe and Japan*. Cambridge: Cambridge University Press.

Curry, J. M. (2015). *Legislating in the Dark: Information and Power in the House of Representatives*. Chicago: University of Chicago Press.

Dagan, D., & Teles, S. M. (2016). *Prison Break: Why Conservatives Turned Against Mass Incarceration*. Oxford: Oxford University Press.

Dahl, R. (1961). *Who Governs? Democracy and Power in an American City.* New Haven, CT: Yale University Press.

Dar, L., & Lee, D.-W. (2014). "Partisanship, Political Polarization, and State Higher Education Budget Outcomes," *Journal of Higher Education,* 85/4: 469–98. DOI: 10.1353/jhe.2014.0023

Davis, S. J., Cao, L., Caldeira, K., & Hoffert, M. I. (2013). "Rethinking Wedges," *Environmental Research Letters,* 8/1: 011001. DOI: 10.1088/1748-9326/8/1/011001

Davis, S. J., Lewis, N. S., Shaner, M., Aggarwal, S., Arent, D., Azevedo, I. L., Benson, S. M., et al. (2018). "Net-Zero Emissions Energy Systems," *Science,* 360/6396. DOI: 10.1126/science.aas9793

DellaVigna, S., & Kaplan, E. (2007). "The Fox News Effect: Media Bias and Voting," *Quarterly Journal of Economics,* 122/3: 1187–234.

Delmas, M. A., & Montes-Sancho, M. J. (2011). "U.S. State Policies for Renewable Energy, Context and Effectiveness," *Energy Politics,* 39: 2273–88.

Delucchi, M. A., & Jacobson, M. Z. (2011). "Providing All Global Energy With Wind, Water, and Solar Power, Part II: Reliability, System and Transmission Costs, and Policies," *Energy Policy,* 39/3: 1170–90.

Devine, M., Chartock, M., Gunn, E. M., & Huettner, D. A. (1987). "PURPA 210 Avoided Cost Rates: Economic and Implementation Issues," *Energy Systems and Policy,* 11/2: 85–101.

Dietz, T. (2010). "Narrowing the US Energy Efficiency Gap," *Proceedings of the National Academy of Sciences,* 107/37: 16007–8.

Dimanchev, E. G., Paltsev, S., Yuan, M., Rothenberg, D., Tessum, C. W., Marshall J. D., & Selin N. E. (2019). "Health Co-benefits of Sub-national Renewable Energy Policy in the US," *Environmental Research Letters,* 14: 08-5012.

Dinca, C., Badea, A., Rousseaux, P., & Apostol, T. (2007). "A Multi-Criteria Approach to Evaluate the Natural Gas Energy Systems," *Energy Policy,* 35/11: 5754–65.

Downie, C. (2017). "Fighting for King Coal's Crown: Business Actors in the US Coal and Utility Industries," *Global Environmental Politics,* 17/1: 21–39.

Drutman, L. (2015). *The Business of America Is Lobbying: How Corporations Became Politicized and Politics Became More Corporate.* Oxford: Oxford University Press.

Duane, T. P. (2002). "Regulation's Rationale: Learning from the California Energy Crisis," *Yale Journal on Regulation,* 19/2: 471–540.

Dunlap, R., & McCright, A. (2008). "A Widening Gap: Republican and Democratic Views on Climate Change," *Environment,* 50/6: 26–36.

Dyer, R. A. (2009). *The History of Electric Deregulation in Texas: The Unfulfilled Promise of Utility Restructuring.* The Colony, TX: Cities Aggregation Power Project, Texas Coalition for Affordable Power.

Dyer, R. A. (2011). "The Story of ERCOT: The Grid Operator, Power Market & Prices Under Texas Electric Deregulation," The Steering committee of cities served by Oncor & The Texas Coalition for Affordable Power. Dallas, Texas: Oncor.

Edwards, M. R., & Trancik, J. E. (2014). "Climate Impacts of Energy Technologies Depend on Emissions Timing," *Nature Climate Change,* 4: 347–52. DOI: 10.1038/NCLIMATE2204

Erikson, R. S., Wright, G. C., & McIver, J. P. (1993). *Statehouse Democracy: Public Opinion and Policy in the American States.* Cambridge: Cambridge University Press.

Faden, V. (2000). "Net Metering of Renewable Energy: How Traditional Electricity Suppliers Fight to Keep You in the Dark," *Widener Journal of Public Law,* 10/1: 109–34.

Fairfield, T., & Charman, A. E. (2017). "Explicitly Bayesian Analysis for Process Tracing: Guidelines, Opportunities, and Caveats," *Political Analysis,* 25: 363–80. DOI: 10.1017/pan.2-17.14

Farrell, J. (2015). "Network Structure and Influence of the Climate Change Counter-movement," *Nature Climate Change,* 6: 370–4. DOI: 10.1038/nclimate2875

Farrell, J. (2016). "Corporate Funding and Ideological Polarization About Climate Change," *Proceedings of the National Academy of Sciences,* 113/1: 92–7. DOI: 10.1073/pnas.1509433112

Feigenbaum, J., Hertel-Fernandez, A., Williamson, V., Blair, P., Derenoncourt, E., Finan, F., Simon, J., et al. (2018). "From the Bargaining Table to the Ballot Box: Political Effects of Right to Work Laws." NBER Working Paper Series 24259. National Bureau of Economic Research, Cambridge, MA. DOI: 10.3386/w24259

Fenno, R. (1978). *Home Style: House Members in Their Districts*. New York: Longman.

Fernández, J. J., & Jaime-Castillo, A. M. (2013). "Positive or Negative Policy Feedbacks? Explaining Popular Attitudes Towards Pragmatic Pension Policy Reforms," *European Sociological Review*, 29/4: 803–15.

Fiorino, D. J. (2011). "Explaining National Environmental Performance: Approaches, Evidence, and Implications," *Policy Sciences*, 44/4: 367–89.

Fischlein, M., Wilson, E. J., Peterson, T. R., & Stephens, J. C. (2013). "States of Transmission: Moving Towards Large-Scale Wind Power," *Energy Policy*, 56: 101–13.

Fishkin, J. S. (2011). "Why Deliberative Polling? Reply to Gleason," *Critical Review*, 23/3: 393–403.

Fouirnaies, A., & Hall, A. B. (2018). "How Do Interest Groups Seek Access to Committees?" *American Journal of Political Science*, 62/1: 132–47.

Fri, R. W. (2003). "The Role of Knowledge: Technological Innovation in the Energy System," *Energy Journal*, 24/4: 51–74.

Fuss, S., Canadell, J. G., Peters, G. P., Tavoni, M., Andrew, R. M., Ciais, P., Jackson, R. B., et al. (2014). "Betting on Negative Emissions," *Nature Climate Change*, 4/10: 850–3.

Galbraith, K., & Price, A. (2013). *The Great Texas Wind Rush: How George Bush, Ann Richards, and a Bunch of Tinkerers Helped the Oil and Gas State Win the Race to Wind Power*. Austin: University of Texas Press.

Garlick, A. (2017). "National Policies, Agendas, and Polarization in American State Legislatures: 2011 to 2014," *American Politics Research*, 45/6: 939–79.

Gaventa, J. (1980). *Power and Powerlessness: Quiescence and Rebellion in an Appalachian Valley*. Urbana: University of Illinois Press.

Gelman, A. (2009). *Red State, Blue State, Rich State, Poor State: Why Americans Vote the Way They Do-Expanded Edition*. Princeton: Princeton University Press

George, A. L., & Bennett, A. (2005). *Case Studies and Theory Development in the Social Sciences*. Cambridge, MA: MIT Press.

Gerber, A. S. (2004). "Does Campaign Spending Work?: Field Experiments Provide Evidence and Suggest New Theory," *American Behavioral Scientist*, 47/5: 541–74.

Gerber, A., Green, D., & Larimer, C. (2008). "Social Pressure and Voter Turnout: Evidence From a Large-Scale Field Experiment," *American Political Science Review*, 102/1: 33–48.

Ghosh, S., & Apostolakis, G. (2005). "Organizational Contributions to Nuclear Power Plant Safety," *Nuclear Engineering and Technology*, 37/3: 207–20.

Gilens, M., & Page, B. I. (2014). "Testing Theories of American Politics: Elites, Interest Groups, and Average Citizens," *Perspectives on Politics*, 12/3: 564–81.

Gold, R. (2014). *The Boom: How Fracking Ignited the American Energy Revolution and Changed the World*. New York: Simon and Schuster.

Goss, K. A. (2008). *Disarmed: The Missing Movement for Gun Control in America*. Princeton, NJ: Princeton University Press.

Goss, K. A. (2010). "Civil Society and Civic Engagement: Towards a Multi-Level Theory of Policy Feedbacks," *Journal of Civil Society*, 6/2: 119–43.

Greenburg, L., Field, F., Erhardt, C. L., Glasser, M., & Reed, J. I. (1967). "Air Pollution, Influenza, and Mortality in New York City," *Archives of Environmental Health: An International Journal*, 15/4: 430–8.

Greenstone, M., Mcdowell, R., Nath, I., Greenstone, M., & Mcdowell, R. (2019). "Do Renewable Portfolio Standards Deliver?" BFI Working Paper, Becker Friedman Institute, Chicago.

Griscom, B. W., Adams, J., Ellis, P. W., Houghton, R. A., Lomax, G., Miteva, D. A., Schlesinger, W. H., et al. (2017). "Natural Climate Solutions," *Proceedings of the National Academy of Sciences*, 114/44: 11645–50.

Grübler, A. (2010). "The Costs of the French Nuclear Scale-Up: A Case of Negative Learning by Doing," *Energy Policy*, 38/9: 5174–88.

Grumbach, J. M. (2015). "Polluting Industries as Climate Protagonists: Cap and Trade and the Problem of Business Preferences," *Business and Politics*, 17/4: 633–59.

Grumbach, J. M. (2018). "From Backwaters to Major Policymakers: Policy Polarization in the States, 1970–2014," *Perspectives on Politics*, 16/2: 416–35.

Grumbach, J. M. (2019). "Interest Group Activists, Party Insiders, and the Polarization of State Legislatures," *Legislative Studies Quarterly*, forthcoming.

Guber, D. L. (2012). "A Cooling Climate for Change? Party Polarization and the Politics of Global Warming," *American Behavioral Scientist*, 57/1: 93–115. DOI: 10.1177/0002764212463361

Hacker, J. S. (2002). *The Divided Welfare State: The Battle Over Public and Private Social Benefits in the United States*. Cambridge: Cambridge University Press.

Hacker, J. S. (2004). "Privatizing Risk Without Privatizing the Welfare State: The Hidden Politics of Social Policy Retrenchment in the United States," *American Political Science Review*, 98/2: 243–60.

Hacker, J. S. (2005). "Policy Drift: The Hidden Politics of US Welfare State Retrenchment." Streeck, W., & Thelen, K. (eds) *Beyond Continuity: Institutional Change in Advanced Political Economies*, pp. 40–82. New York: Oxford University Press.

Hacker, J. S., & Pierson, P. (2002). "Business Power and Social Policy: Employers and the Formation of the American Welfare State," *Politics & Society*, 30/2: 277–325.

Hacker, J. S., & Pierson, P. (2006). *Off Center: The Republican Revolution & the Erosion of American Democracy*. New Haven, CT: Yale University Press.

Hacker, J. S., & Pierson, P. (2010a). *Winner-Take-All Politics*. New York: Simon and Schuster.

Hacker, J. S., & Pierson, P. (2010b). "Winner-Take-All Politics: Public Policy, Political Organization, and the Precipitous Rise of Top Incomes in the United States," *Politics & Society*, 38/2: 152–204.

Hacker, J. S., & Pierson, P. (2014). "After the 'Master Theory': Downs, Schattschneider, and the Rebirth of Policy-Focused Analysis," *Perspectives on Politics*, 12/3: 643–62.

Han, H. (2014). *How Organizations Develop Activists: Civic Associations and Leadership in the 21st Century*. Oxford: Oxford University Press.

Hansen, J. (1991). *Gaining Access: Congress and the Farm Lobby, 1919–1981*. Chicago: University of Chicago Press.

Hargadon, A., & Douglas, Y. (2001). "When Innovations Meet Institutions: Edison and the Design of the Electric Light," *Administrative Science Quarterly*, 46: 476–501.

Harley, K. (2011). "Mercurial but not Swift U.S. EPA's Initiative to Regulate Coal Plant Mercury Emissions Changes Course Again as It Enters a Third Decade," *Chicago-Kent Law Review*, 86: 277–90.

Harrison, C. (2013). "The Historical-Geographical Construction of Power: Electricity in Eastern North Carolina," *Local Environment*, 18/4: 469–86.

Harrison, C. (2016). "Race, Space, and Electric Power: Jim Crow and the 1934 North Carolina Rural Electrification Survey," *Annals of the American Association of Geographers*, 106/4: 909–31. DOI: 10.1080/24694452.2016.1151335

Hawken, P. (2017). *Drawdown: The Most Comprehensive Plan Ever Proposed to Reverse Global Warming*. New York: Penguin.

Heard, B. P., Brook, B. W., Wigley, T. M. L., & Bradshaw, C. J. A. (2017). "Burden of Proof: A Comprehensive Review of the Feasibility of 100% Renewable-Electricity Systems," *Renewable and Sustainable Energy Reviews*, 76: 1122–33. DOI: 10.1016/j.rser.2017.03.114

Heclo, H. (1974). *Modern Social Politics in Britain and Sweden: From Relief to Income Maintenance*. New Haven, CT: Yale University Press.

Heclo, H. (1978). "Issue Networks and the Executive Establishment." King, A. (ed.), *The New American Political System*, pp. 87–124. Washington, DC: American Enterprise Institute for Policy Research.

Hedke, D. (2011). *The Audacity of Freedom*. Mustang, OK: Tate Publishing.

Hertel-Fernandez, A. (2014). "Who Passes Business's 'Model Bills'? Policy Capacity and Corporate Influence in U.S. State Politics," *Perspectives on Politics*, 12/3: 582–602. DOI: 10.1017/S153759s2714001601

Hertel-Fernandez, A. (2016). "Explaining Liberal Policy Woes in the States: The Role of Donors," *PS—Political Science and Politics*, 49/3: 461–5. DOI: 10.1017/S1049096516000706

Hertel-Fernandez, A. (2018). *Politics at Work: How Companies Turn Their Workers Into Lobbyists.* Oxford: Oxford University Press.

Hertel-Fernandez, A. (2019). *State Capture: How Conservative Activists, Big Businesses, and Wealthy Donors Reshaped the American States—and the Nation.* Oxford: Oxford University Press.

Hertel-Fernandez, A., Mildenberger, M., & Stokes, L. C. (2019). "Legislative Staff and Representation in Congress," *American Political Science Review*, 113/1: 1–18. DOI: 10.1017/S0003055418000606

Hertel-Fernandez, A., Skocpol, T., & Lynch, D. (2016). "Business Associations, Conservative Networks, and the Ongoing Republican War Over Medicaid Expansion," *Journal of Health Politics, Policy and Law*, 41/2: 239–86. DOI: 10.1215/03616878-3476141

Hinton, D. D., & Olien, R. M. (2002). *Oil in Texas: The Gusher Age, 1895–1945.* Austin: University of Texas Press.

Hirsh, R. F. (1989). *Technology and Transformation in the American Electric Utility Industry.* Cambridge: Cambridge University Press.

Hirsh, R. F. (1999a). *Power Loss: The Origins of Deregulation and Restructuring in the American Electric Utility System.* Cambridge, MA: MIT Press.

Hirsh, R. F. (1999b). "PURPA: The Spur to Competition and Utility Restructuring," *Electricity Journal*, 12/7: 60–72.

Hirsh, R. F. (2013). "Fifteen Years Later: Whither Restructuring in the American Electric Utility System? A Postscript to Power Loss: The Origins of Deregulation and Restructuring in the American Electric Utility System," *Technology's Stories*, December, 2013.

Hirsh, R. F. (2018). "Shedding New Light on Rural Electrification: The Neglected Story of Successful Efforts to Power Up Farms in the 1920s and 1930s," *Agricultural History*, 92/3: 296–327. DOI: 10.3098/ah.2018.092.3.296

Hirth, L. (2016). "What Caused the Drop in European Electricity Prices? A Factor Decomposition Analysis," *USAEE Working Papers*, 16/282: 143–58. DOI: 10.5547/01956574.39.1.lhir

Hoffert, M. I., Caldeira, K., Benford, G., Criswell, D. R., Green, C., Herzog, H., Jain, A. K., et al. (2002). "Advanced Technology Paths to Global Climate Stability: Energy for a Greenhouse Planet," *Science*, 298/5595: 981–7. DOI: 10.1126/science.1072357

Hogan, M. T. (2008). *Running in Place: Renewable Portfolio Standards and Climate Change.* PhD Thesis. Cambridge, MA: Massachusetts Institute of Technology.

Hojnacki, M., Kimball, D. C., Baumgartner, F. R., Berry, J. M., & Leech, B. L. (2012). "Studying Organizational Advocacy and Influence: Reexamining Interest Group Research," *Annual Review of Political Science*, 15: 379–99. DOI: 10.1146/annurev-polisci-070910-104051

Hopkins, D. J. (2018). *The Increasingly United States: How and Why American Political Behavior Nationalized.* Chicago: University of Chicago Press.

Hopkins, D. J., & Ladd, J. M. (2012). "The Consequences of Broader Media Choice: Evidence From the Expansion of Fox News," *Quarterly Journal of Political Science*, 9/1: 115–35.

Hopper, J. (1976). "A Legislative History of the Texas Public Utility Regulatory Act of 1975," *Baylor Law Review*, 28/4: 777–822.

Howe, P. D., Mildenberger, M., Marlon, J. R., & Leiserowitz, A. (2015). "Geographic Variation in US Climate Change Opinion at State and Local Scales," *Nature Climate Change*, 5/4: 596–603.

Hubbard, E. (1916). *Little Journeys to the Homes of Good Men and Great*, memorial ed. New York: The Roycrofters.

Huber, G., & Arceneaux, K. (2007). "Identifying the Persuasive Effects of Presidential Advertising," *American Journal of Political Science*, 51/4: 957–77.

Huber, J., & Shipan, C. (2002). *Deliberate Discretion? The Institutional Foundations of Bureaucratic Autonomy*. Cambridge: Cambridge University Press.

Hudson, P., & Rowe, E. (2005). "Mandate & Market: Texas Electric Restructuring Act of 1999, An Environmental Case Study Six Years Into Implementation," *Environmental & Energy Law & Policy Journal*, 1/1: 235–50.

Hughes, T. P. (1969). "Technological Momentum in History: Hydrogenation in Germany 1898–1933," *Past and Present*, 44/1: 106–32.

Hughes, T. P. (1983). *Networks of Power: Electrification in Western Society, 1880–1930*, 1st ed. Baltimore, MD: Johns Hopkins University Press.

Hughes, T. P. (2004). *American Genesis: A Century of Invention and Technological Enthusiasm, 1870–1970*. Chicago: Chicago University Press.

Hughes, T. P. (2012). "The Evolution of Large Technological Systems." Bijker, W. E., Hughes, T. P., & Pinch, T. (eds) *The Social Construction of Technological Systems: New Directions in the Sociology and History of Technology*, pp. 45–76. Cambridge, MA: MIT Press.

Hurlbut, D. (2008). "A Look Behind the Texas Renewable Portfolio Standard: A Case Study," *Natural Resources Journal*, 48/1: 129–61.

Intergovernmental Panel on Climate Change. (2018). "Summary for Policymakers." *Global Warming of 1.5 C*. Special Report. Geneva, Switzerland: IPCC. DOI: 10.1017/CBO9781107415324.004

Abu Dhabi, United Arab Emirates: International Renewable Energy Agency.

Iyer, G., Clarke, L., Edmonds, J., Kyle, P., Ledna, C., Mcjeon, H., & Wise, M. (2017). *GCAM-USA Analysis of U.S. Electric Power Sector Transitions*. Technical Report PNNL-26174. Richland, WA: Pacific Northwest National Laboratory.

Jackson, R. B., Le Quéré, C., Andrew, R. M., Canadell, J. G., Korsbakken, J. I., Liu, Z., Peters, G. P., et al. (2018). "Global Energy Growth Is Outpacing Decarbonization," *Environmental Research Letters*, 13/12. DOI: 10.1088/1748-9326/aaf303

Jacobs, A. M., & Weaver, R. K. (2015). "When Policies Undo Themselves: Self-Undermining Feedback as a Source of Policy Change," *Governance*, 28/4: 441–57. DOI: 10.1111/gove.12101

Jacobs, L. R., & Callaghan, T. (2013). "Why States Expand Medicaid: Party, Resources, and History," *Journal of Health Politics, Policy and Law*, 38/5: 1023–50. DOI: 10.1215/03616878-2334889

Jacobs, L. R., & King, D. S. (2016). *Fed Power: How Finance Wins*. Oxford: Oxford University Press.

Jacobs, L. R., & Shapiro, R. Y. (2000). *Politicians Don't Pander: Political Manipulation and the Loss of Democratic Responsiveness*. Chicago: University of Chicago Press.

Jacobs, L. R., & Skocpol, T. (2015). *Health Care Reform and American Politics: What Everyone Needs to Know*. Oxford: Oxford University Press.

Jacobson, M. Z., Delucchi, M. A., Bazouin, G., Bauer, Z. A. F., Heavey, C. C., Fisher, E., Morris, S. B., et al. (2015). "100% Clean and Renewable Wind, Water, Sunlight (WWS) All-Sector Energy Roadmaps for the 50 United States." *Energy & Environmental Science*, 8: 2093–117.

Jacobson, M. Z., & Delucchi, M. A. (2011). "Providing All Global Energy With Wind, Water, and Solar Power, Part I: Technologies, Energy Resources, Quantities and Areas of Infrastructure, and Materials," *Energy Policy*, 39/3: 1154–69. DOI: 10.1016/j.enpol.2010.11.040

Jacobson, M. Z., Delucchi, M. A., Cameron, M. A., & Frew, B. A. (2015). "Low-Cost Solution to the Grid Reliability Problem With 100% Penetration of Intermittent Wind, Water, and Solar for All Purposes," *Proceedings of the National Academy of Sciences*, 112/49: 15060–5. DOI: 10.1073/pnas.1510028112

Jacobson, M. Z., Delucchi, M. A., Cameron, M. A., & Frew, B. A. (2017). "The United States Can Keep the Grid Stable at Low Cost With 100% Clean, Renewable Energy in All Sectors Despite Inaccurate Claims," *Proceedings of the National Academy of Sciences*, 114/26: E5021–3. DOI: 10.1073/pnas.1708069114

Jacques, P. J., Dunlap, R. E., & Freeman, M. (2008). "The Organisation of Denial: Conservative Think Tanks and Environmental Scepticism," *Environmental Politics*, 17/3: 349–85. DOI: 10.1080/09644010802055576

Jaffe, A. B., & Stavins, R. N. (1994). "The Energy-Efficiency Gap: What Does It Mean?" *Energy Policy*, 22/10: 804–10.

Jamieson, D. (2011). "Energy, Ethics, and the Transformation of Nature." Arnold, D. G. (ed.), *The Ethics of Global Climate Change*, pp. 16–37. Cambridge: Cambridge University Press.

Jenkins, J. (2015). *Financing Mega-Scale Energy Projects: A Case Study of the Petra Nova Carbon Capture Project*. Chicago: Paulson Institute.

Jenkins, J. D. (2017). "What's Killing Nuclear Power in U.S. Electricity Markets?" Working Paper Series CEEPR WP 2018-001. Cambridge, MA: Massachusetts Institute of Technology.

Jenkins, J. D., Luke, M., & Thernstrom, S. (2018). "Getting to Zero Carbon Emissions in the Electric Power Sector," *Joule*, 2/12: 2498–510. DOI: 10.1016/j.joule.2018.11.013

Johnstone, B. (2011). *Switching to Solar: What We Can Learn From Germany's Success in Harnessing Clean Energy*. Amherst, NY: Prometheus Books.

Jones, B. D., & Baumgartner, F. R. (2005). *The Politics of Attention: How Government Prioritizes Problems*. Chicago: University of Chicago Press.

Jones, C. O. (1975). *Clean Air: The Policies and Politics of Pollution Control*. Pittsburgh: University of Pittsburgh Press.

Joskow, P. L. (1976). "Contributions to the Theory of Marginal Cost Pricing," *Bell Journal of Economics*, 7/1: 197–206.

Joskow, P. L. (1997). "Restructuring, Competition and Regulatory Reform in the U.S. Electricity Sector," *Journal of Economic Perspectives*, 11/3: 119–38.

Joskow, P. L. (2001). "California's Electricity Crisis," *Oxford Review of Economic Policy*, 17/3: 365–88. DOI: 10.1093/oxrep/17.3.365

Joskow, P. L. (2003). "The Difficult Transition to Competitive Electricity Markets in the U.S." *Deregulation: Where Do We Go From Here?*, pp. 1–107. Washington, DC: Aei Press.

Joskow, P. L. (2006). "Markets for Power in the United States: An Interim Assessment," *Energy Journal*, 27/1: 1–36.

Joskow, P. L., & Schmalensee, R. (1983). *Markets for Power: An Analysis of Electrical Utility Deregulation*. Cambridge, MA: MIT Press.

Kahn, A. E. (1971). *The Economics of Regulation: Principles and Institutions*. New York: John Wiley & Sons.

Kalla, J. L., & Broockman, D. E. (2016). "Campaign Contributions Facilitate Access to Congressional Officials: A Randomized Field Experiment," *American Journal of Political Science*, 60/3: 545–58. DOI: 10.1111/ajps.12180

Kalt, J. P., & Zupan, M. A. (1984). "Capture and Ideology in the Economic Theory of Politics," *American Economic Review*, 74/3: 279–300.

Kamarck, E. C., & Wallner, J. (2018). "Anticipating Trouble: Congressional Primaries and Incumbent Behavior," R Street Policy Study. Washington, DC: Brookings Institution.

Kao, S.-C., Sale, M. J., Ashfaq, M., Uria Martinez, R., Kaiser, D. P., Wei, Y., & Diffenbaugh, N. S. (2015). "Projecting Changes in Annual Hydropower Generation Using Regional Runoff Data: An Assessment of the United States Federal Hydropower Plants," *Energy*, 80: 239–50. DOI: 10.1016/j.energy.2014.11.066

Karol, D. (2019). *Red, Green, and Blue: The Partisan Divide on Environmental Issues*. Cambridge: Cambridge University Press.

Kassakian, J. G., & Schmalensee, R. (2011). *The Future of the Electric Grid: An Interdisciplinary MIT Study*. MIT Energy Initiative. Cambridge, MA: MIT Press.

Kim, S. E., Urpelainen, J., & Yang, J. (2015). "Electric Utilities and American Climate Policy: Lobbying by Expected Winners and Losers," *Journal of Public Policy*, 36/2: 251–75. DOI: 10.1017/S0143814X15000033

Kim, S. E., Yang, J., & Urpelainen, J. (2016). "Does Power Sector Deregulation Promote or Discourage Renewable Energy Policy? Evidence from the States, 1991–2012." *Review of Policy Research*, 33/1: 22–50.

Kind, P. (2013). *Disruptive Challenges: Financial Implications and Strategic Responses to a Changing Retail Electric Business*. Washington, DC: Edison Electric Institute.

King, G., Keohane, R. O., & Verba, S. (1994). *Designing Social Inquiry: Scientific Inference in Qualitative Research*. Princeton, NJ: Princeton University Press.

Kingdon, J. W. (2011). *Agendas, Alternatives, and Public Policies*, 2nd ed. Boston: Little, Brown.

Klass, A. B., & Wilson, E. J. (2012). "Interstate Transmission Challenges for Renewable Energy: A Federalism Mismatch," *Vanderbilt Law Review*, 65/6: 1801–73.

Kollman, K. (1998). *Outside Lobbying: Public Opinion and Interest Group Strategies*. Princeton, NJ: Princeton University Press.

Kroeger, M. (2015). "Plagiarizing Policy: Model Legislation in State Legislatures," Presented at Annual State Politics and Policy Conference, Sacramento, California.

Laird, F. N. (2001). *Solar Energy, Technology Policy, and Institutional Values*. Cambridge: Cambridge University Press.

Laird, F. N., & Stefes, C. (2009). "The Diverging Paths of German and United States Policies for Renewable Energy: Sources of Difference," *Energy Policy*, 37/7: 2619–29. DOI: 10.1016/j.enpol.2009.02.027

Langniss, O., & Wiser, R. (2003). "The Renewables Portfolio Standard in Texas: An Early Assessment," *Energy Policy*, 31/6: 527–35.

Langniss, O., & Wiser, R. (2005). "The Design and Impacts of the Texas Renewables Portfolio Standard." Lauber, V. (ed.), *Switching to Renewable Power: A Framework for the 21st Century*, pp. 187–202. New York: Earthscan.

Lauber, V. (2004). "REFIT and RPS: Options for a Harmonised Community Framework," *Energy Policy*, 32/12: 1405–14. DOI: 10.1016/S0301-4215(03)00108-3

Lax, J. R., & Phillips, J. H. (2009). "Gay Rights in the States: Public Opinion and Policy Responsiveness," *American Political Science Review*, 103/03: 367–86. DOI: 10.1017/S0003055409990050

Lax, J. R., & Phillips, J. H. (2012). "The Democratic Deficit in the States," *American Journal of Political Science*, 56/1: 148–66. DOI: 10.1111/j.1540-5907.2011.00537.x

Layzer, J. A. (2011). "Cold Front: How the Recession Stalled Obama's Clean-Energy Agenda." Skocpol, T., & Jacobs, L. R. (eds) *Reaching for a New Deal*. New York: Russell Sage Foundation.

Layzer, J. A. (2012). *Open for Business: Conservatives' Opposition to Environmental Regulation*. Cambridge, MA: MIT Press.

Leiserowitz, A., Feinberg, G., Howe, P., & Rosenthal, S. (2013). *Climate Change in the Ohioan Mind*. New Haven, CT: Yale Project on Climate Change Communication.

Lenz, G. S. (2012). *Follow the Leader? How Voters Respond to Politicians' Policies and Performance*. Chicago: University of Chicago Press.

Leonard, C. (2019). *Kochland: The Secret History of Koch Industries and Corporate Power in America*. New York: Simon & Schuster.

Leshy, J. D. (1988). "The Making of the Arizona Constitution," *Arizona State Law Journal*, 20/1: 1–52.

Lesser, J. A., & Su, X. (2008). "Design of an Economically Efficient Feed-In Tariff Structure for Renewable Energy Development," *Energy Policy*, 36/3: 981–90. DOI: 10.1016/j.enpol.2007.11.007

Levitt, T. (1960). "Marketing Myopia," *Harvard Business Review*, 38: 24–47. DOI: 10.1108/09600030210415270

Lewis, J. I., & Wiser, R. H. (2007). "Fostering a Renewable Energy Technology Industry: An International Comparison of Wind Industry Policy Support Mechanisms," *Energy Policy*, 35/3: 1844–57. DOI: 10.1016/j.enpol.2006.06.005

Lifset, R. D. (2014). "A New Understanding of the American Energy Crisis of the 1970s," *Historical Social Research*, 39/4: 22–42. DOI: 10.12759/hsr.39.2014.4.22-42

Lindblom, C. E. (1959). "The Science of 'Muddling Through,'" *Public Administration Review*, 19/2: 79–88.

Lindblom, C. E. (1977). *Politics and Markets: The World's Political–Economic Systems*. New York: Basic Books.

Littel, D., Kadoch, C., Baker, P., Bharvirkar, R., Dupuy, M., Hausauer, B., Linvill, C., et al. (2017). *Next-Generation Performance-Based Regulation: Emphasizing Utility Performance to Unleash Power Sector Innovation*. NREL/TP-6A50-68512. Golden, CO: National Renewable Energy Laboratory.

Lockwood, M. (2013). "The Political Sustainability of Climate Policy: The Case of the UK Climate Change Act," *Global Environmental Change*, 23/5: 1339–48. DOI: 10.1016/j.gloenvcha.2013.07.001

Loiter, J., & Norberg-Bohm, V. (1999). "Technology Policy and Renewable Energy: Public Roles in the Development of New Energy Technologies," *Energy Policy*, 27/2: 85–97.

Lopez, A., Roberts, B., Heimiller, D., Blair, N., & Porro, G. (2012). *U.S. Renewable Energy Technical Potentials: A GIS-Based Analysis*. NREL/TP-6A20-51946. Golden, CO: National Renewable Energy Laboratory.

Lovering, J. R., Yip, A., & Nordhaus, T. (2016). "Historical Construction Costs of Global Nuclear Power Reactors," *Energy Policy*, 91: 371–82. DOI: 10.1016/j.enpol.2016.01.011

Lovins, A. B. (1976). "Energy Strategy: The Road Not Taken?" *Foreign Affairs*, 55/1: 65. DOI: 10.2307/20039628

Lowi, T. J. (1972). "Four Systems of Policy, Politics, and Choice," *Public Administration Review*, 32/4: 298–310.

Lowi, T. J. (1979). *The End of Liberalism: The Second Republic of the United States*. New York: Norton.

Luskin, R. C., Fishkin, J. S., & Plane, D. L. (1999). "Deliberative Polling and Policy Outcomes: Electric Utility Issues in Texas." Annual Meeting of the Association for Public Policy Analysis and Management, Washington, DC, November 4-7, 1999.

MacDonald, A. E., Clack, C. T. M., Alexander, A., Dunbar, A., Wilczak, J., & Xie, Y. (2016). "Future Cost-Competitive Electricity Systems and Their Impact on US CO_2 Emissions," *Nature Climate Change*, January: 1–6. DOI: 10.1038/nclimate2921

Mahoney, J., & Thelen, K. (2009). "A Theory of Gradual Institutional Change." Thelen, K., & Mahoney, J. (eds) *Explaining Institutional Change: Ambiguity, Agency and Power*, pp. 1–37. Cambridge: Cambridge University Press.

Malhotra, N. (2008). "The Impact of Public Financing on Electoral Competition: Evidence From Arizona and Maine," *State Politics and Policy Quarterly*, 8/3: 263–81. DOI: 10.1177/153244000800800303

March, J. G., & Olsen, J. P. (1976). *Ambiguity and Choice in Organizations*. Oslo, Norway: Universitetsforlaget.

March, J. G., & Simon, H. A. (1993). *Organizations*. Oxford: Blackwell.

Martin, S. A. (1983). "Problems With PURPA: The Need for State Legislation to Encourage Cogeneration and Small Power Production," *Boston College Environmental Affairs Law Review*, 11/1: 149–202.

May, P. J. (1992). "Policy Learning and Failure," *Journal of Public Policy*, 12/4: 331–54.

McCarty, N. (2007). "The Policy Effects of Political Polarization." *The Transformation of American Politics: Activist Government and the Rise of Conservatism*, pp. 223–55. Princeton, NJ: Princeton University Press.

McCarty, N. (2014). "Complexity, Capacity, and Capture." Carpenter, D., & Moss, D. A. (eds) *Preventing Regulatory Capture—Special Interest Influence and How to Limit It*, pp. 99–123. New York: Cambridge University Press.

McCarty, N., Poole, K. T., & Rosenthal, H. (2006). *Polarized America: The Dance of Ideology and Unequal Riches*. Cambridge, MA: MIT Press.

McCarty, N., & Schickler, E. (2018). "On the Theory of Parties," *Annual Review of Political Science*, 21: 175–93. DOI: 10.1146/annurev-polisci-061915-123020

McCraw, T. K. (1971). *TVA and the Power Fight, 1933-1939*. Philadelphia: Lippincott.

McDonald, F. (1962). *Insull: The Rise and Fall of a Billionaire Utility Tycoon*. Chicago: University of Chicago Press.

McDowall, W., Ekins, P., Radošević, S., & Zhang, L. (2013). "The Development of Wind Power in China, Europe and the USA: How Have Policies and Innovation System

Activities Co-evolved?" Technology Analysis and Strategic Management, 25/2: 163–85. DOI: 10.1080/09537325.2012.759204

McKinsey & Company. (2009). *Unlocking Energy Efficiency in the U.S. Economy. Energy.* New York: McKinsey & Company.

McNerney, J., Farmer, J. D., & Trancik, J. E. (2011). "Historical Costs of Coal-Fired Electricity and Implications for the Future," *Energy Policy*, 39/6: 3042–54.

Merton, R. K. (1936). "The Unanticipated Consequences of Purposive Social Action," *American Sociological Review*, 1/6: 894–904.

Mettler, S. (2002). "Bringing the State Back in to Civic Engagement: Policy Feedback Effects of the G.I. Bill for World War II Veterans," *American Political Science Review*, 96/2: 351–65.

Mettler, S. (2005). *Soldiers to Citizens: The GI Bill and the Making of the Greatest Generation.* Oxford: Oxford University Press.

Mettler, S., & Soss, J. (2004). "The Consequences of Public Policy for Democratic Citizenship: Bridging Policy Studies and Mass Politics," *Perspectives on Politics*, 2/1: 55–73.

Mildenberger, M. (2020). *Carbon Captured: How Business and Labor Control Climate Politics.* Cambridge, MA: MIT Press.

Mildenberger, M., & Leiserowitz, A. (2017). "Public Opinion on Climate Change: Is There an Economy–Environment Tradeoff?," *Environmental Politics*, 26/5: 801–24.

Mildenberger, M., Marlon, J. R., Howe, P. D., & Leiserowitz, A. (2017). "The Spatial Distribution of Republican and Democratic Climate Opinions at State and Local Scales," *Climatic Change*, 145/3–4: 539–48.

Mitchell, B. M., Manning, G., & Acton, J. P. (1980). *Peak-Load Pricing: European Lessons for U.S. Energy Policy.* Cambridge, MA: Ballinger.

Moe, T. M. (1989). "The Politics of Bureaucratic Structure." Chubb, J. E., & Peterson, P. E. (eds) *Can the Government Govern?* pp. 267–330. Washington, DC: Brookings Institution.

Moe, T. (2005). "Power and Political Institutions," *Perspectives on Politics*, 3/2: 215–33.

Moe, T. M. (2015). "Vested Interests and Political Institutions," *Political Science Quarterly*, 130/2: 277–318.

Moeller, J. (2004). "Of Credits and Quotas: Federal Tax Incentives for Renewable Resources, State Renewable Portfolio Standards, and the Evolution of Proposals for a Federally Renewable Portfolio Standard," *Forham Environmental Law Review Journal*, 15/1: 320–32.

Morris, G. (2000). *Biomass Energy Production in California: The Case for a Biomass Policy Initiative.* Golden, CO: National Renewable Energy Laboratory.

Moynihan, D. P., & Soss, J. (2014). "Policy Feedback and the Politics of Administration," *Public Administration Review*, 74/3: 320–32. DOI: 10.1111/puar.12200

Mullin, M. (2009). *Governing the Tap: Special District Governance and the New Local Politics of Water.* Cambridge, MA: MIT Press.

Nall, C. (2015). "The Political Consequences of Spatial Policies: How Interstate Highways Facilitated Geographic Polarization," *Journal of Politics*, 77/2: 394–406.

Nemet, G. F. (2006). "Beyond the Learning Curve: Factors Influencing Cost Reductions in Photovoltaics," *Energy Policy*, 34/17: 3218–32.

Nemet, G. F. (2009). "Demand-Pull, Technology-Push, and Government-Led Incentives for Non-Incremental Technical Change," *Research Policy*, 38/5: 700–9.

Nemet, G. F. (2012). "Solar Water Heater Innovation in the US." Grubler, A., Aguayo, F., Gallagher, K. S., Hekkert, M., Jiang, K., Mytelka, L., Neij, L., et al. (eds) *The Global Energy Assessment.* Cambridge: Cambridge University Press.

Nemet, G. F., & Kammen, D. M. (2007). "U.S. Energy Research and Development: Declining Investment, Increasing Need, and the Feasibility of Expansion," *Energy Policy*, 35/1: 746–55.

Oliver, T. R., Lee, P. R., Lipton, H. L., & Francisco, S. (2004). "A Political History of Medicare and Prescription Drug Coverage," *Milbank Quarterly*, 82/2: 283–354.

Olson, L. K. (2010). *The Politics of Medicaid.* New York: Columbia University Press.

Olson, M. (1965). *The Logic of Collective Action: Public Goods and the Theory of Groups.* Cambridge, MA: Harvard University Press.

Oreskes, N., & Conway, E. M. (2010). *Merchants of Doubt: How a Handful of Scientists Obscured the Truth on Issues From Tobacco Smoke to Global Warming.* New York: Bloomsbury Press.

Pacala, S. (2004). "Stabilization Wedges: Solving the Climate Problem for the Next 50 Years With Current Technologies," *Science,* 305/5686: 968–72.

Patashnik, E. M. (2003). "After the Public Interest Prevails: The Political Sustainability of Policy Reform," *Governance,* 16/2: 203–34.

Patashnik, E. M. (2008). *Reforms at Risk: What Happens After Major Policy Changes Are Enacted.* Princeton, NJ: Princeton University Press.

Patashnik, E. M., & Zelizer, J. (2009). "When Policy Does Not Remake Politics: The Limits of Policy Feedback," Working Paper. Presented at Annual Meeting of the American Political Science Association, Toronto, Canada.

Patashnik, E. M., & Zelizer, J. E. (2013). "The Struggle to Remake Politics: Liberal Reform and the Limits of Policy Feedback in the Contemporary American State," *Perspectives on Politics,* 11/4: 1071–87.

Pawson, R., Wong, G., & Owen, L. (2011). "Known Knowns, Known Unknowns, Unknown Unknowns: The Predicament of Evidence-Based Policy," *American Journal of Evaluation,* 32/4: 518–46.

Pierson, P. (1993). "When Effect Becomes Cause: Policy Feedback and Political Change," *World Politics,* 45/4: 595–628.

Pierson, P. (1994). *Dismantling the Welfare State? Reagan, Thatcher, and the Politics of Retrenchment.* Cambridge Studies in Comparative Politics. Cambridge: Cambridge University Press.

Pierson, P. (2000). "Increasing Returns, Path Dependence, and the Study of Politics," *American Political Science Review,* 94/2: 251–67.

Pierson, P. (2004). *Politics in Time: History, Institutions, and Social Analysis.* Princeton, NJ: Princeton University Press.

Pierson, P. (2006). "Public Policies as Institutions." Shapiro, I., Skowronek, S., & Galvin, D. (eds) *Rethinking Political Institutions: The Art of the State,* pp. 114–34. New York: New York University Press.

Polanyi, K. (1944). *The Great Transformation: The Political and Economic Origins of Our Time.* Boston: Beacon Press.

Powell, L. W. (2012). *The Influence of Campaign Contributions in State Legislatures: The Effects of Institutions and Politics.* Ann Arbor: University of Michigan Press.

Prior, M. (2013). "Media and Political Polarization," *Annual Review of Political Science,* 16/1: 101–27.

Quoidbach, J., Gilbert, D. T., & Wilson, T. D. (2013). "The End of History Illusion," *Science,* 339/6115: 96–8.

Rabe, B. G. (2004). *Statehouse and Greenhouse: The Emerging Politics of American Climate Change Policy.* Washington, DC: Brookings Institution Press.

Rabe, B. G. (2018). *Can We Price Carbon?* Cambridge, MA: MIT Press.

Rabe, B. G., & Borick, C. P. (2012). "Carbon Taxation and Policy Labeling: Experience From American States and Canadian Provinces," *Review of Policy Research,* 29/3: 358–82.

Rader, N., Boley, K., Borson, D., Bossong, K., & Saleska, S. (1989). *Power Surge: The Status and Near Term Potential of Renewable Energy Technologies.* Washington, DC: Public Citizen.

Rader, N., & Hempling, S. (2001). *The Renewables Portfolio Standard: A Practical Guide.* Washington, DC: National Association of Regulatory Utility Commissions.

Rader, N., & Norgaard, R. (1996). "Efficiency and Sustainability in Restructured Electricity Markets: The Renewables Portfolio Standard," *Electricity Journal,* 9/6: 37–49.

Rauch, J., & La Raja, R. J. (2017). *Re-engineering Politicians: How Activist Groups Choose Our Candidates—Long Before We Vote.* Washington, DC: Brookings Institution.

Raymond, L. (2016). *Reclaiming the Atmospheric Commons: The Regional Greenhouse Gas Initiative and a New Model of Emissions Trading.* Cambridge, MA: MIT Press.

Reichelstein, S., & Yorston, M. (2013). "The Prospects for Cost Competitive Solar PV Power," *Energy Policy,* 55: 117–27.

Rhodium Group. (2019). *Preliminary US Emissions Estimates for 2018.* Retrieved from https://rhg.com/research/preliminary-us-emissions-estimates-for-2018/

Richards, J., & Cole, W. J. (2017). "Assessing the Impact of Nuclear Retirements on the U.S. Power Sector," *Electricity Journal*, 30/9: 14–21.

Ricke, K., Drouet, L., Caldeira, K., & Tavoni, M. (2018). "Country-Level Social Cost of Carbon," *Nature Climate Change*, 8/10: 895–900.

Righter, R. W. (1996a). *Wind Energy in America: A History.* Norman: University of Oklahoma Press.

Righter, R. W. (1996b). "Pioneering in Wind Energy: The California Experience," *Renewable Energy*, 9/1–4: 781–4.

Rittenhouse, K., & Zaragoza-Watkins, M. (2017). "Anticipation and Environmental Regulation." Working Paper Series CEEPR WP 2017-004. Cambridge, MA: Massachusetts Institute of Technology.

Roberts, J. M., & Smith, S. S. (2003). 'Procedural contexts, party strategy, and conditional party voting in the U.S. House of representatives, 1971-2000', *American Journal of Political Science*, 47/2: 305–17.

Rockström, J., Gaffney, O., Rogelj, J., Meinshausen, M., Nakicenovic, N., & Schellnhuber, H. J. (2017). "A Roadmap for Rapid Decarbonization," *Science*, 355/6331: 1269–71.

Rogner, H.-H. (1997). "An Assessment of World Hydrocarbon Resources," *Annual Review of Energy and the Environment*, 22/1: 217–62.

Ross, M. L., Hazlett, C., Mahdavi, P., Gupta, S., Mahler, W., Bacon, R., Coady, D., et al. (2017). "Global Progress and Backsliding on Gasoline Taxes and Subsidies," *Nature Energy*, 2/1: 16201.

Rudolph, R., & Ridley, S. (1986). *Power Struggle: The Hundred-Year War Over Electricity.* New York: Harper & Row.

Sabatier, P. A. (1988). "An Advocacy Coalition Framework of Policy Change and the Role of Policy-Oriented Learning Therein," *Policy Sciences*, 21/2–3: 129–68.

Sabatier, P. A. (1993). "Policy Change Over a Decade or More." Sabatier, P. A., & Jenkins-Smith, H. C. (eds) *Policy Change and Learning: An Advocacy Coalition Approach*, pp. 13–39. Boulder, CO: Westview Press.

Sabin, P. (2005). *Crude Politics: The California Oil Market, 1900–1940.* Berkeley: University of California Press.

Sawyer, S. (1985). "State Renewable Energy Policy: Program Characteristics, Projections, Needs," *State & Local Government Review*, 17/1: 147–54.

Schattschneider, E. E. (1935). *Politics, Pressures and the Tariff: A Study of Free Private Enterprise in Pressure Politics, as Shown in the 1929 1930 Revision of the Tariff.* Hamden: Prentice Hall.

Schattschneider, E. E. (1942). *Party Government: American Government in Action.* New York: Rinehart and Company.

Schattschneider, E. E. (1960). *The Semisovereign People: A Realist's View of Democracy in America.* New York: Holt Rinehart and Winston.

Schenk, T., & Stokes, L. C. (2013). "The Power of Collaboration: Engaging All Parties in Renewable Energy Infrastructure Development," *IEEE Power and Energy Magazine*, 11/3: 56–65.

Schickler, E. (2001). *Disjointed Pluralism: Institutional Innovation and the Development of the US Congress.* Princeton, NJ: Princeton University Press.

Schmidt, T. S., & Sewerin, S. (2017). "Technology as a Driver of Climate and Energy Politics," *Nature Energy*, 2/6: 17084.

Schneider, A., & Ingram, H. (1993). "Social Construction of Target Populations: Implications for Politics and Policy," *American Political Science Review*, 87/2: 334–47.

Setzer, J., & Byrnes, R. (2019). *Global Trends in Climate Change Litigation: 2019 Snapshot.* London: London School of Economics and Political Science.

Shepsle, K. A. (2003). "Losers in Politics (and How They Sometimes Become Winners): William Riker's Heresthetic," *Perspectives on Politics*, 1/2: 307–15.

Shor, B. (2015). "Polarization in American State Legislatures." Thurber, J. A. & Yoshinaka, A. (eds) *American Gridlock: The Sources, Character, and Impact of Political Polarization*, pp. 203–21. New York: Cambridge University Press.

Sinclair, B. (2014). *Party Wars: Polarization and the Politics of National Policy Making.* Norman: University of Oklahoma Press.

Skocpol, T. (1992). *Protecting Soldiers and Mothers: The Political Origins of Social Policy in the United States.* Cambridge, MA: Harvard University Press.

Skocpol, T., Ganz, M., & Munson, Z. (2000). "A Nation of Organizers: The Institutional Origins of Civic Voluntarism in the United States," *American Political Science Review,* 94/3: 527–46.

Skocpol, T., & Hertel-Fernandez, A. (2016). "The Koch Network and Republican Party Extremism," *Perspectives on Politics,* 14/3: 681–99.

Slovic, P., Flynn, J. H., & Layman, M. (1991). "Perceived Risk, Trust, and the Politics of Nuclear Waste," *Science,* 254/5038: 1603–7.

Smil, V. (2003). *Energy at the Crossroads: Global Perspectives and Uncertainties.* Cambridge, MA: MIT Press.

Smil, V. (2010). *Energy Transitions: History, Requirements, Prospects.* Santa Barbara, CA: Praeger.

Smith, C. D. (2013). "Fragmentation and Policy Change: The Case of Wind Energy in California." Unpublished Manuscript.

Smith, M. A. (2000). *American Business and Political Power: Public Opinion, Elections, and Democracy.* Chicago: University of Chicago Press.

Soss, J. (1999). "Lessons of Welfare: Policy Design, Political Learning, and Political Action," *American Political Science Review,* 93/2: 363–80.

Soss, J., & Schram, S. F. (2007). "A Public Transformed? Welfare Reform as Policy Feedback," *American Political Science Review,* 101/1: 111–27.

Spencer, D. M., & Wood, A. K. (2014). "Citizens United, States Divided: An Empirical Analysis of Independent Political Spending," *Indiana Law Journal,* 89: 315–72.

Spinak, A. (2013). "'Not Quite so Freely as Air': Comparative Social Visions of Rural Electrification in the United States and Canada," Presented at the Society for American City and Regional Planning History Conference, Cambridge, MA. https://sacrph.org/conferences-2013/schedule/friday

Spinak, A. (2014). *Infrastructure and Agency: Rural Electric Cooperatives and the Fight for Economic Democracy in the United States.* PhD dissertation, Massachusetts Institute of Technology.

Starrs, T. A. (1988). "Legislative Incentives and Energy Technologies: Government's Role in the Development of the California Wind Energy Industry," *Ecology Law Quarterly,* 15/1: 103–58.

Stelzer, I. M. (1982). "Electric Utilities—Next Stop for Deregulators?" *Regulation,* 6/4: 29–35.

Stigler, G. J. (1971). "The Theory of Economic Regulation," *Bell Journal of Economics and Management Science,* 2/1: 3–21.

Stigler, G. J., & Friedland, C. (1962). "What Can Regulators Regulate? The Case of Electricity," *Journal of Law & Economics,* 5: 1–16.

Stimson, J. A. (2004). *Tides of Consent: How Public Opinion Shapes American Politics.* Cambridge: Cambridge University Press.

Stimson, J. A., MacKuen, M. B., & Erikson, R. S. (1995). "Dynamic Representation," *American Political Science Review,* 89/3: 543–65.

Stokes, L. C. (2013). "The Politics of Renewable Energy Policies: The Case of Feed-In Tariffs in Ontario, Canada," *Energy Policy,* 56: 490–500.

Stokes, L. C. (2015). *Power Politics: Renewable Energy Policy Change in US States.* PhD dissertation, Massachusetts Institute of Technology.

Stokes, L. C. (2016). "Electoral Backlash Against Climate Policy: A Natural Experiment on Retrospective Voting and Local Resistance to Public Policy," *American Journal of Political Science,* 60/4: 958–74.

Stokes, L. C., & Breetz, H. L. (2018). "Politics in the U.S. Energy Transition: Case Studies of Solar, Wind, Biofuels and Electric Vehicles Policy," *Energy Policy,* 113: 76–86.

Stokes, L. C., & Warshaw, C. (2017). "Renewable Energy Policy Design and Framing Influence Public Support in the United States," *Nature Energy,* 2/17107.

Stone, D. (2002). *Policy Paradox: The Art of Political Decision Making,* 3rd ed. New York: W. W. Norton.

Stoutenborough, J. W., & Beverlin, M. (2008). "Encouraging Pollution-Free Energy: The Diffusion of State Net Metering Policies," *Social Science Quarterly*, 89/5: 1230–51.

Sunter, D. A., Castellanos, S., & Kammen, D. M. (2019). "Disparities in Rooftop Photovoltaics Deployment in the United States by Race and Ethnicity," *Nature Sustainability*, 2/1: 71–6.

Supran, G., & Oreskes, N. (2017). "Assessing ExxonMobil's Climate Change Communications," *Environmental Research Letters*, 12/8: 084019.

Susskind, L., & Cruikshank, J. (1987). *Breaking the Impasse: Consensual Approaches to Resolving Public Disputes.* New York: Basic Books.

Teles, S. M. (2012). *The Rise of the Conservative Legal Movement: The Battle for Control of the Law.* Princeton, NJ: Princeton University Press.

Tetlock, P. (2005). *Expert Political Judgment: How Good Is It? How Can We Know?* Princeton, NJ: Princeton University Press.

Thelen, K. (1999). "Historical Institutionalism in Comparative Politics," *Annual Review of Political Science*, 2: 369–404.

Thelen, K. (2004). *How Institutions Evolve: The Political Economy of Skills in Germany, Britain, the United States, and Japan.* Cambridge: Cambridge University Press.

Theriault, S. M. (2008). *Party polarization in congress.* Cambridge: Cambridge University Press.

Tobey, R. (1996). *Technology as Freedom: The New Deal and the Electrical Modernization of the American Home.* Berkeley: University of California Press.

Tong, D., Zhang, Q., Zheng, Y., Caldeira, K., Shearer, C., Hong, C., Qin, Y., et al. (2019). "Committed Emissions From Existing Energy Infrastructure Jeopardize 1.5 °C Climate Target," *Nature*, 572: 373–7. DOI: 10.1038/s41586-019-1364-3

Trancik, J. E., Chang, M. T., Karapataki, C., & Stokes, L. C. (2014). "Effectiveness of a Segmental Approach to Climate Policy," *Environmental Science & Technology*, 48/1: 27–35.

Trancik, J. E., & Cross-Call, D. (2013). "Energy Technologies Evaluated Against Climate Targets Using a Cost and Carbon Trade-off Curve," *Environmental Science & Technology*, 47/12: 6673–80.

Troesken, W. (2006). "Regime Change and Corruption. A History of Public Utility Regulation." Glaeser, E. L., & Goldin, C., (eds) *Corruption and Reform: Lessons From America's Economic History.* Chicago: University of Chicago Press.

Upton, G. B., & Snyder, B. F. (2017). "Funding Renewable Energy: An Analysis of Renewable Portfolio Standards," *Energy Economics*, 66: 205–16.

Vajjhala, S. P., & Fischbeck, P. S. (2007). "Quantifying Siting Difficulty: A Case Study of US Transmission Line Siting," *Energy Policy*, 35/1: 650–71.

Valentino, N. A., & Sears, D. O. (2005). "Old Times There Are Not Forgotten: Race and Partisan Realignment in the Contemporary South," *American Journal of Political Science*, 49/3: 672–88.

Velandy, S. M. (2014). "The Energy Pivot: How Military-Led Energy Innovation Can Change the World," *Vermont Journal of Environmental Law*, 15/2: 672–726.

Victor, D. G. (2009). *The Politics of Fossil-Fuel Subsidies.* Winnipeg, Canada: International Institute for Sustainable Development.

Victor, D. G. (2011). *Global Warming Gridlock: Creating More Effective Strategies for Protecting the Planet.* Cambridge: Cambridge University Press.

Vogel, D. (1995). *Trading Up: Consumer and Environmental Regulation in a Global Economy.* Cambridge, MA: Harvard University Press.

Vogel, D. (2018). *California Greenin'.* Princeton, NJ: Princeton University Press.

Volden, C., Ting, M. M., & Carpenter, D. P. (2008). "A Formal Model of Learning and Policy Diffusion," *American Political Science Review*, 102/3: 319–32.

Walker, E. T. (2014). *Grassroots for Hire: Public Affairs Consultants in American Democracy.* Cambridge: Cambridge University Press.

Watkiss, J. D., & Smith, D. W. (1993). "The Energy Policy Act of 1992—A Watershed for Competition in the Wholesale Power Market," *Yale Journal on Regulation*, 10/2: 447–92.

Weaver, K. (2010). "Paths and Forks or Chutes and Ladders? Negative Feedbacks and Policy Regime Change," *Journal of Public Policy*, 30/2: 137–62.

Weaver, V. M. (2007). "Frontlash: Race and the Development of Punitive Crime Policy," *Studies in American Political Development*, 21: 230–65.

Weisman, A. (2008). *The World Without Us*. New York: Macmillan.

Williams, J. H., Haley, B., Kahrl, F., Moore, J., Jones, A. D., Torn, M. S., & McJeon, H. (2014). *Pathways to Deep Decarbonisation in the United States 2050*. San Francisco: Energy and Environmental Economics.

Wilson, J. Q. (1980). "The Politics of Regulation." Wilson, J. Q. (ed.), *The Politics of Regulation*, pp. 357–94. New York: Basic Books.

Wilson, J. Q. (1989). *Bureaucracy: What Government Agencies Do and Why They Do It*. New York: Basic Books.

Wiser, R., & Bolinger, M. (2014). *2013 Wind Technologies Market Report*. Washington, DC: US Department of Energy.

Wiser, R., & Pickle, S. (1997). *Financing Investments in Renewable Energy: The Role of Policy Design and Restructuring*. Berkeley, CA: Lawrence Berkeley National Laboratory.

Wiser, R., Pickle, S., & Goldman, C. (1998). "Renewable Energy Policy and Electricity Restructuring: A California Case Study," *Energy Policy*, 26/6: 465–75.

Wiser, R., Porter, K., & Clemmer, S. (2000). "Emerging Markets for Renewable Energy: The Role of State Policies During Restructuring," *Electricity Journal*, 13/1: 13–24.

Wolak, F. A. (2003). "Diagnosing the California Electricity Crisis," *Electricity Journal*, 16/7: 11–37.

Woo, C. K., Zarnikau, J., Moore, J., & Horowitz, I. (2011). "Wind Generation and Zonal-Market Price Divergence: Evidence From Texas," *Energy Policy*, 39/7: 3928–38.

Xi, F., Davis, S. J., Ciais, P., Crawford-Brown, D., Guan, D., Pade, C., Shi, T., et al. (2016). "Substantial Global Carbon Uptake by Cement Carbonation," *Nature Geoscience*, 9/12: 880–3.

Xu, Y., Ramanathan, V., & Victor, D. G. (2018). "Global Warming Will Happen Faster Than We Think," *Nature*, 564/7734: 30–2.

Yackee, J. W., & Yackee, S. W. (2006). "A Bias Towards Business? Assessing Interest Group Influence on the U.S. Bureaucracy," *Journal of Politics*, 68/1: 128–39.

Yakubovich, V., Granovetter, M., & McGuire, P. (2005). "Electric Charges: The Social Construction of Rate Systems," *Theory and Society*, 34/5–6: 579–612.

Yergin, D. (2011). *The Quest: Energy, Security, and the Remaking of the Modern World*. New York: Penguin.

Zahariadis, N. (2007). "The Multiple Streams Framework: Structure, Limitations, Prospects." Sabatier, P. A. (ed.), *Theories of the Policy Process*, 2nd ed., pp. 65–92. Boulder, CO: Westview Press.

Zarnikau, J. (2011). "Successful Renewable Energy Development in a Competitive Electricity Market: A Texas Case Study," *Energy Policy*, 39/7: 3906–13.

INDEX

Tables and figures are indicated by *t* and *f* following the page number

For the benefit of digital users, indexed terms that span two pages (e.g., 52–53) may, on occasion, appear on only one of those pages.

100% clean energy targets, 16, 26–27, 29, 166–67, 225, 226–27, 228, 238, 249, 251
45Q program, 21
60 Plus Association, 178–79

Advanced Research Projects Agency-Energy (ARPA-E), 15
Affordable Care Act (ACA), 47, 49–50
afforestation, 22
Air Liquide America, 129, 202–3
air pollution, 12, 177, 179, 197, 219, 232, 243, 256–57
Air Products and Chemicals Inc., 129
Airgas, 202–3
Altura Energy, 111
America's Pledge Initiative, 238
American Electric Power (AEP)
  climate denial, 97–98
  federal taxes, 56
  in Ohio, 196–97, 205, 208–9, 213, 215–16, 218, 219–20
  in Texas, 130–31
  lawsuits, 87, 255
American Legislative Exchange Council (ALEC), 6, 58–60, 98, 230, 249
  in Arizona, 174, 188
  in Kansas, 141–42, 149–51, 156, 162–63, 234–35
  in Ohio, 33, 59–60, 195, 206–7, 208
  model legislation, 6–7, 103–4, 229, 240
American Recovery and Reinvestment Act (ARRA) of 2009, 102
American Wind Energy Association (AWEA)
Americans for Prosperity (AFP), 6–7, 229–30, 249
  in Kansas, 32, 59–60, 142, 150–51, 157, 161
Americans for Tax Reform, 150–51, 210–11, 229
anti-wind, 19–20, 33, 144, 160–61, 205, 210, 213, 219, 254

Anzia, Sarah, 11, 40
Apple, Pat, 152, 153–54, 159–60
Arch Coal, 207
Arizona Attorney General, 166, 185, 188, 193, 231–32
Arizona Constitution, 167–68
Arizona Corporation Commission (ACC), 164, 167
  elections, 174–75, 184–85, 189, 245
  net metering policy, 171, 176, 177, 180–84, 186, 190
  regulatory capture, 174, 177, 188–89, 192
  renewable energy policy, 168–69, 175–76, 180, 185–86, 190
Arizona Free Enterprise Club, 189
Arizona Proposition 127, 166, 193
Arizona Public Service (APS)
  election interventions by, 32–33, 174–75, 184–85, 188–89, 193, 230, 234–35
  fossil fuel dependence, 167, 177, 191–92
  lack of support for clean energy, 32–33, 168, 170, 171, 175, 190
  lobbying public against renewables, 166, 178–79, 192
  net metering, 171, 173, 176, 177, 180–81, 183, 185–86
  opposition to distributed energy, 170
  rate cases, 177, 180, 181
  reduced RPS for, 176
  regulatory capture of ACC, 176, 185, 188, 189, 190, 234–35
  solar energy policies, 165–66, 168, 183–84, 187
Arizona Republic, 174, 182
Arizona Solar Energy Freedom Act, 189
Arizona Solar Energy Industries Association (AriSEIA), 169–70, 171, 173
Arizona State University, 185
Arnold, R. Douglas, 40–41, 49